Lecture Notes in Artificial Intelligence 2782

Edited by J. G. Carbonell and J. Siekmann

Subseries of Lecture Notes in Computer Science

Springer
Berlin
Heidelberg
New York
Hong Kong
London
Milan
Paris
Tokyo

Matthias Klusch   Andrea Omicini
Sascha Ossowski   Heimo Laamanen (Eds.)

Cooperative Information Agents VII

7th International Workshop, CIA 2003
Helsinki, Finland, August 27-29, 2003
Proceedings

Springer

Series Editors

Jaime G. Carbonell, Carnegie Mellon University, Pittsburgh, PA, USA
Jörg Siekmann, University of Saarland, Saarbrücken, Germany

Volume Editors

Matthias Klusch
DFKI GmbH, German Research Center for Artificial Intelligence
Stuhlsatzenhausweg 3, 66123 Saarbrücken, Germany
E-mail: klusch@dfki.de

Andrea Omicini
University of Bologna, DEIS
Viale Risorgimento 2, 40136 Bologna, Italy
E-mail: andrea.omicini@ieee.org

Sascha Ossowski
University Rey Juan Carlos, School of Engineering (ESCET)
Campus de Mostoles, Calle Tulipan s/n, 28933 Madrid, Spain
E-mail: S.Ossowski@escet.urjc.es

Heimo Laamanen
TelioSonera Finland
P.O. Box 970, 00051 Sonera, Finland
E-mail: Heimo.Laamanen@teliasonera.com

Cataloging-in-Publication Data applied for

A catalog record for this book is available from the Library of Congress.

Bibliographic information published by Die Deutsche Bibliothek
Die Deutsche Bibliothek lists this publication in the Deutsche Nationalbibliografie;
detailed bibliographic data is available in the Internet at <http://dnb.ddb.de>.

CR Subject Classification (1998): I.2.11, I.2, H.4, H.3.3, H.2, C.2.4, H.5

ISSN 0302-9743
ISBN 3-540-40798-7 Springer-Verlag Berlin Heidelberg New York

Springer-Verlag Berlin Heidelberg New York
a member of BertelsmannSpringer Science+Business Media GmbH

http://www.springer.de

© Springer-Verlag Berlin Heidelberg 2003
Printed in Germany

Typesetting: Camera-ready by author, data conversion by PTP-Berlin GmbH
Printed on acid-free paper   SPIN: 10931530   06/3142   5 4 3 2 1 0

Preface

These are the proceedings of the 7th International Workshop on Cooperative Information Agents (CIA 2003), held at the Sonera Conference Center in Helsinki, Finland, August 27–29, 2003. It was co-located with the 4th Agentcities Information Days.

One key challenge of developing advanced agent-based information systems is to balance the autonomy of networked data and knowledge sources with the potential payoff of leveraging them by the appropriate use of intelligent information agents on the Internet. An information agent is a computational software entity that has access to one or multiple, heterogeneous, and distributed data and information sources; proactively searches for and maintains relevant information on behalf of its human users or other agents, preferably just-in-time. In other words, it is managing and overcoming the difficulties associated with information overload in the open and exponentially growing Internet and Web. Depending on the application and tasks at hand information agents may collaborate in open, networked data and information environments to provide added value to a variety of applications in different domains. Thus, research and development of information agents is inherently interdisciplinary: It requires expertise in information retrieval, artificial intelligence, database systems, human-computer interaction, and Internet and Web technology.

Initiated in 1997, the purpose of the annual international workshop series on cooperative information agents (CIA) is to provide an interdisciplinary forum for researchers, software developers, and managers to get informed about, present, and discuss the latest high-quality results in advancements of theory and practice in information agent technology for the Internet and Web. Each event of this renowned series attempts to capture the intrinsic interdisciplinary nature of this research area by calling for contributions from different research communities, and by promoting open and informative discussions on all related topics. Since 2001, the series also issues a Best Paper Award, and a System Innovation Award, to acknowledge highly innovative research and development, respectively, in the domain of intelligent information agents.

In keeping with its tradition, this year's workshop featured a sequence of regular and invited talks of excellence given by leading experts in the field. These talks covered a broad area of topics of interest, such as pervasive information service provision; information agents and peer-to-peer computing; and information gathering and integration. Other topics were methods for negotiation and interaction; collaborative search and filtering; as well as issues of trust and engineering of information agent systems.

This year the *CIA System Innovation Award* and the *CIA Best Paper Award* were sponsored by Whitestein Technologies AG, Switzerland, and Elsevier Science, The Netherlands, respectively. The Spanish Association for Artificial Intelligence (AEPIA) provided limited financial support to its members who were co-authors of accepted papers so that they could give their presentations at CIA 2003.

CIA 2003 featured 2 invited, 17 regular (long), and 6 short papers selected from 60 submissions. The result of the peer-review of all contributions is included in this volume, rich in interesting, inspiring, and advanced work on research and development of intelligent information agents worldwide. All workshop proceedings have been published by Springer-Verlag as Lecture Notes in Artificial Intelligence volumes: 1202 (1997), 1435 (1998), 1652 (1999), 1860 (2000), 2182 (2001), and 2446 (2002).

The CIA 2003 workshop was organized in cooperation with the Association for Computing Machinery (ACM). In addition, we are very much indebted to our sponsors, whose financial support made this event possible and contributed to its success. The sponsors of CIA 2003 were:

TELIASONERA, Finland
NOKIA, Finland
WHITESTEIN TECHNOLOGIES, Switzerland
ELSEVIER SCIENCE, The Netherlands
SPANISH ASSOCIATION FOR ARTIFICIAL INTELLIGENCE, Spain

We are also grateful to the authors and invited speakers for contributing to this workshop, as well as to all the members of the program committee and the external reviewers for their very careful, critical, and thoughtful reviews of all submissions. Finally, a deep thanks goes to each of the brave members of the local organization team at TeliaSonera in Helsinki for their hard work in providing CIA 2003 with a modern, comfortable location, and an exclusive social program.

We hope you enjoyed CIA 2003, and were inspired!

August 2003   Matthias Klusch, Andrea Omicini,
                                                Sascha Ossowski, Heimo Laamanen

Co-chairs

Matthias Klusch   DFKI, Germany, *General Chair*
Andrea Omicini   University of Bologna, Italy
Sascha Ossowski   University of Rey Juan Carlos in Madrid, Spain
Heimo Laamanen   TeliaSonera, Finland, *Local Chair*

Program Committee

Elisabeth Andre   University of Augsburg, Germany
Ricardo Baeza-Yates   University of Chile, Chile
Wolfgang Benn   TU Chemnitz, Germany
Sonia Bergamaschi   University of Modena, Italy
Brahim Chaib-draa   Laval University, Canada
Rose Dieng   INRIA, France
Frank Dignum   University of Utrecht, The Netherlands
Fausto Giunchiglia   University of Trento, Italy
Rune Gustavsson   Blekinge TH, Sweden
Heikki Helin   Sonera, Finland
Mike Huhns   University of South Carolina, USA
Toru Ishida   University of Kyoto, Japan
Manfred Jeusfeld   University of Tilburg, The Netherlands
Catholijn Jonker   Free University of Amsterdam, The Nether-
                       lands
Hillol Kargupta   UMBC, USA
Larry Kerschberg   George Mason University, USA
Sarit Kraus   University of Maryland, USA
Daniel Kudenko   University of York, UK
Victor Lesser   University of Massachusetts, USA
Mike Luck   University of Southampton, UK
Martti Mäntylä   Helsinki Institute for Information Technology,
                       Finland
Dennis McLeod   University of Southern California, USA
Werner Nutt   Heriot-Watt University Edinburgh, UK
Eugenio Oliveira   University of Porto, Portugal
Terry Payne   University of Southampton, UK
Michal Pechoucek   TU Prague, Czech Republic
Paolo Petta   Austrian Research Institute for AI, Austria
Enric Plaza   CSIC AI Research Lab, Spain
Alun Preece   University of Aberdeen, UK
Kimmo Raatikainen   Nokia Research Center, Finland
Roope Raisamo   University of Tampere, Finland
Omer F. Rana   University of Wales, UK
Volker Roth   Fraunhofer IGD, Germany

Heiko Schuldt	ETH Zurich, Switzerland
Onn Shehory	IBM Research, Israel
Amit Sheth	University of Georgia, USA
Carles Sierra	CSIC AI Research Lab, Spain
Von-Wun Soo	National Tsing Hua University, Taiwan
Leon Stirling	University of Melbourne, Australia
Rudi Studer	University of Karlsruhe, Germany
Henry Tirri	University of Helsinki, Finland
Steven Willmott	UPC Barcelona, Spain
Mike Wooldridge	University of Liverpool, UK
Eric Yu	University of Toronto, Canada
Chengqi Zhang	University of Technology Sydney, Australia
Ning Zhong	Maebashi Institute of Technology, Japan

Local Organizing Committee

Heikki Helin	TeliaSonera, Finland
Heimo Laamanen	TeliaSonera, Finland
Mikko Laukkanen	TeliaSonera, Finland
Martti Mäntylä	Helsinki Institute of Information Technology, Finland
Kimmo Raatikainen	University of Helsinki, Finland
Roope Raisamo	University of Tampere, Finland
Henry Tirri	University of Helsinki, Finland

External Reviewers

Tibor Bosse	Ralf Neubert
Seokkyung Chung	Guilherme Pereira
Pilar Dellunde	Jan Peters
Otmar Görlitz	Enric Plaza
Mario Gomez	Avi Rosenfeld
Francesco Guerra	Luis Sarmento
Meirav Hadad	Teresa Solchaga
Aizhong Lin	Nenad Stojanovic
Maria-Victoria Belmonte Martinez	Maurizio Vincini
Rebecca Montanari	

Table of Contents

Information Gathering and Integration

Collaborative Search and Filtering

Collaboration in Open Environments

Issues of Trust in Agent-Based Information Provision

Information Agent Systems Engineering (1)

Information Agent Systems Engineering (2)

ACCESS: An Agent Architecture for Ubiquitous Service Delivery

Conor Muldoon, Gregory O'Hare, Donnacha Phelan, Robin Strahan, and
Rem Collier

Department of Computer Science, University College Dublin (UCD), Belfield, Dublin 4,
Ireland
{conor.muldoon, gregory.ohare, donnacha.phelan, robin.strahan,
rem.collier}@ucd.ie
http://www.cs.ucd.ie/

Abstract. This paper introduces the Agents Channeling ContExt Sensitive Services (ACCESS) architecture, an agent-based architecture that supports the development and deployment of context sensitive services. Specifically, ACCESS is comprised of two sub-systems: a run-time system that delivers the minimum functionality necessary to execute ACCESS Agents, and a development environment that delivers structured tool-based support for the creation, development, and visualization of u-commerce services.

1 Introduction

This paper introduces the Agents Channeling ContExt Sensitive Services (ACCESS) architecture, an agent-based architecture that supports the development and deployment of context sensitive services. User context is considered an aggregation of their location, previous activities, and preferences. This paper describes ACCESS and specifically how it integrates with and compliments the Agent factory system upon which it is constructed. Specifically, the Agent Factory Run-Time Environment and the ACCESS Management Agents provide horizontal technology layers that are utilized to deploy ACCESS-compliant services. This generic technology strata facilitates the rapid design and deployment of agent based context aware services.

2 Related Work

Considerable research has been invested of late in the deployment of agents in the ubiquitous and mobile computing arena. Many such systems deliver context sensitive services. Agents2Go [12] is representative in this respect and constitutes an agent based distributed system that provides mobile users with location dependent services and information. It consists of a PalmApp, residing on the PDA, together with several server side components namely the Agents2Go Server, the Locator and the Agents2Go

M. Klusch et al. (Eds.): CIA 2003, LNAI 2782, pp. 1–15, 2003.

Information Repository. An initial prototype delivers restaurant based information. Thus two further components are used to provide this specific service, the Restaurant Broker and the Restaurant Agent. The Agent2Go Server handles all communication to and from the PalmApp. The user's location is determined by simple base cell identification. Static information about the restaurants (such as their address, phone number, etc) is stored on the Information Repository. Dynamic content (such as the menu and prices) is handled by the Restaurant Broker.

Each restaurant has a Restaurant Agent that allows them to update the information in the Broker. Restaurants are assigned to a Broker that handles a specified region. This facilitates system scalability. A user's request for information to the Agent2Go Server is passed to the Locator, which determines the Broker best suited to respond to the request. The Broker then formulates a response from its store of dynamic information. This response is sent to the Agent2Go Server, which combines it with static content from the Information Repository to form the complete response which is dispatched to the PalmApp.

Numerous m-commerce applications have been developed including Agora [5], Impulse [15] and Easishop [6]. Agora is based on the Zeus Agent Framework [8] and permits shoppers equipped with a PDA to interact with services offered by stores at a mall, whether they are at the mall or in close proximity to it. Stores and shoppers are represented by agents. The shopper agent acts as a personal shopping assistant and bidder. When the user enters the mall they indicate to the mall server what product(s) they wish to purchase. The user chooses the product and quantity together with the maximum price they are willing to pay. This information is passed to an English Auction agent. The auction agent holds auctions on behalf of store agents for the requested products. It allows any number of bidding agents to participate in an English auction of fixed length. If the user wins the auction, payment for the product is made and the transaction is completed. Easi-shop utilises the Agent Factory system [3, 4, 10] and similarly provides a *market place* where shopper agents may migrate in order to participate in an auction process on behalf of the user.

The Impulse project developed at MIT Media Lab [15] in contrast uses the Hive [14] system of agents, also developed by MIT Media Lab merely assists the user in the location of products and does not support auctioning or purchase.

Mihailescu and Binder [7] have proposed an m-commerce framework based on mobile agents. It provides three agent types *Device, Service and Courier* agents. The *Device agent* resides fixed on the mobile device, handling the presentation of information to the user and communication between the device and Service Agents. *Service Agents* handle user requests to service providers. Service agents typically store information from prior user interactions in order to personalise future content. *Courier Agents* are single hop lightweight agents that are transmitted to the mobile devices by the Service Agents. They carry information that can be displayed to the user and can be destroyed once reaching their target. but the Device Agent can also cache them to aid storing the current status of a transaction in case of failure.

Of the five systems all but one involve determining the user's location in order to provide context sensitive information. However no two systems use the same method of doing so. Agents2Go uses cell-based location; Agora uses infrared sensors embedded in the physical environment while Impulse uses GPS and Easishop uses a combination of GPS and Bluetooth.

The systems offer varying degrees of expandability. Agents2Go expansion is limited without a major revision of the existing components. This is primarily due to the limited nature of the interface, which would be unable to display graphical media such as product pictures, or maps. Agora and Easishop are primarily an aid to a shopper in a mall and as such rely on infrared/Bluetooth communication which is unusable outside the enabled mall. Thus the expansion of its services beyond the scope of the mall would be inherently difficult. Impulse suffers from restrictions similar to the Agents2Go together with a restrictive communication protocol.

The system that has the most potential for expansion is the framework proposed by Mihailescu and Binder. As the Courier Agents determine what the Device Agent displays, it is possible to create Service Agents of varying natures that in turn create Courier Agents that communicate different media, as there is no predetermined communication protocol.

Table 1. Comparasion of Agent-based U-Commerce Systems.

System Name	Agent System	Migration	Autonomy	Personalisation of Content	Multiple Use	Context Sensitive
Agents2Go	Agents2Go	✖	✖	✖	✖	✔
Agora	Zeus	✖	✖	✖	✖	✖
Impulse	Hive	✖	✔	✖	✖	✔
MB Framework	Aglets/ KVM	✔	✖	✔	✔	✖
EasiShop	Agent Factory	✔	✔	✔	✔	✔
ACCESS	Agent Factory	✔	✔	✔	✔	✔

The ubiquitous agent-based architecture that we propose in this paper, ACCESS, will exhibit some of the properties of the MB framework. One of the main objectives and motivations behind the ACCESS architecture is that it will provide a generic framework upon which a wide range of ubiquitous context sensitive services can be developed. ACCESS will utilise the Agent Factory system and will offer a multi-user environment offering personalization of content, by user profiling and context, support for mobile lightweight intentional agents and intelligent prediction of user service needs .

3 The ACCESS Architecture

The Agents Channeling ContExt Sensitive Services (ACCESS) architecture is an agent-based architecture that supports the development and deployment of context sensitive services. ACCESS has been realized as an extension of a pre-existing framework for agent development, known as *Agent Factory* [3, 4, 10].

Agent Factory is a cohesive framework that delivers structured support for the development and deployment of agent-oriented applications. Specifically, Agent Factory supports the fabrication of a type of software agent that is: autonomous, situated, socially able, intentional, rational, and mobile [3]. Practically, this has been achieved through the design and implementation of an agent programming language and associated interpreter. Together, the language and interpreter facilitate the expression of the current behaviour of each agent through the mentalistic notions of belief and commitment. These are augmented with a set of commitment rules that describe the dynamics of the agents' behaviour through the definition of the conditions under which the agent should adopt commitments. This approach is consistent with the well-documented BDI-agent model [2][11].

The framework itself is comprised of four-layers that deliver: the agent programming language, a distributed run-time environment that delivers support for the deployment of agent-oriented applications, an integrated toolkit that delivers a visually intuitive set of tools, and a software engineering methodology that specifies the sequence of steps required to develop and deploy agent-oriented applications with the preceding layers. Additionally, Agent Factory provides FIPA-compliance through an Agent Management System (AMS) agent and a Directory Facilitator (DF) agent. Agent-oriented applications built using Agent Factory use these prefabricated agents to gain access to the infrastructure services provided by the run-time environment (i.e. yellow and white pages services, migration services).

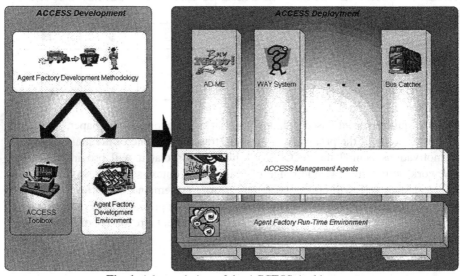

Fig. 1. A layered view of the ACCESS Architecture.

Conversely, ACCESS augments the basic infrastructure delivered by Agent Factory through the implementation of additional agents, which deliver infrastructure services that are relevant to m-commerce applications. These agents form a cohesive management layer into which multiple m-commerce services may be plugged. This facilitates m-commerce service developers by enabling them to focus on the implementation of their service, and not the infrastructure required to deliver it.

Figure 1 illustrates the structure of the ACCESS architecture. Specifically, it can be seen that the Agent Factory Run-Time Environment and the ACCESS Management Agents provide strata or horizontal technology layers that are utilized to deploy ACCESS-compliant services. These services are represented by the vertical layers, which implement the associated business logic. Finally, ACCESS Development is supported through the augmentation of the existing Agent Factory Development Methodology. Specifically, we have developed the ACCESS Toolbox, a set of pre-fabricated components that aid the developer in the development of ACCESS-compliant services.

3.1 ACCESS Management Agents

The ACCESS Management agents implement the core functionality of the ACCESS architecture, which includes context management, user profiling, map generation, content delivery, account management, and location sensing. A discussion of all these functional areas is beyond the scope of this paper. Consequently, the following sections focus on the user profiling, content management, and map generation functionality of ACCESS. Figure 2 below outlines the ACCESS Management agent community.

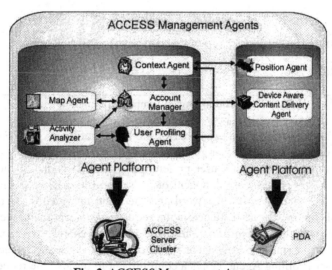

Fig. 2. ACCESS Management Agents.

3.1.1 User Profiling

The User Profiling Agent provides a mechanism to enable agents request user preferences, which are used to configure user specific services. A distinct user profile exists for every registered user. User profile information is obtained explicitly from the user preference form and implicitly from the activity analyzer. One advantage of requiring the user to complete a preference form is that it allows the personalisation of services to begin immediately, allowing applications to begin tailoring their services to the needs of specific users prior to observing users' behaviour and preferences. The personalisation process is then further refined as the profile is implicitly developed as the user interacts with the system. Examples of explicit profile information include age, sex, smoking/non-smoking etc. this information is used to stereotype the user, or the users preferences. Implicit profile information is obtained using data mining techniques on recorded user activity, for instance when examining service usage its noted what was used, when it was used, and where is was used. The User Profiling Agent also communicates with the Context Agent to create user specific hotspots. For example hotspots may be created around cinemas if the user indicates on the registration form that they like cinema or if the user often accesses applications that have a semantic relationship to cinemas. The former relates to hotspot creation based on explicit profile information while the later refers to hotspot creation based on implicit profile information.

```
BELIEF(requested_achieve(getProfileInfo(?keyword,?agent
ToInform),?agent))
=>
COMMIT(Self,Now,GetProfileInfo(?keyword,?agentToInform)
)


BELIEF(profileInfo(?data,?agentToInform))
=>
COMMIT(Self,Now,inform(?agentToInform(?data)))
```

Fig. 3. User Profiling Agent commitment rules.

By way of an example of the behaviour of the User Profiling Agent, Figure 3 outlines the two commitment rules that govern the interaction between the User Profiling Agent and another agent seeking user preferences. The first commitment rule illustrates how an agent requests a component of a user profile that is associated with a specific keyword. Note that the keyword and the agent to which the corresponding information should be sent are included in the request. An agent may specify another agent to which the requested information should be sent, although it is more common for the requesting agent to be the agent to which the data is sent. On receiving this request the User Profiling Agent adopts a commitment to retrieve the requested information, causing the invocation of a get profile information actuator.

The second commitment rule demonstrates how the User Profiling agent returns the requested information to the relevant agent. Once the User Profiling Agent adopts the belief that it has retrieved the requested information, it adopts a commitment to send this data to the agent. This task is undertaken by the inform actuator.

3.1.2 Context Management

Within the ACCESS architecture, a users context is a combination of their location, previous activities, and preferences. Context is used to help ACCESS understand where and when to provide services, and more specifically, what services the user may need.

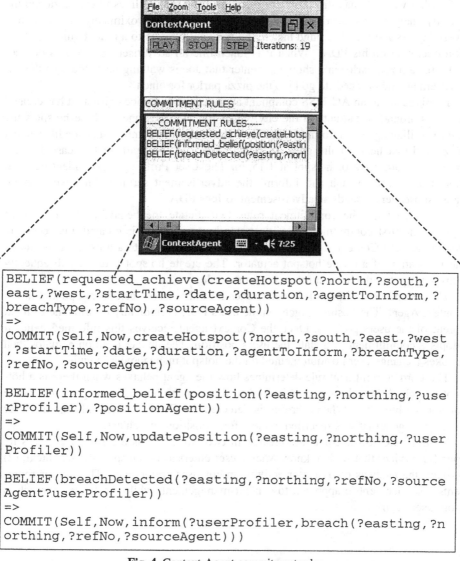

```
BELIEF(requested_achieve(createHotspot(?north,?south,?
east,?west,?startTime,?date,?duration,?agentToInform,?
breachType,?refNo),?sourceAgent))
=>
COMMIT(Self,Now,createHotspot(?north,?south,?east,?west
,?startTime,?date,?duration,?agentToInform,?breachType,
?refNo,?sourceAgent))

BELIEF(informed_belief(position(?easting,?northing,?use
rProfiler),?positionAgent))
=>
COMMIT(Self,Now,updatePosition(?easting,?northing,?user
Profiler))

BELIEF(breachDetected(?easting,?northing,?refNo,?source
Agent?userProfiler))
=>
COMMIT(Self,Now,inform(?userProfiler,breach(?easting,?n
orthing,?refNo,?sourceAgent)))
```

Fig. 4. Context Agent commitment rules.

The Context Agent is responsible for handling *context sensitive hotspots* within the ACCESS architecture. Specifically, a hotspot is a region of space-time that is limited by specified bounds (e.g. an area of 100 square meters centered around a particular shop, during the shops business hours). Once a user breaches a hotspot the Context Agent informs the User Profiling Agent, which may then decipher weather the hotspot breach is relevant to the user.

The following scenario illustrates how the Context Agent uses hotspots to manage context. Consider for example a user called Joe. Joe is on holiday in a city that he is unfamiliar with. He has stated on a registration form that he likes to eat pizza and the activity analyzer has identified that he goes for lunch at approximately the same time everyday. As Joe travels around the city he frequently refers to a tourist guide application operating on his PDA. When it is lunchtime an advertisement appears on Joes PDA for a pizza parlor in a shopping center that Joe is walking past. Joe sees the advertisement and proceeds to go in to the pizza parlor for lunch.

In this scenario an ACCESS compliant advertisement service exists that has created hotspots around restaurants in the city. Once Joe breaches one of these hotspots the User Profiling agent is informed. The User Profiling Agent knows that Joe likes to eat pizza and that he normally goes for lunch between 1 an 2pm. In this case Joe has breached a pizza parlor hotspot at 1.15pm. The User Profiling Agent identifies that this is a relevant breach and informs the advertisement service. An advertisement agent subsequently sends an advertisement to Joes PDA.

Fig. 4 contains the commitment rules that dictate the behavior of the Context Agent. The first commitment rule illustrates how a hotspot is created. On receiving this request the Context Agent adopts a commitment to create a hotspot. This causes the invocation of a create hotspot actuator. The create hotspot actuator subsequently adds a hotspot to the hotspot management module.

The second commitment rule determines how the users position is updated in the Context Agent. The Position Agent on the users PDA periodically informs the Context Agent of the users position. Once the Context agent receives this informed belief it adopts a commitment to update the users position. The update position actuator then invokes a change user position method on the hotspot management module.

The third commitment rule determines how the agent behaves when there is a hotspot breach. A breach preceptor is used to monitor the hotspot management module for hotspot breaches. When a breach is detected the Context Agent informs the User Profiling Agent that was specified in the inform position speech act.

Within ACCESS hotspots are created in two ways: (1) as a result of requests by specific services that wish to know when a user enters a certain space-time context, (2) through the analysis of past user activity and/or user preferences. The former represents a service-centric approach to context management, while the latter approach is more user-centric.

3.1.3 Map Generation

The Map Agent dynamically generates maps for a specified location. The generated maps are subsequently merged with service specific content overlay. The Map Agents exist as part of a community of peers, this enables the distribution of load and also allows the Map Agents to be geographically bound i.e. Map Agents are not responsible for generating Maps for the entire globe, they have specified bounds for their locality. When a generate map request from a service agent is made, the size of the map and its location are specified. The Map agent contacts its map server, to retrieve the map segments required to generate a Map centered on the location specified. The Map Agent merges the segments and requests the service specific content from a service agent. This content is received as a list of instructions that determine what overlays to place on top of the map. Once the draw instructions have been executed and the content overlay has been merged with the generated map, a jpeg file is created. An agent specified in the generate map request is then informed of the jpegs URL.

3.1.4 Location Sensing, Content Delivery and Account Management

We now consider briefly each of the Position Agent, the Account Manager and the Device Aware Content Delivery Agent (DACDA). The Position Agent is responsible for periodically informing the Context Agent of the users position. It is a lightweight agent that resides on the users PDA. It currently uses GPS, however it is envisaged that in the future other position sensing technologies may be used.

The Device Aware Content Delivery Agent performs the roles of interface and content manager. It monitors the users interaction with the GUI and provides a means to deliver content. All communication with the user is done through the DACDA. The DACDA has the responsibility of registering the user with the system at start up and also registering the user with the services they wish to avail of.

Within the ACCESS architecture there are a number of instance agents that exist on a one per user basis, which must be created the first time the user uses the system. The Account Managers role is to drive the creation of the user's initial profile. The following gives a description of the sequence of events involved. The user runs the ACCESS software on their PDA for the first time. Instances of the DACDA and Position Agent are created on the PDA. The DACDA requests the name of an Account Manager from the Directory Facilitator. The Directory Facilitator informs the DACDA of an Account Managers name. The DACDA requests that the Account Manager create a user account. The Account Manager requests that the User Profiling Agent create a new user profile. It then informs the DACDA of the instance agents' names.

3.2 The Service Provider Contract

The Service Provider Contract forms the minimum requirements necessary for a service to be considered ACCESS compliant. Roles that must be filled as part of the

Service Provider Contract include the Service Manager, the Service User Agent and the Service Usage Agent. These components constitute prefabricated components of the ACCESS development framework and may be extended to provide service specific functionality (see figure 5). Although the Service Provider Contract gives three roles that must be provided, it does not limit the service developer from adding additional roles and agents that are specific to the application they are developing.

The Service Manager is responsible for registering the service with the system. It communicates with the DACDA when a user wishes to use the service. Once the DACDA initiates a conversation the service manager creates an instance Service User Agent, which will be the DACDAs communication entry point for the service. In addition to creating the Service User Agent, the Service Manager creates other instance agents that are not defined in the contract but are necessary for the particular service. The Service Manager also informs interested Activity Analyzers of the Service Usage Agents name when requested.

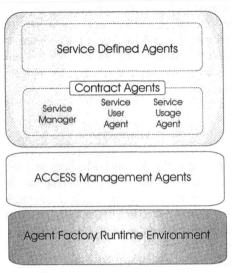

Fig. 5. Layered service provision.

The Service User Agent is responsible for communicating with the DACDA. It interprets speech acts coming from the DACDA and collaborates with the other service agents to deliver the required application. The functionality of the Service User Agent will primarily be service specific, but from the point of view of the contract it is viewed as the functional data block that handles or represents the user in the service.

The Service Usage Agents role is to identify user activity patterns that are specific to the particular service with which it belongs to. It is an expert only in its own service. The Activity Analyzer carries out the generic activity analysis that is related to the users general behavior as opposed to behavior within a particular service. If the Activity Analyzer identifies behavior that it believes is service specific it may request the Service Usage Agents expert opinion. Once the Service Usage Agent receives this request it analyses the data and informs the Activity Analyzer of its opinion.

3.3   ACCESS Management Agent and Service Provider Interaction

The ACCESS architecture is composed of reusable social behavior patterns, which have been encoded into the system. Examples include service creation, activity analysis, periodic position update, user registration, setup interface, context creation, activity recording and so forth. A number of these patterns are made up of components from both the ACCESS Management Agents and Contract Agent roles. Fig. 6 gives an example of an Agent UML [9] collaboration diagram for the service creation behaviour pattern.

The purpose of the service creation behavior pattern is to create the service specific infrastructure required to deliver a service to the user. It is assumed that the Service Manager and Service Usage Agent are already in existence, the diagram shows how the user specific components are created the first time the user uses the service. These components include the Contract Service User Agent, the service specific user agents and a profile relating to the service in the User Profiling Agent.

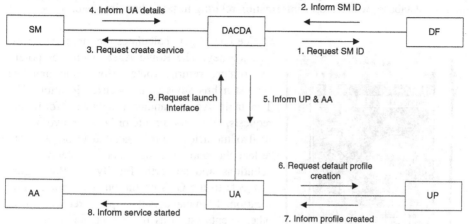

Fig. 6. Create service collaboration diagram.

Initially the DACDA requests the Service Managers ID from the Directory Facilitator. Once the ID has been received it requests the Service Manager to create the service. The Service Manager creates a Service User Agent in addition to other instance service agents that may be required. It informs the DACDA of the Service User Agents details. The DACDA informs the Service User Agent of the Activity Analyzer and User Profiling Agent information. The Service User Agent requests the User Profiling Agent to create a default profile for the service. The Activity Analyzer is then informed that the service has started. Finally the DACDA is requested to launch the interface.

4   Case Study

In order to animate the ACCESS system we briefly introduce an ACCESS-compliant service that has been deployed on top of the generic ACCESS system. The Bus Catcher [13] service is an agent-based ubiquitous service hosted on a PDA. Bus Catcher delivers real time bus network information that is relevant to the transportation and movement of the user. Features include: fare calculation, timetable information and route planning. In addition, Bus Catcher is an agent-based application endowed with the ability to act autonomously and proactively anticipate the travel information needs of the mobile user.

The Bus Catcher Application (Fig. 8) consists of seven Service Agents, including three *contract agents* required to satisfy the contract rules of the ACCESS architecture (section 3.2). The contract agents, namely: the Bus Catcher Service Manager, the Bus Catcher User Agent, and the Bus Catcher Usage Agent are supplemented by agents designed specifically for the Bus catcher application. These include: the Fare Agent, the Timetable Agent, the Route Agent and the Bus Agent. The application also includes a database, which stores information relating to fares, bus times etc.

Fig. 7. Image to represent user and bus location

The Fare Agent calculates the fare for a specified journey. The Route Agent identifies potential routes, returns route information and the nearest *n* bus stops to a specified location. The Timetable Agent handles timetable information requests, either for a route or between two points. It also modifies static timetable information to reflect the real time state updates, delays, cancellations and so forth. Finally the Bus Agent connects to the GPS on the bus and monitors its location. It manages subscription requests from other agents (such as the Timetable Agent) and informs the subscribed agents of bus delays/progress. These four agents connect to the database and issue SQL statements to retrieve the required data.

The agent-oriented approach adopted has resulted in a variety of advantages over an earlier non-agent design. These include increased flexibility and extensibility of the application (adding new functionality/services is primarily a matter of creating and deploying additional agents); improved robustness and adaptivity (the application agents can dynamically re-organize themselves at run-time or migrate to different hosts in order to survive or to aid load balancing). Perhaps the most important advantage is that of autonomy. The agents are capable of intelligently anticipating the user's information needs and can proactively obtain it without any user interaction. The agents can also query the User Profile Agent providing personalised content.

In evaluating the system 30 members of the public were asked to use it and then complete a questionnaire on their experiences with it. A seven point Likert scale was used to measure the extent to which a person agrees or disagrees with the questions posed. The trials were carried out over two days, at two distinct locations, one in UCD Belfield Campus and the other on Grafton Street in the Dublin city centre. Among the users who participated in the Grafton Street trials, roughly half were tourists or visitors to Dublin, one of the possible target markets for Bus Catcher.

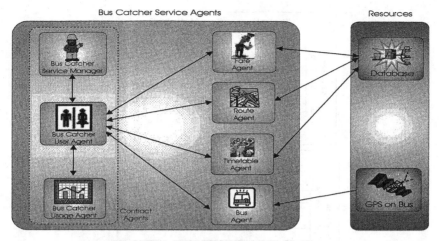

Fig. 8. Bus Catcher application architecture

All users found the system to be helpful with nearly 80% finding it very helpful, furthermore users were similarly enthusiastic about the level of improvement it offered Dublin bus travelers over those services currently available.

With a view to productising Bus Catcher, users were also asked if they would consider using and buying it. Interestingly, while the vast majority said they would use it, a lower number said they would be willing to pay for it. Many thought that this should be provided free of charge by the transport network provider. This provides a motivation for the development of intelligent, targeted advertising as a revenue stream by which the service could be cross-subsidised. This feature is facilitated by the ACCESS architecture's user profiling and context management capabilities. More detailed descriptions of user evaluations are provided elsewhere in the literature [1].

5 Conclusions

Within this paper, we have introduced the Agents Channeling ContExt Sensitive Services (ACCESS) architecture, an agent-based architecture that supports the development and deployment of m-commerce services. This has been achieved through the extension of a pre-existing framework for agent development, known as Agent Factory.

Specifically, ACCESS augments the basic infrastructure of Agent factory through the implementation of additional agents, which deliver infrastructure services that are relevant to m-commerce applications. This facilitates m-commerce service developers by enabling them to focus upon the implementation of their service, and not the infrastructure required to deliver it. To achieve this, we introduce the *Service Provider Contract* – a set of constraints, specified as agent roles, that m-commerce services must satisfy to be compliant with the ACCESS Architecture.

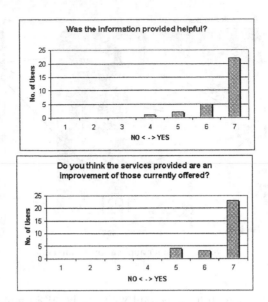

Fig. 9. Assessing the helpfulness of the Bus Catcher system

Work on the ACCESS architecture is ongoing. Specifically, efforts are currently directed at the fabrication of an array of u-commerce service demonstrators, and at the refinement and improvement of the existing community of ACCESS Management Agents.

Acknowledgements. We would gratefully acknowledge the kind support of Enterprise Ireland through their grant ATRP/01/209 to the E=mC^2: Empowering the mobile Citizen Creatively project.

References

1. Bertolotto, M., O'Hare, G., Strahan, R., Brophy, A., Martin, A., McLoughlin, E.: Bus Catcher: a Context Sensitive Prototype System for Public Transportation Users. Proceedings Second International Workshop on Web and Wireless Geographical Information Systems (W2GIS), Singapore, December 2002 (in press)
2. Busetta, P., Howden, N., Ronnquist, R., and Hodgson, A.: Structuring BDI Agents in Functional Clusters, in Intelligent Agents VI: Theories, Architectures and Languages, LNAI Volume 1757 (N. Jennings & Y. Lesperance eds), pp 277–289, Springer-Verlag, Heidelberg, Germany (2000)
3. Collier, R.: Agent Factory: A Framework for the Engineering of Agent-Oriented Applications, Ph.D. Thesis, Department of Computer Science, University College Dublin, Ireland (2001)

4. Collier, R.W., O'Hare G.M.P., Lowen, T., Rooney, C.F.B., Beyond Prototyping in the Factory of the Agents, 3rd Central and Eastern European Conference on Multi-Agent Systems (CEEMAS'03), Prague, Czech Republic (2003)

5. Fonseca S., Griss M., Letsinger R.: An Agent-Mediated E-Commerce Environment for the Mobile Shopper. HP Technical Report HPL-2001-157 (2001)

6. Keegan, K. & O'Hare, G.M.P. (2002) "EasiShop: Context sensitive Shopping for the Mobile User through Mobile Agent Technology", Proceedings of PIMRC 2002 13th IEEE International Symposium on Personal Indoor and Mobile Radio Communications, IEEE Press. Sept. 15th-18th, Lisbon, Portugal

7. Mihailescu P., Binder W.: A Mobile Agent Framework for M-Commerce, Proceedings of Agents in E-Business (AgEB'01), Vienna, Austria (2001)

8. Nwana H., Ndumu D., Lee L.: ZEUS: A Tool-Kit for Building Distributed Multi-Agent Systems, Applied Artificial Intelligence Journal, Vol. 13(1) 129–186 (1999)

9. Odell, J., Parunak, H. and Bauer, B.: Extending UML for agents. Proceedings Agent-Oriented Information System Workshop at the 17th National Conference on Artificial Intelligence (2000)

10. O'Hare, G.M.P.: Agent Factory: An Environment for the Fabrication of Distributed Artificial Systems, in O'Hare, G.M.P. and Jennings, N.R.(Eds.), Foundations of Distributed Artificial Intelligence, Sixth Generation Computer Series, Wiley Interscience Pubs, New York (1996)

11. Rao, A.S., Georgeff, M.P.: BDI Agents: From Theory to Practice, in Proceeding of the First International Conference on Multi-Agent Systems (ICMAS-96), pp 312–319, San Francisco, CA, June (1996)

12. Ratsimore O., Korolev V., Joshi A.,Finin T.: Agents2Go: An infrastructure for Location-Dependent Service Discovery in the Mobile Electronic Commerce Environment. First ACM Mobile Commerce Workshop, Rome (2001)

13. Strahan, R., Muldoon, C., O'Hare, G., Berolotto, M., Collier, R.: An Agent-Based Architecture for Wireless Bus Travel Assistants. Proceedings The Second International Workshop on Wireless Information Systems (WIS 2003), Angers France, April 2003, (in press)

14. Taylor D.: Agents that move for things that hink. IEEE Intelligent Systems, March/April 2000, pp. 4–6 (2000)

15. Youll J., Morris J., Krikorian R., Maes P.: Impulse: Location-based Agent Assistance, Software Demos, Proceedings of the Fourth International Conference on Autonomous Agents (Agents 2000), Barcelona, Spain, (2000)

Adaptive Agent-Based Service Composition for Wireless Terminals

Sasu Tarkoma [1] and Mikko Laukkanen [2]

[1] Helsinki Institute for Information Technology
P.O. Box 9800, FIN-02015 HUT, Finland
sasu.tarkoma@hiit.fi

[2] TeliaSonera Finland
P.O.Box 970 (Teollisuuskatu 13)
FIN-00051 SONERA
+358 40 5073358
mikko.laukkanen@teliasonera.com

Abstract. Software agents are one of the building blocks of ambient intelligence and pervasive computing. Adaptation to changes in the execution context is necessary in order to provide continuous and smooth provision of services for wireless clients. In this paper, we present a system for adapting a service consisting of multiple agents based on application, terminal and communication models and profiles. The system adapts and composes the service by finding the best combination of local and external agents to contact. The context models are based on experimentation with actual devices and environments. We present a theoretical cost model for runtime service composition, and examine experimental results that are based on an example scenario.

1 Introduction

Software agents are one of the building blocks of ambient intelligence and pervasive computing [13]. Agents are autonomous and proactive entities that are capable of reacting and adapting to changes in their environment. Agent technology relies on asynchronous messaging that is used in order to facilitate agent communication in multi-agent systems [6]. Therefore, improving messaging and minimizing communication latency are key requirements for improving the performance and response time of agent-based services and applications. This optimisation requires that agents adapt to their communication context, and react to changes perceived in the communication link, message transport and the agent execution environment.

Adaptation to changes in the execution context is necessary in order to provide continuous and smooth provision of services for wireless clients. In this paper, we present a system for adapting a service that consists of multiple agents for wireless clients. The adaptation mechanism uses application, terminal and communication models that allow the system to examine different usage strategies for contacting the

M. Klusch et al. (Eds.): CIA 2003, LNAI 2782, pp. 16–29, 2003.

agents of the service. The system adapts the service by finding the best combination of local and external agents to contact. Local agents are available on the client terminal, and external agents reside on fixed-network systems, and require the use of a communication mechanism that may or may not be limited in terms of bandwidth and latency. The context models are based on experimentation with devices and environments. We present a theoretical cost model for service composition. We have focused on the dynamic service composition or partitioning decision, whether to request part of a service from a local agent or an external agent. Mobile agents or agent download is not considered, and we assume that the agents are available locally and that the service requests are stateless. Stateless operation allows the system to change the usage strategy without costly state transfer between agents.

In this paper service composition and partitioning are synonymous; however, service composition could also have more requirements, such as application requirements that would need to be considered. Moreover, we have assumed that the structure of the service being composed is available; however, in multi-vendor scenarios the client or initial service provision agent may need to negotiate the service structure by, for example, participating in auctions.

This paper is structured as follows: Section 2 presents the system overview and examines various models and how they are used in service composition. Section 3 presents the experimental application scenario: the recommendation service. Finally, Section 4 presents the conclusions.

1.1 Background and Related Work

Service composition has been the subject of many research projects, such as the Ninja project [5] and SAHARA [12]. In addition, W3C is specifying the Semantic Web, which includes specifications for WSDL, SOAP and other protocols that may be used to describe, access, execute, and discover services on the Web [8]. The Semantic Web effort provides mechanisms that may be used to realize automatic service composition and they are a building block for interoperable multi-agent systems and complement the existing agent standards, such as the FIPA architecture [3].

Agents have been considered for service composition both in fixed-network environments and in mobile environments [1,2]. Mobile agents and fixed-network proxies have been considered for application partitioning [14]. In addition, service partitioning in wireless and mobile environments with FIPA agents has been examined in [9]. A theoretical examination of selecting the best communication protocol has been presented in [11] in the context of service provision. One of the conclusions of the paper is that local decisions by agents in minimizing load lead to globally good behaviour. Agent-based service composition based on negotiation in multiple auctions has been examined in [10].

The work presented in this paper is based on the FIPA architecture [3], which aims to improve agent interoperability by standardizing the agent platform and the external interfaces of agents and platforms, such as: message transport protocols, message envelopes, agent communication language (ACL), content languages and interaction protocols.

MicroFIPA-OS is an agent development toolkit and platform based on the FIPA-OS agent toolkit. The system targets medium to high-end PDA devices that have sufficient resources to execute a PersonalJava compatible virtual machine. MicroFIPA-OS allows the use of FIPA-OS components such as AMS and DF, and supports the rapid prototyping of agents in PDA environments without modifying agent code with tradeoffs between portability, and performance and resource consumption [15].

Previous performance measurements [15] with MicroFIPA-OS indicate that high-end PDAs are capable of supporting multiple agents on a single device; however, with a cost in system latency and memory. The wireless connections are the critical part of the system being considerably slower than messaging within devices. Since the messaging environment is constrained by the capabilities of the device and the limitations of the wireless link, the system needs to decide what is transmitted and when [7,15].

2   Adaptive Service Composition

Service composition and adaptation to changes in the client communication context requires that the agent or agent execution environment on the terminal has a model of the environment, and the different components that are available. The model is used as the basis for decision-making in selecting the best way of using the components. Fig. 1 presents an overview of different aspects of the environment. The changeable parameters that may be used for optimization are illustrated using italics. Observable parameters are highlighted using the bold type. In this paper, a service is composed of a number of agents, which are available locally, remotely or both to the service-requesting agent on a terminal device.

We propose a system that finds an optimal usage pattern for the agents that can be used either locally or externally. The primary goal of this system is to minimize application-level latency, which is important in order to provide reasonable response times when slow and unreliable communication links are used. The system provides a flexible way to partition a service between terminals and servers thus reducing server load when clients have enough processing power to execute parts of the service.

We assume that one agent requests service from the other agents. The service experienced by this agent is composed of one or more agents. Some of the agents may or must be local to the requesting agent, and some agents may or must be external.

There are many different possible adaptation techniques. Table 1 identifies three possible adaptation techniques in an agent execution environment. We focus on service composition. Dynamic selection of the MTP and different message encodings create a more complex scenario.

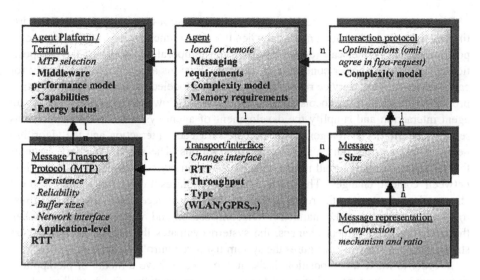

Fig. 1. Dependencies of various components of an agent system and an overview of the observable (bold) and changeable (italics) parameters

Table 1. Adaptation techniques in an agent execution environment

Adaptation Decision	Description
Service composition	Find the optimal location of agents, and their parameters. Agents are non-mobile, stateless and available locally, or remotely. The execution environment may support this transparently using information stored in application profiles.
Selection of MTP	The system can change MTP to a more suitable protocol when the link properties change. In addition, MTP may support message prioritization, and various messaging strategies (push/pull). Selection of MTP is not addressed in this paper.
Message representation	The message representation and compression can be changed to optimize the number of bits transmitted and the communication latency. Message representation issues are not addressed in this paper.

2.1 Service Composition

Agent-based services can be implemented using a number of agents that co-operate in the realization of the service functionality. An agent wishing to use the service needs to know at least one agent that provides the service. It is assumed that a service consists of N agents, and some may be local and some external. External agents are required, because many service elements cannot be provided locally because of their nature. On the other hand, it is not reasonable to use some components externally if they are locally available and the execution environment is fast enough.

The service composition decision can be made at start-time or at run-time. Start-time decisions may become unoptimal when the environment changes. Run-time composition can be further categorized based on the temporal properties of the composition decision: one-shot or continuous. One-shot decisions are evaluated separately for each service request. Service requests are typically modeled using different interaction protocols. Interaction protocols specify the message flow and possible states of an agent interaction and simplify the development of agent systems. One-shot decisions require that the decision algorithm is executed for each interaction and the algorithm needs to take into account also the other interactions. The second category assumes that the decision holds for all interactions for a certain period of time, usually the time between context changes. The latter approach requires information about context changes in order to start the re-evaluation of the service access strategy. Fig. 2 illustrates the continuous and dynamic service composition and adaptation process. When the execution environment changes, the system evaluates the current service access strategy and possibly re-configures the system using a control mechanism.

In order to make a composition decision, we need to have a model of the application behaviour: the type, volume and frequency of interactions. The modelling of application behaviour is difficult and may require input from the authors of the application and run-time performance monitoring and modelling. The execution environment may support service composition transparently using information stored in application profiles. The applications profiles need to include information about the location, availability and requirements of various components.

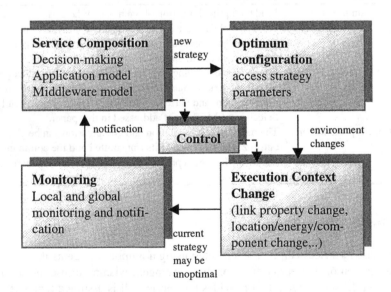

Fig. 2. Service composition in a dynamic environment

2.2 Application Model

For one-shot interactions, we need to model the expected number of bytes that are sent and received, and the expected processing time of each request. Complex functionality or interactions require more complex models for the communication. The adaptation engine uses this model in deciding whether external or local agent is used. We assume that all agents that are components of a service are available on the local system, so the download time is not taken into account, which is a factor in real-life situations. The main metric is the total time spent in messaging, which should be minimized. Additional metrics are memory and resource use on the local system. The experimental model is presented in Section 3.

2.3 Theoretical Cost Model

Equation 1 presents the one-shot external cost in seconds for accessing an external agent using the fipa-request interaction protocol [4] with the agree performative omitted. Srv denotes the processing time of the request on the server in seconds, M_{req} is the request size in bytes and M_{res} is the response size in bytes, is the bandwidth (bps) and δ is the link latency in seconds. We assume symmetric communication links and all variables are non-negative and finite. In addition, there may be only one service request active at a time or the effect of existing messaging needs to be taken into account in the bandwidth:

$$E(C_E) = E(Srv) + 2\delta + \frac{8(E(M_{req}) + E(M_{res}))}{\tau}.$$

(1)

Equation 2 presents the cost of accessing a local agent with the same interaction protocol. L_{cl} denotes the expected local processing time of the agent to be contacted, and C_{Lreq} is the expected cost in seconds for the local request operation that is middleware specific:

$$E(C_L) = E(L_{cl}) + E(C_{Lreq}).$$

(2)

2.4 Composition Decision

Context-aware service composition may be represented as a decision theoretic problem. Let $A = \{Ai \text{ for } i = 1,2,...,M\}$ be a finite set of decision alternatives, different ways that agents of a service may be contacted, and $G = \{G_j \text{ for } j = 1,2,...,N\}$ a finite set of goals that represent the agents that need to be contacted. A decision matrix is used to represent the decision problem. An element a_{ij} of (MxN) decision matrix represents the performance of alternative A_i when it is evaluated in terms of the goal G_j. In order to solve the problem and find A^*, the optimal configuration of local and external components, we use the weighted sum model (WSM), which is a common approach for single dimensional problems under the additive utility assumption [16]:

$$A^* = Min_i \sum_{j=1}^{N} a_{ij} \,. \tag{3}$$

Since each agent may be used locally or remotely, each goal may take either the value of 0 (local) or 1 (remote). There are $M = 2^N$ possible configurations, and therefore M rows in the decision matrix. Let a' denote an element of a second MxN matrix that represents the different decision alternatives, the different binary N-strings. Equation 4 presents how an element a_{ij} of the decision matrix is calculated:

$$a_{ij} = a'_{ij} E(C_E(j)) + (1 - a'_{ij}) E(C_L(j)) \,. \tag{4}$$

In equation 4, functions $C_E(j)$ and $C_L(j)$ represent the cost of requesting service from the agent j externally and locally, respectively. In addition to response time, we may also consider the overhead of using the components locally. Let β denote the threshold, in percentage, that the cumulative local resource overhead must not exceed, and let R_{local} denote the local resource overhead increment by using the given resource locally. Equation 5 presents the resource overhead for the decision alternative i, which must be below β:

$$\varphi(i) = \sum_{j=1}^{N} \left(1 - a'_{ij}\right) R_{local}(j) \,. \tag{5}$$

A^* may be found by exhaustion by going through all the 2^N subsets and finding the sequence that solves the problem with the smallest response time, possibly taking into account the overhead as well. Equation 5 allows us to remove rows of the decision matrix that do not satisfy the inequality $(\varphi(i) < \beta)$. The decision matrix and A^* are found using the following steps:

1. Create a temporary (M,N) matrix T' and each row a'_i of T' contains a binary decision alternative for N goals. If a component j can only be used remotely, its value in $a'_{ij} \in T'$ is set to 1. Duplicate rows are removed from T'.
2. Let E denote the set of rows that do not satisfy the inequality; thus $x \in E$, $\varphi(x) \geq \beta$, and it follows $M = |A \backslash E|$. Rows in E are removed from T'.
3. Create a (M,N) matrix using Equation 4.
4. Sum all rows of the decision matrix.
5. Select the row (A^*) with the minimum sum (Equation 3).

2.5 Discussion

The dynamic service composition and partitioning problem is challenging, because the environment changes over time. The proposed model is relatively simple and more complex models would reflect service usage better. We have focused on decisions based on the measurements of interactions for stateless agents one strategy at a time. The evaluation of longer and more complicated communication patterns may require support for context prediction and communication pattern duration estimation, because the system needs to know for what period of time the strategy is evaluated. Stateful agents require that a certain adopted communication pattern is maintained as long as the state is maintained by the service agent.

This approach requires that the service requests are sequential in nature and they can utilize the given bandwidth of the link. If the requests are not sequential the usage decision may become unoptimal, because the link characteristics do not reflect the current situation of the communication link, which may be congested and have additional latencies due to message buffering. Simultaneous requests require additional information in making the usage decision, such as the average request rate for each interaction. Another approach is to monitor the bandwidth and latency, and when a long-term change is perceived a context change event is fired and a new usage strategy is formulated using the new estimates of the link characteristics.

3 Example Scenario: Recommendation Service

We have created a simple adaptive service scenario based on the ideas presented in Section 2. The experimental scenario used to examine service composition in wireless environments consists of a location-based recommendation service. The service takes the location of the client, accesses an external database that contains location specific information, such as nearby restaurants and their menus, and creates a map image of the neighborhood with the nearby location highlighted. The results presented in this section are based on a prototype Java implementation of the components of the map service, and the MicroFIPA-OS platform [15]. The service configuration is illustrated Fig. 3 and the system consists of the following components:

- Client agent that orchestrates the service usage and has knowledge of its location,
- Proxy DB-agent that caches map information and retrieves information from location-information database located on the fixed network,
- Map-agent that takes the location-information from the database and builds an image of the neighbourhood,
- Proximity agent that calculates distances between objects and returns the identifiers of nearby objects, and
- Database-agent that manages location-based information.

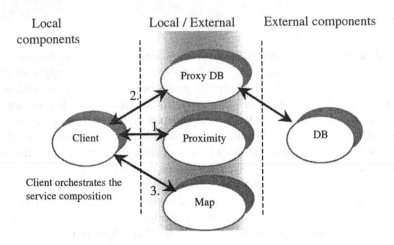

Fig. 3. Overview of the service configuration space

In Fig. 3, the client agent uses the other agents in order to create a map of nearby locations. First, the client sends the coordinates to the Proximity agent that returns the
identifiers of the nearby locations (1). After this, the client sends the identifiers of the
locations to the Proxy DB/Database-agent (2), which returns their names and other
relevant information. Finally, the client sends the data to the Map-agent, which creates an image of the nearby locations with the coordinates highlighted on the map.
Table 2 presents the equipment that was used in the experimentation. All the local
processing times were measured with a laptop and a Compaq iPAQ, and in the network performance tests the peer computer was another laptop. The client system used
Nokia D211 for WLAN/GPRS connectivity.

Table 2. The equipment used in the measurements

Device	Hardware	Software
Windows terminal	HP Omnibook 6100 512MB RAM 1GHz CPU	Windows 2000 Professional Service Pack 3, RC 3.136 JDK1.1.8
Linux terminal	HP Omnibook 6100 512MB RAM 1GHz CPU	Linux 2.4.18 JDK1.1.8
Handheld terminal	Compaq iPAQ H3630 32MB RAM 206 MHz CPU	Linux 2.4.3 JDK1.1.8
Network peer	Toshiba Portege 7020 128MB RAM 366 MHz CPU	Linux 2.2.18 JDK1.1.8

Table 3 presents a summary of the output data of the components and their average processing times. These measurements were made using 1000 replications. The input arguments to the Proximity-agent were longitude, latitude, and the diameter, and the output was a list of identifiers. The identifiers were the input to the Database-agent, which returned a list of strings. The Map-agent input was a list of strings and coordinates, and the output was a byte array consisting of the compressed image (GIF-format). In the experiments we omitted the overhead caused by the agent platform, because the components are generic service objects. The network performance measurements were performed in two environments: WLAN and GPRS. The WLAN was a private network consisting of a WLAN access point connecting the terminal with the network peer. In the case of GPRS, on the other hand, a live and public production network was used. Table 4 presents the results of wireless access of the same components using WLAN and GPRS on top of the MicroFIPA-OS execution environment. The wireless measurements were made using 20 replications.

This experimental data is the basis for the application profile that is used in deciding what components are used and where. The application profile consists of the FIPA-request protocol information: the types of FIPA-request messages sent and received, their estimated frequency, processing times locally and remotely, and an estimated size for the request and reply messages of each type. This information is used to evaluate the cost of local and external communication.

Table 3. Summary of output data and average processing time of the three components on three different devices

Case	Setup	Output vector size	Output size (bytes)	Avg. Processing time (ms)
Proximity	Laptop (Win)	1	22	0.0014
		50	1103	0.06439
		100	2234	0.13019
	Laptop (Linux)	1	22	0.0032
		50	1103	0.15486
		100	2234	0.31019
	iPAQ (Linux)	1	22	1.408
		50	1103	73.263
		100	2234	144.042
Database	Laptop (Win)	1	16	0.0018
		50	802	0.0698
		100	1533	0.1381
	Laptop (Linux)	1	16	0.02405
		50	802	0.50064
		100	1533	0.98662
	iPAQ (Linux)	1	16	0.332
		50	802	5.702
		100	1533	11.19
Map	Laptop (Win)	50x50	3639	9.474
		200x200	46159	46.096
	Laptop (Linux)	50x50	3639	16.575
		200x200	46159	198.979
	iPAQ (Linux)	50x50	3639	35151
		200x200	46159	121981

Table 4. Remote performances of the three components using WLAN and GPRS on MicroFI-PA-OS with FIPA-request (agree message omitted)

Case	Network	Output	Avg. time (ms)	Standard Deviation
Proximity	GPRS	1	3713.9	110.27
		50	4387.58	63.51
		100	4615.05	201.11
	WLAN	1	37.8	7.25
		50	55	5.55
		100	72.4	6.88
Database	GPRS	1	3715.58	121.87
		50	3815.21	436.95
		100	4418.26	696.69
	WLAN	1	38.55	6.45
		50	47.8	4.94
		100	59.25	5.38
Map	GPRS	50x50	5454.95	406.21
		200x200	19705.79	409.57
	WLAN	50x50	122.75	5.24
		200x200	1223.8	15.86

Table 5 presents the decision matrix with the 2^3 decision alternatives and the approximate response time. The number 0 denotes that the component is used locally, and 1 that it is used externally. The database column denotes the database proxy agent when the local component is used, and the actual database agent when the external component is used. For these results we have used the laptop-based network measurements, because the wireless link is slower than local processing. We have previously measured the approximate local fipa-request latency of the MicroFIPA-OS system on the iPAQ as 144 ± 22 ms using the interoperable FIPA-OS API, and 37.3 ± 0.48 ms using the minimal messaging API that lacks conversation management [15]. Table 5 includes the approximate response time calculated using the latter latency.

In runtime operation, the system may use Equation 1 to calculate an estimate for the remote interaction if the application profile contains information about processing times and message sizes. We plan to take the memory overhead of the components into account in the future.

The results of Table 5 indicate that we may gain considerable benefits by finding the best access pattern for the components of a service. The smallest response times are highlighted using underlining and bold type. The selected strategy for WLAN offers 18.7% (2% if local latency is taken into account) improvement in response time when compared with the strategy in which all components are external, and it is 192 (160) times faster than all-local operation. Similarly, the selected strategy for GPRS offers 60% (59%) improvement from the all-external scenario, and it is 6.4 (6.3) times faster than all-local operation. The service latency is lowest for the iPAQ when the client does not orchestrate the service, but only fetches the image from the fixed-network side; however, this kind of approach does not provide any functionality when the client is disconnected.

Table 5. Decision matrix for the experimental scenario on iPAQ with WLAN and GPRS (50x50 image with output vector size 50)

		Proximity	Database	Map	Response time (ms)	Response time with local latency (ms)
1	WLAN	0 (73.263)	0 (5.702)	0 (35151)	35229.97	35341.87
	GPRS	0 (73.263)	0 (5.702)	0 (35151)	35229.97	35341.87
2	WLAN	0 (73.263)	0 (5.702)	1 (122.75)	201.715	276.315
	GPRS	0 (73.263)	0 (5.702)	1 (5454.95)	*5533.915*	*5608.5*
3	WLAN	0 (73.263)	1 (47.8)	0 (35151)	35272.06	35346.66
	GPRS	0 (73.263)	1 (3815.21)	0 (35151)	39039.47	39114.07
4	WLAN	1 (55)	0 (5.702)	0 (35151)	35211.7	35286.3
	GPRS	1 (4387.58)	0 (5.702)	0 (35151)	39544.28	39618.88
5	WLAN	0 (73.263)	1 (47.8)	1 (122.75)	243.813	281.113
	GPRS	0 (73.263)	1 (3815.21)	1 (5454.95)	9343.423	9380.723
6	WLAN	1 (55)	1 (47.8)	0 (35151)	35253.8	35291.1
	GPRS	1 (4387.58)	1 (3815.21)	0 (35151)	43353.79	43391.09
7	WLAN	1 (55)	0 (5.702)	1 (122.75)	*183.452*	*220.752*
	GPRS	1 (4387.58)	0 (5.702)	1 (5454.95)	9848.232	9885.532
8	WLAN	1 (55)	1 (47.8)	1 (122.75)	225.55	225.55
	GPRS	1 (4387.58)	1 (3815.21)	1 (5454.95)	13657.74	13657.74

In this scenario, the bottleneck component is the map component, which is slow in local operation. The results are similar with 200x200 images and with output vector size of 100 on the iPAQ. On a laptop, however, the all-local configuration has the lowest response time and the all-external the highest response time, because wireless communication is slow. These results show that neither the all-external nor the all-local configurations are optimal for a small device given that the service is orchestrated from the client-side. In addition, the results motivate using local components and service logic with slow links and reasonably powerful client systems, such as GPRS and the laptop used in this study.

4 Conclusions

One of the key requirements for applications and services is to minimize the delay experienced by the user. In this paper, we have investigated how the latency of services that consist of multiple agents can be improved by adaptive service composition. In the proposed model, the agent responsible for service composition decides whether to contact an agent externally or locally. This decision is made when the execution context changes. We have assumed that the agents are locally available, and that they are stateless. We presented a method for formulating a decision matrix and making the usage decision, and an example service scenario. The experimental results show that the client agent may gain substantial improvement in latency by selecting the best combination of local and external resources.

This kind of approach may also be used to implement partial fault tolerance, in which part of the service functionality can still be provided even if network connectivity is lost. In the future we plan to examine service composition and reconfiguration in mobile and wireless environments, context events for triggering reconfiguration, and sensitivity analysis of the composition and partitioning decision.

Acknowledgements. This work has been funded by the National Technology Agency of Finland (Tekes), Elisa Communications, Ericsson, Nokia, TeliaSonera, More Magic Software, and Movial. We thank Heikki Helin and Jaakko Kangasharju for valuable comments.

References

1. Chakraborty, D., Joshi, A. Dynamic Service Composition: State-of-the-Art and Research Directions. Technical Report TR-CS-01-19. CSEE. University of Maryland, Baltimore County. December 2001
2. Chen, H., Joshi, A., Finin, T. Dynamic Service Discovery for Mobile Computing: Intelligent Agents Meet Jini in the Aether. Cluster Computing, Volume 4, Number 4, pages 343–354, 2001
3. Foundation for Intelligent Physical Agents (FIPA). The FIPA Architecture, Geneva, Switzerland, 2003. Available at http://www.fipa.org
4. Foundation for Intelligent Physical Agents (FIPA). FIPA Request Interaction Protocol Specification. Available at http://www.fipa.org/specs/fipa00026/
5. Gribble, S. D., Welsh, M., von Behren, R., Brewer, E. A., Culler, D., Borisov, N., Czerwinski, S., Gummadi, R., Hill, J., Joseph, A. D., Katz, R. H., Mao, Z., Ross, S., and Zhao, B. The Ninja Architecture for Robust Internet-Scale Systems and Services, Special Issue of Computer Networks on Pervasive Computing, March 2001, 473–497
6. Jennings, N., Sycara, K., Wooldridge, M. A Roadmap of Agent Research and Development, Autonomous Agents and Multi-Agent Systems (275-306), Kluwer Academic Publishers, Boston, 1998
7. Laukkanen, M., Helin, H., Laamanen, H. Supporting Nomadic Agent-based Applications in the FIPA Agent Architecture. In Cristiano Castelfranci and W. Lewis Johnson, editors, Proceedings of the First International Joint Conference on Autonomous Agents & Multi-Agent Systems (AAMAS 2002) pages 1348–1355, July, 2002, Bologna, Italy
8. McIlraith, S., Son T., Zeng, H. Semantic Web Services. IEEE Intelligent Systems, Special Issue on the Semantic Web, Volume 16, No. 2, pp. 46–53, March/April, 2001
9. Koskimies, O., Raatikainen, K. Partitioning Applications with Agents. In the Second International Workshop on Mobile Agents for Telecommunication Applications (MATA2000), pages 79-93. Lecture Notes in Computer Science, Springer Verlag, September 2000
10. Preist, C., Byde, A., Bartolini, C., Piccinelli, G. Towards Agent-Based Service Composition through Negotiation in Multiple Auctions. HP report, HPL-2001-71
11. Preist, C., Pearson, S. An Adaptive Choice of Messaging Protocol in Multi Agent Systems. Foundations and Applications of Multi-Agent Systems, LNAI 2403, Springer, 2002

12. Raman, B., Agarwal, S., Chen,Y., Caesar, M., Cui, W., Johansson, P., Lai, K., Lavian, T., Machiraju, S., Mao, Z.M., Porter, G., Roscoe, T., Seshadri, M., Shih, J., Sklower, K., Subramanian, L., Suzuki, T., Zhuang, S., Joseph, A.D., Katz, R.H., and Stoica, I. The SAHARA Model for Service Composition Across Multiple Providers. Pervasive Computing, August 2002. Lecture Notes in Computer Science LNCS 2414, Springer, 2002
13. Satyanarayanan, M. Pervasive computing: vision and challenges. IEEE Personal Communications, August 2001
14. Schill, A., Held, A., Ziegert, T., Springer, T. A Partitioning Model for Applications in Mobile Environments. In Todd Papaioannou and Nelson Minar, editors, Proceedings. Mobile Agents in the Context of Competition and Cooperation (MAC3), a workshop at Autonomous Agents '99, pages 34–41, 1999
15. Tarkoma, S., Laukkanen, M. Facilitating Agent Messaging on PDAs. Fourth International Workshop on Mobile Agents for Telecommunication Applications (MATA-2002), Barcelona, Spain. Lecture Notes in Computer Science (LNCS) 2521, Springer 2002
16. Triantaphyllou, E., Shu, B., Nieto Sanchez, S., and Ray, T. Multi-Criteria Decision Making: An Operations Research Approach. Encyclopedia of Electrical and Electronics Engineering, (J.G. Webster, Ed.), John Wiley & Sons, New York, NY, Vol. 15, pp. 175–186, 1998

An Information Notification Model with VPC on KODAMA in an Ubiquitous Computing Environment, and Its Experiment

Tadashige Iwao[1], Satoshi Amamiya[2], Kenichi Takahashi[2], Guoqiang Zhong[2],
Tatsuya Kainuma[3], Lusheng Ji[4], and Makoto Amamiya[2]

[1] Web Technology Laboratory, Fujitsu Laboratories Ltd.,
4-1-1 Kamikodanaka, Nakahara-ku, 211-8588 Kawasaki, Japan
`iwao@labs.fujitsu.com`
[2] Graduate School of Information Science and Electrical Engineering,
Kyushu University,
6-1 Kasuga-Koen, Kasuga, 816 Fukuoka, Japan
`{roger, tkenichi, amamiya}@is.kyushu-u.ac.jp`
[3] 2nd Development Division, Fujitsu Prime Soft Technologies Ltd.,
1-16-38 Aoi, Higashi-ku, 461-0004 Nagoya, Japan
`kainuma@pst.fujitsu.com`
[4] Fujitsu Laboratories of America College Park, 301-486-0978 College Park, MD
`lji@fla.fujitsu.com`

Abstract. The notification of useful information to users is necessary to keep them aware of their environment and is of particular benefit in a ubiquitous computing environment. However, the amount and nature of information to be provided depends on circumstances. Too much information will confuse users. Systems used to disseminate information in a ubiquitous computing environment should not provide all information to all users, and should instead modify information disseminated depending on circumstances and context. In addition, systems designed for use in a ubiquitous computing environment need a security function for various reasons including privacy protection. For these reasons, we have developed an information dissemination model, called *VPC on KO-DAMA*. The model enables systems to provide an appropriate amount of information to users depending on circumstances and contains a security function. Using this model, we performed a large-scale experiment involving approximately one thousand participants. This paper contains the results of and discussions regarding this experiment.

1 Introduction

The device and network infrastructure necessary to create a truly ubiquitous computing environment is rapidly reaching maturity. In the near future, ubiquitous computing might well become a reality. Should this occur, the computing environment will be available not only at home, but also in shopping malls, service stations and other locations as well. In a ubiquitous computing environment, the quality and utility of the information disseminated to users is very

M. Klusch et al. (Eds.): CIA 2003, LNAI 2782, pp. 30–45, 2003.

important. The dissemination of useful information to users is necessary to keep them aware of their environment. However, the amount and nature of information to be provided depends on circumstances. Too much information will simply confuse users. For instance, there are many shops, facilities, and products available in a shopping mall. If information on all of these is provided to users, overload occurs; users become confused and may abandon use of the system. For this reason, systems designed for operation in a ubiquitous computing environment should not disseminate all available information to user, and should instead change information the volume and nature of the information provided depending on circumstances. In addition, systems designed for use in a ubiquitous computing environment should be equipped with a security function. In the context of dissemination, the security function should protect user's privacy and prevent them from being harassed from illegal or unwanted solicitations such as those contained in SPAM emails. Of course, determining whether information dissemination from the environment will be of actual benefit to users in the real world is a big question to begin with. Only an actual field test can answer this question.

We propose a new model, called *VPC on KODAMA*, that enables notifyee in ubiquitous computing environment to receive appropriate information without disclosure notifyee's information. VPC [1,2] and KODAMA [3,4] have been developed independently. VPC (*Virtual Private Community*) provides a framework that filters information in notifyee side using notifyee's profile. Notification information in VPC is packed as a *policy package* that includes not only notification contents, but also policy of notification. Notification policies that are rule base are defined as contents change depending on user's profile by notifyer. In VPC, each notifyee is regarded as a member in a community. Notiyees are agents in VPC, and have their own *roles* in communities. Roles are to see contents here. The roles change depending on notifyee's profile. A policy package is sent to notifyees who attempt to join in the community. A VPC platform that works on user's terminal devices evaluates the policy package and determines appropriate contents according to the rule in the policy package and user's profile.

KODAMA provides a framework of hierarchy structure for communities. Members in a community are agents that have a self-contained community. Messages are relayed to lower communities one after another. At each step agents have message filtering policies and filter messages according those policies. Agents that represent communities are called as *portal agents*.

By unifying VPC and KODAMA, agents in VPC reside in communities that are represented by portal agents. Messages in KODAMA are regarded as policy packages in VPC. Policy packages are filtered by portal agents. Communities are assigned based on factors such as location and shops. Agents change communities according to physical change of users. Policy packages are sent from a root community, and are disseminated down through lower communities via portal agent filters. Unnecessary policy packages and illegal policy packages are filtered out by the portal agents. Agents in VPC can receive filtered context-dependent policy packages without disclosing profile information.

We performed a large-scale experiment of VPC on KODAMA in Nagoya, Japan over a period lasting approximately two months. About one thousand people participated to this experiment. The service provided in this experiment consisted on advertisements that were specifically related to the user's profile and location. The results of this experiment showed that shop sales increased with the quality of information disseminated.

We discuss notification model in section 2. VPC, KODAMA and their unification are described in section 3. The experiment is shown in section 4. Section 5 describes related works.

2   Filtering Notifcation of Information

In a ubiquitous computing environment, reflection of the physical environment to the logical environment is important. All information disseminated should reflect any change of the context of physical environment such as change of location. Hence, the filtering policy for disseminated information should change according to context. Systems for filtering disseminated information need be capable of changing filters according to context. The security of this system should also be able to ensure user privacy.

Generally speaking, there are two ways to filtering information; Information provider side filtering and participating user side filtering. In information provider side information filtering, the information provider needs to know what information is required by participating users. This requires participating users to disclose personal data, and as a result, the possibility of information leakage occurs.

In participating user side information filtering, participating users receive information and filters it themselves. This method does not require participating users to disclose any personal information, but results in a massive initial information dump that makes it very difficult for participating users to locate information relevant to their needs. Additionally, filtering policies change depending on circumstances and contexts, resulting in even more information overload.

Thus, simply put, filtering by participating users results in information overload on the user while filtering by information provider is susceptible to misuse in terms of privacy and security. To address these concerns and realize a truly ubiquitous computing environment, we need a method that does not require participating users to disclose personal information while protecting them from information overload. The method should also support changes to filtering policies, depending on circumstances and context, in order to reflect any change to the physical environment with the logical environment.

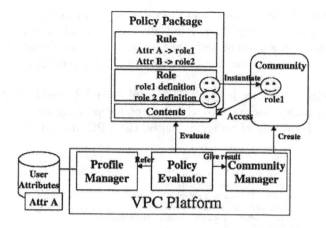

Fig. 1. Overview of VPC

3   Virtual Private Community (VPC) and KODAMA

3.1   VPC

VPC Basic Model. Figure 1 shows a VPC basic model. In the basic model, a policy package defines contents of information to disseminate, notification policies, and roles that examine the contents. Policy packages are activated by *VPC platforms* (VPC-Ps) that manage user attributes, evaluate policy packages according to the user attributes, decide appropriate roles, and create the community. Roles are programs that examine notified contents. Each role has a name, and is bound to a content. For instance, only users who have role A can see content A when role A is assigned content A. In addition, users who have attribute a can see content A, when a dissemination policy is set that allows users who have attribute a can have role A. Thus, information providers can define notification policies.

The primary parts of a VPC-P consist of a profile manager, a policy evaluator, and community manager. Profile managers manage the user profile contained in tamper-resistant devices such as Java Card [5]. The policy evaluator determines roles depending on user attributes. The community manager executes selected agents, and connects with any community managers on other VPC-Ps that utilize the same policy packages. VPC supports both the propagation and utilization phases as well as both the stand-alone and interaction models in the utilization phase. In the stand-alone mode, the community manager will not connect with the others, even if others have the same community.

Policy Package. Figure 2 depicts a structure of policy packages. A policy package consists of a set of rules as a condition table, a set of roles as transitions, and a set of contents. A rule consists of a condition and role names. A condition is described with logical expressions using attributes. An attribute consists of a database name, a variable name, and the value of the variable. A role consists of a role name, a program name, and an initialization method. A content consists of a content name, and a content path that locates the real content data. Content includes program codes that implements roles. Policy packages are written in XML.

Policy packages are encoded by S/MIME [6]. S/MIME enables VPC to detect falsification of policy packages by checking policy package hash codes . When VPC detects falsification of policy packages, the VPC discards the policy packages.

```
<policy package>  ::= <rules> <roles> <contents>
<rules>           ::= <rule> | <rule> <rules>
<rule>            ::= <condition> <role names>
<role names>      ::= <role name> | <role name> <role names>
<condition>       ::= "TRUE"
                   |  "and" <condition> <condition>
                   |  "not" <condition>
                   |  "eq" <attribute> | "<" <attribute>
<attribute>       ::= <variable name> <value>
<roles>           ::= <role> | <role> <roles>
<role>            ::= <role name> <program name> <init description>
<contents>        ::= <content> | <content> <contents>
<content>         ::= <content name> <content path>
```

Fig. 2. Structure of Policy Packages

3.2   KODAMA

Relationships among communities. All agents in KODAMA form the logical world which is completely separated from the physical world consisting of agent host machines. As illustrated in Figure 3, agents are organized and located into various agent communities, which in turn are linked together to form a directed acyclic graph (DAG) structure, in the logical world. Each community has a portal agent that represents the community. Portal agents work as a gateway or a router that dispatches messages to agents in their own community and filters messages according to a filtering policy.

On the other hand, agents are programs running on different machines and need to exchange various kinds of data over networks in real time. The network themselves are full of latencies, congestion, overload and unforeseen failure. Building a multi-agent system directly on top of distributed networks, therefore, is very difficult, time-consuming, and costly. To solve this problem, a new generic agent communication infrastructure (or agent infrastructure, infrastructure for short) has been introduced. Once the interface between agent infrastructure and agents is defined, agents can send/receive messages to/from any other peer without concern about network issues. It is also true to say that agents are not physical-network-aware.

In this way, the low-level network implementation details can be successfully hidden from the high-level agent implementation [8]. While agent-level logic

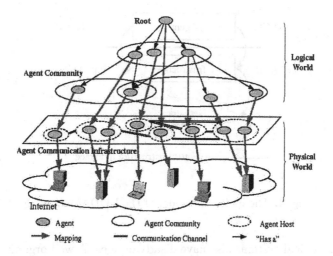

Fig. 3. Overview of the KODAMA system

Table 1. Agent-level and Network-level Logic

	problem solving
	self-learning
	decision making
agent-level logic	interaction pattern
	socia relationship
	name addressing (logical world)
	agent name resolution (physical world)
	agent message deliver
network-level logic	quality of service management
	network security

deals with the problem of when and with whom to interact, network-level logic concentrates on the problem of how to interact (see Table 1 for some examples). Of course, both agent-level logic and network-level logic can be independently abstracted, implemented and updated.

Multi-tier Model. The relations among agents, agent communication infrastructure and networks can be summarized by a multi-tier model, as illustrated in Figure 4. In a multi-tiered system, each layer provides services to the layer above it and serves as a client to the layer below it, and interfaces between adjacent layers determine how layers will interact. Usually, interfaces are well defined so that higher layers are hidden from lower ones.

Agent Layer. To cope with openness and uncertainty, all agents in KODAMA are logically organized and located in a hierarchical structure. Theoretically, a hierarchical structure is an efficient technique for tackling complexity in scalable systems and hierarchical systems are more flexible and evolve more quickly than non-hierarchical ones.

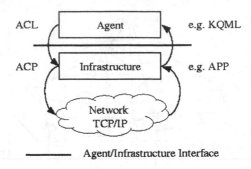

Fig. 4. The multi-tier model of the KODAMA system

But hierarchical systems also have disadvantages. A well-organized structure eventually leads to a top element, say an unnamed root, which is the origin of all elements. It is here, at the root, that undesirable centralized control over the system may take place. To solve this problem, an original agent model, the portal agent model, has been introduced.

The primary feature of this model is that a portal agent allows all agents in one community to be treated as one single normal agent outside the community. It is also true to say that a portal agent is the local root of its community, and the management of all agents is carried out by all distributed portal agents. There is one more thing worth noting here, which is that a portal agent can be requested by any agent inside the community to act as its proxy so that that agent can be hidden from outside.

Agent Communication Infrastructure. Next comes the agent infrastructure layer, which plays a vital role in connecting the agent layer (the logical world) with the network layer (the physical world). Such connection is guaranteed and realized by two well-defined interfaces, one between the agent layer and this infrastructure, and the other between this infrastructure and the network layer.

Agents are self-contained entities in the logical world and not physical-network-aware. Indeed, they rely on the agent infrastructure to provide transparent support for network communication. Once agent messages are passed from agents to the agent infrastructure, they should be delivered to their destination without further interaction with agents. This raises the need to provide two fundamental services - agent name resolution and agent message delivery - in the agent infrastructure.

Network Layer. The lowest layer is the network layer, which can be seen as the transport service provider, since data transmission from source machines to destination machines through networks is realized in this layer. In our design, it is a physical world consisting of agent host machines. There is a de facto standard for the transport service provider on the Internet, namely TCP/IP.

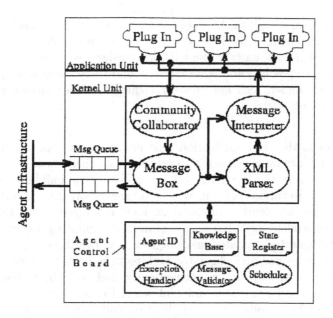

Fig. 5. A plug-and-play agent architecture

Most Internet applications implement their own protocols on top of TCP/IP which also is the default protocol of the network layer in KODAMA.

Plug and play agents. An agent is made up of a kernel unit and an application unit, as illustrated in Figure 5. Both units are highly modularized and made up of components.

Kernel Unit. The kernel unit encapsulates the common modules that can be shared by all agents. In terms of the layered architecture, this unit consists of the communication, cooperation and control subsystems as well as the individual and social knowledge bases. Specifically, its typical modules and their functions are as follows:

- Message Queue: a mutual message queue of incoming and outgoing messages. It is the only message I/O of an agent.
- Message Box: a message buffer that can have various priorities so that messages with higher priorities can be handled first.
- Message Interpreter: an interpreter that extracts the semantics of incoming messages written in ACL and initiates the local problem-solving processes or cooperation processes.
- Community Collaborator: the cooperation subsystem in the layered architecture.

– Agent Control Board: the brain of the kernel unit, and the major part of the control subsystem in the layered architecture. In our design, it consists of three kinds of data, namely agent ID, knowledge base (individual knowledge and social knowledge) and state register, and three components, namely an exception handler, message valuator (which validates incoming messages) and scheduler.

Application Unit. The application unit encapsulates application-dependent modules that differ from one agent to another. In other words, this unit is the action subsystem in the layered architecture. The basic building blocks of application units are various plug-ins which can seamlessly plug into kernel units. To this end, the application-independent logic is entirely separated from the application-dependent logic. In the case of mobile computing, for example, plug-ins can be transmitted, updated and plugged in at run-time.

Since it is a layered and pluggable architecture, both the kernel and application units (or plug-ins) can be independently analyzed, abstracted and implemented. Either can be reused in different ways. Kernel units, on the one hand, are widely used by various agents. Application units, on the other hand, are set up by embedding one or more plug-ins which in turn are reusable. It is appropriate to say that the more plug-ins we have, the easier. It is to construct agents. As the number of available plug-ins expands, the capabilities of agent systems are enlarged.

3.3 Unification of VPC and KODAMA

On one hand, KODAMA provides logical relationships among communities and a filtering message method. On the other hand, VPC provides a method that enables information providers to define dissemination information as rule base while protecting the privacy of participating users. Unifying VPC and KODAMA allows filtering information to be disseminated depending on context.

Figure 6 shows overview of VPC on KODAMA. Each community has its own policy package. Community portal agents have their own policy packages, and provide the policy package to users who wish to join into the communities. Portal agents for users interface communities receive the policy package, evaluate them, and determine appropriate roles for them depending on agent's attributes. Roles that are assigned to users are appended into communities that are created according to policy packages when users join into the communities. Roles in communities that are created by one policy package collaborate with each other as if they are members of the same community. Thus, these communities form one virtual community. Roles that are assigned to users generate message requests to response roles. Portal agents route messages. Generated messages are filtered by each portal agent the messages pass through. Each portal agent can be set with its own message filter policy.

VPC on KODAMA allows users to join in to several communities at the same time, and provides fine grain access control. Role assignment provides role-based

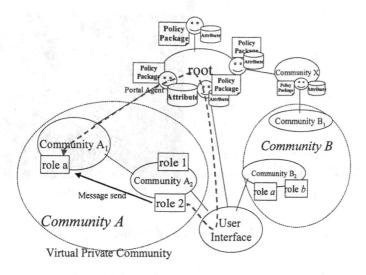

Fig. 6. Overview of VPC on KODAMA

access control. Only agents that satisfy a rule of policy packages can have roles. On the other side, message filtering provides discretionary access control. Only those messages authorized by portal agents pass through the communities and reach to response roles. Hence, VPC on KODAMA provides both role-based access control and discretionary access control. The hierarchy of communities represents context such as location, state of systems and/or devices. Users join several communities at the same time according to state, and change communities depending on any change of state.

Agents can send a policy package as a message to other agents. Policy packages are filtered by portal agents through communities. Thus, VPC on KODAMA filters disseminated information by context.

4 Experiment with Practical Application

We performed large-scale experiment of our VPC and KODAMA unification system in an shopping town in Nagoya city (Japan) over a period of about two months (03/08/2003-04/30/2003). This experiment aimed at determining the effectiveness of the VPC and Kodama unification model.

In the experiment, users were able to obtain information on shops and products depending on user profiles and user locations. The user's terminals were their own mobile phones. Users could receive information on such topics as price discounts, shop locations, and messages from other users, on their mobile phones, while walking around the shopping town. The information disseminated to each user varied depending on information contained in the user's profile such as age, gender and interest category.

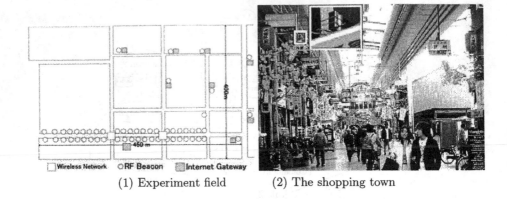

(1) Experiment field   (2) The shopping town

Fig. 7. Overview of the field

About one thousand people participated in this field trial over a month-long period. About 20% of the participants purchased products that were recommended by this system.

4.1   System Overview

The Figure 7-(1) shows an overview of the location of this experiment. The size of the location is about 450m x 400m. About one hundred shops participated to this experiment. We deployed about 100 RF beacon receivers that reported any detected user ID to a server. Detection data on user position was collected and sent to a server via the Internet. Upon receipt of this information, the server then calculated the user's position based on the position of the RF receivers that could detect the user ID. The accuracy of the detected position is about 3-4m. The Figure 7-(2) shows an Image of the shopping town. The wireless network was build using SNOWNET [9]. SNOWNET provided a secure wireless backbone network.

The system architecture is shown as Figure 9. Our target devices in this experiment were the user's mobile phone. In an ideal system, it is advisable that VPC and Kodama work on other user's devices such as PCs or PDAs. This is because, current mobile phones do not have sufficient resources to operate the VPC and KODAMA system on them, even though Java works on some products. Because of this, we employed a method in which main functions of the system were exported to servers. The servers were set up to behave as part of the user's own system when accessed by the user. In other words, the user's mobile phones were simply used as interfaces. Despite this, users were able to access the server using the World Wide Web, via such systems as i-mode, and e-mail. Thus, we can report that we have developed a virtual user terminal system, which VPC and Kodama works, with mobile phones.

The system works as the followings. Each user has its own RF beacon transmitter that contains a unique ID. The RF beacon transmitters (8-(1)) broadcast

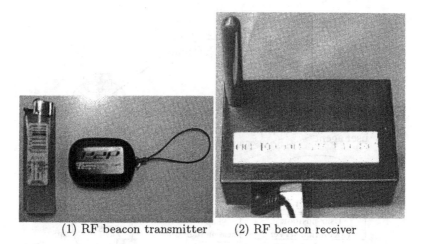

(1) RF beacon transmitter   (2) RF beacon receiver

Fig. 8. RF beacon

their own IDs every seven seconds. RF beacon receivers (8-(2)) that are deployed in the area detect the broadcast ID and send it to a user position calculation server. Then, the user position calculation server computes the position of the user with locations of RF beacon receivers, and updates position data in the user profile database. In our experiment, we employed a method, in which the user position is a coordination of center of detected receivers. VPC for web is a VPC platform that has customized module for web applications. This module returns role outputs that are determined by requested user's profile and policy packages, as a HTTP request response.

The module determines the community, into which the user should go, depending on a shop location file and the user location. Once a community is determined, the module receives a community policy package. In this case, policy packages consisted of advertisements that changed contents depending on the user profiles. There were several categories including those with information on fashion, food, books, and PCs. The policy packages were then sent to user's mobile phones as e-mail.

The e-mails contain the URL of the products and the shops. The system can detect what users read because users can access the URL through the VPC for Web. The system then evaluates the policy package, and determines advertisements according to the user profile. For instance, if user is a 20-year-old male, he may see an advertisement for an electric shaver in the following policy package. In addition, the system determines which users read which URLs and provides feedback to user profiles. The system can thus modify user interest categories based on the feedback data.

```
<rules>
  <rule>  <condition>  <and>
    <condition>  < AGE 18    </condition>
    <condition>  eq GENDER MALE    </condition>
```

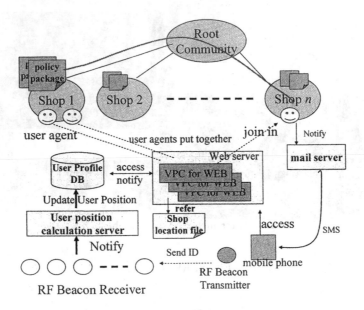

Fig. 9. System overview

```
    </and> </condition>
      <role> shaver </role> </rule>
  <rule>   <condition> <and>
    <condition> < AGE 18    </condition>
    <condition> eq GENDER FEMALE    </condition>
    </and> </condition>
      <role>  cosmetic </role> </rule>
</rules>
```

Users can receive advertisements from other shops that have relationship between them. For example, a shoes shop and a dress shop might collaborate and propose a total fashion package to users. Users in a dress shop might be able to get information on shoes that match clothes. In another example, customers in a PC shop might be offered a cup of free coffee from a coffee shop, when the owner of both shops is the same.

Only advertisements that are agreed upon by both shops can be exchanged beyond the set communities in this system. Shops that agree to advertisement exchange have filtering policy of portal agents.

4.2   Results and Discussion

The result for one month is the followings. About two months have passed from start of the experiment. The total number of participants is 901 people (male: 631, female: 270). The number of participants per age is shown as the Table 2. Number of categories of advertisements and interest is shown as Figure 10-(1). The number of persons of each category reflects the category of the shops

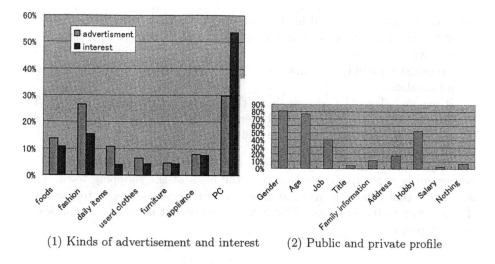

(1) Kinds of advertisement and interest   (2) Public and private profile

Fig. 10. Result

in this shopping town. The number of withdrawal of RF beacon transmitter is 693. 165 persons in the set bought products in the shopping town by the mail, and payed 2,517,272 yen as total. Hence, the system have affected about 23% (=165/693 *100) of visitors in the shopping town. Each person payed about 15,256 (=2,517,272/165) yen as the average.

Table 2. Number of participants per age

Age	10s	20s	30s	40s	50s	60s
Number	200	278	244	131	42	6

We enumerate the followings information as a general profile for a person; gender, age, job, title, family information, address, hobby, and salary. We asked users which information you can disclose. Figure 10-(2) shows the rate of information which people can disclose. Almost persons think that they can disclose gender and age according to the graph. We can say that gender and age are public information. Also, about 50 % people think hobby and job are disclosable. hobby and job are public information depending on persons. Title, family information, and salary are private information. It seems that people do not want to open their information, that is easier to identify the individual. People who do not want to open any information is only 7%. As the result, people can disclose their information to get reasonable information unless the information specifies the individual.

The followings are comments from users.

- I became more interested in the contents of the shops.
- It is very interesting because information mails provide an opportunity to talk with store clerks.
- I received a lot of useful information, but there was also a lot of unnecessary information.
- It was fun. I could find new shops that I had not entered previously. The information in the mails is insufficient. I would probably check the URLs, if the information contained in the mails was richer.

Based on this experiment, we believe that VPC on Kodama works well. This system made a positive contribution to the sales of the shopping town. Thus, we can say that providing information and advertisements directly to users is an effective way to increase sales. The location of context is necessary and desired by most people.

5 Related Work

Context-aware [10,11] is a concept that software adapts according to its location of use, the collection of nearby people and objects, as well as changes to those objects over time. SLP (Service Location Protocol) [12] provides a protocol for finding services depending on the location of a user device in a mobile environment. Jini [13] provides a framework plug-and-play framework using a look up server. UPnP[14] provides a framework which service description include control and presentation based on HTTP.

Context-aware has focus on system works after specific services starting. SLP is a protocol for "searching" services in their immediate surroundings. It is not notification. Users can not know services unless users search. Both of them lack the view point of notification and security. VPC on KODAMA provides concepts of context-notification and security to them.

Jini assumes that there is a look up server in network. However, we can not assume servers such as look up servers in everywhere. Users, also, may begin services ad hoc on the spot. Jini and UPnP lack views of security. The security issue will be very important in these areas. Services have to be protected from illegal users, and users have to be protected from illegal services. VPC has a policy package that allows defining security control, and KODAMA has message filtering. VPC on KODAMA provides a security framework and a distributed architecture to these architectures.

6 Summary

W proposed a model for notification of information, called *VPC on KODAMA*. The model enables systems to notify appropriate information to users depending on circumstances, and also have security function. We had performed large scale experiment of VPC on KODAMA at Nagoya Japan for about two months.

About one thousand people participated to this experiment. Service in this experiment is that users can receive advertisements according to user's profile and location. According to this experiment, sales of shops increased by notification of information.

Acknowledgments. This work was done under a grant to the "Research on Management of Security Policies in Mutual Connection" from the Telecommunications Advancement Organization (TAO) of Japan.

References

1. T. Iwao, Y. Wada, S. Yamasaki, M. Shiouchi, M. Okada, and M. Amamiya, "Collaboration among Agents in Logical Network of Peer-To-Peer Services, SAINT2002, pp. 6–7, IEEE (2002)
2. T. Iwao, et al, "Large Scale Peer-to-Peer Experiments with Virtual Private Community Framework", CIA2002, LNAI 2442, pp. 66–81, 2002
3. G. Zhong, et al, "The design and implementation of KODAMA system", IEICE Transactions on Information and Systems, E85-D(4):637–646, April 2002
4. Guoqiang Zhong, Ken'ichi Takahashi, Tarek Helmy, Kouichirou Takaki, Tsunenori Mine, Shigeru Kusakabe, and Makoto Amamiya. KODAMA: As a distributed multi-agent system. In Proc. of the Seventh International Conference on Parallel and Distributed Systems: Workshops, pp. 435–440. IEEE Computer Society Press, 2000.
5. Sun Microsystems, "Java Card 2.1.1 Platform", http://www.java.sun.com/products/javacard/javacard21.html,
6. B. Ramsdell, Editor, "S/MIME Version 3 Message Specification", http://www.faqs.org/rfcs/rfc2633.html, 1999
7. Stephen Kent, and Tim Polk, "Public-Key Infrastructure", http://www.ietf.org/html.charters/pkix-charter.html, 2000
8. Guoqiang Zhong, Tsunenori Mine, Tarek Helmy, and Makoto Amamiya. The design and implementation of agent communication in KODAMA. In Proc. of the International Conference on Artifical Intelligence, volume 2, pages 673-679, 2000.
9. L. Ji, J. Agre, S. Thakkar, and A. Mishra, Secure Nomadic Wireless Networks (SNOWNET), FLA-PCRTM03-01
10. Schilit B, Theimer M. Disseminating active map information to mobile hosts. IEEE Network 1994; 8:22–32
11. Schilit B, Adams N, Want R. Context-aware computing applications. In: First International Workshop on Mobile Computing Systems and Applications, 1994; 85–90
12. Veizades, J., Guttman, E., Perkins, C., and S. Kaplan, "Service Location Protocol", RFC 2165 June 1997.
13. The Jini ServiceUI Project. http://www.artima.com/jini/serviceui/
14. Universal Plug and Play. http://www.upnp.org/

Multi-agent Systems and Peer-to-Peer Computing: Methods, Systems, and Challenges

Manolis Koubarakis

Intelligent Systems Laboratory
Dept. of Electronic and Computer Engineering
Technical University of Crete
73100 Chania, Crete, Greece
www.intelligence.tuc.gr/~manolis

Abstract. In this paper we comment on the relationship between multi-agent systems and peer-to-peer systems. We point out that work in the frontiers of these two areas can be beneficial to both P2P computing and multi-agent systems, and survey recent research that is already addressing these issues. Then we summarize the work of our group at the Technical University of Crete on the topic of selective information dissemination using P2P networks of middle-agents.

1 Introduction

In P2P systems a very large number of autonomous computing nodes (the *peers*) pool together their resources and rely on each other for *data* and *services*. Popular systems such as Napster[1] (now in a transition state), Gnutella[2], Freenet[3], Kazaa[4], Morpheus[5] and others have made this model of interaction popular. Ideas from P2P computing can also be applied to other areas beyond data sharing such as Grid computation (e.g., SETIHome[6] or DataSynapse[7]), collaboration networks (e.g., Groove[8]) and even new ways to design Internet infrastructure that supports sophisticated patterns of communication and mobility [54].

The wealth of business opportunities promised by P2P networks has generated much industrial interest, and has resulted in the creation of various re-

---

[1] http://www.napster.com
[2] http://gnutella.wego.com
[3] http://freenet.sourceforge.net
[4] http://www.kazaa.com
[5] http://www.musiccity.com
[6] http://www.setiathome.ssl.berkeley.edu
[7] http://www.datasynapse.com
[8] http://www.groove.net

M. Klusch et al. (Eds.): CIA 2003, LNAI 2782, pp. 46–61, 2003.
© Springer-Verlag Berlin Heidelberg 2003

search and industrial projects[9], startup companies, and special interest groups.[10] Researchers from distributed computing, networks, multi-agent systems and databases have also become excited with the P2P vision, and papers tackling open problems in this area have started appearing in high-quality venues (such as ICDCS, SIGCOMM, INFOCOM, CIDR, SIGMOD, VLDB, etc.) but also new specialized conferences and workshops.[11]

The multi-agent systems (MAS) community has reacted rather slowly to the P2P wave as pointed out in the call for papers for the First International Workshop on Agents and Peer-to-Peer Computing (AAMAS-2002, Bologna, Italy). This reality is in direct contrast with other disciplines such as distributed systems and networks that have jumped on the P2P bandwagon and have led the development of the second generation of P2P networks based on distributed hash tables (DHT). It is also disappointing given that deployed P2P systems can be considered an interesting case of MAS as pointed out originally in [25].

In the first part of this paper we point out that the basic concepts underlying P2P systems and MAS are very similar and make a case for a *synthesis* of research agendas that would benefit both areas. Given the current state of the art, MAS can readily offer concepts and techniques that can be useful to P2P computing at the *application modeling* and *design level* (e.g., ontologies for describing network resources in a semantically meaningful way, protocols for meaning negotiation, P2P system modeling and design methodologies etc.). On the other hand, P2P computing can offer readily *popular application domains*, *sophisticated implementation techniques* and *prototype infrastructure components* for implementing and deploying MAS. As more intense cross-fertilization among these two areas takes place, we expect to see researchers from MAS and P2P crossing into each other's territory with their contributions (e.g., models of trust developed in the area of P2P systems could find applications in MAS or resource allocation algorithms pioneered in MAS can find applications to P2P computing etc.).

In the second part of the paper we summarize some of our work in the area of MAS and P2P carried out at the Intelligent Systems Laboratory of the Technical University of Crete since early 2001. The results presented emphasize the use of ideas from P2P systems to the implementation of middle-agent networks for *selective dissemination of information (SDI)*. For more details the interested

---

[9] See the European projects DIET (http://www.dfki.de/diet), BISON (http://www.cs.unibo.it/bison/)), MMAPPS (http://www.mmapps.org), SWAP (http://swap.semanticweb.org/) and the recent US project IRIS (http://iris.lcs.mit.edu/).

[10] For example, see the activities of the P2P working group of the Global Grid forum at http://www.gridforum.org.

[11] For example, see the 1st and 2nd IEEE International Conference on P2P Computing (http://www.ida.liu.se/conferences/p2p/p2p2002), the International Workshop on Agents and P2P Computing (http://p2p.ingce.unibo.it), the 1st and 2nd International Workshop on Peer-to-Peer Systems (http://iptps03.cs.berkeley.edu) and so on.

reader should consult the papers [37,41,38,39] and technical reports [60,33] (all of them are available on our Web site).

The rest of the paper is organized as follows. Section 2 surveys recent work at the frontiers of MAS and P2P systems and makes a case for a synthesis of ideas from these two areas. Section 3 presents the P2P middle-agent architecture we have used in our work on SDI. Then Section 4 summarizes our contributions in this area. Finally, Section 5 presents our conclusions.

2 P2P Computing and MAS: A Synthesis

Since their inception, MAS have always been thought of as *networks of equal peers*. Today, the concept of agent in MAS offers the right kind of abstraction for *enriching* the concept of peer as implemented in today's P2P systems. MAS is an appropriate framework for realizing all popular P2P applications mentioned in the introduction of this paper and many more. The typical properties associated with *agency* (e.g, *autonomy, social ability, reactivity* and *pro-activeness* [65]) are some of the characteristics that one would wish to have in the peers of next generation P2P systems. Other *society-level* properties such as *emergence of complex behaviours* and *self-organization* typically stressed in *bottom-up* approaches to MAS [23] are also very important in this context because these are exactly the kind of properties exhibited by deployed P2P networks [2,52,34,4].

In the rest of this section, we survey previous work that synthesizes concepts from MAS and P2P computing and demonstrates that results from each area can be beneficially used in the other. Our presentation is selective and we concentrate on research that is closest to our work presented in Section 3 and 4.[12] We also point out some open research questions.

2.1 P2P for MAS

Existing P2P system technology can be utilized in the development of MAS in many ways. First, P2P networks can provide *infrastructure* for deploying MAS. For example, P2P networks can be used to provide Internet-wide discovery services as originally proposed for the agent-to-agent (A2A) framework of RETSINA where agents participate as nodes in the existing public Gnutella network to increase their reachability of other agent-provided services (e.g., agent name servers or middle-agents) [43]. The basic idea of [43] is in the right direction, but today there are even better choices for the P2P networks to be used. The Gnutella network is known to have scalability problems because of its use of flooding for broadcasting messages. Thus if one wishes to deploy MAS on a publicly available P2P network, one could use the more recent super-peer based P2P

---

[12] For example, we do not deal at all with the problem of resource allocation in P2P systems and do not discuss what MAS research has to offer to this problem. We also do not discuss other interesting problems at the frontiers of these two areas such as the existence of *non-cooperative, selfish* and *malicious* agents (peers) and the associated problems of *trust, reputation* and *security*.

networks (e.g., Morpheus[13] – currently the most popular P2P network according to [67]).

An even better alternative would be to use one of the DHT-based second generation P2P networks such as Chord that provide much better *scalability, self-organization, availability, fault-tolerance* and *load balancing* [55]. DHT-based systems could easily provide Internet-wide agent name services for MAS because all that is needed in this case is a facility for mapping agents to their IP addresses given some identifying agent feature usually a *name* [57].

Other kinds of MAS infrastructure such as middle-agent networks can also be implemented using techniques from P2P networks. While middle-agents can be classified in various different dimensions [63,40], their basic functionality is to match *requests* for agents with a certain capability with *advertisements* specifying available capabilities. As an example, [39,41,38] (and Sections 3 and 4) present the theoretical principles and implementations techniques of DIAS, a distributed SDI system for digital libraries based on a P2P network of middle-agents. The middle-agent network of DIAS can be understood to follow the *content-based routing* protocol of [42], but it has been implemented using the routing algorithms of the P2P pub/sub system SIENA [13].

It is currently an open question how to use a DHT to implement more sophisticated kinds of MAS infrastructure e.g., the middle-agents of RETSINA [57] that are using service description languages such as LARKS [58] or DAML-S [49].

2.2   MAS for P2P

It is instructive to think of P2P systems in terms of MAS concepts both at the *modeling* and *design* level and at the *system architecture* and *implementation* level.

At the modeling and design level, the concept of agent and its associated properties (autonomy, social ability, reactivity, pro-activeness) can be understood as an extension of the concept of peer in today's P2P systems. Also, as shown by recent measurement studies, deployed P2P networks are self-organizing societies of agents (peers) with various emergent properties [2,52,34,4]. These observations have given rise to various proposals for implementing P2P systems using MAS techniques as we will see below. What is a largely open question in this area, is how to extend current agent-based software engineering methodologies [64,14] to the case of P2P systems. Some preliminary steps towards this area are taken in [8] where it is shown how to apply the agent-oriented software engineering methodology Tropos [14] to the development of distributed knowledge management applications on current P2P platforms such as JXTA.

At the system architecture and implementation level, Tim Finin and Yannis Labrou have suggested to think of Napster servers as *matchmakers*, a special kind of middle-agents operating using appropriate KQML protocols and a simple ontology for MP3 files [25]. Today, the use of schemas or ontologies for describing network resources will allow P2P systems to cross into the world of *semantics*

---

[13] http://www.musiccity.com

and take advantage of recently developed Semantic Web technologies.[14] This is in fact the main goal of project EDUTELLA [47] where RDFS schemata and RDF metadata can be used to annotate P2P resources, and query languages such as RDF-QEL [47] or RQL [35] can be used for search. EDUTELLA is built on top of Sun's P2P platform JXTA[15] and its current application domain is the exchange of learning materials.

In the context of the Semantic Web, *globally shared* schemas or ontologies are used to annotate Web content so that agents can operate on it in more effective ways. In the context of P2P systems, this notion of global commonly agreed ontologies can be relaxed in favour of *local* ontologies and local translations among ontologies of neighbouring peers [1,36,31,30]. Through appropriate P2P communication, local agreements on semantics can give rise to *global agreement* in a *bottom-up emergent* manner [1]. It is an open question what concepts, algorithms and methodologies are appropriate for making progress in this problem.

Implementation techniques from the area of agent systems can also be used beneficially for the development of a new generation of P2P systems. BestPeer is a prototype P2P system implemented at the National University of Singapore that uses *mobile agents* as its implementation technology [48]. Routing in BestPeer is performed using flooding and TTLs like in Gnutella. However, BestPeer uses *mobile code* as its communication unit and achieves a number of advantages against first generation P2P systems such as Gnutella. First, BestPeer can achieve a finer granularity of data sharing. Local nodes can "mask" their content using *active objects* and can provide different replies to identical requests depending on the identity or privileges of the requester. Furthermore, requesters can ship code that contains *filtering subroutines* to another peer's site to select the content that will be returned based on the requester's own criteria. This feature is especially useful when the language for requests supported by the P2P system does not allow requesters to express their preferences in an effective way. By moving filtering to the provider's site, BestPeer increases bandwidth utilization because useless data is never returned to the requester. Additionally, BestPeer uses a distributed network of servers to allow *location independent global name lookup*. Using these servers, peers can maintain their unique identity even after disconnecting from the network and reconnecting from another IP address. Finally, BestPeer allows a peer to *reconfigure* its direct connections in the network to *get closer* to preferred peers (where preference can be based on criteria such maximum number or quality of answers). [48] demonstrates experimentally that this self-configuration capability allows BestPeer to outperform Gnutella in query answering performance. Leaving aside the usual permission/security considerations raised for every mobile agent system, BestPeer offers a nice agent-based framework for the development of P2P applications.

Shehory [53] presents a theoretical analysis of the practical problem of finding the location of an agent with certain capabilities in an open MAS that is like the Gnutella P2P network (i.e., there are no middle-agents so each agent keeps

---

[14] http://www.w3.org/2001/sw/
[15] http://www.jxta.org

a local list of other agents and their capabilities). [53] considers situations where agents are connected in a lattice-like rectangular graph structure, and shows that dramatic improvements in the number of communication operations is possible by randomly connecting a small number of pairs of nodes in the original graph. Additionally, Shehory gives some evidence that these results apply to larger classes of graphs as well. The practical relevance of this work is that it shows that if there is enough structure in the topology of the MAS then approaches with no middle-agents may result in very small communication costs.

Bottom-up Approaches to MAS. An important subarea of MAS research that is expected to play an important role in the development of future P2P systems is the bottom-up approach [23] and the closely related area of *complex adaptive systems* [61,26]. Bottom-up approaches to MAS emphasize that it is rather impossible to understand many application domains by traditional *top-down decomposition:* breaking them into components, understanding what each component does and deducing the behaviour of the whole system from the behaviour of its components. In such societies of agents the whole is greater than the sum of the parts, and the behaviour of the whole can only be understood by understanding the *interactions* between the autonomous agents that make up the whole and lead to *emergent global behaviours*.

European projects DIET[16] [44,32] and BISON[17] [6] were the first to point out that P2P networks are clearly an instance of CAS and follow a *nature-inspired* computing approach [9,26] to their development.

DIET started in July 2002 and one of its first results were the implementation of a MAS platform inspired by *natural ecosystems* and bottom-up approaches to Artificial Intelligence [44,32]. In the context of DIET, an ecosystem is composed of one or more communities of living organisms interacting with each other and with the physical environment that they inhabit. At the implementation level, the DIET platform offers a minimal *core layer* that allows the development of *lightweight mobile agents* (the living organisms) occupying *environments* that are parts of *worlds* (there is one world for each Java Virtual Machine on a user's computer). Similarly with natural ecosystems, DIET agents may be very simple but their collective behaviours and the overall functionality arising from their interactions exceed the capacities of any individual agent. DIET agents can *migrate* to other environments in the same or a remote machine, and can communicate with each other using *local* or *remote* communication mechanisms. Additional application functionality can be implemented on top of the core layer. The DIET platform has been shown to scale to large numbers of lightweight agents [32] and to form a nice basis for developing various efficient, robust and adaptive applications based on the P2P paradigm: information retrieval [28], information dissemination [38,41], content-sharing [59], community self-organization and group formation [32,62] and distributed look-up infrastructures [10].

---

[16] http://www.dfki.de/diet

[17] http://www.cs.unibo.it/bison/

BISON is a European project that has commenced in January 2003. Its partners have already designed and implemented a mobile agent system called Anthill [6] which can be used to construct P2P applications based on the *swarm-intelligence* paradigm of Dorigo and colleagues [9]. The Anthill model is based on the concepts of nest and ant. A *nest* is a middleware component written in Java that can host resources and can perform computations. A P2P application built on Anthill is organized as an overlay network of interconnected nests. Nests can interact with local instances of one or more *applications* and provide them with various *services* by generating *ants* that travel the overlay network to perform the required task. Anthill is built on top of JXTA and currently includes a *run-time environment* for developing working systems and a *simulation* environment for experimenting with P2P algorithms before deploying them. Ant implementations can be the same in the run-time and simulation environments to avoid duplicate effort in developing applications.

Up to this point, Anthill has been used to develop a file-sharing application called Gnutant, and a load-balancing application called Messor [6,45,46]. Gnutant is similar to Freenet in functionality and is described in more detail in [6]. Messor provides an ant algorithm for balancing the load in a simple Grid computing system aimed for highly-parallel, time intensive computations in which the workload can be decomposed into many independent jobs [45,46]. The main idea behind Messor is to have ants travelling a network of nests which host computational resources, trying to "disperse" jobs in order to balance the load throughout the network. Essentially, Messor carries out the opposite function to the one performed by several species of real ants that are known to collectively gather objects in their environments to form piles [51].

DIET and Anthill have shown the way, but there is still a lot of work to be done in this area. The first interesting problem is to compare the approaches taken by DIET and Anthill with standard ways of developing P2P applications and to evaluate the benefits and deficiencies of each approach. Furthermore, one should work towards the development of a methodology for the application of nature-inspired techniques to P2P networks. This will allow us to move away from the current *harvesting* approach where we pick an interesting heuristic from nature (e.g., the behaviour of ant colonies mentioned above) and apply it to a P2P problem (e.g., load-balancing), to a *synthesis* phase where we have a methodology for guiding the search for CAS that lead to the desired global behaviour. This is one of the goals of the BISON project as presented by Ozalp Babaoglu in [5]. Finally, let us point out that the results of this research will strongly support the "shift in paradigm" for software engineering research envisioned in [68] where it is conjectured that we are witnessing a move from the current "design-based mechanical" foundation of software engineering to a more "physics-based" or "intentional" foundation. They will also lead to the development of methodologies for the design and implementation of P2P systems, an open problem we have mentioned at the beginning of this section.

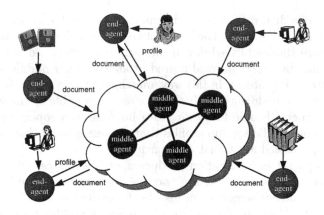

Fig. 1. A P2P agent architecture for SDI

Here we finish our survey of recent research on the frontiers of MAS and P2P. It is our belief that a synthesis of the research agendas of these two areas will be very beneficial to both.

3 P2P Middle-Agent Networks for SDI

Let us now turn to summarizing some of our recent results on MAS and P2P systems. The work presented here starts from the observation that the main application scenario of recent P2P data sharing systems is that of *ad-hoc querying*: a user poses a query (e.g., "I want MPEGs with video-clips of Jennifer Lopez") and the system returns a list of pointers to matching files owned by various peers in the network. Then, the user can go ahead and download files of interest. The complementary scenario of *selective information dissemination (SDI)* or *selective information push* [27] has so far been considered by very few P2P systems [38, 50,29]. In an SDI scenario, a user posts a *profile* or *continuous query* to the system to receive notifications whenever certain *events* of interest take place (e.g., when a video-clip of Jennifer Lopez becomes available). SDI can be as useful as ad-hoc querying in many target applications of P2P networks ranging from file sharing, to more advanced applications such as alert systems for digital libraries, e-commerce networks etc.

We envision an information dissemination scenario in the context of a *distributed peer-to-peer (P2P) agent architecture* like the one shown in Figure 1. This architecture was originally proposed in [12] in the context of the P2P *event notification system* SIENA.[18] This agent architecture has been adopted by our group since early 2001 and it was first presented in [38].

In the scenario of Figure 1 users utilize their *end-agents* to post *profiles* or *documents* (expressed in some appropriate language) to some *middle-agents*.

---

[18] SIENA uses the term *server* instead of middle-agent but the idea is exactly the same.

End-agents play a dual role: they can be information producers and information consumers at the same time. The P2P network of middle-agents is the "glue" that makes sure that published documents arrive at interested subscribers. To achieve this, middle-agents forward posted profiles to other middle-agents using an appropriate P2P protocol. In this way, matching of a profile with a document can take place at a middle-agent that is as close as possible to the origin of the incoming document. Profile forwarding can be done in a sophisticated way to minimize network traffic e.g., no profiles that are less general than one that has already been processed are actually forwarded.

In their capacity as information producers, end-agents can also post *advertisements* that describe in a "concise" way the documents that will be produced by them. These advertisements can also be forwarded in the P2P network of middle-agents to *block* the forwarding of *irrelevant* profiles towards a source. Advertisement forwarding can also be done in a sophisticated way using ideas similar to the ones for profile forwarding.

Most of the concepts of the architecture sketched above are explicit (or sometimes implicit) in the KQML literature and subsequent MAS based on it [24, 42,22,56,58]. Unfortunately the emphasis in most of these systems is on a single central middle-agent, making the issues that would arise in a distributed setting difficult to appreciate. In our opinion, the best presentation of these concepts available in the literature can be found in [12] and our paper [38].

4   Summary of Our Results

Our work on P2P middle-agent networks for SDI has been driven by the following considerations:

- The next generation of P2P data sharing systems should be developed in a *principled* and *formal* way and classical results from logic and theoretical computer science should be applied. Most of the current work on P2P systems has not emphasized such theoretical considerations at all, as witnessed by the recent survey of [21].
- Performance and scalability must be a primary consideration in the design of any realistic system that supports SDI with P2P networks.
- Implementations of P2P systems should be based on modern technologies that would enable rapid application development and reuse.

In the rest of this section we discuss our work up to now and what we have done to address these considerations.

4.1   Data Models and Query Languages

We have developed the data models $\mathcal{WP}, \mathcal{AWP}$ and $\mathcal{AWPS}$, and their corresponding languages for specifying queries and notifications. $\mathcal{WP}$ is based on free text and its query language is based on the *boolean model with proximity operators*. The concepts of $\mathcal{WP}$ extend the traditional concept of proximity in IR [7,

16,17] in a significant way, and utilize it in a query language targeted at SDI for distributed digital libraries. Data model $\mathcal{AWP}$ is based on *attributes* with finite-length strings as values. Its query language is an extension of the query language of data model $\mathcal{WP}$. Finally, the model $\mathcal{AWPS}$ extends $\mathcal{AWP}$ by introducing a "similarity" operator based on the IR vector space model [7].

Our data modelling work complements recent proposals for querying textual information in SDI systems [12,11] by using linguistically motivated concepts such as *word* and traditional IR operators (instead of strings and their operators). Our data models and query languages are more expressive than the one used in the centralized SDI system SIFT [66] where documents are free text and queries are conjunctions of keywords. On the other hand, we have only considered notifications that have *flat* structure, thus our query languages are weaker than the XML-based query languages of [3,15]. Notice that the similarity concept of $\mathcal{AWPS}$ has also been used in database systems with IR influences (e.g., WHIRL [19]) and more recently in the XML query language ELIXIR [18]. We note that both WHIRL and ELIXIR target information retrieval and integration applications, and pay no attention to information dissemination and the concepts/functionality needed in such applications. Finally, notice that although our data models deal with *textual information* only, they can be easily combined with models for expressing other kinds of information (e.g., arithmetic information for modelling prices in an e-commerce application).

4.2 Algorithms and Computational Complexity

In [37,41,38,39] we point out that in order to have a scalable implementation of a P2P SDI architecture like the one in Figure 1, the following four algorithmic problems need to be formalized and solved efficiently (for a start!). The first problem is the *satisfiability problem*: deciding whether a profile can ever be satisfied by an incoming notification. The second problem is the *satisfaction problem*: Deciding whether a notification satisfies (or matches) a profile. The third problem (which includes the second one) is the *filtering problem*: Given a database of profiles db and a notification n, find all profiles $q \in db$ that match n. This functionality is very crucial at each middle-agent because we expect deployed information dissemination systems to handle hundreds of thousands or millions of profiles. The fourth problem is the *entailment problem*: Deciding whether a profile is more or less "general" than another. This functionality is crucial if we want to minimize profile forwarding as sketched above.

[41] presented PTIME worst-case upper bounds for the complexity of satisfaction and filtering for the case of models $\mathcal{WP}$ and $\mathcal{AWP}$. In [39] we extend these results and study the computational complexity of query satisfiability and entailment for models $\mathcal{WP}$ and $\mathcal{AWP}$. Our results show that the satisfiability and entailment problems for queries in $\mathcal{WP}$ is NP-complete and coNP-complete respectively. Our results for $\mathcal{AWP}$ show that even for queries in some "canonical" form, satisfiability is NP-complete and query entailment is coNP-complete.

4.3 Implementation

In [38] our group has proposed DIAS, a distributed information alert system for digital libraries that follows the architecture of Figure 1 and employs conjunctive queries in $\mathcal{AWPS}$. Work on DIAS has resulted in the implementation of a prototype *super-peer* system called P2P-DIET that combines ad-hoc querying as found in other P2P networks and SDI as discussed above [33]. P2P-DIET has been developed on top of the mobile agent system DIET Core presented in [32]. P2P-DIET is currently available only to partners of project DIET but we plan to make it freely available to all interested parties as soon as the underlying platform DIET Core becomes open source.

4.4 Performance and Scalability

Let us now briefly discuss the data structures, algorithms and protocols that regulate how P2P-DIET nodes work together so that all published notifications are delivered to interested consumers. Our implementation uses a combination of the following techniques: *sophisticated routing* of profiles and notifications by utilizing the reverse path forwarding algorithm of [20] and a poset data structure encoding profile entailment, and *very fast indexing* at each node for detecting the set of profiles that match an incoming notification. Preliminary evaluation of these techniques by us (and previously by SIENA researchers [12]) show that P2P-DIET is a scalable super-peer system that goes beyond the ones envisioned in [67].

In [39] we study the problem of filtering for model $\mathcal{AWP}$ and present a simple but efficient profile indexing algorithm called PINDEX. PINDEX utilises a two-level index over profiles expressed in $\mathcal{AWP}$ and its detailed data structures are discussed in [60]. We have tested PINDEX in a digital library SDI application using documents downloaded from *ResearchIndex*[19] and realistic profiles, consisting of terms extracted from the documents. As it is shown in Figure 2, PINDEX can deal with 2.5 million profiles in less than 500 milliseconds and compares very favourably with the obvious brute-force algorithm BF. In our experiments profiles and documents are stored in main memory and time measured is the mean matching time for one hundred incoming documents. The experiments were run on a standard PC with Pentium III 1.6GHz processor and 1GB RAM, running Linux. In recent work we have extended these algorithms to the model $\mathcal{AWPS}$ and the results appear in a forthcoming paper.

5 Conclusions

We have pointed out that the basic concepts underlying P2P systems and MAS are very similar and made a case for a synthesis of the respective research agendas that would benefit both areas. To drive our point home, we presented some

---

[19] http://www.researchindex.org

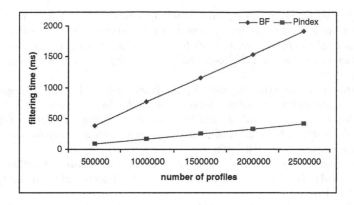

Fig. 2. Matching time vs. number of indexed profiles for $\mathcal{AWP}$ queries

of our work in the area of MAS and P2P that starts from SDI scenarios studied in traditional MAS research and tackles them with middle-agent networks implemented with state-of-the-art techniques from P2P systems.

Acknowledgements. I would like to thank the organizers of CIA-2003 for giving me the opportunity to present my ideas on P2P Computing and MAS.

The research presented here was carried out as part of the DIET (Decentralised Information Ecosystems Technologies) project (IST-1999-10088), within the Universal Information Ecosystems initiative of the Information Society Technology Programme of the European Commission. I would like to thank the other participants of the DIET project and especially my students at TUC for their comments and contributions. Lots of thanks to Thodoros Koutris and Christos Tryfonopoulos whose experimental work resulted in the graph of Figure 2 (and many more!).

References

1. K. Aberer, P. Cudre-Mauroux, and M. Hauswirth. The Chatty Web: Emergent Semantics Through Gossiping. In *Twelfth International World Wide Web Conference (WWW2003)*, May 2003.
2. Eytan Adar and Bernardo A. Huberman. Free Riding on Gnutella. *First Monday*, October 2000.
3. M. Altinel and M.J. Franklin. Efficient filtering of XML documents for selective dissemination of information. In *Proceedings of the 26th VLDB Conference*, 2000.
4. Fred S. Annexstein, Kenneth A. Berman, and Mihajlo A. Jovanovic. Latency Effects on Reachability in Large-scale Peer-to-Peer Networks. In *Proceedings of ACM Symposium on Parallel Algorithms and Architectures*, pages 84–92, 2001.
5. O. Babaoglu. BISON: Biology-inspired techniques for self-organization in dynamic networks, November 2002. Presentation at the launch meeting of the Network of Excellence on Complex Systems (EXYSTENCE) in Torino, Italy.

6. Ozalp Babaoglu, Hein Meling, and Alberto Montresor. Anthill: A framework for the development of agent-based peer-to-peer systems. In *Proceedings of IEEE International Conference on Distributed Computer Systems*, pages 15–22, 2002.

7. R. Baeza-Yates and B. Ribeiro-Neto. *Modern Information Retrieval*. Addison Wesley, 1999.

8. D. Bertolini, P. Busetta, A. Molani, M. Nori, and A. Perini. Designing peer-to-peer applications: an agent-oriented approach. In *Proceeding of International Workshop on Agent Technology and Software Engineering (AgeS)-Net Object Days 2002 (NODe02)*, volume 2592 of *Lecture Notes in Artificial Intelligence*, pages 1–15. Springer, October 7–10 2002.

9. Eric Bonabeau, Marco Dorigo, and Guy Theraulaz. *Swarm Intelligence: From Natural to Artificial Systems*. SFI Studies in the Sciences of Complexity. Oxford University Press, 1999.

10. Erwin Bonsma and Cefn Hoile. A distributed implementation of the SWAN look-up system using mobile agents. In *Proceedings of the AAMAS 2002 Workshop on Agents and Peer-to-Peer Computing*, 2002. Forthcoming volume in Lecture Notes in Computer Science, G. Moro and M. Koubarakis (eds.).

11. A. Campailla, S. Chaki, E. Clarke, S. Jha, and H. Veith. Efficent filtering in publish-subscribe systems using binary decision diagrams. In *Proceedings of the 23rd International Conference on Software Engineering*, Toronto, Ontario, Canada, 2001.

12. A. Carzaniga, D. S. Rosenblum, and A. L. Wolf. Achieving scalability and expressiveness in an internet-scale event notification service. In *Proceedings of the 19th ACM Symposium on Principles of Distributed Computing (PODC'2000)*, pages 219–227, 2000.

13. Antonio Carzaniga, David S. Rosenblum, and Alexander L Wolf. Design and evaluation of a wide-area event notification service. *ACM Transactions on Computer Systems*, 19(3):332–383, August 2001.

14. J. Castro, M. Kolp, and J. Mylopoulos. Towards requirements-driven software development methodology: The Tropos project. *Information Systems*, 27(6):365–389, June 2002.

15. C.-Y. Chan, P. Felber, M. Garofalakis, and R. Rastogi. Efficient Filtering of XML Documents with XPath Expressions. In *Proceedings of the 18th International Conference on Data Engineering*, pages 235–244, February 2002.

16. C.-C. K. Chang, H. Garcia-Molina, and A. Paepcke. Boolean Query Mapping across Heterogeneous Information Sources. *IEEE Transactions on Knowledge and Data Engineering*, 8(4):515–521, 1996.

17. C.-C. K. Chang, H. Garcia-Molina, and A. Paepcke. Predicate Rewriting for Translating Boolean Queries in a Heterogeneous Information System. *ACM Transactions on Information Systems*, 17(1):1–39, 1999.

18. T. T. Chinenyanga and N. Kushmerick. Expressive retrieval from XML documents. In *Proceedings of SIGIR'01*, September 2001.

19. William W. Cohen. WHIRL: A word-based information representation language. *Artificial Intelligence*, 118(1-2):163–196, 2000.

20. Y. Dalal and R. Metcalfe. Reverse Path Forwarding of Broadcast Packets. *Communications of the ACM*, 21(12):1040–1048, 1978.

21. N. Daswani, H. Garcia-Molina, and B. Yang. Open problems in data sharing peer-to-peer systems. In *Proceedings of the 9th International Conference on Database Theory (ICDT 2003)*, volume 2572 of *Lecture Notes in Computer Science*, pages 1–15. Springer, January 2003.

22. K. Decker, K. Sycara, and M. Williamson. Middle-agents for the internet. In *Proceedings of IJCAI-97*, 1997.
23. J. Ferber. *Multi-Agent Systems: An introduction to Distributed Artificial Intelligence.* Addison-Wesley, 1999.
24. T. Finin, R. Fritzson, D. McKay, and R. McEntire. KQML as an Agent Communication Language. In N. Adam, B. Bhargava, and Y. Yesha, editors, *Proceedings of the 3rd International Conference on Information and Knowledge Management (CIKM'94)*, pages 456–463, Gaithersburg, MD, USA, 1994. ACM Press.
25. T.W. Finin and Y. Labrou. Napster as a Multi-Agent System. Presentation at the 18th FIPA meeting, University of Maryland Baltimore County, July 2000.
26. Gary William Flake. *The Computational Beauty of Nature: Computer Explorations of Fractals, Chaos, Complex Systems, and Adaptation.* MIT Press, 2000.
27. M. J. Franklin and S. B. Zdonik. "Data In Your Face": Push Technology in Perspective. In *Proceedings ACM SIGMOD International Conference on Management of Data*, pages 516–519, 1998.
28. A. Galardo-Antolin, A. Navia-Vasquez, H.Y. Molina-Bulla, A.B. Rodriquez-Gonzalez, F.J. Valvarde-Albacete, A.R. Figueiras-Vidal, T. Koutris, A. Xiruhaki, and M. Koubarakis. I-Gaia: an Information Processing Layer for the DIET Platform. In *Proceedings of the 1st International Joint Conference on Autonomous Agents & Multiagent Systems (AAMAS 2002)*, pages 1272–1279, July 15–19 2002.
29. Bugra Gedik and Ling Liu. PeerCQ: A Decentralized and Self-Configuring Peer-to-Peer Information Monitoring System. In *Proceedings of the 23rd IEEE International Conference on Distributed Computer Systems*, May 2003.
30. Fausto Giunchiglia and Ilya Zaihrayeu. Making peer databases interact - a vision for an architecture supporting data coordination. In *Proceedings of the 6th International Workshop on Cooperative Information Agents (CIA 2002)*, volume 2446 of *Lecture Notes in Computer Science*. Springer, September 2002.
31. Alon Y. Halevy, Zachary G. Ives, Dan Suciu, and Igor Tatarinov. Schema Mediation in Peer Data Management Systems. In *Proceedings of the 19th International Conference on Data Engineering*, March 2003.
32. Cefn Hoile, Fang Wang, Erwin Bonsma, and Paul Marrow. Core specification and experiments in DIET: a decentralised ecosystem-inspired mobile agent system. In *Proceedings of the 1st International Joint Conference on Autonomous Agents & Multiagent Systems (AAMAS 2002)*, pages 623–630, July 15–19 2002.
33. S. Idreos and M. Koubarakis. P2P-DIET: A Query and Notification Service Based on Mobile Agents for Rapid Implementation of P2P Applications. Technical report, Intelligent Systems Laboratory, Dept. of Electronic and Computer Engineering, Technical University of Crete, June 2003.
34. Mihajlo A. Jovanovic. Modeling Large-scale Peer-to-Peer Networks and a Case Study of Gnutella. Master of Science, University of Cincinnati, June 2001.
35. Greg Karvounarakis, Sofia Alexaki, Vassilis Christophides, Dimitris Plexousakis, and Michel Scholl. RQL: A Declarative Query Language for RDF. In *Proceedings of the 11th International World Wide Web Conference.* May 2002.
36. Anastasios Kementsietsidis, Marcelo Arenas, and Renee J. Miller. Mapping Data in Peer-to-Peer Systems: Semantics and Algorithmic Issues. In *Proceedings of the ACM SIGMOD International Conference on Management of Data*, June 2003.
37. M. Koubarakis. Boolean Queries with Proximity Operators for Information Dissemination. Proceedings of the Workshop on Foundations of Models and Languages for Information Integration (FMII-2001), Viterbo, Italy , 16-18 September, 2001. In LNCS (forthcoming).

38. M. Koubarakis, T. Koutris, P. Raftopoulou, and C. Tryfonopoulos. Information Alert in Distributed Digital Libraries: The Models, Languages and Architecture of DIAS. In *Proceedings of the 6th European Conference on Research and Advanced Technology for Digital Libraries (ECDL 2002)*, volume 2458 of *Lecture Notes in Computer Science*, pages 527–542, September 2002.

39. M. Koubarakis and C. Tryfonopoulos. Peer-to-peer agent systems for textual information dissemination: algorithms and complexity, December 2002. In the *UK Workshop on Multiagent Systems (UKMAS-2002)*, Liverpool, UK.

40. M. Koubarakis, C. Tryfonopoulos, and Y. Labrou. Agent middleware: A survey, 2003. Forthcoming paper.

41. M. Koubarakis, C. Tryfonopoulos, P. Raftopoulou, and T. Koutris. Data models and languages for agent-based textual information dissemination. In *Proceedings of 6th International Workshop on Cooperative Information Systems (CIA 2002)*, volume 2446 of *Lecture Notes in Computer Science*, pages 179–193, September 2002.

42. D. R. Kuokka and L. P. Harada. Issues and extensions for information matchmaking protocols. *International Journal of Cooperative Information Systems*, 5(2-3):251–274, 1996.

43. B. Langley, M. Paolucci, and K. Sycara. Discovery of infrastructure in multi-agent systems. In *Proceedings of the Second Workshop on Infrastructure for Agents, MAS and Scalable MAS*, 2001.

44. P. Marrow, M. Koubarakis, R.H. van Lengen, F. Valverde-Albacete, E. Bonsma, J. Cid-Suerio, A.R. Figueiras-Vidal, A. Gallardo-Antolin, C. Hoile, T. Koutris, H. Molina-Bulla, A. Navia-Vazquez, P. Raftopoulou, N. Skarmeas, C. Tryfonopoulos, F. Wang, and C. Xiruhaki. Agents in Decentralised Information Ecosystems: The DIET Approach. In M. Schroeder and K. Stathis, editors, *Proceedings of the AISB'01 Symposium on Information Agents for Electronic Commerce, AISB'01 Convention*, pages 109–117, University of York, United Kingdom, March 2001.

45. Alberto Montresor, Ozalp Babaoglu, and Hein Meling. Towards adaptive, resilient and self-organizing peer-to-peer systems. In *Web Engineering and Peer-to-Peer Computing, NETWORKING Workshops 2002, Pisa, Italy, May 19-24*, number 2376 in Lecture Notes in Computer Science, pages 300–305. Springer, 2002.

46. Alberto Montresor, Hein Meling, and Ozalp Babaoglu. Messor: load balancing through a swarm of intelligent agents. In *Proceedings of the AAMAS 2002 Workshop on Agents and Peer-to-Peer Computing*, 2002. Forthcoming volume in Lecture Notes in Computer Science, G. Moro and M. Koubarakis (eds.).

47. W. Neidl, B. Wolf, C. Qu, S. Decker, M. Sintek, A. Naeve, M. Nilsson, M. Palmer, and T. Risch. EDUTELLA: A P2P networking infrastructure based on RDF. In *Proceedings of the 11th International World Wide Web Conference*. May 2002.

48. Wee Siong Ng, Beng Chin Ooi, and Kian Lee Tan. BestPeer: A Self-Configurable Peer-to-Peer System . In *Proceedings of the 18th International Conference on Data Engineering*, February 2002.

49. M. Paolucci, T. Kawamura, T.R. Payne, and K. Sycara. Semantic Matching of Web Services Capabilities. In *Proceedings of the 1st International Semantic Web Conference (ISWC2002)*, volume 2342 of *LNCS*, pages 333–347, 2002.

50. P. R. Pietzuch and J. Bacon. Hermes: A Distributed Event-Based Middleware Architecture. Proceedings of the International Workshop on Distributed Event-Based systems (DEBS'02), July 2-3, 2002, Vienna, Austria.

51. M. Resnick. *Turtles, Termites and Traffic Jams: Explorations into Massively Parallel Microworlds*. MIT Press, 1994.

52. S. Saroiu, K. Gummadi, and S. Gribble. A measurement study of peer-to-peer file sharing systems. In *Proceedings of Multimedia Conferencing and Networking*, January 2002.
53. O. Shehory. A Scalable Agent Location Mechanism. In *Proceedings of ATAL 1999*, pages 162–172, 1999.
54. I. Stoica, D. Adkins, S. Ratnasamy, S. Shenker, S. Surana, and S. Zhuang. Internet indirection architecture. In *Proceedings of ACM SIGCOMM'02*, pages 73–86, August 2002.
55. Ion Stoica, Robert Morris, David Karger, M. Frans Kaashoek, and Hari Balakrishnan. Chord: A scalable peer-to-peer lookup service for internet applications. In *Proceedings of the ACM SIGCOMM '01 Conference*, San Diego, California, August 2001.
56. K. Sycara, M. Klusch, S. Widoff, and J. Lu. Dynamic Service Matchmaking Among Agents in Open Information Environments. *SIGMOD Record (ACM Special Interest Group on Management of Data)*, 28(1):47–53, 1999.
57. K. Sycara, M. Paolucci, M. van Velsen, and J. Giampapa. The RETSINA MAS Infrastructure. *Autonomous Agents and Multi-Agent Systems*, 7(1/2), July 2003.
58. K. Sycara, S. Widoff, M. Klusch, and J. Lu. LARKS: Dynamic Matchmaking Among Heterogeneous Software Agents in Cyberspace. *Autonomous Agents and Multi-Agent Systems*, 5:173–203, 2002.
59. P. Triantafillou, C. Xiruhaki, M. Koubarakis, and N. Ntarmos. Towards high-performance peer-to-peer content and resource sharing systems. In *Proceedings of the First Biennial Conference on Innovative Data Systems Research (CIDR 2003)*, January 2003.
60. C. Tryfonopoulos and M. Koubarakis. Agent-based textual information dissemination: Data models, query languages, algorithms and computational complexity. Technical report, Intelligent Systems Laboratory, Dept. of Electronic and Computer Engineering, Technical University of Crete, October 2002.
61. Mitchell M. Waldrop. *Complexity: The Emerging Science at the Edge of Order and Chaos*. Touchstone Books, 1993.
62. F. Wang. Self-organising Communities Formed by Middle Agents. In *Proceedings of the 1st International Joint Conference on Autonomous Agents & Multiagent Systems (AAMAS 2002)*, pages 1333–1339, July 15–19 2002.
63. H. Chi Wong and K. Sycara. A Taxonomy of Middle-Agents for the Internet. In *Proceedings of 4th International Conference on Multi Agent Systems (ICMAS-2000)*, pages 465–466, Boston, Massachusetts, USA, July 2000.
64. M. Wooldridge, N. R. Jennings, and D. Kinny. The Gaia Methodology for Agent-Oriented Analysis and Design. *Journal of Autonomous Agents and Multi-Agent Systems*, 3(3):285–312, 2000.
65. Michael Wooldridge and Nicholas R. Jennings. Intelligent Agents: Theory and Practice. *The Knowledge Engineering Review*, 10(2):115–152, 1995.
66. T.W. Yan and H. Garcia-Molina. The SIFT information dissemination system. *ACM Transactions on Database Systems*, 24(4):529–565, 1999.
67. B. Yang and H. Garcia-Molina. Designing a super-peer network. In *Proceedings of the 19th International Conference on Data Engineering (ICDE 2003)*, March 5–8 2003.
68. Franco Zambonelli and H. Van Dyke Parunak. From design to intention: signs of a revolution. In *Proceedings of the 1st International Joint Conference on Autonomous Agents & Multiagent Systems (AAMAS 2002)*, pages 455–456, July 15–19 2002.

A Peer-to-Peer Approach to Resource Discovery in Multi-agent Systems

Vassilios V. Dimakopoulos and Evaggelia Pitoura

Department of Computer Science, University of Ioannina
GR 45110 Ioannina, Greece
{dimako,pitoura}@cs.uoi.gr

Abstract. A multi-agent system is a network of software agents that cooperate to solve problems. In *open* multi-agent systems, the agents that need resources provided by other agents are not aware of which agents provide the particular resources. We propose a fully distributed approach to this resource discovery problem. Each agent A maintains a limited size local cache in which it keeps information about k different resources, that is, for each of the k resources, it stores the contact information of one agent that provides it. The agents in the cache of agent A are called A's neighbors. An agent searching for a resource contacts its local cache and if there is no information for the resource, it contacts its neighbors, which in turn contact their neighbors and so on until the resource is found in some cache. We consider variations of this flooding-based search and develop and verify by simulation analytical models of their performance for both uniformly random resource requests and for requests in the case of hot spots. Finally, we introduce two approaches to the problem of updating the caches: one that uses flooding to propagate the updates and one that builds on the notion of an inverted cache.

1 Introduction

In a multi-agent system (MAS), agents cooperate with each other to fulfill a specified task. As opposed to *closed* MAS where each agent knows all other agents it needs to interact with, in *open* MAS such knowledge is not available. To locate an agent that provides a particular resource, most open MAS infrastructures follow a central directory approach. With this approach, agents register their resources to a central directory (e.g., a middle agent [14]). An agent that requests a resource contacts the directory which in turn replies with the contact information of some agent that provides the particular resource. However, in such approaches, the central directories are potential bottlenecks of the system both from a performance and from a reliability perspective.

In this paper, we advocate a new approach to the resource discovery problem in open MAS inspired by search procedures in peer-to-peer systems. Each agent maintains a limited size local cache with the contact information for k different resources (i.e., for each of the k resources, one agent that offers it). This results in a fully distributed directory scheme, where each agent stores part of the

M. Klusch et al. (Eds.): CIA 2003, LNAI 2782, pp. 62–77, 2003.
© Springer-Verlag Berlin Heidelberg 2003

directory. The agents in the cache of an agent A are called its *neighbors*; they are the agents that A knows about. We model this system as a directed graph. Each node of the graph corresponds to an agent and there is a directed edge from a node A to all its neighbors.

We consider flooding-based approaches to searching for a resource. An agent that searches for a particular resource checks the entries of its local cache. If there is no information for the resource, the agent contacts its neighbors which in turn check their own caches and if no information is found, they contact their neighbors. This search procedure continues until either the resource is located in some agent's local cache or a maximum number of steps is reached. If the resource cannot be found, the agent has to resort to some other (costly) mechanism (e.g., to a middle agent) which is guaranteed to reply with the needed information. We provide a number of variations of the search procedure based on which subset of an agent's neighbor is contacted at each step.

Caching can be seen as complementary to directories. Small communities of agents knowing each other can be formed. Such a fully distributed approach eliminates the bottleneck of contacting a central directory. It is also more resilient to failures since the malfunction of a node does not break down the whole network. Furthermore, the system is easily scalable with the number of agents and resources.

We provide analytical estimations of the performance of the proposed search procedures and validate them by simulation. We study both uniformly random requests and requests in the case of hot spots. In the former case, we assume that the entries in the cache are random, that is the entries of each cache is a uniformly random subset of the available resources. In the latter case, we assume that some resources (i.e., the hot spots) appear in a large number of caches.

We also consider the problem of cache updates. We outline two approaches. One approach is based on the notion of an inverted cache: in addition to its local cache, each agent A maintains a list of the agents that have A as their neighbor (i.e., the agents that have A's contact information in their caches) and uses this cache to propagate the updates. The other approach is symmetric to the search procedure: when an agent either changes its location or its resources, it propagates these updates to its neighbors, which in turn contact their neighbors.

The remainder of this paper is structured as follows. In Section 2, we present local caches, in Section 3, search procedures and their analysis and in Section 4, cache updates. A summary of related work is given in Section 5, while conclusions are provided in Section 6.

2 P2P-Based Directories in Multi-agent Systems

2.1 Multi-agent Systems

A multi-agent system (MAS) is a loosely coupled network of software agents that cooperate to solve problems that may be beyond the individual capacities or knowledge of each particular agent. In a MAS, computational resources are distributed across a network of interconnected agents. When compared to a centralized system, a MAS does not suffer from the single point of failure problem. Furthermore, a MAS has less performance bottlenecks or resource limitations. Finally, MAS efficiently retrieves, filters, and globally coordinates information from sources that are spatially distributed.

To fulfill their goals, agents in a MAS need to use resources provided by other agents. To use a resource, an agent must contact the agent that provides it. However, in an *open* MAS, an agent does not know which agents provide which resources. Furthermore, it does not know which other agents participate in the system. A common approach to the resource discovery problem is to introduce middle agents or directories that maintain information about which agents provide which resources. Thus to find a resource, an agent has first to contact the middle agent.

However, middle agents can become bottlenecks and contradict the distribution goals set by a MAS along the dimensions of computational efficiency, reliability, extensibility, robustness, maintainability, responsiveness, and flexibility.

2.2   Peer-to-Peer Systems

Recently, peer-to-peer (p2p) computing [8] has evolved as a new distributed computing paradigm of sharing resources available at the edges of the network. A p2p system is a fully-distributed cooperative network in which nodes collectively form a system without any supervision. P2p systems offer robustness in failures, extensive resource sharing, self-organization, load balancing and anonymity.

An issue central to p2p systems is discovering a peer that offers a particular resource. There are two types of p2p systems depending on the way resources are located in the network. In *structured p2p systems*, resources are not placed at random peers but at peers at specified locations. Most resource discovery procedures in structured p2p systems (such as CAN [9], Chord [13], Past [10] and Tapestry [15]) build a distributed hash table. With distributed hashing, each resource is associated with a key and each node (peer) is assigned a range of keys. In *unstructured p2p*, resources are located at random points. In this context, flooding-based approaches to resource discovery have been proposed, in which each peer searching for a resource contacts all peers in its neighborhood. Gnutella [4] is an example of such an approach.

In this paper, we apply fully-decentralized, unstructured p2p search approaches to the problem of resource discovery in open agent systems. Such approaches distribute the load, increase tolerance to failures, are extensible and scalable to the number of agents and resources.

2.3   Distributed Caches

We assume a multi-agent system with N nodes/agents, where each agent provides a number of resources. We assume that there are R different types of resources. Each agent can locally store part of what a middle agent knows. In

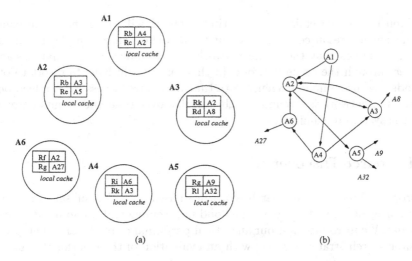

Fig. 1. Part of the cache network: (a) agents with their caches, (cache entries are of the form (Rx, Ai), where Rx is a resource (type) and Ai is the contact information of an agent that offers the resource Rx), and (b) the corresponding directed graph (the cache network).

particular, we assume that each agent has a private cache of size k. Each agent A stores in its cache information about k different resources, that is, for each of the k resources the contact information of one agent that provides it. The agents in the cache of agent A are called A's *neighbors*.

The system is modeled as a directed graph $G(V, E)$, called the *cache network*. Each node corresponds to an agent along with its cache. There is an edge from node A to each of A's neighbors. There is no knowledge about the size of V or E. An example is shown in Figure 1. An agent may provide two or more resources, thus the same agent may appear more than once in another agent's cache. Consequently, there may be less that k outgoing edges from a node, i.e. a node has *at most* k neighbors.

We address the following problem: Given this cache network, how can an agent A that needs a particular type of resource x, find an agent that provides it? Agent A initially searches its own cache. If it finds the resource there, it extracts the corresponding contact information and the search ends. If resource x is not found in the local cache, A sends a message querying a *subset* of its neighbors, which in turn propagate the message to a subset of their neighbors and so on.

Due to the possibility of non-termination, we limit the search to a maximum number of steps, t (similar to the Time To Live (TTL) parameter in p2p systems). In particular, the search message contains a counter field initialized to t. Any intermediate agent that receives the message first decrements the counter by 1. If the counter value is not 0, the agent proceeds as normal; while if the counter value is 0 the agent does not contact its neighbors and sends a positive (negative) response to the inquiring agent if x is found (not found) in its cache.

When the search ends, the inquiring agent A will either have the contact information for resource x or a set of negative responses. In the latter case, agent A assumes that the cache network is *disconnected*, i.e., that it cannot locate x through the cache network. In this case, it will have to resort to other methods, e.g. use a middle agent. Note that disconnectedness may indeed occur because the network is dynamic: caches evolve over time and agents enter and leave the system dynamically.

3   Resource Discovery

We propose three different search strategies based on which subset of its neighbors each agent contacts, namely the flooding, teeming and random paths search strategies. We introduce first our analytical performance model and then present the three search strategies along with an evaluation of their performance.

3.1   Our Perfomance Model

We evaluate the performance of each search strategy with respect to the following three metrics.

- The probability, Q_t, that the resource is found within the t steps. This probability determines the frequency with which an agent avoids using the other locating mechanisms available.
- The average number of steps, $\overline{S_t}$, needed for locating a resource (given that the resource is found).
- The average number of message transmissions, $\overline{M_t}$, occurring during the course of the search. Efficient search strategies should require as few messages as possible in order to not saturate the resources of the underlying network (which, however, may lead to a higher number of steps).

Table 1 summarizes the notation used.

The network of caches is assumed to be in steady-state, all caches being full, meaning that each node knows of exactly k resources (along with the agents that provide them).

If s_i is the probability of locating a resource x at exactly the ith step of a search strategy, then the probability of locating x in any step (up to a maximum of t steps) is given by:

$$Q_t = \sum_{i=0}^{t} s_i. \tag{1}$$

Given that a resource is located within t steps, the probability that we locate it at the ith step is given by s_i/Q_t, and the average number of steps is given by:

$$\overline{S_t} = \sum_{i=1}^{t} i \frac{s_i}{Q_t} = \frac{1}{Q_t} \sum_{i=1}^{t} i s_i. \tag{2}$$

Table 1. Notation used.

Input Parameters	
R	number of resource types
N	number of agents (caches)
k	cache size per agent/node
t	maximum allowable number of steps
h	fraction of caches at which a hot spot appears
r_h	percentage of the resources that are hot spots
Output Parameters	
$PC(j)$	probability that a particular resource is in at least one of j given caches
Q_t	prob. of locating a resource within t steps
$\overline{S_t}$	average # steps needed to locate a resource
$\overline{M_t}$	average # of message transmissions
a	$= 1 - k/R$ (random resource requests) $= 1 - h$ (search for a hot resource) $= 1 - \frac{(k/R)-hr_h}{1-r_h}$, (search for a cold resource)

Let $PC(1)$ be the probability of finding x in any given cache. Then, the probability of finding x is in at least one of j given caches is:

$$PC(j) = 1 - (1 - PC(1))^j \tag{3}$$

that is, 1 minus the probability of not finding x in any of the j caches.

Next, we compute $PC(1)$ for two types of resource request distributions.

Uniformly Random Requests. The content of each cache is assumed to be completely random; in other words the cache's k known resources are a uniformly random subset of the R available resources.

Given a resource x, the probability that x is present in a particular cache is equal to:

$$PC(1) = P[x \in \text{cache}] = 1 - P[\text{every cache entry} \neq x].$$

The number of ways to choose k elements out of a set of R elements so that a particular element is not chosen is $\binom{R-1}{k}$. Since the k elements of the cache are chosen completely randomly, the last probability above is equal to: $\binom{R-1}{k}/\binom{R}{k} = (R-k)/R$, which, gives $PC(1) = k/R$. In what follows, we let $a = 1 - k/R$, so that $PC(1) = 1 - a$.

Requests with Hot Spots. In practice, some resources *(hot spots)* are needed more frequently than others *(cold spots)*. In such cases, it is expected that hot spots will appear in a large number of caches. In particular, we assume that a hot spot will appear in a (high) fraction h of all caches, $h \leq 1$. Let a portion r_h of the resources be hot spots, i.e., a total of $r_h R$ resources are hot spots (with the remaining $(1 - r_h)R$ being cold spots).

Searching for hot spots: The probability of finding a particular hot spot in a particular cache is:

$$PC(1) = h = 1 - a \quad \text{where } a \text{ in this case is equal to } 1 - h.$$

Searching for cold spots: We now estimate the probability $PC(1)$ of finding a particular cold spot in a particular cache. Given N agents (caches), each one holding contact information for k resources, there are in total kN cache entries in the whole network. Each hot spot appears in hN caches, and thus $r_h RhN$ entries are occupied by hot spots, in total. The rest will be occupied by cold spots, which means that each of the cold resources appears on the average:

$$\frac{kN - r_h RhN}{R - r_h R} = \frac{N(k - r_h Rh)}{R(1 - r_h)}$$

times, or equivalently, in a portion of

$$\frac{N(k - r_h Rh)}{R(1 - r_h)} \bigg/ N$$

of the caches. Consequently, we obtain:

$$PC(1) = \frac{k - hr_h R}{R(1 - r_h)} = \frac{(k/R) - hr_h}{1 - r_h}.$$

Again, we set $a = 1 - \frac{(k/R) - hr_h}{1 - r_h}$, so that $PC(1)$ becomes equal to $1 - a$.

3.2   Flooding

In flooding, agent A that searches for a resource x checks its cache, and if the resource is not found there, A contacts *all* its neighbors (i.e., all the agents listed in its cache). In turn, A's neighbors check their caches and if the resource is not found locally, they propagate the search message to *all* their neighbors. The procedure ends when either the resource is found or a maximum of t steps is reached. The scheme, in essence, broadcasts the inquiring message.

As the search progresses, a k-ary tree is unfolded rooted at the inquiring node A. An example is shown in Figure 2(a). The term "tree" is not accurate in graph-theoretic terms since a node may be contacted by two or more other nodes but we will use it here as it helps to visualize the situation. This search tree has (at most) k^i different nodes in the ith level, $i \geq 0$, which means that at the ith step of the search algorithm there will be (at most) k^i different caches contacted. Since an agent A may offer more than one resource, it may appear more than once in another node's cache. Also, there may exist more than one

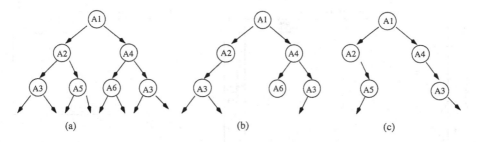

Fig. 2. Searching the cache network of Figure 1: (a) flooding, (b) teeming, (c) random paths ($p = 2$)

caches that know of A. Both these facts may limit the number of different nodes in the ith level of the tree to less than k^i.

Suppose that we are searching at the ith level of this tree for a particular resource x. The probability that we find it there is approximately given by $\ell_i = PC(k^i)$ since in the ith level there are k^i caches. The approximation overestimates the probability since, as noted above, the number of different caches may be less than k^i. However, it simplifies the analysis and does not introduce significant error as shown by our simulation results. Table 2 shows the three performance metrics for flooding. Details for their derivation can be found in [2]. As anticipated, the flooding algorithm requires an exponential number of messages with respect to the cache size (k).

Table 2. Performance of flooding (a is given in Table 1).

Q_t	$1 - a^{\frac{k^{t+1}-1}{k-1}}$
S_t	$\frac{1}{Q_t}\left(a - (t+1)(1 - Q_t) + \sum_{i=2}^{t+1} a^{\frac{k^i-1}{k-1}}\right)$
M_t	$c^t + c + c(c + 1 - a)\frac{c^{t-1}-1}{c-1}, \quad c = ak.$

Figure 3 shows the performance of flooding with respect to the maximum number of steps. The flooding scheme has a number of disadvantages. One is the excessive number of messages that have to be transmitted, especially if t is not small. Another drawback is the way disconnectedness is determined. The inquiring agent has to wait for all possible answers before deciding that it cannot locate the resource. This introduces a number of problems. There is a large number of negative replies. Furthermore, since the network is not synchronized, messages propagate with unspecified delays. This means that the reply of one or more nodes at the tth level of the tree may take quite a long time. One solution is the use of timeout functions; at the end of the timeout period the inquiring

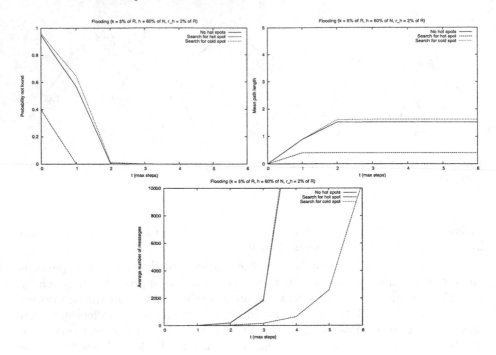

Fig. 3. Performance of flooding (for random distribution (no hot spots), and for hot and cold spots in the case of skewed distribution: probability of not finding the resource $(= 1 - Q_t)$, mean path length $(= \overline{S_t})$ and average number of message transmissions $(= \overline{M_t})$.

agent A decides that the resource cannot be located, even if it has not received all answers.

3.3   Teeming

To reduce the number of messages, we propose a variation of flooding that we call *teeming*. With teeming, at each step, if the resource is not found in the local cache of a node, the node propagates the inquiring message only to a *random subset* of its neighbors. We denote by ϕ the fixed probability of selecting a particular neighbor. In contrast with flooding, the search tree is not a k-ary one any more (Figure 2(b)). A node in the search tree may have between 0 to k children, $k\phi$ being the average case. Flooding can be seen as a special case of teeming for which $\phi = 1$.

   In teeming, a node propagates the inquiring message to each of its neighbors with a fixed probability ϕ. If the requested resource x is not found, it is due to two facts. First, the inquiring node does not contain it in its cache (occurring with probability $1 - PC(1)$). Second, none of the k "subtrees" unfolding from the inquiring node's neighbors replies with a positive answer. Such a subtree has

$t - 1$ levels; it sends an affirmative reply only if it asked by the inquiring node and indeed locates the requested resource.

Based on the above observations, one can derive the three performance metrics of teeming shown in Table 3 (their detailed derivation can be found in [2]). Teeming also requires an exponential number of messages, which however grows slower than in the case of flooding; its rate is controlled by the probability ϕ.

Table 3. Performance of teeming (a is given in Table 1).

Q_t	$1 - a\left(1 - \phi Q_{t-1}\right)^k$
S_t	$t - \frac{1}{Q_t}\sum_{i=0}^{t-1} Q_i$
M_t	$c^t + c + c(c+1-a)\frac{c^{t-1}-1}{c-1}, \; c = ak\phi$

3.4 Random Paths

Although, depending on ϕ, teeming can reduce the overall number of messages, it still suffers from the rest of the problems of flooding. One approach to eliminate these drawbacks is the following: each node contacts only one of its neighbors (randomly). The search space formed ends up being a single random path in the network of caches. This scheme propagates one single message along the path and the inquiring agent will be expecting one single answer.

We generalize this scheme as follows: the root node (i.e., the inquiring agent A) constructs $p \geq 1$ random paths. In particular, if x is not in its cache, A asks p out of its k neighbors (not just one of them). All the other (intermediate) agents construct a simple path as above, by asking (randomly) exactly one of their neighbors. This way, we end up with p different paths unfolding concurrently (Figure 2(c)). The search algorithm produces less messages than flooding or teeming but needs more steps to locate a resource.

When using the random paths algorithm, the inquiring node transmits the message to $p \geq 1$ of its neighbors. Each neighbor then becomes the root of a randomly unfolding path. There is a chance that those p paths meet at some node(s), thus they may not always be disjoint. However, for simplification purposes we assume that they are completely disjoint and thus statistically independent. This approximation introduces negligible error (especially if p is not large) as our experiments showed.

At each step i, $i > 0$, of the algorithm, p different caches are contacted (one in each of the paths). The probability of finding resource x in those caches is $PC(p) = 1 - a^p$. One can then derive the three performance metrics for the random paths search strategy shown in Table 4. Details for their derivation can be found in [2].

Table 4. Performance of random paths (a is given in Table 1).

Q_t	$1 - a^{pt+1}$
$\overline{S_t}$	$\frac{a-(1+t-ta^p)(1-Q_t)}{(1-a^p)Q_t}$
$\overline{M_t}$	$ap + ap\frac{1-a^t}{1-a}$

3.5   Performance Comparison

The three performance measures are shown in Figure 4 for all the proposed strategies. In the plots we have assumed cache sizes equal to 5% of the total number of resources R, which was taken equal to 200. The graphs show the random paths strategy for $p = 4$ paths. For the teeming algorithm, we chose $\phi = 1/\sqrt{k}$, that is, on the average $\sqrt{k}$ children receive the message each time. Larger values of ϕ will yield less steps but more message transmissions.

Note that the flooding and teeming algorithms depend on k (the cache size) while the random paths algorithm is only dependent on the ratio k/R (as can be seen by Table 4 for the values of a given in Table 1). The reported results are for searching hot spots. They suggest that caching hot spots is very efficient since for all approaches 2 steps suffice to locate them with very high probability. Although teeming as compared to random paths, yields higher probabilities of locating the requested resource and with a smaller number of steps, the number of message transmissions is excessive. This is because even if the resource is found, some agents may continue to propagate the request, since they are not informed about the successful location of the resource by some other agent.

To validate the theoretical analysis, we developed simulators for each of the proposed strategies. Our simulation results show that our analysis matches the simulation results closely; the approximations made produce negligible error which only shows up in cases of small cache sizes. Figure 5 reports both the analytical estimation and the simulation results for the average number of messages metric. A more detailed discussion can be found in [2].

4   Updates and Mobility

Open MASs are by nature dynamic systems. Agents may move freely, they may offer additional resources or may cease offering some resources. In effect, this gives rise to two types of updates that can make the cache entries obsolete: (i) updates of the contact details (i.e., location) of an agent (for example, when the agent is mobile and moves to a new network site), or (ii) updates of the resources offered by an agent. Note that the second type of updates models also the cases in which an existing agent leaves the MAS (cease to offer all its resources) or a new agent joins the MAS (offers additional resources).

An approach to handling updates due to agent mobility is to change the type of cache entries. In particular, instead of storing in the cache the location

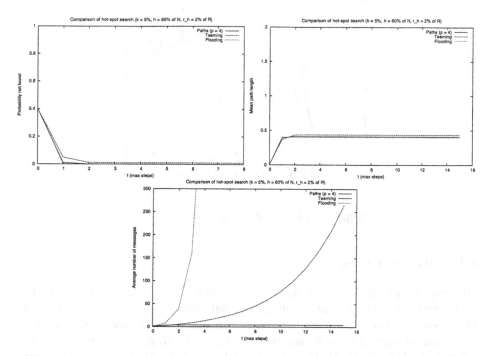

Fig. 4. Comparison of the proposed algorithms: probability of not finding the resource ($= 1 - Q_t$), mean path length ($= \overline{S_t}$) and average number of message transmissions ($= \overline{M_t}$). The teeming algorithm uses $\phi = 1/\sqrt{k}$. The resource searched for is a hot spot.

of an agent, we may maintain just its name. An additional location server is then needed that maintains a mapping between agent names and their locations. In this case, updates of an agent's location do not affect any of the caches. However, this approach adds the additional overhead of contacting the location server, which can now become a bottleneck. In this paper, we consider only decentralized approaches. We also focus on location updates; similar considerations hold for resource updates as well.

Any cache updates are initiated from the agent that moves. The agent may either send an invalidation update message or a propagation update message. In the *invalidation* case, the agent just sends a message indicating the update, so that the associated entries in the caches are marked invalid. In the *propagation* case, the agent also sends its new location. In this case, the associated cache entries are updated with the new location. Invalidation messages are smaller than propagation messages and work well with frequent moving agents. A hybrid approach is also possible. For instance, a frequent moving agent sends an invalidation message first, and a propagation message containing its new location later after settling down at a location.

Next, we consider two approaches to cache invalidation: one based on the notion of an inverted cache and one based on flooding.

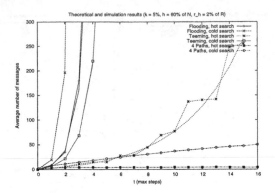

Fig. 5. Validation of our analytical models.

4.1   Inverted Cache

One approach is to maintain an "inverted" cache at each agent. In particular, each agent A maintains a list of all agents that know about A, that is, all agents that have A in their cache. Figure 6 shows an example instance of such a cache.

When an agent moves, it uses the inverted cache to find out which agents it needs to contact. Then, it sends an invalidation (propagation) message to them. In the example of Figure 6, when $A5$ moves, it needs to inform agents $A2$ and $A7$. In terms of the corresponding graph, the dissemination of the updates follows the dotted arrows. Note, that only the agents in the inverted cache need to be contacted.

For "popular" agents, that is, agents with resources that are hot spots, the size of the inverted cache may become very large. Also, the maintenance of an inverted cache makes cache management harder, since each time an entry for a resource offered by B is cached at an agent A, A needs to inform B so that B includes A in its inverted cache. Another consideration is whether the inverted cache should be used in resource discovery: should the agents in an agent's inverted cache be contacted during search?

4.2   Flooding-Based Dissemination of Updates

It is possible to disseminate invalidation (or propagation messages) using an approach similar to the proposed approaches for resource discovery. When an agent A moves, it informs some of its neighbors (i.e., the k agents that are in its cache) by sending an invalidation (propagation) message to them. Each one of them, checks whether agent A is in their cache, and if so it invalidates the corresponding entry (or updates it with A's new location). Then, it forwards the message to some of its neighbors. This process continues until a maximum number of steps is reached. Based on which subset of its neighbors an agent selects to inform at each step, we may have flooding, teeming or random path variations of this procedure.

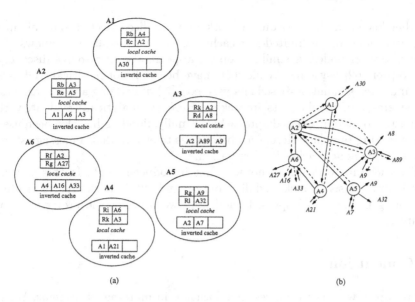

(a)   (b)

Fig. 6. The extended cache: (a) agents, (b) corresponding graph (dotted edges correspond to inverted cache entries)

How many cache entries will be informed depends on the maximum number of steps. It also depends on the topology of the cache network, since in our model, the neighbor relationship is not symmetric; that is, B may be a neighbor of A (i.e., B may be in A's cache), while A is not a neighbor of B (i.e., A is not in B's cache). For example, this is the case when A needs resources offered by B, while B does not need any of A's resources. With flooding-based dissemination, some entries may still be obsolete. In this case, an agent discovers this fact when attempting to contact an agent using an outdated location. The agent may invalidate the entry and continue the search.

5   Related Work

The only other studies of the use of local caches for resource location in MAS that we are aware of are [1] and [12]. In [1], a depth first traversal of what corresponds to our cache network is proposed. Experimental results are presented that show that this approach is more efficient in terms of the number of messages than flooding for particular topologies, in particular, the ring, star, and complete graph topologies. There are no analytical results. In [12], the complexity of the very limited case of lattice-like graphs (in which each agent knows exactly four other agents in such a way that a static grid is formed) is analyzed.

The problem that we study in this paper can be seen as a variation of the resource discovery problem in distributed networks [6], where nodes learn about other nodes in the network. However, there are important differences: (i) we are interested in learning about one specific resource as opposed to learning about all other known nodes, (ii) our network may be disconnected and (iii) in our case, each node has a limited-size cache, so at each instance, it knows about at most k other nodes. A similar problem appears also in resource discovery in peer-to-peer (p2p) systems. While there have been a lot of empirical studies (e.g. [11]) and some simulation-based analysis (e.g. [7]) of flooding and its variants for p2p systems, analytical results are lacking. Here, we analytically evaluate various alternatives of flooding-based approaches. Finally, flooding has also been used in ad-hoc routing (e.g. [5]). Here, the objective is to ensure that a message starting from a source node reaches its destination.

The cache network for agents was first introduced in [3]. In this paper, we extend our analysis for a skewed distribution and obtain performance results for discovering hot and cold spots. In addition, we consider the problem of cache updates.

6   Conclusions

In this paper, we focused on resource location in multi-agent systems. We proposed a fully distributed approach, in which each agent maintains in a local cache information about a number of resources. We introduce and analytically estimated the performance of a number of variations of flooding-based search using these caches for both a random and a skewed distribution. A problem that was not addressed in this paper is how to choose which resources to cache at each agent. This is an interesting problem that we are currently pursuing. We are also implementing a prototype of our system in a mobile agent platform.

Acknowledgments. This work was partially funded by the Information Society Technologies programme of the European Commission, Future and Emerging Technologies under the IST-2001-32645 DBGlobe project and by a Greek Ministry of Education program for Supporting Graduate Studies in Computer Science (EPEAEK II).

References

1. M. A. Bauer and T. Wang. Strategies for Distributed Search. In *CSC '92, ACM Conference on Computer Science*, 1992.
2. V. V. Dimakopoulos and E. Pitoura. A Peer-to-Peer Approach to Resource Discovery in Multi-Agent Systems (Extended Vesrion). Technical Report TR2003, Univ. of Ioannina, Dept. of Computer Science, June 2003. Also available at: http://www.cs.uoi.gr/~pitoura/pub.html.
3. V. V. Dimakopoulos and E. Pitoura. Performance Analysis of Distributed Search in Open Agent System. In *IPDPS '03, International Parallel and Distributed Processing Symposium*, 2003.
4. Gnutella website. http://gnutella.wego.com. Technical report.
5. Z. Haas, J. Y. Halpern, and L. Li. Gossip-Based Ad Hoc Routing. In *IEEE Proc. of INFOCOM 2002*, pages 1707–1716, 2002.

6. M. Harchol-Balter, T. Leighton, and D. Lewin. Resource Discovery in Distributed Networks. In *PODC '99, Principles of Distributed Computing*, pages 229–337, 1999.

7. Q. Lv, P. Cao, E. Cohen, K. Li, and S. Shenker. Search and Replication in Unstructured Peer-to-Peer Networks. In *Proc. ICS2002, 16th ACM Int'l Conf. on Supercomputing*, pages 84–95, 2002.

8. D. S. Milojicic, V. Kalogeraki, R. Lukose, K. Nagaraja, J. Pruyne, B. Richard, S. Rollins, and Z. Xu. Peer-to-Peer Computing. Technical Report HPL2002-57, HP Technical Report, 2002.

9. S. Ratnasamy, P. Francis, M. Handley, R. Karp, and S. Schenker. A Scalable Content-Addressable Network. In *Proc. of ACM SIGCOMM*, pages 161–172, 2001.

10. A. Rowstron and P. Druschel. Storage Management and Caching in PAST, a Large-scale, Persistent Peer-to-Peer Storage Utility. In *Proc. of SOSP 2001, 18th ACM Symp. on Operating System Priciples*, pages 188–201, 2001.

11. S. Saroiu, P. K. Gummadi, and S. D. Gribble. A Measurement Study of Peer-to-Peer File Sharing Systems. In *Proc. MMCN '02, Multimedia Computing and Networking 2002*, 2002.

12. O. Shehory. A scalable agent location mechanism. In *Proc. ATAL '99, 6th Int'l Workshop on Intelligent Agents, Agent Theories, Architectures, and Languages*, volume 1757 of *LNCS*, pages 162–172. Springer, 2000.

13. I. Stoica, R. Morris, D. Karger, M. F. Kaashoek, and H. Balakrishnan. Chord: A Scalable Peer-to-Peer Lookup Service for Internet Applications. In *Proc. of ACM SIGCOMM*, pages 149–160, 2001.

14. K. Sycara, M. Klusch, S. Widoff, and J. Lu. Dynamic Service Matchmaking Among Agents in Open Information Environments. *SIGMOD Record*, 28(1):47–53, March 1999.

15. B. Y. Zhao, J. D. Kubiatowicz, and A. D. Joseph. Tapestry: An Infrastructure for Fault-tolerant Wide-area Location and Routing. Technical Report UCB/CSD-01-1141, U. C. Berkeley, April 2001.

Ostensive Automatic Schema Mapping for Taxonomy-Based Peer-to-Peer Systems

Yannis Tzitzikas* and Carlo Meghini

Istituto di Scienza e Tecnologie dell' Informazione [ISTI]
Consiglio Nazionale delle Ricerche [CNR], Pisa, Italy
{tzitzik|meghini}@iei.pi.cnr.it

Abstract. This paper considers Peer-to-Peer systems in which peers employ taxonomies for describing the contents of their objects and for formulating semantic-based queries to the other peers of the system. As each peer can use its own taxonomy, peers are equipped with inter-taxonomy mappings in order to carry out the required translation tasks. As these systems are ad-hoc, the peers should be able to create or revise these mappings on demand and at run-time. For this reason, we introduce an ostensive data-driven method for automatic mapping and specialize it for the case of taxonomies.

1 Introduction

There is a growing research interest on peer-to-peer systems like Napster, Gnutella, FreeNet and many others. A peer-to-peer (P2P) system is a distributed system in which participants (the peers) rely on one another for service, rather than solely relying on dedicated and often centralized servers. Many examples of P2P systems have emerged recently, most of which are wide-area, large-scale systems that provide content sharing [4], storage services [19], or distributed "grid" computation [2,1]. Smaller-scale P2P systems also exist, such as federated, server-less file systems [10,7] and collaborative workgroup tools [3].

Existing peer-to-peer (P2P) systems have focused on specific application domains (e.g. music file sharing) or on providing file-system-like capabilities. These systems do not yet provide semantic-based retrieval services. In most of the cases, the name of the object (e.g. the title of a music file) is the only means for describing the contents of the object. Semantic-based retrieval in P2P systems is a great challenge. In general, the language that can be used for indexing the objects of the domain and for formulating semantic-based queries, can be *free* (e.g natural language) or *controlled*, i.e. object descriptions and queries may have to conform to a specific vocabulary and syntax. The first case, resembles distributed Information Retrieval (IR) systems and this approach is applicable in the case where the objects of the domain have a textual content (e.g. see [23]). In this paper we focus on the second case where the objects of a peer are

---

* Work done during the postdoctoral studies of the author at CNR-ISTI as an ERCIM fellow.

M. Klusch et al. (Eds.): CIA 2003, LNAI 2782, pp. 78–92, 2003.

indexed according to a specific conceptual model represented in a data model (e.g. relational, object-oriented, logic-based, etc), and content searches are formulated using a specific query language. This approach, which can be called "database approach", starts to receive noteworthy attention by the researchers, as is believed that the database and knowledge base research has much to contribute to the P2P grand challenge through its wealth of techniques for sophisticated semantics-based data models and query processing techniques (e.g. see [14,9,18,15,32]). A P2P system might impose a single conceptual model on all participants to enforce uniform, global access, but this will be too restrictive. Alternatively, a limited number of conceptual models may be allowed, so that traditional information mediation and integration techniques will likely apply (with the restriction that there is no central authority). The case of fully heterogeneous conceptual models makes uniform global access extremely challenging and this is the case that we are interested in.

The first and basic question that we have to investigate is which conceptual modeling approach is appropriate for the P2P paradigm. We would like a scalable conceptual modeling approach which also allows bridging the various kinds of heterogeneity in a systematic and easy manner. As there are no central servers, or mediators, each participating source must have (or be able to create) *mappings*, or articulations, between its conceptual model and the conceptual models of its neighbors in order to be able to translate the received queries to queries that can be understood (and thus answered) by the recipient sources. These mapping could be established manually (as in the case of Semantic Web [8]) but the more appropriate approach for a P2P network, and the more challenging, is the *automatic mapping*. For all these reasons, a simple, conceptually clear, and application-independent conceptual modeling approach seems to be advantageous.

In this paper we consider the case where peers employ *taxonomies*. Note that it is quite easy to create a taxonomy for a source or a mediator. Even ordinary Web users can design this kind of conceptual model. Taxonomies can be constructed either from scratch, or by extracting them from existing taxonomies (e.g. from the taxonomy of Yahoo! or ODP) using special-purpose languages and tools (e.g. see [30]). Furthermore, the design of taxonomies can be done more systematically if done following a faceted approach (e.g. see [27,26]). In addition, thanks to techniques that have emerged recently [31], taxonomies of compound terms can be also defined in a flexible and systematic manner. However, the more important for P2P systems, advantage of taxonomies is that their simplicity and modeling uniformity allows integrating the contents of several sources without having to tackle complex structural differences. Indeed, as it is shown in [32], inter-taxonomy mappings offer a *uniform* method for bridging *naming*, *contextual* and *granularity* heterogeneities between the taxonomies of the sources. Given this conceptual modeling approach, a mediator does not have to tackle complex structural differences between the sources, as it happens with relational mediators (e.g. see [22,21]) and Description Logics-based mediators (e.g. see [17,11]). Moreover, it allows the integration of *schema* and *data* in a uniform manner. Another advantage of this conceptual modeling approach is that query evaluation in taxonomy-based sources and mediators can be done efficiently (polynomial time).

In this paper we introduce a data-driven method for automatic taxonomy articulation. We call this method *ostensive* because the meaning of each term is explained by ostension, i.e. by pointing to something (here, to a set of objects) to which the term applies. For example, the word "rose" can be defined ostensively by pointing to a rose and saying "that is a rose". Instead, the verbal methods of term definition (e.g. the synonyms or the analytic method) presuppose that the learner already knows some other terms and, thus, they are useless to someone who does not know these terms; e.g. verbal word definitions are useless to a small child who has not learnt any words at all.

Specifically, in this paper we describe an ostensive articulation method that can be used for articulating both single terms and queries, and it can be implemented efficiently by a communication protocol. However, ostensive articulation is possible in a P2P system only if the domain of the peers is not disjoint. If it is disjoint then we cannot derive any articulation. This problem can be tackled by employing *reference collections*. For instance, each peer can have its own taxonomy, but before joining the network it must first index the objects of a small reference object set. Consequently, peers can build automatically the desired articulations by running the articulation protocol on this reference collection.

The rest of this paper is organized as follows: Section 2 introduces a general formal framework for ostensive articulation. Section 3 specializes and describes ostensive articulation for taxonomy-based sources. Section 4 discusses the application of ostensive articulation in P2P systems of taxonomy-based sources, and finally, Section 5 concludes the paper.

2   Ostensive Articulation

Let us first introduce the general framework. We view a source S as a function $S : Q \rightarrow A$ where Q is the set of all queries that S can answer, and A is the set of all answers, i.e. $A = \{ S(q) \mid q \in Q \}$. As we focus on retrieval queries, we assume that A is a subset of $\mathcal{P}(Obj)$ where Obj is the set of all objects stored at the source.

The ostensive articulation technique that we shall introduce requires a "naming service", i.e. a method for computing one (or may more) name (e.g. query) for each set of objects $R \subseteq Obj$. Let Q_N denote the set of all names. In general, $Q_N = Q$, however we introduce Q_N because we may want names to be queries of a specific form. For supporting the naming service we would like a function $n : \mathcal{P}(Obj) \rightarrow Q_N$ such that for each $R \subseteq Obj$, $S(n(R)) = R$. Having such a function, we would say that $n(R)$ is an exact name for R. Note that if S is an *onto* function and $Q_N = Q$, then the naming function n coincides with the inverse relation of S, i.e. with the relation $S^{-1} : \mathcal{P}(Obj) \rightarrow Q$. However, this is not always the case, as more often than not, S is not an onto function, i.e. $A \subset \mathcal{P}(Obj)$. For this reason we shall introduce two naming functions, a *lower* naming function n^- and an *upper* naming function n^+. To define these functions, we first need to define an ordering over queries. Given two queries, q and q' in Q, we write $q \leq q'$ if $S(q) \subseteq S(q')$, and we write $q \sim q'$, if both $q \leq q'$ and $q' \leq q$ hold. Note that $\sim$ is an equivalence relation over Q, and let $Q_\sim$ denote the set of equivalence classes induced by $\sim$ over Q. Note that $\leq$ is a partial order over $Q_\sim$.

Now we can define the function n^- and n^+ as follows:

$$n^-(R) = lub\{\, q \in Q_N \mid S(q) \subseteq R\,\}$$
$$n^+(R) = glb\{\, q \in Q_N \mid S(q) \supseteq R\,\}$$

where R is any subset of Obj. Now let R be a subset of Obj for which both $n^-(R)$ and $n^+(R)$ are defined (i.e. the above lub and glb exist). It is clear that in this case it holds:

$$S(n^-(R)) \subseteq R \subseteq S(n^+(R))$$

and that $n^-(R)$ and $n^+(R)$ are the best "approximations" of the exact name of R. Note that if $S(n^-(R)) = S(n^+(R))$ then both $n^-(R)$ and $n^+(R)$ are exact names of R.

If Q_N is a query language that (a) supports disjunction ($\vee$) and conjunction ($\wedge$) and is closed with respect to these, and (b) has a top ($\top$) and a bottom ($\perp$) element such that $S(\top) = Obj$ and $S(\perp) = \emptyset$, then the functions n^- and n^+ are defined for every subset R of Obj. Specifically, in this case $(Q_\sim, \leq)$ is a complete lattice, thus these functions are defined as:

$$n^-(R) = \bigvee \{\, q \in Q_N \mid S(q) \subseteq R\,\}$$
$$n^+(R) = \bigwedge \{\, q \in Q_N \mid S(q) \supseteq R\,\}$$

As Q_N is usually an infinite language, $n^-(R)$ and $n^+(R)$ are queries of infinite length. This means that in practice we also need for a method for computing a query of finite lenght that is equivalent to $n^-(R)$ and another one that is equivalent to $n^+(R)$.

If however Q_N does not satisfy the above ((a) and (b)) conditions, then $n^-(R)$ and $n^+(R)$ may not exist. For example, this happens if we want to establish relationships between single terms of two taxonomy-based sources, or between atomic concepts of two Description Logics-based sources. For such cases, we can define n^- and n^+ as follows:

$$n^-(R) = max\{\, q \in Q_N \mid S(q) \subseteq R\,\}$$
$$n^+(R) = min\{\, q \in Q_N \mid S(q) \supseteq R\,\}$$

where max returns the maximal element(s), and min the minimal(s). Clearly, in this case we may have several lower and upper names for a given R.

We can now proceed and describe the ostensive articulation. Consider two sources $S_i : Q_i \rightarrow \mathcal{P}(Obj_i)$, and $S_j : Q_j \rightarrow \mathcal{P}(Obj_j)$. Ostensive articulation is possible only if their domains are not disjoint, i.e. if $Obj_i \cap Obj_j \neq \emptyset$. Let C denote their common domain, i.e. $C = Obj_i \cap Obj_j$. The method that we shall describe yields relationships that are extensionally valid in C.

Suppose that S_i wants to establish an articulation $a_{i,j}$ to a source S_j. An articulation $a_{i,j}$ can contain relationships of the form:

(i) $q_i \geq q_j$,
(ii) $q_i \leq q_j$

where $q_i \in Q_i$, $q_j \in Q_j$. These relationships have the following meaning:

(i) $q_i \geq q_j$ means that $S_i(q_i) \cap C \supseteq S_j(q_j) \cap C$
(ii) $q_i \leq q_j$ means that $S_i(q_i) \cap C \subseteq S_j(q_j) \cap C$

Before describing ostensive articulation let us make a couple of remarks. The first is that the form (i or ii) of the relationships of an articulation depends on the internal structure and functioning of the source that uses the articulation. For instance, suppose that S_i acts as a mediator over S_j. If S_i wants to compute *complete* (with respect to C) answers, then it should use only relationships of type (i) during query translation. On the other hand, if S_i wants to compute *sound* (with respect to C) answers then it should use relationships of type (ii) (e.g. see [21]).

Another interesting remark is that if S_i is a mediator that adopts a *global-as-view* modeling approach, then all q_i that appear in $a_{i,j}$ are primitive concepts. On the other hand, if S_i adopts a *local-as-view* approach then all q_j that appear in $a_{i,j}$ are primitive concepts of S_j.

Below we describe ostensive articulation for the more general case where S_i is interested in relationships of both, (i) and (ii), types, and where q_i, q_j can be arbitrary queries. Let n_j^- and n_j^+ be the naming functions of S_j as defined earlier. Also let $S_i^c(q) = S_i(q) \cap C$ and $S_j^c(q) = S_j(q) \cap C$. Now suppose that S_i wants to articulate a query $q_i \in Q_i$. The query q_i should be articulated as follows:

$$- \; q_i \geq n_j^-(S_i^c(q_i)) \text{ if } S_i^c(q_i) \supseteq S_j^c(n_j^-(S_i^c(q_i)))$$
$$- \; q_i \leq n_j^-(S_i^c(q_i)) \text{ if } S_i^c(q_i) \subseteq S_j^c(n_j^-(S_i^c(q_i)))$$
$$- \; q_i \geq n_j^+(S_i^c(q_i)) \text{ if } S_i^c(q_i) \supseteq S_j^c(n_j^+(S_i^c(q_i)))$$
$$- \; q_i \leq n_j^+(S_i^c(q_i)) \text{ if } S_i^c(q_i) \subseteq S_j^c(n_j^+(S_i^c(q_i)))$$

Observe the role of the naming functions. S_j instead of checking all queries in Q_j, it just uses its naming functions in order to compute the lower and the upper name of the set $S_i(q_i) \cap C$. Recall that the naming functions (by definition) return the most precise (semantically close) mapping for q_i, thus this is all that we need.

Furthermore, as we shall see below, the above relationships can be obtained without extensive communication. In fact, they can be obtained by a quite simple and efficient (in terms of exchanged messages) distributed protocol. The protocol is sketched in Figure 1. Note that only two messages have to be exchanged between S_i and S_j for articulating the query q_i.

S_i :   (1) $A := S_i(q_i)$;
          (2) $\text{SEND}_{S_i \to S_j}(A)$

S_j :   (3) $F := A \setminus Obj_j$
          (4) $A := A \cap Obj_j$;
          (5) $down := n_j^-(A)$; $Bdown := S_j(down)$;
          (6) $up := n_j^+(A)$; $Bup := S_j(up)$;
          (7) $\text{SEND}_{S_j \to S_i}(F, down, Bdown, up, Bup)$

S_i :   (8)   If $(A \setminus F) \supseteq (Bdown \cap Obj_i)$ then set $q_i \geq down$;
          (9)   If $(A \setminus F) \subseteq (Bdown \cap Obj_i)$ then set $q_i \leq down$;
          (10) If $(A \setminus F) \supseteq (Bup \cap Obj_i)$ then set $q_i \geq up$;
          (11) If $(A \setminus F) \subseteq (Bup \cap Obj_i)$ then set $q_i \leq up$

Fig. 1. The ostensive articulation protocol

Another interesting point is that S_i and S_j do not have to a-priori know (or compute) their common domain C, as C is "discovered" during the run of the protocol (this is the reason why S_j stores in F and sends to S_i those terms that do not belong to Obj_j).

In the case where $Q_N \subset Q$, the only difference is that the message that S_j sends to S_i may contain more than one up and $down$ queries.

A source can run the above protocol in order to articulate one, several or all of its terms (or queries).

3   Ostensive Articulation for Taxonomy-Based Sources

Here we shall specialize ostensive articulation for the case of taxonomy-based sources. Examples of this kind of sources include Web Catalogs (like Yahoo!, Open Directory) and Classification Schemes used in Library and Information Science

We view a taxonomy-based source S as a quadruple $S = \langle T, \preceq, I, Q \rangle$ where:

- T is a finite set of names called *terms*, e.g. Caranies, Birds.
- $\preceq$ is a reflexive and transitive binary relation over T called *subsumption*, e.g. Canaries $\preceq$ Birds.
- I is a function $I : T \to \mathcal{P}(Obj)$ called *interpretation* where Obj is a finite set of objects. For example $Obj = \{1, ..., 100\}$ and $I(\text{Canaries}) = \{1, 3, 4\}$.
- Q is the set of all queries defined by the grammar $q ::= t \mid q \wedge q' \mid q \vee q' \mid \neg q \mid (q)$ where t is a term in T.

Figure 2 shows an example of a source consisting of 8 terms and 3 objects[1].

We assume that every terminology T also contains two special terms, the *top term*, denoted by $\top$, and the *bottom term*, denoted by $\bot$. The top term subsumes

---

[1]   We illustrate only the Hasse diagram of the subsumption relation.

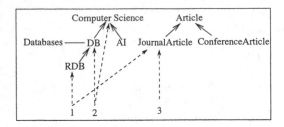

Fig. 2. Graphical representation of a source

every other term t, i.e. $t \preceq \top$. The bottom term is strictly subsumed by every other term t different than top and bottom, i.e. $\bot \preceq \bot$, $\bot \preceq \top$, and $\bot \prec t$, for every t such that $t \neq \top$ and $t \neq \bot$. We also assume that $I(\bot) = \emptyset$ in every interpretation I.

The answer $S(q)$ of a query q is defined as follows (for more see [33]):

$$S(t) = \bigcup \{ I(t') \mid t' \preceq t\}$$
$$S(q \wedge q') = S(q) \cap S(q')$$
$$S(q \vee q') = S(q) \cup S(q')$$
$$S(\neg q) = Obj \setminus S(q)$$

For example, in Figure 2 we have $S(\mathtt{DB}) = \{1, 2\}$, as $S(\mathtt{DB}) = I(\mathtt{DB}) \cup I(\mathtt{Databases}) \cup I(\mathtt{RDB}) = \{1, 2\}$, and $S(\mathtt{DB} \wedge \mathtt{JournalArticle}) = \{1\}$. We define the *index* of an object o with respect to an interpretation I, denoted by $D_I(o)$, as follows: $D_I(o) = \bigwedge\{t \in T \mid o \in I(t)\}$. For example, in the source of Figure 2 we have $D_I(3) = \mathtt{JournalArticle}$ and $D_I(1) = \mathtt{RDB} \wedge \mathtt{JournalArticle}$.

Let us now define the naming functions for this kind of sources. We define the set of names Q_N as follows: $Q_N = \{ q \in Q \mid q$ does not contain negation "$\neg$" $\}$. We exclude queries with negation because, as showed in [32], if such queries appear in articulations then we may get systems which do not have a unique minimal model and this makes query evaluation more complicated and less efficient.

The lower and upper name of a set $R \subseteq Obj$ are defined as in the general framework and clearly $(Q_N, \leq)$ is a complete lattice. What remains is to find finite length queries that are equivalent to $n^-(R)$ and $n^+(R)$.

Theorem 1.

$$n^-(R) \sim \bigvee \{ D_I(o) \mid o \in R,\ S(D_I(o)) \subseteq R\}$$
$$n^+(R) \sim \bigvee \{ D_I(o) \mid o \in R\}$$

The proof is given in [34]. It is clear that the above queries have finite length, hence they are the queries that we are looking for. For this purpose, hereafter we shall use $n^-(R)$ and $n^+(R)$ to denote the above queries. Note that if the

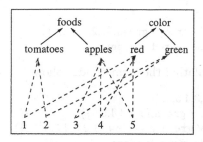

Fig. 3. Example of a source

set $\{o \in R,\ S(D_I(o)) \subseteq R\}$ is empty then we consider that $n(R)^- = \bot$. Some examples from the source shown in Figure 3 follow:

$$n^+(\{1,3\}) = (\mathtt{tomatoes} \wedge \mathtt{red}) \vee (\mathtt{apples} \wedge \mathtt{green})$$
$$n^-(\{1,3\}) = (\mathtt{tomatoes} \wedge \mathtt{red}) \vee (\mathtt{apples} \wedge \mathtt{green})$$
$$n^+(\{1,3,5\}) = (\mathtt{tomatoes} \wedge \mathtt{red}) \vee (\mathtt{apples} \wedge \mathtt{green}) \vee (\mathtt{apples} \wedge \mathtt{red})$$
$$n^-(\{1,3,5\}) = (\mathtt{tomatoes} \wedge \mathtt{red}) \vee (\mathtt{apples} \wedge \mathtt{green})$$

Let us now demonstrate the articulation protocol for taxonomy-based sources. Consider the sources shown in Figure 4 and suppose that S_1 wants to articulate its terms with queries of S_2. In the following examples we omit the set F (from the message of line (7) of Figure 1) as it is always empty.

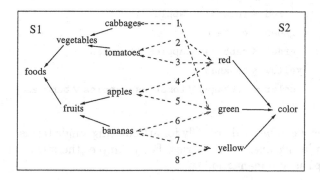

Fig. 4. An example of two sources S_1 and S_2

The steps for articulating the term `cabbages` follow:

$$
\begin{array}{ll}
S_1 \rightarrow S_2 & : \{1\} \\
S_2 \rightarrow S_1 & : (\bot, \emptyset), (\mathtt{green}, \{1,5,6\}) \\
S_1 & : \mathtt{cabbages} \preceq \mathtt{green}
\end{array}
$$

The steps for articulating the term `apples` follow:

$$S_1 \to S_2 \quad : \{4, 5\}$$
$$S_2 \to S_1 \quad : (\perp, \emptyset), (\text{red} \vee \text{green}, \{1,2,3,4,5,6\})$$
$$S_1 \qquad\quad : \text{apples} \preceq \text{red} \vee \text{green}$$

The steps for articulating the term foods follow:

$$S_1 \to S_2 \quad : \{1,2,3,4,5,6,7\}$$
$$S_2 \to S_1 \quad : (\text{red} \vee \text{green}, \{1,2,3,4,5,6\}),$$
$$\qquad\qquad\quad (\text{red} \vee \text{green} \vee \text{yellow}, \{1,2,3,4,5,6,7,8\})$$
$$S_1 \qquad\quad : \text{foods} \succeq \text{red} \vee \text{green},$$
$$\qquad\qquad\quad \text{foods} \sim \text{red} \vee \text{green} \vee \text{yellow}$$

If S_1 runs the protocol for each term of its taxonomy, it will infer the following relationships:

$$\text{cabbages} \preceq \text{green}$$
$$\text{tomatoes} \preceq \text{red}$$
$$\text{apples} \preceq \text{red} \vee \text{green}$$
$$\text{bananas} \preceq \text{green} \vee \text{yellow}$$
$$\text{vegetables} \preceq \text{green} \vee \text{red}$$
$$\text{fruits} \preceq \text{red} \vee \text{green} \vee \text{yellow}$$
$$\text{foods} \succeq \text{red} \vee \text{green}$$
$$\text{foods} \sim \text{red} \vee \text{green} \vee \text{yellow}$$

If S_2 runs this protocol for each term of its taxonomy, it will infer the following relationships:

$$\text{red} \succeq \text{tomatoes}$$
$$\text{red} \preceq \text{tomatoes} \vee \text{apples}$$
$$\text{green} \succeq \text{cabbages}$$
$$\text{green} \preceq \text{cabbages} \vee \text{apples} \vee \text{bananas}$$
$$\text{yellow} \preceq \text{bananas}$$
$$\text{color} \sim \text{cabbages} \vee \text{tomatoes} \vee \text{apples} \vee \text{bananas}$$

The protocol can be used not only for articulating single terms to queries, but also for articulating queries to queries. For example, the steps for articulating the query apples $\vee$ bananas follow:

$$S_1 \to S_2 \quad : \{4, 5, 6, 7\}$$
$$S_2 \to S_1 \quad : (\text{red} \vee \text{green} \vee \text{yellow}, \{1,2,3,4,5,6,7,8\})$$
$$S_1 \qquad\quad : \text{apples} \vee \text{bananas} \preceq \text{red} \vee \text{green} \vee \text{yellow}$$

Now consider the case where we do not want to articulate terms with queries, but terms with *single terms* only, i.e. consider the case where $Q_N = T$. Note that now $lub\{t \in T \mid S(t) \subseteq R\}$ and $glb\{t \in T \mid S(t) \supseteq R\}$ do not always exist. For example, consider the source shown in Figure 5.(a). Note that $n^+(\{1\}) = glb\{t, t'\}$ which does not exist. For the source shown in Figure 5.(b) note that

$n^-(\{1,2\}) = lub\{t, t'\}$ which does not exist. Therefore, we can define the upper and lower *names* of a set R as follows: $n^-(R) = max(\{t \in T \mid S(t) \subseteq R)\})$ and $n^+(R) = min(\{t \in T \mid S(t) \supseteq R)\})$. Consider for example the source shown in Figure 5.(c). Here we have:

$$n^-(\{1,2,3\}) = max(\{c, d, e, b\}) = \{b\}$$
$$n^+(\{1,2,3\}) = min(\{b, a\}) = \{b\}$$

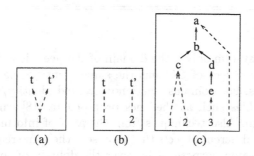

(a)   (b)   (c)

Fig. 5. An example of three sources

Certainly, the relationships obtained by the term-to-term articulation are less expressive than the relationships obtained by the term-to-queries articulation. For instance, suppose that we want to articulate the terms of the source S_1 in each one of the three examples that are shown in Figure 6. Table 1 shows the articulation $a_{1,2}$ that is derived by the *term-to-term* articulation and the *term-to-queries* articulation in each of these three examples.

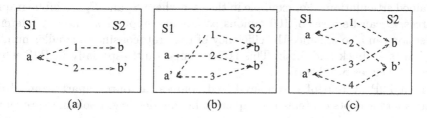

(a)   (b)   (c)

Fig. 6. Three examples

4   Ostensive Articulation in Taxonomy-Based P2P Systems

We demonstrated how ostensive articulation can be applied on taxonomy-based sources for constructing inter-taxonomy articulations. Ostensive articulation is

Table 1. *Term-to-term* vs *term-to-query* articulation

Example	$a_{1,2}$	
	term-to-term art.	*term-to-query* art.
Figure 6.(a)	$a \succeq b$	$a \sim b \vee b'$
	$a \succeq b'$	
Figure 6.(b)	$a \preceq b$	$a \sim b \wedge b'$
	$a \preceq b'$	$a' \preceq b \vee b'$
Figure 6.(c)		$a \preceq b \vee b'$
		$a' \preceq b \vee b'$

possible in a P2P system only if the domain of the peers is not disjoint. We also assume that every object of Obj has the same identity (e.g. object identifier, URI) in all sources. For domains where no accepted identity/naming standards exist, mapping tables such as the ones proposed in [18] can be employed to tackle this problem. Also techniques from the area of information fusion (that aim at recognizing different objects that represent the same reality) could be also employed for the same purpose. If however the domain of the peers is disjoint then we cannot derive any articulation. One method to tackle this problem is to employ *reference collections*. For instance, each peer can have its own taxonomy, but before joining the network it must first index the objects of a small object set. Consequently, peers can build automatically the desired articulations by running the articulation protocol on this reference collection. Running the protocol on the reference collection C means that the sources S_1 and S_2 instead of using $S_1(q_1)$ and $S_2(q_2)$, they use $S_1(q_1) \cap C$ and $S_2(q_2) \cap C$ respectively. Also note that the employment of reference collections can: (a) *enhance the accuracy* of the resulting articulation, and/or (b) *enhance efficiency*. For instance, if C corresponds to a well known, thus well-indexed set of objects then it can improve the quality of the obtained articulations. For example in the case where S_1 and S_2 are bibliographic sources, C can be a set of 100 famous papers in computer science. A reference collection can also enhance the efficiency of the protocol since a smaller number of objects go back and forth. This is very important, especially in P2P where involved sources are distant.

In a P2P system of taxonomy-based sources, a source apart from object queries now accepts content-based queries, i.e. queries (e.g. boolean expressions) expressed in terms of its taxonomy. For answering a query a source may have to query the neighbor sources. The role of articulations during query evaluation has been described in [33] (for the mediator paradigm) and in [32] (for the P2P paradigm). Roughly, a source in a P2P network can serve any or all of the following roles: primary source, mediator, and query initiator. As a *primary* source it provides original content to the system and is the authoritative source of that data. Specifically, it consists of a taxonomy (i.e. a pair $(T, \preceq)$) plus an object base (i.e. an interpretation I) that describes a set of objects (Obj) in terms of the taxonomy. As a *mediator* it has a taxonomy but does not store or provide any content: its role is to provide a uniform query interface to other sources, i.e. it forwards the received queries after first selecting the sources to be queried and formulating the query to be sent to each one of them. These tasks are determined by the articulations of the mediator. As a *query initiator* it acts as client in the system and poses new queries. Figure 7 sketches graphically the architecture of a network consisting of four peers $S_1, ..., S_4$; two primary sources (S_3 and S_4), one mediator (S_2) and one source that is both primary and mediator (S_1). Triangles denote taxonomies, cylinders object bases, and circles inter-taxonomy mappings. S_2 is a mediator over S_1, S_3 and S_4, while S_1 is a mediator over S_2 and S_3. For more about this architecture and the associated semantics and query evaluation methods please refer to [32].

$$S_1 = (T_1, \leq_1, I_1, a_{1,2}, a_{1,3})$$

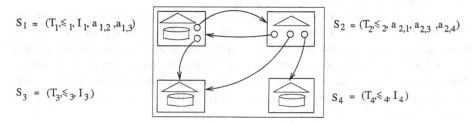

$$S_2 = (T_2, \leq_2, a_{2,1}, a_{2,3}, a_{2,4})$$

$$S_3 = (T_3, \leq_3, I_3)$$

$$S_4 = (T_4, \leq_4, I_4)$$

Fig. 7. A P2P network based on taxonomies and inter-taxonomy mappings

5   Conclusion

The contribution of this paper is a formal framework for ostensive data-driven articulation. Roughly, the approaches for linking two conceptual models or taxonomies can be broadly classified as either *model*-driven or *data*-driven.

The model-driven approach starts with a (theoretical) model of how the two taxonomies are constructed and how they are used. Subsequently, the mapping approaches have to address the compatibility, structural and semantic differences and heterogeneities that exist. This is done using software tools (that usually rely on lexical resources) that assist the designer during the articulation process (e.g. see [25,29,5,24]).

On the other hand, in the *data-driven* approach the mappings are *discovered* by examining how terms are used in indexing the objects. The advantage of such an approach is that it does not make any assumptions on how the two taxonomies are constructed, or how they are used. All it requires is the presence of two databases that contain several objects in common. However, the data-driven approach does have inherent difficulties. First, unless one has a large collection of objects that have been indexed using *both* taxonomies, spurious correlation can result in inappropriate linking. Second, if a term is not assigned to any of the common objects, one cannot establish a link for that term. Third, rarely occurring terms can result in statistically insignificant links. Finally, the validation of data-driven approaches can only be statistical in nature. In spite of these inherent difficulties, data-driven approaches can be formalized and automated. However, most of the data-driven approaches that can be found in the literature are applicable only if the domain is a set of documents (texts) (e.g. [6,16,12,20, 28]), and they cannot establish mappings between queries.

The technique described in this paper is quite general and expressive as it can be used for articulating not only single terms but also queries. Furthermore, it can be used for articulating the desired set of terms or queries (it is not obligatory to articulate the entire taxonomies). Another distinctive feature of this technique is that it can be implemented efficiently by a communication protocol, thus the involved sources do not have to reside on the same machine. Therefore it seems appropriate for automatic articulation in P2P systems which is probably the more challenging issue in P2P computing [9].

We also demonstrated how it can be applied to taxonomy-based sources. An interesting remark is that the proposed method can be applied not only to manually constructed taxonomies but also to taxonomies derived automatically on the basis of an inference service. For instance, it can be applied on sources indexed using taxonomies of compound terms which are defined algebraically [31]. Furthermore it can be applied on concept lattices formed using Description Logics (DL) [13].

One issue for further research, is to investigate how a source that wants to articulate a set $F \subseteq Q$ must use the described protocol in order to obtain the desired articulation with the minimal number of exchanged messages and the less network throughput. Another issue for further research is to investigate ostensive articulation for other kinds of sources.

Acknowledgements. The first author wants to thank his wife Tonia for being an endless source of happiness and inspiration.

References

1. "About LEGION – The Grid OS"(www.appliedmeta.com/legion/about.html), 2000.
2. "How Entropia Works"(www.entropia.com/how.asp), 2000.
3. "Groove" (www.groove.net), 2001.
4. "Napster"(www.naptster.com), 2001.
5. Bernd Amann and Irini Fundulaki. "Integrating Ontologies and Thesauri to Build RDF Schemas". In *Proceedings of the Third European Conference for Digital Libraries ECDL'99*, Paris, France, 1999.
6. S. Amba. "Automatic Linking of Thesauri". In *Proceeding of SIGIR'96*, Zurich, Switzerland, 1996. ACM Press.
7. T.E. Anderson, M. Dahlin, J. M. Neefe, D. A. Patterson, D. S. Roselli, and R. Wang. "Serveless Network File Systems". *SOSP*, 29(5), 1995.
8. Tim Berners-Lee, James Hendler, and Ora Lassila. "The Semantic Web". *Scientific American*, May 2001.
9. Philip A. Bernstein, F. Giunchiglia, A. Kementsietsidis, J. Mylopoulos, L. Serafini, and I. Zaihrayeu. "Data Management for Peer-to-Peer Computing: A Vision". In *Proceedings of WebDB02*, Madison, Wisconsin, June 2002.

10. W. J. Bolosky, J. R. Douceur, D. Ely, and M. Theimer. "Feasibility of a Serveless Distributed File System Deployed on an Existing Set of Desktop PCs". In *Proceedings of Measurement and Modeling of Computer Systems*, June 2000.

11. Diego Calvanese, Giuseppe De Giacomo, and Maurizio Lenzerini. A framework for ontology integration. In *Proc. of the 2001 Int. Semantic Web Working Symposium (SWWS 2001)*, pages 303–316, 2001.

12. A. Doan, J. Madhavan, P. Domingos, and A. Halevy. "Learning to Map between Ontologies on the Semantic Web". In *Proceedings of the World-Wide Web Conference (WWW-2002)*, 2002.

13. F.M. Donini, M. Lenzerini, D. Nardi, and A. Schaerf. *"Reasoning in Description Logics"*, chapter 1. CSLI Publications, 1997.

14. Steven Gribble, Alon Halevy, Zachary Ives, Maya Rodrig, and Dan Suiu. "What can Databases do for Peer-to-Peer?". In *Proceedings of WebDB01*, Santa Barbara, CA, 2001.

15. Alon Halevy, Zachary Ives, Peter Mork, and Igor Tatarinov. "Piazza: Data Management Infrastructure for Semantic Web Applications". In *Proceedings of WWW'2003*, May 2003.

16. Heiko Helleg, Jurgen Krause, Thomas Mandl, Jutta Marx, Matthias Muller, Peter Mutschke, and Robert Strogen. "Treatment of Semantic Heterogeneity in Information Retrieval". Technical Report 23, Social Science Information Centre, May 2001. (http://www.gesis.org/en/publications/ reports/iz_working_papers/).

17. Vipul Kashyap and Amit Sheth. "Semantic Heterogeneity in Global Information Systems: the Role of Metadata, Context and Ontologies ". In *Cooperative Information Systems: Trends and Directions*. Academic Press, 1998.

18. A. Kementsietsidis, Marcelo Arenas, and Rene J. Miller. "Mapping Data in Peer-to-Peer Systems: Semantics and Algorithmic Issues". In *Int. Conf. on Management of Data, SIGMOD'2003*, San Diego, California, June 2003.

19. J. Kubiatowicz, D. Bindel, Y. Chen, S. Czerwinski, P. Eaton, D. Geels, R. Gummadi, S. Rhea, H. Weatherspoon, W. Weimer, C. Wells, and B. Zhao. "Oceanstore: An Architecture for Global-Scale Persistent Storage". In *ASPLOS*, November 2000.

20. M. Lacher and G. Groh. "Facilitating the Exchange of Explicit Knowledge Through Ontology Mappings". In *Proceedings of the 14th Int. FLAIRS Conference*, 2001.

21. Maurizio Lenzerini. Data integration: A theoretical perspective. In *Proc. ACM PODS 2002*, pages 233–246, Madison, Wisconsin, USA, June 2002.

22. Alon Y. Levy. "Answering Queries Using Views: A Survey". *VLDB Journal*, 2001.

23. Bo Ling, Zhiguo Lu, Wee Siong Ng, BengChin Ooi, Kian-Lee Tan, and Aoying Zhou. "A Content-Based Resource Location Mechanism in PeerIS". In *Proceedings of the 3rd International Conference on Web Information Systems Engineering, WISE 2002*, Singapore, December 2002.

24. Bernardo Magnini, Luciano Serafini, and Manuela Speranza. "Making Explicit the Hidden Semantics of Hierarchical Classification". In *Atti dell'Ottavo Congresso Nazionale dell'Associazione Italiana per l'Intelligenza Artificiale, LNCS. Springer Verlag*, 2003.

25. P. Mitra, G. Wiederhold, and J. Jannink. "Semi-automatic Integration of Knowledge sources". In *Proc. of the 2nd Int. Conf. On Information FUSION*, 1999.

26. Ruben Prieto-Diaz. "Implementing Faceted Classification for Software Reuse". *Communications of the ACM*, 34(5), 1991.

27. S. R. Ranganathan. "The Colon Classification". In Susan Artandi, editor, *Vol IV of the Rutgers Series on Systems for the Intellectual Organization of Information*. New Brunswick, NJ: Graduate School of Library Science, Rutgers University, 1965.

28. I. Ryutaro, T. Hideaki, and H. Shinichi. "Rule Induction for Concept Hierarchy Allignment". In *Proceedings of the 2nd Workshop on Ontology Learning at the 17th Int. Conf. on AI (IJCAI)*, 2001.

29. Marios Sintichakis and Panos Constantopoulos. "A Method for Monolingual Thesauri Merging". In *Proceedings of 20th International Conference on Research and Development in Information Retrieval, ACM SIGIR'97*, Philadelphia, PA, USA, July 1997.

30. Nicolas Spyratos, Yannis Tzitzikas, and Vassilis Christophides. "On Personalizing the Catalogs of Web Portals". In *15th International FLAIRS Conference, FLAIRS'02*, Pensacola, Florida, May 2002.

31. Yannis Tzitzikas, Anastasia Analyti, Nicolas Spyratos, and Panos Constantopoulos. "An Algebraic Approach for Specifying Compound Terms in Faceted Taxonomies". In *13th European-Japanese Conference on Information Modelling and Knowledge Bases*, Kitakyushu, Japan, June 2003.

32. Yannis Tzitzikas, Carlo Meghini, and Nicolas Spyratos. "Taxonomy-based Conceptual Modeling for Peer-to-Peer Networks". In *Proceedings of 22th Int. Conf. on Conceptual Modeling, ER'2003*, Chicago, Illinois, October 2003.

33. Yannis Tzitzikas, Nicolas Spyratos, and Panos Constantopoulos. "Mediators over Ontology-based Information Sources". In *Second International Conference on Web Information Systems Engineering, WISE 2001*, Kyoto, Japan, December 2001.

34. Yannis T. Tzitzikas. *"Collaborative Ontology-based Information Indexing and Retrieval"*. PhD thesis, Department of Computer Science – University of Crete, September 2002.

Proposal-Based Negotiation in Convex Regions

Marco Cadoli

Dipartimento di Informatica e Sistemistica
Università di Roma "La Sapienza"
Via Salaria 113, I-00198 Roma, Italy
cadoli@dis.uniroma1.it
www.dis.uniroma1.it/~cadoli

Abstract. In this work we analyze negotiation between two partially cooperative agents, which are supposed to find an agreement which satisfies both of them minimizing the number of iterations. Our goal is to understand the role that reasoning can play in speeding up the search for an agreement. We do not put any limit on the number of shared variables and constraints, and analyze the negotiation problem under the hypothesis that the admissibility regions for each agent are convex. Under such a framework, we show how an agent can perform a sophisticated form of reasoning, which can be formalized by means of *projections* on the other agent's proposals. The main technical result of this paper is that projections can be very effective in speeding up negotiation; in particular, we show by means of several examples that reasoning about the other agent's reasoning using projections allows a protocol which is, in some cases, very efficient. We also investigate the intrinsic limits of the methodology, showing that there are some worst-case scenarios in which the number of exchanged proposals is exponential both in the number of variables and in the number of constraints.

1   Introduction

Automated negotiation is an important area in the field of Distributed Artificial Intelligence, which has been widely studied in the past years (cf., e.g., [4,8, 9,11,13,14]). It has been frequently noted in the literature that the need for negotiation arises in several applications, such as distributed resource allocation problems [2] and distributed scheduling [10].

Of course the relatively recent interest in e-business provides a very interesting scenario for negotiation techniques. As noted in [6,8], when two automated agents belonging to different enterprises need to interact, they are typically self-motivated, but may benefit from cooperation. In other words, in business interaction the *buying* and the *selling* agents have their own specifications in terms of handled variables, constraints that they are supposed to honor, and expected benefits that they want to maximize. Nevertheless, they are forced to cooperate, because a mutually satisfactory agreement has to be found before the business transaction can take place.

M. Klusch et al. (Eds.): CIA 2003, LNAI 2782, pp. 93–108, 2003.

As noted in, e.g., [12], finding an agreement can be modeled as a *distributed constraint satisfaction problem* (DCSP), i.e., a constraint satisfaction problem (CSP) where variables and constraints are naturally distributed among different automated agents. It is in fact interesting to model a negotiation problem as a DCSP rather than a generic CSP because gathering information in a single agent may be undesirable –or even impossible– for security or privacy reasons. As a matter of facts, it is unrealistic to model a business transaction pretending that both partners are willing to share the totality of their goals and constraints.

Important factors in defining protocols and algorithms for negotiation are, among others, cf. [6,8]: the negotiation objects, the agents' decision making models, the level of cooperation among the agents, the number of agents, and the communication and computation costs. In this work we focus on the specific case of two agents, partially cooperative, which are supposed to find an agreement which satisfies both of them minimizing the number of iterations.

Other researchers, cf., e.g., [7,12], have considered the case in which there are several agents, but the number of shared variables is somewhat limited. On the other hand, here we do not put any limit on the number of shared variables and constraints, and focus on the specific case of "peer to peer" interaction, which is probably the most common pattern for e-commerce, and involves just two agents.

The goal of this paper is twofold:

1. to describe in a systematic, and adequately general, way the kind of interaction that could happen between the agents;
2. to study in detail a specific case of interaction, trying to understand the role that reasoning can play in speeding up the search for an agreement.

In Section 2 we focus on the former goal, while in Sections 3 and 4 we focus on the latter one. In particular, we analyze the negotiation problem under the hypothesis that the admissibility regions for each agent are *convex*, i.e., that all points between two acceptable variable assignments are acceptable as well. Under such a framework, we study how an agent can learn from the other agent's *proposals*, where a proposal is a single point in the space of variable assignments. In particular, the agents can perform a sophisticated form of reasoning, which can be formalized by means of *projections*. The main technical result of this paper is that projections can be very effective in speeding up negotiation; in particular, we show by means of several examples that reasoning about the other agent's reasoning using projections allows a protocol which is, in some cases, very efficient. We also investigate the intrinsic limits of the methodology, showing that there are some worst-case scenarios in which the number of exchanged proposals is exponential both in the number of variables and in the number of constraints. In Section 5 we conclude the paper, and present current research.

2   Nature of the Interaction

When dealing with negotiation, everyday experience shows that there are several aspects that must be taken into account. In this section we list some of the most important aspects, without claiming the list to be exhaustive.

Variables: typically, when two agents start a negotiation, they already agree on the relevant variables (or issues). As an example, when a book is supposed to be bought via the Internet, buying and selling agents may agree that there are three relevant variables:
   - the price (p, a positive real);
   - the number of days for the delivery (d, a positive integer);
   - the possibility of returning the book (r, a boolean).
   We assume that for each negotiation there is a finite list of typed variables that are involved. Usually variables are numeric (integer or real); boolean variables –analyzed in, e.g., [11]– are special cases of the integer ones.

Constraints: each agent involved in the negotiation may be willing to accept an agreement as long as some constraints are satisfied. Returning to the previous example, here is a possible situation:
   - the buying agent wants:
     • to be able to return the book, if it is expensive, e.g.,

$$(p > 25) \rightarrow (r = true),$$

   and
     • the book to be delivered soon, e.g.,

$$d < 4;$$

   - the selling agent wants:
     • the price to be greater than or equal to a fixed amount, plus a fee for delivery which decreases with respect to delivery time, e.g.,

$$p \geq 20 + 20/d,$$

   and
     • not to bother with returns of cheap books, e.g.,

$$(r = true) \rightarrow (p > 23).$$

It is worthwhile to notice that an entity knowing the entire set of constraints could obtain a solution pretty soon, using standard Mathematical Programming and Constraint Programming techniques. However, realistically the two agents are not willing to share the constraints, therefore the problem is much more complex.

In general, we assume that each agent has her own *feasibility region*, which is the set of assignments to the variables that she is willing to accept (admissible solutions). Each agent has her own syntax for expressing constraints, which may determine the shape of the feasibility region. Important cases are those of *connected* and *convex* regions.

Objective function: an agent may prefer a solution rather than another one. Continuing our example:
- an anxious reader may be upset by long waits, e.g., she wants to minimize the function

$$p + 2 \cdot d,$$

- a wise merchant may want to maximize the income, i.e., the function p. We remark that, also in this case, it is reasonable to assume that each agent ignores the other agent's preferences.

Exchanged information: since there are circumstances in which agents –even if partially cooperating– are not willing to share the whole set of constraints, the question of what kind of information they are supposed to exchange arises.

One possibility is to exchange *proposals*, i.e., single points in the space of variable assignments. Returning to our running example, one agent may propose

$$\langle p = 22, d = 3, r = true \rangle.$$

Obviously, the other agent may either accept or decline the proposal.
Another possibility, studied in, e.g., [11], is to communicate a constraint, i.e., a whole region in the space of assignments, e.g.,

$$d \leq 3.$$

Protocol rules: before establishing precisely the way agents are supposed to interact, it is necessary to clarify which rules must be always respected.
"*No cheat*" seems to be a reasonable rule: an agent cannot make a proposal which she is not willing to accept. This assumption is adopted in e.g., [4]. If constraints, and not proposals, are exchanged, an agent should not be allowed to communicate a constraint which is inconsistent with her own set of constraints.
Other aspects are less clear. As an example, are we supposed to accept the first proposal which is in our feasibility region? Can we decline it, but only for a predefined maximum number of times, after which we must accept?

Strategy: each agent follows her own strategy during negotiation. Reasonable strategies are:
- trying to minimize the number of iterations,
- try to reach an optimal point with respect to the objective function,
- a combination of the above ones.

Variability with respect to time: people tend to "change their mind" when a negotiation lasts for a long time. As an example, if after three months I am not able to find a flat with three bedrooms, I may relax such a constraint; similarly, I may modify my preferences, i.e., the objective function. A crucial choice is either to allow or deny such changes, in a problem formulation.

Amount of resources: reasoning on other agents' reasoning, and in particular about the deductions that can be done by others, may be very useful. A typical assumption is that each agent is *logically omniscient*, i.e., she is able to compute all logical consequences of the information she has [5,3].

Willingness to cooperate: assuming that an optimal algorithm for negotiation is known, each agent may be willing to use it –being in this way totally cooperative– or not. As an example, an agent may decide not to be cooperative, by making proposals that –although not cheating– are obviously useless, since it is possible to infer that the other agent will never accept them.

3   Proposals in Convex Regions

In this section, we introduce a special case of interaction which will be studied throughout the paper. Albeit simple, the interaction we study offers the opportunity to make interesting considerations. To the best of our knowledge, this case has not been analyzed in the literature before.

Variables and constraints: there are two agents A and B who agreed beforehand on the variables, which are all *real*. Constraints are such that feasibility regions (denoted with R_A and R_B, respectively) are convex, i.e., all points between two acceptable variable assignments are acceptable as well.

Obviously, agent A knows R_A. About R_B, A just knows that it is convex (same for B, exchanging roles). In particular, both R_A and R_B may be described in terms of a set of *linear* dis-equations.

Objective function: for the sake of simplicity, there is no objective function. In other words, all points in the feasibility region are equally acceptable from the point of view of an agent.

Exchanged information: agents exchange proposals, i.e., single points.

Protocol rules: agents do not cheat, i.e., they must make proposals in their feasibility region, and must accept the first feasible proposal that they receive.

Strategy: we assume that the agent that initiates the negotiation (conventionally, A) wants to finish it using the minimum number of iterations. For the purpose of generality, we do not ascribe such a behavior to B. Concluding a negotiation means either to find a point (called *agreement*) in $R_A \cap R_B$, or to logically prove that there is no such a point.

Variability with respect to time: for the sake of simplicity, both R_A and R_B do not change.

Amount of resources: we assume that both A and B are able to compute all logical consequences of the information they have. We also assume that both of them know that the other agent has such a feature.

Willingness to cooperate: we assume that both A and B are, at least partially, cooperative. As an example, we forbid B to make twice a proposal P. The rationale behind it is that, since 1) P has been previously rejected by A, 2) R_A has not changed in the meanwhile, and 3) B can make logical inferences, B knows that A would reject P again. We remark that we do not assume the agents to follow an "optimal" strategy but rather we forbid "obstructionism".

Few comments about these assumptions are in order. Assuming that there is no objective function simplifies the scenario a lot: as an example, it makes the "accept-first" protocol the only reasonable one. We do not claim that having no objective function is always reasonable, and we plan to eventually drop such an assumption. In the conclusions, we spend few words about it. For the moment, we claim that studying the simplified scenario is a mandatory starting point for more complex investigations.

Figure 1 shows a potential situation with two variables; there is a potential agreement, since $R_A \cap R_B \neq \emptyset$. In what follows, we try to figure out conditions which imply that A and B may effectively find an agreement.

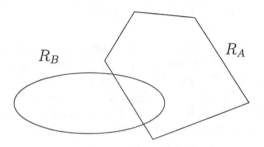

Fig. 1. Feasibility regions on a 2-variable space

3.1   One-Variable Regions

The case in which there is only one variable is simple. Nevertheless, it is complex enough to let most issues emerge. According to the previous assumption on constraints, both R_A and R_B are convex; we assume that they are closed, i.e., intervals, including boundaries. Figure 2 illustrates a potential sequence of interaction:

1. agent A proposes one of her extremal points, i.e., a "vertex", e.g., the left one (A_1);
2. if $A_1 \in R_B$, then agent B must accept it, thus ending the negotiation; let us assume it is not the case, and that B proposes one of her points (B_1, not necessarily a vertex);
3. agent A proposes the other vertex (A_2);
4. interaction must stop after two more steps:
   a) if $R_B \cap \overline{A_1 A_2} \neq \emptyset$ then B (who knows that R_A is convex and therefore must contain the segment $\overline{A_1 A_2}$) will make a proposal $B_2 \in \overline{A_1 A_2}$, which A accepts;
   b) otherwise, B will make a proposal $B_2 \notin \overline{A_1 A_2}$; at this point A will know that there is no possible agreement, and is supposed to officially close the negotiation (obviously, exhibiting the logical proof).

R_A

Fig. 2. A possible sequence of proposals in a one-variable space

Few comments about the above example are in order:

- In order to find an agreement, both A and B must *keep* the other agent's proposals, i.e., store them in some format.
- Moreover, they must *reason*, taking into account both their feasibility region and the other agent's one.

  As an example, in point 4b of the sequence illustrated previously, A is able to conclude that there is no agreement because she knows that:
  - B knows that $\overline{A_1 A_2} \supseteq R_A$ (*convexity*);
  - if $R_B \cap \overline{A_1 A_2} \neq \emptyset$, then B should propose a point in such a region (*partial cooperation*);
  - since B makes a proposal $B_2 \notin \overline{A_1 A_2}$, then A knows that $R_B \cap \overline{A_1 A_2} = \emptyset$ (*logical omniscience*).

It is now possible to specify more precisely what "partially cooperative" means: we want to be sure that B uses all the information she has when making the second proposal B_2. In particular, if $R_B \cap \overline{A_1 A_2} \neq \emptyset$, we do not allow B to make a proposal outside $\overline{A_1 A_2}$, i.e., to be "obstructive".

It is easy to show that, in the case of a single variable, negotiation stops always in five steps or less, provided that the agent starting negotiation (A) proposes her vertices. It is interesting to note that this holds also if the other agent (B) does not propose her vertices, but just internal points.

3.2 Multi-variable Regions

The first aspect to be noted in the case of two or more variables is that the vertex-based interaction can be done only in the case of polyhedral feasibility regions. Referring to Figure 1, only R_A is polyhedral.

On top of that, even in the case of polyhedral regions the vertex-based interaction is not completely satisfactory, since the number of vertices grows exponentially with the number of variables. As an example, the set of $2n$ constraints $0 \leq x_i,\ x_i \leq 1\ (1 \leq i \leq n)$ on the n variables x_i describes a hypercube with 2^n vertices. An interesting problems can be stated as follows:

- Let us assume that the feasibility regions are finite and described by means of linear constraints. Are there proposal-based protocols which are guaranteed to terminate in polynomially many iterations (with respect to the number of variables)?

In what follows we analyze the above problem, and our goal is to determine whether agents can terminate negotiation without proposing all their vertices. We show a sophisticated form of reasoning that, in many cases, allows to save a large number of iterations. In this section we present a detailed example which highlights the main features of the reasoning; for the sake of simplicity, the example refers to a negotiation involving just two variables.

We refer to the following example; R_A is described by means of the constraints:

$$x \geq 0, \quad x \leq 10, \quad y \geq 0, \quad y \leq 10.$$

We use the following abbreviations for some interesting points (A_1-A_4 are the four vertices of R_A, cf. Figure 3):

$$A_1 \equiv (0,0), A_2 \equiv (10,10), A_3 \equiv (10,0), A_4 \equiv (0,10), B_1 \equiv (0,15), B_2 \equiv (5,15).$$

Assuming that the sequence of interaction starts with the proposal (from A) of the point A_1 and continues with B_1 (from B), A_2 and B_2, we represent the negotiation knowledge base of A by means of the following assertions:

$$\alpha : offer(A_1); \quad \beta : receive(B_1); \quad \gamma : offer(A_2); \quad \delta : receive(B_2).$$

It is interesting to note that the assertions in the knowledge base allow A to infer new constraints, which add on those of R_A. An obvious example is:

$$\alpha \wedge \beta \vdash A_1 \notin R_B,$$

since B, offering B_1, implicitly rejects A_1.

A more interesting example is the following one:

$$\alpha \wedge \beta \wedge \gamma \wedge \delta \vdash R_B \cap s_1 \overline{A_1 A_2} s_2 = \emptyset, \tag{1}$$

where s_1 is the ray with endpoint in A_1 and of equation:

$$y = 3x, \quad y \leq 0,$$

and s_2 is the ray with endpoint in A_2 of equation:

$$x + 2y = 15, \quad y \leq 10.$$

Note that (cf. Figure 3) that B_1 and B_2 are aligned with s_2 and s_1, respectively. The reason why A is able to make the deduction in (1), i.e., that R_B has no point in the infinite region delimited by the two rays s_1, s_2 and by the line segment $\overline{A_1 A_2}$, can be synthesized in this way:

- $\alpha \wedge \gamma$ implies that (by the convexity hypothesis) B knows that $R_A \supseteq \overline{A_1 A_2}$;
- since B proposes B_2, A knows that $R_B \cap \overline{A_1 A_2} = \emptyset$ must hold;
- let us assume that there is a point $P \in R_B \cap s_1 \overline{A_1 A_2} s_2$; from the last constraint, and from the convexity hypothesis, R_B must contain all points of the triangle $B_1 \widehat{P} B_2$; now, since such a triangle contains at least on point of the line segment $\overline{A_1 A_2}$, a contradiction arises.

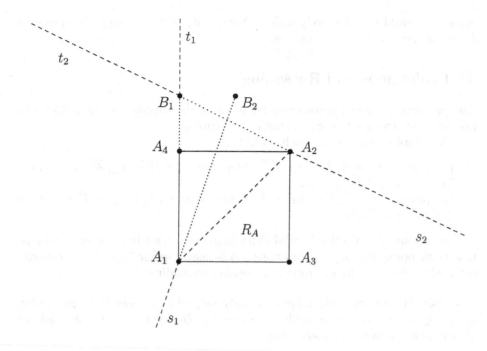

Fig. 3. Sequence of proposals and inferred constraints

A practical consequence of this deduction is that A will not propose the vertex A_3, which lies in the "forbidden region" $s_1\overline{A_1A_2}s_2$: A is partially cooperative, and wants to minimize the number of iterations for concluding the negotiation.

Agent B, on the other hand, is able to infer that:

$$\alpha \wedge \beta \wedge \gamma \vdash R_A \cap t_1 t_2 = \emptyset, \tag{2}$$

where t_1 and t_2 are the rays (both with endpoint in B_1) of equation (respectively):

$$x = 0, \quad y \geq 15, \qquad\qquad x + 2y = 15, \quad y \geq 15.$$

It is worthwhile to note (cf. Figure 3) that A_1 is aligned with t_1, and that s_2 is aligned with t_2.

The reason why B is able to make the deduction in (2), i.e., that R_A has no points in the infinite region delimited by the two rays t_1 e t_2, can, using the convexity hypothesis, be summarized in this way:

- since A does not accept B_1, B knows that $R_A \cap t_1 = \emptyset$ must hold;
- since A proposes A_2, B knows that $R_A \cap t_2 = \emptyset$ must hold;
- $\alpha \wedge \gamma$ implies that B knows that $R_A \supseteq \overline{A_1A_2}$;
- from the last constraint, $R_A \cap t_1 t_2 \neq \emptyset$ would imply a contradiction.

A practical consequence of such a deduction is that B, being –by hypothesis– partially cooperative, will not propose any point in the "forbidden region" $t_1 t_2$, since this would be completely useless. Note that, in our example, the proposal B_2 is coherent with this hypothesis.

4   Projections and Reasoning

The previous example suggests the definition of the concept of "projection of a line segment over another one", shown in Figure 4.

The figure highlights two such projections:

1. the projection of $\overline{A_1 A_2}$ over $\overline{B_1 B_2}$ (denoted with $\Pi(\overline{B_1 B_2}, \overline{A_1 A_2})$, and delimited by $r_2\overline{B_1 B_2}r_1$), and
2. the projection of $\overline{B_1 B_2}$ over $\overline{A_1 A_2}$ (denoted with $\Pi(\overline{A_1 A_2}, \overline{B_1 B_2})$, and delimited by $s_1\overline{A_1 A_2}s_2$).

The notion of projection is valid also when one or both line segments collapse in a single point. Moreover, projections can be easily defined also for spaces with n variables using n-ples of proposals, possibly coinciding.

Our claim is that projections are extremely helpful in reasoning. In particular, if A_1, A_2 are two proposals made by A and B_1, B_2 are two proposals made by B (the order does not matter), then:

- A is supposed to infer that $R_B \cap \Pi(\overline{B_1 B_2}, \overline{A_1 A_2}) = \emptyset$, and
- B is supposed to infer that $R_A \cap \Pi(\overline{A_1 A_2}, \overline{B_1 B_2}) = \emptyset$.

As shown by the previous example, reasoning by means of projections can be effectively used for terminating negotiation without having to propose all vertices. Referring to Figure 3, agent A can close the negotiation by proposing A_4: if B rejects the proposal, then there is no agreement.

In some cases, reasoning by projection allows to obtain large savings in terms of number of proposed vertices. As an example, Figure 5 refers to a negotiation in which the sequence of proposals is $\langle A_1, B_1, A_2, B_2 \rangle$, and only R_A is shown. Since $R_A \subseteq \Pi(\overline{B_1 B_2}, \overline{A_1 A_2})$, A is sure that $R_A \cap R_B = \emptyset$, i.e., there is no possible agreement, and can close the negotiation after just four steps.

In general, if there have been –among possibly others– proposals A_i, B_j, A_k, B_l, in any order, then:

1. if $R_B \subseteq \Pi(\overline{A_i A_k}, \overline{B_j B_l})$, then B can close the negotiation,
2. if $R_A \subseteq \Pi(\overline{B_j B_l}, \overline{A_i A_k})$, then A can close the negotiation.

The above argumentation suggests that reasoning about the other agent's reasoning using projections seems to yield a more efficient protocol, since inferred constraints allow –at least in some cases– to avoid unnecessary proposals. More formally, reasoning using projections for the agent A amounts to:

1. add to the set of constraints describing the original admissibility region, i.e., R_A, constraints forbidding points in $\Pi(\overline{B_j B_l}, \overline{A_i A_k})$, where A_i, B_j, A_k, B_l is any subset of the proposals made so far, and possibly $A_i = A_k$ and $B_j = B_l$;

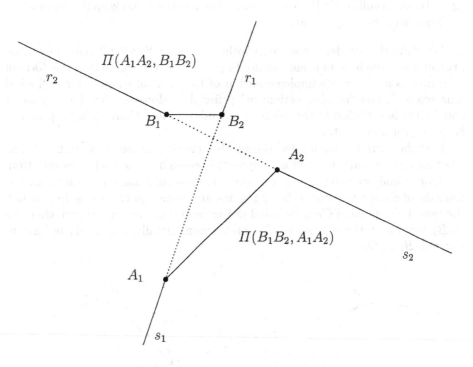

Fig. 4. Projections of line segments

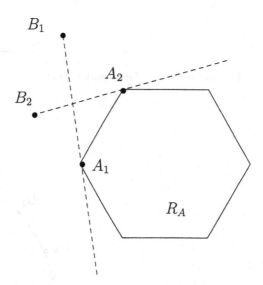

Fig. 5. Reasoning with projections

2. solve the resulting CSP problem, make the proposal, and keep the negotiation knowledge base up-to-date.

We claim that, under the set of hypothesis listed in Section 2, reasoning using projections is the best an agent can do. In particular, we believe that this form of reasoning is a reasonable implementation of the "partial cooperation", "logical omniscience", and "no obstructionism" principles. Moreover, for the purpose of concluding negotiation in the minimum number of iterations, A is supposed to keep on proposing vertices.

It is therefore interesting to address the question raised in Section 3.2, i.e., whether a polynomial number of proposals is enough to conclude a negotiation.

To this end, we show a scenario which is especially bad for projections. For the sake of clarity, the admissibility regions are defined in two steps. In Figure 6 the two circles C_A and C_B have equal radius, and their distance is such that line $A_1 B_0$ is tangent through A_1 to C_A, and, symmetrically, line $B_1 A_0$ is tangent through B_1 to C_B.

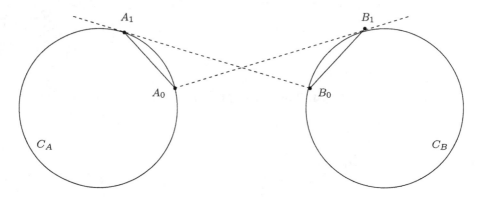

Fig. 6. Worst case for negotiation (I)

Fig. 7. Worst case for negotiation (II)

Now, let's consider two arbitrary sets of points $S_A = \{A_2, \ldots A_n\}$ and $S_B = \{B_2, \ldots B_m\}$, lying on the two circumferences, between points A_0 and A_1, and B_0 and B_1, respectively. Figure 7 shows an example with $n = m = 3$. Note that points A_i and B_j (except for $i, j = 0, 1$) need not be symmetric. Admissibility regions R_A and R_B are simply defined as the convex hull of points $\{A_0, \ldots, A_n\}$ and $\{B_0, \ldots, B_n\}$, respectively.

It is easy to see that, for each quadruple of vertices A_i, A_j ($0 \leq i, j \leq n$), B_k, B_l ($0 \leq k, l \leq m$):

- $\Pi(\overline{B_k B_l}, \overline{A_i, A_j})$ does not have points of R_A, except for A_i and A_j, and
- $\Pi(\overline{A_i, A_j}, \overline{B_k B_l})$ does not have points of R_B, except for B_k and B_l.

In other words, even if both agents propose only vertices, any sequence of proposals does not allow to exclude vertex from the negotiation. As a consequence, in order to reach that no agreement is possible, all vertices have to be proposed.

Although this proves that the number of iterations can be proportional to the number of vertices in the worst case, we still did not prove that the number of iterations can be exponential in the number of variables. Nevertheless it is a simple step to generalize the above example to an arbitrary number of variables, by considering sectors of (hyper-)spheres lying at an appropriate distance. As an example, for the case of three variables it is sufficient to rotate the circles of Figure 6 around their centers, thus obtaining convex solids. The facets of the convex polyhedron are obtained connecting some of the points, e.g., those in Figure 7 and the ones corresponding through rotation. Just taking a couple of intermediate points like in Figure 7, the number of vertices will be exponential in the number of variables. Summing up, reasoning by projection will not avoid to exchange an exponential (in the number of variables) number of proposals, in the worst case.

5   Conclusions, Current Research, and Related Work

In this paper we tackled the problem of negotiation under a set of hypothesis (listed in Section 3), analyzing the efficiency of negotiation protocols in terms of number of iterations. The main results we obtained are the following:

- the basic protocol, i.e., the one in which one agent always proposes vertices of her admissibility region, always converges, because agents can profit from the convexity, the logical omniscience, and the "no obstructionism" hypothesis;
- in the worst case the number of exchanged proposals is exponential both in the number of variables and in the number of constraints;
- the protocol can be improved a lot by means of a sophisticated form of reasoning, named "reasoning using projections", which formalizes the above hypotheses and in many cases is expected to speed up convergence;
- in the worst case also reasoning using projections fails to converge in a polynomial number of iterations, as shown by a specific example.

The current research focuses on the following aspects:

- Protocols based on different criteria are studied. As an example, as opposed to proposing a vertex, an agent could propose a point which is very close to the other agent's proposals. In particular, several variants of this criterion can be studied, e.g., always propose the point closest to the last proposal of the other agent, or the vertex closest to the last proposal, etc. Our goal is to determine whether convergence is guaranteed or not, and, if yes, what is the speed.
- In the current formulation all variables are real, thus implying that convexity is a reasonable assumption. An interesting generalization is to allow some variables to be integer (cf. example in Section 2), and to have convexity only on some variables.
- Some authors, e.g., [7], allow *private* variables, i.e., variables which are not seen by the other agent. It would be interesting to analyze the impact of such variables on the protocols.
- The results of Section 4 seem to put an intrinsic limit on the viability of proposal-based negotiation for large-scale negotiation problems. As a consequence, it would be interesting to determine whether higher levels of efficiency can be achieved by exchanging *constraints*, rather than proposals.
- Since the analyzed protocols require an exponential number of iterations to terminate, and the agents benefit from remembering the sequence of proposals (both made and received), are there algorithms and data structures which allow the agents to store all proposals in polynomial *space*?
- The most problematic assumption, among those listed in Section 3, is probably the absence of the objective function. It is important to note that, if solutions are not all equally good, then it becomes reasonable to reject acceptable proposals. In order to 1) guarantee convergence, and 2) model passing of time a *penalty* function could be introduced for rejected proposals.
- It would be interesting to analyze from the experimental point of view the performance of the various protocols.

Among the papers appearing in the literature, probably the most related to our research are those concerning DCSPs. In particular, [7] analyzes a scenario in which there are several negotiation variables, which either belong to single agents, i.e., are *local*, or are shared between agents. Constraints exist on both types of variables. The focus of their research is to define and analyze different negotiation strategies, which are criteria for selecting variable assignments. The main difference with respect to our formulation is in that they consider negotiation via *argumentation*, i.e., explicit justifications of the proposals, which help in the process of finding an agreement. The paper [12] focus on the case of agents having a single variable, and of binary constraints. Other restricted cases are analyzed in [1]. None of these papers study analytically the speed of convergence of the protocols, but rather focus on the efficiency of the proposed algorithms on some instances.

The issue of convergence and of the relative speed is tackled in [11]. In such a paper the negotiation scenario is described in a formalism rather different from ours; in particular, all variables are boolean, and the agents exchange constraints, i.e., propositional formulae, rather than proposals.

Another related work is [4], in which various strategies and tactics for negotiation are empirically evaluated. In such a paper feasibility regions are necessarily hyper-rectangles, the edges being always parallel to the axes; this makes it possible to find an agreement incrementally, i.e., fixing one variable at the time. Moreover, there is an objective function, which varies with respect to time,

Acknowledgements. This research has been supported by MIUR (Italian Ministry for Instruction, University, and Research) under the FIRB project ASTRO (Automazione dell'Ingegneria del Software basata su Conoscenza). The author thanks Francesco M. Donini, Andrea Schaerf and Marco Schaerf for interesting discussions on negotiation, and Massimiliano Giacomin for pointing out useful references. He is also grateful to the anonymous Referees for their comments and suggestions.

References

1. A. Armstrong and E. H. Durfee. Dynamic prioritization of complex agents in distributed constraint satisfaction. In *Proceedings of the Fifteenth International Joint Conference on Artificial Intelligence (IJCAI'97)*, pages 620–625, 1997.
2. S. E. Conry, K. Kuwabara, and R. A. Lesser, V. R. Meyer. Multistage negotiation for distributed constraint satisfaction. *IEEE Transactions on Systems, Man and Cybernetics*, 21(6):462–477, 1991.
3. Ronald Fagin, Joseph Y. Halpern, Yoram Moses, and Moshe Y. Vardi. *Reasoning about Knowledge*. The MIT Press, 1995.
4. Peyman Faratin, Carles Sierra, and Nick R. Jennings. Negotiation decision functions for autonomous agents. *International Journal of Robotics and Autonomous Systems*, 24(3-4):159–182, 1998.
5. J. Hintikka. *Knowledge and belief*. Cornell University Press, Ithaca, New York, 1962.
6. Nick R. Jennings, Peyman Faratin, and Carles Sierra. Automated negotiation: Prospects, methods and challenges. *Group Decision and Negotiation*, 10:199–215, 2001.
7. Hyuckchul Jung, Milind Tambe, and Kulkarni Shriniwas. Argumentation as distributed constraint satisfaction: applications and results. In *Proceedings of the Fifth International Conference on Autonomous Agents (Agents 2001)*, pages 324–331. ACM Press, 2001.
8. Sarit Kraus. Negotiation and cooperation in multi-agent environments. *Artificial Intelligence*, 94(1-2):79–98, 1997.
9. Jeffrey S. Rosenschein and Gilad Zlotkin. *Rules of Encounter: Designing Conventions for Automated Negotiations Among Computers*. The MIT Press, 1994.
10. K. P. Sycara, S. Roth, N. Sadeh, and M. Fox. Distributed constrained heuristic search. *IEEE Transactions on Systems, Man and Cybernetics*, 21(6):446–461, 1991.

11. Michael Woolridge and Simon Parsons. Languages for negotiation. In *Proceedings of the Fourteenth European Conference on Artificial Intelligence (ECAI 2000)*, pages 393–397, 2000.
12. Makoto Yokoo, Edmund H. Durfee, Toru Ishida, and Kazuhiro Kuwabara. The distributed constraint satisfaction problem: Formalization and algorithms. *IEEE Transactions on Knowledge and Data Engineering*, 10(5):673–685, 1998.
13. Makoto Yokoo and Hirayama Katsutoshi. Algorithms for distributed constraint satisfaction: A review. *Autonomous Agents and Multi-Agents Systems*, 3(2):185–207, 2000.
14. Gilad Zlotkin and Jeffrey S. Rosenschein. Mechanisms for automated negotiation in state oriented domains. *Journal of Artificial Intelligence Research*, 5:163–238, 1996.

A Conversational Component-Based Open Multi-agent Architecture for Flexible Information Trading

Habin Lee, Patrik Mihailescu, and John Shepherdson

Intelligent Systems Laboratory, BT Exact,
Orion Building, MLB1/pp12, Adastral Park, Martlesham Heath, Ipswich, Suffolk, IP5 3RE, UK
{ha.lee,patrik.2.mihailescu,john.shepherdson}@bt.com

Abstract. In a competitive market environment, information service providers try to differentiate their offerings by adopting new kinds of interactions with information consumers. The standardization of languages and interaction protocols used in messages among information agents in electronic commerce frustrates the needs of service providers as they attempt to differentiate their offerings. In this paper a multi-agent architecture (where conversational components are used as the main tool for interactions among participating agents) is proposed to allow an information consumer agent to interact with an information provider agent that supplies a service via an unknown language or interaction protocol.

1 Introduction

Information agents are considered to play a major role in electronic commerce (eCommerce) [1]. Autonomous agents can act on behalf of their human users to buy or sell information, products or services.

As the number of cases where information agents are used as the core technology for an information trade increases, the openness and flexibility of a multi-agent system (MAS) for eCommerce is considered to be one of the critical success factors. The eCommerce environment is dynamic in that new consumers and merchants may appear, new products and services can be introduced frequently, and sometimes the standard languages and transaction rules can be changed. As a result, MAS must be flexible enough to adapt to these frequent changes. Within an eCommerce environment a requirement for a MAS is that it allows agents to participate, disengage, and/or transact with each other using new business rules (subject to some minimum constraints).

One obstacle to producing an open and flexible MAS is the need for all participating agents to use the same *content languages*, *ontologies*, and *interaction protocols (IPs)* in the messages they exchange. This prerequisite makes it impossible for agents providing services based on a new IP, ontology, or content language to participate in existing MAS-based markets. To accommodate such an agent, the MAS

M. Klusch et al. (Eds.): CIA 2003, LNAI 2782, pp. 109–116, 2003.

would need to be re-engineered to allow existing agents to use the new content language, ontology, or IP to request and receive services from the new agent.

In this paper, a MAS architecture (CCoMaa), which allows plug-and-play of conversational components (C-COMs) is proposed to allow information agents to interact with unknown content languages and IPs assuming they have the same understanding on the ontology used within messages. A C-COM is a piece of software that enables the required agent interactions (i.e. request and response) to occur during an information trade. The C-COM consists of two or more role components (according to the roles needed for the interactions) and all the interactions are performed via messages which can be interpreted and composed by the role components. The generic role components Initiator and Respondent (which can be extended according to the application requirements) are aware of the content language, ontology, and IP used for a given information trade. An information provider agent can participate in an existing agent society by providing its Initiator components to information consumer agents via a public mediator facility. An information consumer agent is able to interact with the new information provider agent just by installing the Initiator component for a given information trade, even if it doesn't recognize the required content language or IP. The CCoMaa defines the roles of participating agents and the procedures which they should comply with in order to install C-COMs and to be capable of interacting with the corresponding agents during the information trade.

This paper is organized as follows. The next section examines related work in the area and Section 3 provides of overview of the CCoMaa and the structure of a C-COM. Finally, section 4 summarizes this paper.

2   Related Works

The need for ad-hoc IPs is clear in information-centric agents in e-markets that are characterized by their focus on collecting, processing, analysing, and monitoring information [2]. Decker [3] described information agents as a class of autonomous agents that are closely related with information sources. For these reasons, the conversations with information agents may strictly depend on the nature of information sources that include legacy systems, Web sites and so on, which cannot be supported by a few standard IPs. It was also pointed out that existing IPs are not extensive enough to support all applications and systems [4].

Based on the above requirements, there has been some research on dynamic execution of ad-hoc IPs in a MAS [5][6][7]. Weiliang et al. [5] proposed an XML-based language that can be used to specify a new IP in an XML format which can be executed dynamically by an agent. Iwa et al. [6] and Ahn et al. [7] suggested frameworks that can be used to dynamically exchange and execute IPs. The research described in those three papers has similar motivation to the main objective of the work presented in this paper. However, the proposed models are not proven to be complete to represent complex IPs. Furthermore, C-COM can easily be integrated with Web service technologies such as UDDI [8] and XLANG [9] as a means of service exchange because C-COM is not dependent on any specific IP specification model.

The service component concept for MAS was also adopted in the European 5th Framework project LEAP (Lightweight Extensible Agent Platform) [10]. One objective of LEAP was to develop generic service components which could be reused in similar applications. This was achieved by producing a static library that is used when agents are developed, and is present when they are launched on an agent platform.

3 CCoMaa: A Component-Based Multi-agent Architecture

3.1   C-COM: A Conversational Component for Plug and Play Services in MAS

The basic idea of a C-COM is to abstract similar interactions between agent roles to achieve the same goal as an interaction pattern and to make this pattern a reusable software component that can be installed and executed on the fly.

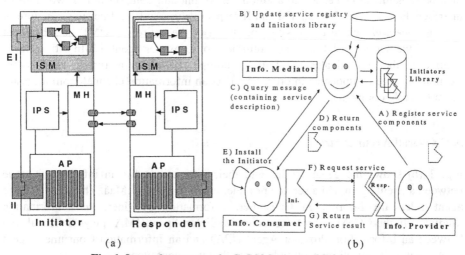

Fig. 1. Internal structure of a C-COM (a) and CCoMaa (b)

The main feature of a C-COM is that it is divided into two or more role components. There are two generic role components for each C-COM - Initiator and Respondent. In particular, the Initiator component can be plugged dynamically into an agent. An agent which installs a role component is called a *master agent* of the role component. From an agent's point of view, the Initiator component is a black box which hides the details of the interaction process (with its designated Respondent components) from its master agent, only exposing an interface which specifies the input and output data needed to execute the role component. However, more than one role component can be plugged into an agent concurrently.

Fig. 1(a) shows the internal structure of a C-COM. The two main building blocks are an IP and the role components. The IP defines the sequence of asynchronous messages sent between the role components, and the role components perform the actions necessary at each stage of the IP to achieve the service goal. The Initiator component starts an interaction by sending a message and the Respondent component is activated when it receives a message from the Initiator component. These two generic role components can be specialised according to the requirements of target applications. Each role component consists of an Interaction Protocol Scheduler (IPS), a Message Handler (MH), an Action Pool (AP) and one or more Interfaces. Each role component is in effect a Finite State Machine, driven by internal state changes, and has a different set of internal states according to the role the component plays in the IP employed for a given C-COM. The IPS schedules and executes all the actions stored in the AP of a role component according to internal state changes. For this purpose, each role component maintains an Interaction State which is managed by the Interaction State Manager (ISM). The MH is responsible for validating outgoing messages and interpreting incoming messages. The role component provides a number of interfaces for customisation purposes. In this paper, an interface is defined as a set of method signatures. An interface must be provided with an implementation of the method signatures to be executed at run time. An Initiator component has two kinds of interface: External and Internal (EI and II respectively). An EI defines the signature of a *trigger method* (which triggers the execution of the entire C-COM), i.e., the input data and the service result which is returned to its master agent. Calling the trigger method in the EI activates the Initiator component which activates all its other Respondent role components in order. An II is an information channel from a master agent to a role component.

3.2 Overall Architecture

Fig. 1 (b) shows the generic roles and their interactions for an information trade between a client agent and a service provider agent in the CCoMaa. The three generic agent roles are Information Consumer, Information Provider, and Information Mediator. In the CCoMaa, an Information Mediator Agent (IMA) plays a critical role between an Information Provider Agent (IPA) and an Information Consumer Agent (ICA) as it mediates all interaction between the two agent types.

The CCoMaa is a multi-agent architecture where agents are able to interact with each other through a C-COM, thus enabling existing agents to interact with new information providing agents by dynamically installing and executing the Initiator components supplied by the new IPAs. To facilitate this dynamic configuration change, the CCoMaa requires special agents with predefined roles.

An IPA registers its service and component description to an IMA (A). The registration process is different from the one defined by FIPA in that the IPA registers not only a service description but also the executable Initiator component and a component description, which is used by an ICA during the installation and execution of the executable Initiator component. The IMA is responsible for maintaining the service registry and Initiator library that contains Initiator components (B). The service registry maintains all the registered service descriptions as defined in FIPA specifications. The Initiator library maintains the pair of component description and the executable Initiator component. The component description specifies the minimum execution environment needed to install and execute the Initiator component. This includes the required runtime environment (e.g. a JVM supporting the CLDC specification) and required computing resources (e.g. 20k storage space, 160x160 screen resolution, etc).

Once the IPA has registered its service(s), any ICA can contact the IMA to retrieve the contact information on any registered IPAs. To retrieve the contact information, an ICA needs to send a query message containing a service description (C). The IMA then tries to match the service description with one provided by an IPA. If a matching service description is found, the IMA returns a tuple containing a component description of the IPA and an executable Initiator component to the ICA (D). If any contact information is returned by the IMA, the ICA installs the executable Initiator component into its Initiator library, based on the component description (E) and executes the Initiator component to get the service result from the IPA (F), (G).

3.3 Component Registration and Matching

Fig. 2(a) shows a sample CCoMaa agent description which is used by an IPA to register the "Book Flight" service and associated Initiator component with an IMA.

A CCoMaa agent description consists of a service description and a component description. The service description consists of name, type, and properties fields. This paper assumes that the ICA and IPA has the same understanding on the service. That is, the ICA expects that the service "Book Flight" will produce ticket information that satisfies the constraints that are given as an input of the service. The component description has three sub-descriptions: Interface, File, and GUI descriptions. The Interface description specifies the trigger method and ontology items that are used as input and output of the trigger method. The File description is used by the ICA to install the downloaded Initiator component in the local device on which the agent is running. Finally, the GUI description is optional. An IPA can provide ICAs with a GUI component which can be used to retrieve additional ontology items (which might not be known to ICAs) used by the Initiator component to pass to the Respondent component.

Once an IPA has registered its service(s) to an IMA, any ICAs can contact the IMA to retrieve the contact information of the IPA. To retrieve the contact information, the ICA sends a message that contains a service description to the IMA. An example of the contents of this type of message is shown in Fig. 2(b).

This type of request message from an ICA to an IMA is different from the message type specified by FIPA when querying the DF registry. Note that the ICA doesn't have to specify either the language or protocol in a service description used for service acquisition. The IMA then tries to match the service description and component description with one provided by any IPAs. If a matching agent description is found, the IMA returns the agent description of the corresponding IPA and an executable Initiator component to the ICA. If any contact information is returned by the IMA, the ICA installs the executable Initiator component into its Initiator library, based on the component description and executes the Initiator component to retrieve the service result from the IPA.

```
<CCOMAgentDescription>
...
<ServiceDescription>
<Name> BookFlight </Name>
<Type> BookingService </Type>
<Ontology> Travel </Ontology>
<Property
name=domain, value=international/>
</ServiceDescription>
<ComponentDescription>
<Interface>
<Method name=getTicket>
<Input order=1, name="Route",
type=Travel.Booking.Route />
<Output type=Travel.Booking.TicketList />
</Method> </Interface>
<File>
<package name="com.travelagent.booking"
mainclass="Flight_initiation.class" />
<MinJVM> CDC </MinJVM>
<FormatType> Jar </FormatType>
<FileName> ticketing.jar </FileName>
<StorageSpace> 10 </StorageSpace>
<StorageMetric> k </StorageMetric>
</File>
<GUI>
<UIPresent> Y </UIPresent>
<UIImplType> Foundation </UIImplType>
<UIScreenWidth> 160 </UIScreenWidth>
<UIScreenHeight 160 </UIScreenHeight>
</GUI>
</ComponentDescription>
```

```
(request
:sender (agent-identifier
         :name SCA@foo.com
:address iiop://foo.com/acc)
:receiver (agent-identifier
          :name Mediator@foo.com
:address iiop://foo.com/md)
:ontology CCOM-Management
:language SL0
:protocol FIPA-Request
:content
(action
 (agent-identifier :name Mediator@foo.com
:address iiop://foo.com/md)
 (search
 (ccom-agent-description
  :services (set (service-description
  :name bookFlight
  :type BookingService
  :properties (set
            (property :name domain
                      :value international))))
     :component     (set     (component-
description
:file (set (storagespace 100)
(storagemetric k))
:gui (set (uiscreenwidth 240)
(set (uiscreenheight 320))
:min-jvm CDC)))))
```

(a)	(b)

Fig. 2. A sample component description (a) and sample ACL message used to match the component description (b)

3.4 Dynamic Download, Installation, and Execution of C-COM

An ICA is equipped with a co-ordination engine which is responsible for downloading, installing, and executing an Initiator component. Fig. 3 shows the structure of the co-ordination engine and its internal process.

The goal of the co-ordination engine is to provide the other components of its master agent with information they request by executing installed Initiator components. The component could be an Initiator, an agent behaviour or a custom component. When an information request arrives from a local component, the co-ordination controller checks a local ontology dictionary to work out which service can provide the required information. The ontology dictionary contains a mapping between ontology items and services which can produce those ontology items. If a successful match is located, the co-ordination controller will activate the load manager module to load an Initiator component that matches the service description taken from the ontology dictionary.

If there is no locally installed Initiator component that matches the service description provided by the co-ordination controller, the load manager will forward a request to the component installer module which will attempt to locate an IMA that contains the required Initiator component via negotiation with an IMA. Once the component installer module locates an Initiator component that matches the given requirements it will begin downloading the Initiator component. After the Initiator component has been successfully downloaded the component installer module will return control back to the load manager module. The load manager module will then request that the package manager module install the Initiator component within the C-COM local library. As part of the installation process the package manager module will also record the service description of the Initiator component so that in future the Initiator component does not need to be downloaded again. Upon completion of its execution, the results from the Initiator component will be passed (by the co-ordination controller) to the component which originally requested the information.

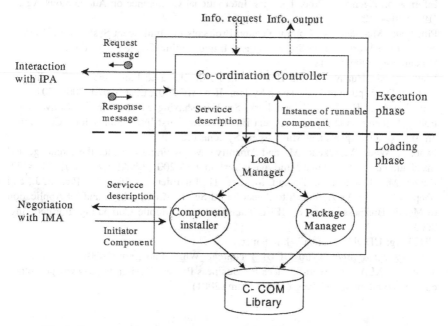

Fig. 3. Component loading and execution procedure in the Co-ordination Engine

4 Conclusion

Within this paper we proposed a component-based multi-agent architecture for open and flexible information exchange among multiple agents. We introduced the concept of a C-COM, which is a plug & play software component, comprising of two or more role components which abstract and hide all the details of interactions among the participating roles. We also introduced the CCoMaa which is a multi-agent architecture where participating agents can interact with each other via a C-COM. The CCoMaa enables an agent to participate in new services that have been added to an existing agent society even if the agent doesn't recognize the IP or language used by the new services. Simply by installing the appropriate role component an agent is able to take advantage of the new services.

References

[1] Maes, P., Guttman, R. H., and Moukas, A. G.: Agents That Buy and Sell", Communication of the ACM, 42(3) (1999) 81–91
[2] Nodine, H. and Chandrasekhara, D.: Agent Communication Languages for Information-Centric Agent Communities. in Proc. Hawaii Int'l Conf. on System Sciences (1999)
[3] Decker, K., Pannu, A., Sycara, K. and Williamson M.: Designing Behaviors for Information Agents. in Proc. The First International Conference on Autonomous Agents (1997) 404–412
[4] Pitt, J. and Mamdani, A.: Communication Protocols in Multi-agent Systems. In Working Notes of the Workshop on Specifying and Implementing Conversation Policies, Seattle, Washington (1999) 39–48
[5] Weiliang, M., Huanye, S. and Huanye, S.: An XML-based Language for Coordination Protocol Description in Multi-agent System, IEA/AEI 2001, LNAI 2070 (2001) 707–717
[6] Ahn, M., Lee, H., Yim, H. and Park, S.: Handshaking Mechanism for Conversation Policy Agreements in Dynamic Agent Environment, First International Joint Conference on Autonomous Agents and Multi-Agent Systems (2002)
[7] Iwao, T., Wada, Y., Okada, M., and Amamiya, M.: A Framework for the Exchange and Installation of Protocols in a Multi-agent System. CIA 2001, LNAI 2182 (2001) 211–222
[8] Berger, M., Buckland, B., Bouzid, M., Lee, H., Lhuillier, N., Olpp, D., Picault, J., and Shepherdson, J.: An Approach to Agent-based Service Composition and its Application to Mobile Business Processes. IEEE Transactions on Mobile Computing, Forthcoming, 2003
[9] UDDI.org: UDDI Technical White Paper, http://www.uddi.org/pubs/Iru_UDDI_Technical_White_Paper.pdf (2000)
[10] Thatte, S.: XLANG – Web Services for Business Process Design. http://www.gotdotnet. com/team/xml_wsspecs/xlang-c/default.htm (2001)

The Search for Coalition Formation in Costly Environments

David Sarne[1] and Sarit Kraus[1,2]

[1] Department of Computer Science, Bar-Ilan University, Ramat-Gan, 52900 Israel
{sarned, sarit}@macs.biu.ac.il
[2] Institute for Advanced Computer Studies
University of Maryland, College Park, MD 20742

Abstract. We study the dynamics of forming coalitions of self-interested autonomous buyer agents, for the purpose of obtaining a volume discount. In our model, agents, representing coalitions of various sizes, may choose to be acquainted with other agents, hopefully ending up with a joint coalition structure, which will improve the overall price. Upon encountering potential partnering opportunities for extended coalitions, the agent needs to decide whether to accept or reject them. Each coalition partnership encapsulates expected benefit for the agent; however the process of finding a potential partner is associated with a cost. We explore the characteristics of the agent's optimal strategies in the equilibrium and develop the equations from which these strategies can be derived. Efficient algorithms are suggested for a specific size-two variant of the problem, in order to demonstrate how each agent's computation process can be significantly improved. These algorithms will be used as an infrastructure from which the general case algorithms can be extracted.

1 Introduction

The growing interest in autonomous interacting agents has given rise to many issues concerning coalition formation. A coalition is a group of self-interested agents that agree to coordinate and cooperate in the performance of a specific task. Through the coalition, the agents as a group are able to perform their task more efficiently, and increase the participants' benefits [2, 6, 15, 16]. The main question in every coalition formation application is how to determine the set of agents each specific agent will be willing to form a coalition with. This is where each agent is associated with a specific type that captures special properties that characterizes it.

We consider environments in which an agent's utility is fully correlated with its type. The agent's type is additive and thus can be improved by forming coalitions with other agents. Agent types are ordered according to their associated utility. The higher the other coalition member's type the higher the agent's utility. Each agent in our model represents a coalition of one or more members. The agents may interact with each other to share information regarding their types. This information is used by each agent in its decision making process of whether to combine its current coalition with another agent's coalition, thereby forming a new coalition of a higher type. Consider, for example, the electronic marketplace where agents represent coalitions of buyers interested in a product. Assume the requested quantities determine the

M. Klusch et al. (Eds.): CIA 2003, LNAI 2782, pp. 117–136, 2003.
© Springer-Verlag Berlin Heidelberg 2003

agent's type, thus the higher the requested quantity the better the price for the coalition members.

The agents' search for coalition opportunities is costly [10]: at each stage of its search an agent has to spend resources in locating and interacting with another agent representing a coalition of a random type. In addition, each stage of the search reflects a coalition coordination cost (communication with its members), which is derived from the number of coalition members.

The agent's willingness to extend the coalition upon encountering a new agent is insufficient. The new coalition will be formed only if it is mutually accepted by both agents' parties. A new agent will be created for the new coalition formed. This new agent will handle and represent all members previously handled by the agents that formed the new coalition. Each member in a given coalition will share the agent's costs relative to its type. It will also share the utility of the final coalition it will be a member of, relative to its type. Recalling that the types are additive and the agent's utility increases with its type, then a decision taken by an agent to form a coalition with another agent to improve its type, will never cause a conflict of interests with any of the members represented by this agent – the higher the increase in the agent's type, the more utility each member will be gaining.

Therefore, each agent, either created for a new coalition, or entering the marketplace as a representative of a single coalition member must consider two major questions: First, is it going to execute its task immediately or is it more beneficial to engage in costly search to extend the coalition? If the latter decision was taken then at each stage of the agent's search process, after reviewing the information regarding the current potential partner, the agent must make a decision whether to terminate the search or to continue. Continuing the search will hopefully yield a higher type partner to continue the process with (the agent will prefer rejecting partnerships reflecting significant future coalition coordination costs). Terminating the search will result in forming a coalition with the current potential partner if it agrees; this new coalition will face the same decisions, as mentioned above, all over again.

We utilize the electronic marketplace environment [16], as a framework for our analysis. The model we present considers buying agents, representing one or more different buyers, possibly interested in extending their coalition for buying a specific product. The benefit for all participants in such a coalition is in their ability to obtain, as a team, a discount price (compared to the price each of them would have paid separately). Each agent gains this utility separately, and the utility is not transferable (no side-payments). Obviously, the larger the quantity an agent is seeking to buy for the current coalition it is representing, the greater the benefit for its potential partners of an extended coalition and vice versa. Whenever a new coalition is created the new agent will seek to minimize the overall costs of such a coalition. The agent's utility (either by purchasing the product or by forming new coalitions) as well as its costs will be split among its represented members, according to their percentage out of the overall requested quantity. Therefore any decision the representative agent will take is the most beneficial for *all* its represented members.

The best price that can be obtained will be through one big coalition in which all agents are members. Yet, the introduction of search costs and coalition management costs into the model prevents this type of solutions, and enforces a genuine cost effectiveness analysis for evaluating each potential new coalition.

The same concepts of coalition formation through partnerships are valid and re-usable in other plausible MIS and CS related applications. Consider, for example, client-server environments, where distributed subroutines are waiting to be processed on a central server. Typically, the server processing time is a function of the query input. Here, there may be an incentive for a subroutine to partner with others to create a combined query for which the processing time over the server is shorter than the aggregated execution of each subroutine separately. Each subroutine's query characteristics can indicate a type, and the combined query possesses similar additive behavior as described above. Adoption of the proposed analysis and the suggested algorithms for such applications is simple once we express the search and coalition coordination costs associated with each application in terms of the coalition benefit.

Looking for a baseline for the coalition through partnerships problem we addressed AI and economic literature, as will be described in section 2. We continue in section 3 by presenting the general model for coalition formation through partnerships with search and coalition coordination costs. We show the general characteristics of equilibrium and develop the equations describing the agents' optimal strategies. In section 4 we utilize the basic two-size coalition variant to suggest algorithms for simplifying the distributed calculation performed by each agent. This is an important step towards extending the algorithms to handle the general case. We conclude and present directions for future work in section 5.

2 Related Work

Coalition formation processes focus a lot of attention on multi-agent systems [11, 13]. In recent years, research has introduced the coalition formation process also into electronic market environments. Recognizing the incentives for both buyers and vendors in volume discounts[1], several different buyer-agents coalition schemes were proposed [7, 12, 15, 16]. Extensions of the transaction-oriented coalitions to long-term ones, were also suggested [2, 3]. However, most research was mainly concerned with the procedures of negotiating the formation of coalitions and division of coalition payoffs. Other related popular research topics were finding the optimal division of agents into coalitions through a central mechanism and enforcement methods for the interaction protocols. The resources associated with agent's search for a coalition, and the influence of this factor over its decisions, were not discussed in this context[2]. Most mechanisms assumed an agent could scan as many agents as needed, or simply a central view of the environment.

The review of economic literature reveals that the model of partnerships with partner search costs was widely studied in traditional marriage markets and job-search applications, which evolved from the area of search theory [8, and references therein]. These models were focused on establishing optimal strategies for the searcher, assuming

---

[1] The vendor agent was also claimed to possess several advantages for selling in bulk, mainly due to decreased advertisement costs and distribution costs.

[2] An exception can be found in [10], discussing settings where there are too many coalition structures to enumerate and evaluate (due to, for example, costly or bounded computation and/or limited time). Instead, agents have to select a subset of coalition structures on which to focus their search.

no mutual search activities and were classified under one-sided searches. In an effort to understand the effect of dual search activities in such models, the "Two-sided" search research followed. This notion was explored within the equilibrium search framework [4]. An interesting analysis through simulation of a two-sided market variant was introduced by Greenwald and Kephart [5].

Another important research area is the one called assortative matching. This area involves a decentralized search of more than two heterogeneous agent types. Becker [1] analyzed a costless matching market, where two different agent types produce a different utility when matched and otherwise no utility. Becker showed that the unique competitive equilibrium has assortative matching – meaning that matched partners are identical (in type), for both the transferable and non-transferable utility cases. Extended models which included some search cost elements for the non-transferable case were proposed by Smith [14] who modeled search "costs" by the discounting of the future flow of gains and Morgan [9] who used additive explicit search costs. The transformation of the suggested concepts in the economical models, into plausible applications over the internet and computerized environments with search and coalition coordination costs is not trivial. All the above economical models assumed no utility for an agent without forming a partnership, and most importantly, they didn't allow coalitions to extend themselves beyond two agents. We will refer to such models in section 4.

3   The Model

We consider an electronic marketplace with numerous heterogeneous buying agents, representing different buyers. Each agent is characterized by the number of buyers it represents and the initial intention of buying a pre-defined quantity of a specific well defined and easily found product. The encapsulated quantity of a coalition representative agent is an aggregation of all the quantities requested by the buyers this agent represents. The product price is a function of the purchased quantity - sellers offer a "discount for quantity" price, aiming to encourage purchase of large quantities in a bulk. Denoting the posted price for a quantity q as P_q, the price function satisfies the following:

$$\frac{dP_q}{dq} < 0 \quad , \quad \frac{d^2P_q}{dq^2} > 0 \qquad (1) \qquad \frac{d(qP_q)}{dq} > 0 \quad , \quad \frac{d^2(qP_q)}{dq^2} < 0 \qquad (2)$$

The first condition ensures the price per unit is a monotonically decreasing function (in a decreasing rate) of the requested quantity. This is mainly because sellers wish to create the incentive to buy wholesale. The second condition ensures basic economic principals of paying in overall more when buying more.

By introducing the above price function, and assuming that any quantity can be supplied, buying agents have an incentive to form a coalition with other buying agents in order to gain the price discount. However, finding a partner has its cost: for each stage of the search the process induces a specific search cost $a+bn$, where n is the number of buyers represented by the agent. The fixed cost a is related to the resources an agent spends on advertising its presence, locating other agents and interacting with them. The variable cost b is associated with the coalition coordination – the agent is required to maintain communication with the buyers it represents throughout the search process.

The agents are homogeneous in the sense that each agent has the same goal (to purchase a specific product at the lowest total cost), however they are heterogeneous in their types. We classify all the agents representing n buyers, who are interested in buying an overall quantity of q of the product, as agents of type (q,n). $(*,k)$ will be used to denote any agent representing k buyers and $(q,*)$ will denote any agent requesting an aggregated quantity q. The (q,n) type agent can either engage in a search to extend its coalition, or buy the requested product, in its current configuration with an overall cost of qP_q. The agents are self-interested and therefore, given several alternatives, they will prefer to select the more beneficial ones.

Since the agent is not concerned with a limited decision horizon and the interaction with other agents doesn't imply any new information about the market structure, then its best search strategy for partners is sequential. Also, in spite of the existence of search costs, the agent's strategy is stationary – an agent of any specific type will not accept an opportunity it has rejected beforehand. At any stage of its search the agent randomly encounters one other agent interested in the same product. At the encounter, both agents will reveal their type (overall requested quantity and number of buyers represented by each agent). Then, each agent will make a decision whether to continue searching or to extend its coalition structure by partnering with the current encountered agent. In the latter case, the new coalition will take effect only if both agents are willing to form the partnership. Upon the creation of a new coalition, a new agent will be created, replacing the two agents in representing the joint coalition. The search and coalition coordination costs accumulated for each agent will be imposed on the buyers represented by it, relative to their requested quantity from the overall quantity. The new agent created, as any other agent in the marketplace, can either buy the product with a total cost of $(q_i + q_j)P_{q_i+q_j}$, or conduct a search to further extend its coalition with search and coordination costs of $a + b(n_i + n_j)$ - see Figure 1.

We start by assuming a continuous flow of new agents to the marketplace, each representing a single buyer. These agents are of type $(q,1)$ where q is defined over the interval $[\underline{q}, \overline{q}]$. Since these are the basic bricks of future coalitions, the potential agent types can be described over the semi-continuous grid in Figure 2 (possible agent types are in gray).

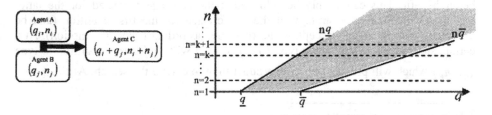

Fig. 1. Coalition Formation   **Fig. 2.** Possible coalitions

Notice that at this stage of the analysis, the gray area has no finite boundaries. This is simply because we consider all possible coalitions, regardless of equilibrium constraints and search profitability. We suggest that the area representing the agents' types engaged in search (of which we are interested in this paper) is actually bounded. Introducing search and coalition coordination costs into the model, we can easily set upper limits for this area. For each point q in the horizontal axis $q > \underline{q}$ we can find an agent type (q,k) for which it will be non-beneficial to engage in search, regardless of the distribution of other agent types currently engaging in search. This is where:

$$q(P_q - P_{q \to \infty}) = a + bk \tag{3}$$

Since the right side expression of (3) increases in k, then obviously all other agents of type (q,n), where $n>k$, will prefer not to engage in search. Therefore the following expression (4) is an upper limit for possible agent types engaged in search in equilibrium:

$$n(q) = \min\left\{ \left\lceil \frac{q}{\underline{q}} \right\rceil, \left\lceil \frac{q(P_q - P_{q \to \infty}) - a}{b} \right\rceil \right\} , \quad q \geq \underline{q} \tag{4}$$

A density function $f(q,n)$ is associated with each type of agents engaged in search and requesting a quantity q. We assume that agents, while ignorant of other individual agents' coalition sizes and requested quantities, are acquainted with the overall distribution of agent types in the market[3]. We also assume that this distribution is time-invariant[4]. Considering the population of agents engaged in search, we prove the following Theorem (1), for the agent's strategy in equilibrium.

Theorem 1. *(a) In equilibrium, an agent of type (q_i, n_i), engaging in a search for potential partners, in order to extend its coalition, will use a reservation value strategy[5] according to a vector $\vec{Q}_{q_i, n_i}$ of quantity values (where $Q_{q_i, n_i}[k]$ represents the reservation quantity to be used when encountering a potential partner of type $(*,k)$). (b) $Q_{q_i, n_i}[k+1] \geq Q_{q_i, n_i}[k]$.*

Sketch of Proof:

(a) Assume that all agents are using a reservation quantity strategy and consider a (q,n) type agent which is willing to accept agent type (q_i, n_i) during the search. Obviously an alternate coalition with an agent (q_j, n_i), where $q_j > q_i$, will yield a better benefit. This can simply be achieved if the new agent created for the latter coalition will imitate the strategy of the one created for the first coalition (and be accepted by all the agents accepting the first one, according to the assumption). At a certain stage of the search, agent type $(q + q_i, n + n_i)$ will evolve to a coalition of type (q_k, n_k) which will prefer to buy the product than to extend the search. At this point,

---

[3] Using market indicators, spectator agents, etc..
[4] The method for maintaining a steady state population of agent type is important but will not be discussed in this context.
[5] A reservation value strategy is one where the searcher follows a reservation-value rule: It accepts all offers greater than or equal to the reservation value, and rejects all those less than this value.

the original members of coalition $(q+q_i, n+n_i)$ will be able to purchase the product at price P_{q_k} in comparison to price $P_{q_k+q_j-q_i}$ for original members of the coalition $(q+q_j, n+n_j)$.

(b)   The search costs of the new coalition, created with the agent representing more users, are higher and therefore $Q_{q_i,n_i}[k+1] \geq Q_{q_i,n_i}[k]$ is true. []

Notice that $Q_{q_i,n_i}[k]$ is a vector of a finite size as the area of potential agents to form a coalition with is finite (see equation (4) above). Denoting the expected cost of agent type (q_i, n_i), when using the optimal reservation vector $\vec{Q}_{q_i,n_i}$ as $V_{q_i,n_i}(\vec{Q}_{q_i,n_i})$, and the optimal cost of a coalition (q_i, n_i) as V_{q_i,n_i}, we obtain:

$$V_{q_i,n_i} = \min\{ V_{q_i,n_i}(\vec{Q}_{q_i,n_i}), \; q_i P_{q_i} \}. \tag{5}$$

Using equation (5) we will be able to determine if an agent will engage in a search, according to its type. Consider agent of type (q_i, n_i) engaged in a search, at any given stage of its search. After reviewing the current potential partner's type (q_j, n_i), it has to make a decision whether to reject this partner and continue the search or partner with this agent in order to extend the coalition. Continuing the search in the current agent configuration will result in an expected future total cost of $V_{q_i,n_i}(\vec{Q}_{q_i,n_i})$. Accepting the partnership, will result in a future cost $(q_i V_{q_i+q_j,n_i+n_j})/(q_i+q_j)$ for agent (q_i, n_i) if the other agent agrees to form a coalition, or otherwise will enforce the agent to keep searching with an expected future total cost of $V_{q_i,n_i}(\vec{Q}_{q_i,n_i})$. Therefore, the optimal reservation value is the quantity $Q_{q_i,n_i}[n_j] = q_j$ where the agent is indifferent to the two options:

$$V_{q_i,n_i}(Q_{q_i,n_i}[n_j]) = V_{q_i,n_i}(\vec{Q}_{q_i,n_i}) \Pr(q_i < Q_{q_j,n_j}[n_i]) + \frac{q_i V_{q_i+q_j,n_i+n_j}}{q_{i+}q_j} \Pr(q_i \geq Q_{q_j,n_j}[n_i]) \tag{6}$$

Resulting in:

$$V_{q_i,n_i}(\vec{Q}_{q_i,n_i}) = V_{q_i,n_i}(Q_{q_i,n_i}[n_j]) = \frac{q_i V_{q_i+Q_{q_i,n_i}[n_j],n_i+n_j}}{q_{i+}Q_{q_i,n_i}[n_j]} \;, \quad n_j = 1,2,... \tag{7}$$

The interpretation of equation (7) is that for any given agent of type (q_i, n_i), the overall cost when using its optimal reservation vector, $\vec{Q}_{q_i,n_i}$, equals its relative part (according to its quantity) in the overall cost of a coalition $(q_i + Q_{q_i,n_i}[n], n_i + n)$, for any n. This characteristic will play a key role in our further analysis.

In order to introduce the agent's search equations, we need to prove some additional characteristics of the equilibrium. First we will show consistency between agents' decision whether to engage in a search (Theorem 2). Then we will prove that for any two agents engaged in a search, the higher type agent (in terms of requested quantity) will use a higher reservation value for each n (Theorem 3). For this purpose first we need to prove Lemma 1.

Lemma 1. *The improvement in an agent's utility when buying the product in a coalition with any given partner, is an increasing function of its own overall requested quantity:*

$$\frac{d\left(q_i P_{q_i} - q_i P_{q_i+q_j}\right)}{dq_j dq_i} = 0 - \frac{dq_i P_{q_i+q_j}}{dq_j dq_i} > 0 \tag{8}$$

The proof for Lemma 1 as well as more detailed proofs for all following theorems, Lemmas and algorithms are available in the full version of the authors' paper[6].

Theorem 2. *If in its optimal strategy, an agent of type* (q_i, n_i) *chooses to engage in a search, then so does any other agent of type* (q, n_i), *where* $q > q_i$.

Sketch of Proof: Consider agents of types (q_i, n_i) and (q, n_i) where $q > q_i$. Since all other agents will use a reservation value strategy (according to Theorem 1) then the latter agent will be accepted by all agents accepting the first. By creating a coalition with any third agent encountered by these two agents, agent (q, n_i) will gain more compared to the other type (according to Lemma 1). Therefore, since both agents search costs are identical, if the first agent preferred to search over buying directly then the second agent's strategy would be the same. []

A necessary step towards Theorem 3, which deals with the dependency of the agent's reservation vector in its quantity is the proof of Lemma 2. Here we will prove the consistency of the different elements in the reservation vectors of two agents.

Lemma 2. *For any two agent types* (q_i, n_i) *and* (q_j, n_i), *where all other agent types use reservation quantities that increase as a function of their requested quantities, the following holds: If* $Q_{q_i,n_i}[k] \geq Q_{q_j,n_i}[k]$ *for a specific k, then* $Q_{q_i,n_i}[v] \geq Q_{q_j,n_i}[v]$ *for any value v. Namely, if one agent's reservation quantity is higher than another's for any coalition size n, then this will be the case for all other coalition sizes.*

Sketch of Proof for Lemma 2: Recursively substitute the cost function of agent types (q_i, n_i) and (q_j, n_i), when using equation (7) with $n=k$ for the first iteration and $n=1$ for each additional step. Eventually one of the agents will reach a coalition for which it will be non-beneficial to engage in a search (according to Theorem 2, it will be agent (q_j, n_i)). This coalition price, will be the expected price per unit that agent (q_j, n_i) will pay (when adding the search costs into calculations), according to (7). The other agent's expected price per unit will be lower, since all other agent types use reservation quantities that increase as a function of their requested quantities. Repeating the same process with $n=v$ will produce a contradictory result. []

Theorem 3. *A unique Nash equilibrium exists for the problem in which each agent engaging in a search uses a reservation value strategy, where the reservation value* $Q_{q_i,n_i}[n]$ *increases with the agent quantity* q_i *for every n.*

Sketch of Proof: Consider an agent of type (q_i, n_i). Assuming all other agents behave according to the theorem, we will prove that the optimal strategy for any single agent of type (q_i, n_i) is to act according to the theorem. We will use the

---

[6] Can be found at www.cs.biu.ac.il/~sarned/cia/

notation: $q_n[q_i, n_i] = \max\{q \mid Q_{q,n}[n] \le q_i\}$, the maximal quantity requested to be purchased by any of the agent types *(*,n)*, accepting agent type (q_i, n_i). $\bar{n}(q_i, n_i)$ will denote the last member of the vector $\vec{Q}_{q_i, n_i}$.

Notice that $V_{q_i, n_i}(\vec{Q}_{q_i, n_i})$ can be written as:

$$V_{q_i, n_i}(\vec{Q}_{q_i, n_i}) = E\left[a + bn_i + \frac{q_i V_{q_i + q_j, n_i + n_j}}{q_{i+} q_j} \bullet 1(dualaccept) + V_{q_i, n_i}(\vec{Q}_{q_i, n_i}) \bullet 1(not(dualaccept))\right] \tag{9}$$

Here 1(*dualaccept*) represents the indicator of the event {both agents accept each other}. If all other agents act according to the theorem, then:

$$\frac{q_i V_{q_i + q_j, n_i + n_j}}{q_{i+} q_j} \bullet 1(dualaccept) = q_i \sum_{n=1}^{\bar{n}(q_i, n_i)} \left(\int_{q = Q_{q_i, n_i}[n]}^{q_n[q_i, n_i]} \frac{V_{q_i + q, n_i + n}}{q_i + q} f(q, n) dq \right) \tag{10}$$

and:

$$V_{q_i, n_i}(\vec{Q}_{q_i, n_i}) \bullet 1(not(dualaccept)) = V_{q_i, n_i}(\vec{Q}_{q_i, n_i}) \left(1 - \sum_{n=1}^{\bar{n}(q_i, n_i)} \left(\int_{q = Q_{q_i, n_i}[n]}^{q_n[q_i, n_i]} f(q, n) dq \right) \right) \tag{11}$$

Substituting (10) and (11) in (9), we obtain:

$$a + bn_i = \sum_{n=1}^{\bar{n}(q_i, n_i)} \left(\int_{q = Q_{q_i, n_i}[n]}^{q_n[q_i, n_i]} \left(V_{q_i, n_i}(\vec{Q}_{q_i, n_i}) - \frac{q_i V_{q_i + q, n_i + n}}{q_i + q} \right) f(q, n) dq \right) \tag{12}$$

and according to (7):

$$a + bn_i = \sum_{n=1}^{\bar{n}(q_i, n_i)} \left(\int_{q = Q_{q_i, n_i}[n]}^{q_n[q_i, n_i]} \left(\frac{q_i V_{q_i + Q_{q_i, n_i}[n], n_i + n}}{q_{i+} Q_{q_i, n_i}[n]} - \frac{q_i V_{q_i + q, n_i + n}}{q_i + q} \right) f(q, n) dq \right) \tag{13}$$

Notice that $q_i + Q_{q_i, n_i}[n] > q_i + q$, for any value of q within the interval boundaries. Therefore, according to theorem (2) either at least one of the agent types $(q_i + Q_{q_i, n}[n], n_i + n)$ and $(q_i + q, n_i + n)$ will engage in a search or both will purchase the product in their current configuration. In the latter case, the integrated function becomes $q_i P_{q_i + Q_{q_i, n_i}[n]} - q_i P_{q_i + q}$, which is an increasing function of q_i for any value of q within the interval boundaries (according to Lemma 1), and a decreasing function of $Q_{q_i, n_i}[n]$ (due to the nature of the price function, as reflected in (1)). Also, since the other agent's reservation quantity is increasing function of q, the interval upper limit, $q_n[q_i, n_i]$, becomes an increasing function of q_i. Thus, increasing q_i must be accompanied with an increase in the interval lower limit $\varrho_{q_i, n_i}[n]$ of at least one of the aggregated integrals, in order to maintain the equality. Using Lemma 2, we conclude that all other elements of $\vec{Q}_{q_i, n_i}$ also increase. []

To conclude the equilibrium analysis, we suggest theorem 4, which complements theorem (2).

Theorem 4. *If in its optimal strategy, an agent of type* (q_i, n_i) *chooses not to engage in a search, then the same holds for any other agent of type* (q, n_i) *where* $q < q_i$.

Sketch of Proof: Consider an agent (q_i, n_i) for which:

$$a + bn_i = \sum_{n=1}^{\bar{n}(q_i,n_i)} \left(\int_{q=nq}^{q_n[q_i,n_i]} \left(q_i P_{q_i} - \frac{q_i V_{q_i+q,n_i+n}}{q_i + q} \right) f(q,n) dq \right) \tag{14}$$

Obviously this agent is indifferent to maintaining a search or purchasing the product in its current coalition structure. Notice that since the lower bound of the equation is not influenced by changes in the agent's type, then according to Lemma 1, the right hand side of the equation is an increasing function of q_i. Therefore, there is a specific agent type (q_i, n_i), where all other agent types (q_j, n_i), where $q_j < q_i$, will never engage in a search. []

Theorems 1-4, fully outline the conditions by which an agent will decide to engage in a search in order to extend its coalition, and the characteristics of its optimal strategy within the search. An important issue to consider is the complexity of the equations from which the equilibrium strategies can be extracted. The different characteristics of the optimal strategies as described in this section can aid us in this task. We will demonstrate such a process using a variant of the problem in the following section.

4 Specific Cases

In this section we discuss some variants of the general coalition formation problem modeled in the previous section. The first variant, in which the coalition coordination costs are negligible, is an upper limit for the agent types that will engage in a search in the general model. The second variant, the two-size coalition is a good example and a test bed for demonstrating possible uses of algorithms for distributed calculation of the agent's optimal strategy parameters in equilibrium.

4.1 Coordination Costs Are Negligible

Consider a marketplace where the agents are not subject to coalition coordination costs, bn, and the only cost associated with the search is the fixed cost per search stage, a. Here, there is no significance to the number of buyers a potential partner agent is representing, and the only relevant decision argument is the partner's overall requested quantity. As long as the agent engages in search it will accept any agent it encounters (the search cost is a sunk cost, and any coalition will increase the coalition quantity).

An agent of type $(q_i, *)$ will choose to search, only if the expected coalition to be reached through the search will benefit more than buying the product in the current coalition configuration. Denoting the overall cost of agent type $(q_i, *)$ if it is conducting a search as $V_{q_i}(search)$, and the cost of purchasing the product without a search as $V_{q_i}(buy)$, we obtain:

$$V_{q_i}(search) = a + E\left[\frac{q_i V_{q_{i+q}}}{q_i + q}\right], \; V_{q_i}(buy) = q_i P_{q_i} \tag{15}$$

Remember that $f(q,n)$ is the distribution function of the agent types engaging in a search, in equilibrium, therefore:

$$E\left[\frac{q_i V_{q_{i+q}}}{q_i + q}\right] = \int_{q=q}^{q_{upper}} \frac{q_i V_{q_{i+q}}}{q_{i+q}} \left(\sum_n f(q,n)\right) dq \tag{16}$$

In the above equation (16), q_{upper} represents the highest quantity for which $f(q,*) > 0$. Agent $(q_i, *)$ will prefer to conduct a search if the following equation (17) holds, and otherwise it will prefer to buy the product in its current configuration:

$$V_{q_i}(buy) - V_{q_i}(search) = q_i P_{q_i} - a - \int_{q=q}^{q_{upper}} \frac{q_i V_{q_{i+q}}}{q_{i+q}} \left(\sum_n f(q,n)\right) dq > 0 \tag{17}$$

Notice that in equilibrium all agents of type q, where $q > q_{upper} - \underline{q}$, will not form further coalitions and though the term $(q_i V_{q_{i+q}})/(q_{i+q})$ can be expressed as $q_i P_{q_{i+q}}$.

4.2 Agent Pairs' Coalitions

In this section we consider a second variant of the problem, concerning coalitions of agent pairs. Each coalition can be seen as a beneficial partnership among two autonomous agents, of specific types $(q,1)$. The reason for limiting the discussion here to coalitions of pairs is twofold. First, the dynamics of the atom (size-two) coalition structures creation processes is a basic infrastructure for the analysis of the larger coalitions. Thus this can be a useful test bed for algorithms that can be extended later to deal with the general case. Second, we identify several applications where an agent can benefit or perform a task only by finding one partner[7].

Consider, for example, a client agent in a Kazaa\Gnutella-like file sharing application, searching for a specific media file A, and offering another specific media file B. The agent can find a partner with complimentary offerings, starting immediately with the download and upload processes. Alternatively, it can look for a better connected agent with the same offering, in order to reduce the download time. At each stage of the search, the agent will have to consider the tradeoff between time saved (on download, by possibly finding a better partner) and time spent (in search for such a partner). In addition, when considering possible better partners, the agent should take into account these agents' own strategies and asses their willingness to form a coalition with its type. A totally different application can be found in VoIP networking. Here, we can utilize the partnership concept, for service providers, looking for partners to form ad-hoc call terminations between two destinations. Each

---

[7] We do understand the difficulties of using the abstract size-two model in these applications. However the analysis given, as well as the algorithms to follow, are unique in the context of coalition formation for these applications.

service provider faces different partners offering different link qualities (jitter, packet loss, etc.). However testing a partner's quality also entails costs.

In the context of the general coalition formation problem in electronic marketplace, as described in section 3, we may consider this specific variant when there might be technical implementation obstacles for creating a representative agent for more than one buyer. Though, for an agent that has decided to engage in a search, at each stage of its search process, after reviewing the information regarding the current potential partner, the agent must make a decision whether to terminate the search or to continue. Terminating the search will result in immediate purchase of the product with the current potential partner, if it agrees, whereas continuing the search will hopefully yield a better type partner.

Notice that since the agent is not concerned with coalition coordination costs, the only relevant parameter for its decision is the other agent's requested quantity. Therefore the agent will be using a reservation quantity Q, instead of the reservation vector $\vec{Q}$ as in the general case. When a mutual acceptance occurs the agent ends its search and purchases the product at price $P_{q_i+q_j}$. Equation (9) can now be expressed as:

$$V_{q_i}(Q) = E\left[k + q_i P_{q_i+q_j} \bullet 1(dualaccept) + V_{q_i}(Q) \bullet 1(not(dualaccept))\right] \qquad (18)$$

where $V_{q_i}(Q) = V_{q_i,1}(Q[1])$ and $k=a+b$.

Theorem 5. *For this variant of the problem a unique Nash equilibrium exists for the agent types engaging in a search, in which each agent uses a reservation value (reservation quantity) strategy, with a lower reservation than its requested quantity (derived by its type), and increases with the agent's type[8].*

Sketch of Proof: The proof methodology resembles the one given for theorem (3). The equivalent to Equation (11) is:

$$V_{q_i}(Q_i) = E\left[k + q_i P_{q_i+q_j} \bullet 1(Q_i \leq q \leq q(q_i)) + V_{q_i}(Q_i) \bullet 1(q_j < Q_i \cup q_i < Q_j)\right] \qquad (19)$$

And using $V_{q_i}(Q_i) = q_i P_{q_i+Q_i}$ (the equivalent to equation (13) of the general case), we obtain:

$$k = q_i \int_{q_j=Q_i}^{q(q_i)} \left(P_{q_i+Q_i} - P_{q_i+q_j}\right) f(q) dq \qquad (20)$$

Concluding that the only way to maintain the equality, when increasing q_i is by increasing Q_i.

Since all buying agents will accept agent type $\overline{q}$, then this agent's type problem becomes a simple problem of choosing the best reservation quantity without any restriction (of acceptance by other agents). This leads to $\overline{Q} < \overline{q}$, and so therefore $Q_i < q_i$ for any q_i. []

As in the general problem, if an agent requesting a quantity q_i finds it beneficial to engage in a search, rather than buy the product as a single buyer, then any other agent

---

[8] Similar characteristics of equilibrium as in theorem 5 are described in [9] for a model concerning the maximization of the agent's utility when searching for pairs.

requesting a quantity $q > q_i$ will find the search process beneficial as well. Consider the agent type q_j, where $V_{q_j} = P_{q_i} q_i$. Since for all agents of type i above q_i, $V_{q_i} = P_{q_i + Q} q_i < P_{q_i} q_i$ holds, then these agents have no incentive to abandon the search. Agents of a type lower than q_j, will prefer to leave the market and not to engage in a search at all. The q_j type can be calculated in the continuous case as follows:

$$k = q_i \int_{q_j = q}^{q(q_i)} \left(P_{q_i} - P_{q_i + q_j}\right) f(q) dq \tag{21}$$

Once agents of a specific type have an incentive to leave the environment, new equilibrium reservation quantities should be computed for the remaining agents. The new calculation should be based on the updated probability function of the remaining agents. This procedure should be repeated until all agents have an incentive to buy through pair coalitions.

Consider equation (20). We have shown that the right hand side of the equation is an increasing function of Q_i, and though once $q(q_i)$ is known, Q_i can be calculated by setting $Q_i = q_i$, and decreasing this value until the right hand side exceeds the value k. Notice that all the agents will accept the highest type agent, $\bar{q}$, since an agent's reservation quantity is always smaller than its requested quantity. This means that agents of type $\bar{q}$ can simply calculate their reservation quantity $\bar{Q}$ by solving (20) for $q(\bar{q}) = \bar{q}$, regardless of the other agents' reservation quantities. This calculation method is valid also for all agents in the perceived interval $[\bar{Q}, \bar{q}]$, since all other agents' reservation quantities are lower than $\bar{Q}$. Furthermore, for each one of the agent types in this interval, a unique finite sequence of reservation values can be obtained. Each member of such sequence (except for the first one) is the reservation quantity of the former sequence member. Each sequence member (except for the last one) is also the highest type agent willing to accept agents of the next sequence member type. Thus, each sequence member can be calculated using (20), with the former sequence member agent as the integral upper bound.

Obviously, calculating all possible sequences will reveal the reservation values for all agent types in the interval $[q, \bar{q}]$. However, having a continuous range of agent types makes the task impossible. A computational algorithm is needed to find a reservation quantity of a given agent of type q_i. Utilizing the unique characteristics of the equilibrium, along with the concept of the sequences, we suggest an algorithm for bounding the optimal reservation quantity, Q_i, into an interval of size ε.

Recall that each agent's reservation quantity is smaller than its requested quantity, and increases as its type increase. Therefore Q_i is bounded by the reservation quantities of two subsequent agents in any sequence. For the purpose of bounding Q_i in an interval of size ε, we should find two agent types q_{i_-} and q_{i_+}, whose reservation quantities difference is smaller than ε. This is done by changing the selection of the two sequence originating types in the interval $[\bar{Q}, \bar{q}]$. Using binary search over this interval will ensure that on each step the interval bounding Q_i is narrowed. The proposed algorithm for computing such a sequence, which is valid for any distribution function $f(q)$, and search price k, is specified below.

Algorithm 4.1 (FindSequence(q_{start}, q_{stop})).

(* Input   (1) An agent type q_{start} to start with ; (2) An agent type q_{stop} to stop with   *)

(* Output   a sequence, represented by an array, q[], where q[0]= q_{start}, and q[last]   *)

is the first sequence member exceeding type q_{stop} from below   *)

```
1.  q[0]:= q_start ;
2.  q[1]:=Q_i, where Q_i solves (20) with q_i=q[0] and q(q_i)=q[0];
3.  i:=1;
4.  While (q[i]≥q_stop) do {i++; q[i]:=Q_i, where Q_i solves (20)
        with q_i=q[i-1] and q(q_i)=q[i-2]; }
5.  return q[];
```

Using the above procedure, the following scheme can be used to calculate the reservation quantity of agent type q_i:

Algorithm 4.1 (CalculateReservation(q_i, ε)).

(* Input   (1) An agent type q_i ; (2) level of precision ε *)

(* Output   the bounded interval for reservation quantity of type q_i *)

```
1.  q_upper:=FindSequence (q̄, q_i);
2.  If (q_i ≥ q_upper[1]) then
a.       Upper=Q_i, where Q_i solves (20) with q_i and q(q_i):=q̄ ;
b.       Return (Upper, Upper);
3.  q_lower = FindSequence (q_upper[1], q_upper[last]);
4.  While (q_upper[last]- q_lower[last]>ε) do
a.       q:=FindSequence((q_upper[0]+q_lower[0])/2, q_upper[last]);
b.       if (q[last]>q_i) then q_upper=q;
c.       else q_lower=q;
5.  return(q_upper[last]+q_lower[last]);
```

Further explanations and proofs regarding the correctness of the algorithms are available in the full version of the authors' paper.

Notice that in the absence of the algorithm, any given agent would have been required to compute reservation values for a continuous interval of types. The proposed algorithm suggests evaluation of the reservation value, in a finite number of steps, for any level of required precision.

4.3 Discrete Environment

The above algorithms are concerned with markets characterized by enumerated types like gold, coffee and chemicals. However for most products in the electronic marketplace, the required quantity can be expressed only in discrete units. In the following paragraphs, we will demonstrate how these algorithms can be adjusted to handle such discrete environments. This can be obtained by proving that the same equilibrium characteristics found for the continuous case are also maintained in the discrete environment.

Theorem 6. *Consider a finite set of n agent types, each characterized by (q_i, g_i), where q_i is the quantity requested by agent type i, and g_i is the proportion of this agent type in the population. Then there is a unique Nash equilibrium for the model, where agents use reservation values as the optimal strategy, and:*

(a) An agent's reservation quantity is an increasing function of its type.

(b) An agent's reservation quantity is lower than its requested quantity.

(c) Type q_i agent's reservation quantity Q_i, satisfies:

$$k = q_i \sum_{q_j=Q_i}^{q(q_i)} \left(P_{q_i+Q_i} - P_{q_i+q_j}\right)g_j \tag{22}$$

Sketch of Proof: Similar proof to the one given in section 4.2, resulting in equation (22). Using Lemma 1 (the Lemma concerns only the price function and its validness is not influenced by the distribution of types), we conclude that in order to keep the above equation valid, Q_i must be an increasing function of q_i. []

As in the continuous case, from lemma 1 we conclude that the right hand side of (22) is an increasing function of Q_i, and though once $q(q_i)$ is known, Q_i can be calculated. Therefore, a similar algorithm to that presented in section 3.2 for finding a reservation quantity of a given agent of type q_i, can be applied in the discrete case, replacing equation (20) with (22). Notice, however, that in the discrete case there is a possibility that calculations based on (22) will result in a reservation quantity Q_i, with no actual agent type j associated to it. Here, any reservation quantity taken from the interval $[Q_i, \min(q_j); q_j \geq Q_i]$ will result in identical expected minimal costs.

Therefore, for each agent we can define a reservation type instead of a reservation quantity. The reservation type defines the lowest agent type an agent will be willing to accept as a partner. An appropriate reservation agent value for an agent i type can be calculated simply by using equation (22): first, find the upper index based on the reservation quantities of higher types (starting with the highest type agent and backward). Then, check the right hand value when setting $Q_i = q_j; j = i, i-1, \ldots$, until the calculated term exceeds the value k. This will require overall (n-j+1) reservation type calculations. Notice that once the reservation type concept has been adopted, an agent's reservation type is a weakly increasing function of the agent's type (several agents may have the same reservation agent). In addition, the agent's reservation type can actually be its own type (and not necessarily a lower type).

For the purpose of calculating Q_i, we can utilize the new acceptance types concept, suggesting a more efficient heuristic. The algorithm works on the array agents[] where each member i, agent[i], holds, in addition to the requested quantity, and type's probability fields, also pointers to the highest agent type that accepts type i, and the lowest type accepted by agent i.

The algorithm uses two functions:

- FindUpper(i,initial) - used to associate a given agent of type i with the highest agent type that will accept it. This value will be used as $q(q_i)$ in the calculation of Q_i in (22).

  The function is initialized with a higher or equal agent type, *initial*, which is known to accept type i.

- FindSequence(q_{start}, q_{stop}) – A similar function as in the continuous case. This time, however, each member is the lowest agent type accepted by the former sequence member. The last member in the array is the first sequence member smaller than type q_{stop}.

Algorithm 4.2 (FindUpper(i,initial)).
(* Input: (1) Agent type i for which the calculation is requested *)
(*   (2) An initial agent type to start with   *)
(* Output: Updating agents[i].upper with appropriate value   *)

```
1. If (agents[i].upper==null)
   then {
2.    j=initial;
3.    While (j<n) do {
4.       i=i+1;
5.       If(CalculateReservation(i)>i)
          agents[i].upper=j-1;
      }
6.    If (i=n) then
         agents[i].upper:=n;
}
```

Algorithm 4.2 (FindSequence(q_{start}, q_{stop})).
(* Input: (1) An agent type q_{start} to start with   *)
(*   (2) An agent type q_{stop} to stop with   *)
(* Output: array, q[], representing a sequence, where q[0]=   *)
(* q_{start}, and q[last]= first agent type smaller than *)
(* q_{stop} belonging to such a sequence   *)

```
1. q[0]:=q_start; FindUpper(q[0],q[0]);
2. q[1]:= CalculateReservation(q[0]);
3. i:=1;
4. While ((q[i]≥q_stop) and (q[i]!=q[i-1])) do{
   a. i++;
   b. FindUpper(q[i-1],q[i-2]);
   c. q[i]:=Q_i, where Q_i solves (22) with
      q_i=q[i-1] and q(q_i)=q[i-2];}
5. return q[];
```

Algorithm 4.2 (CalculateReservation(i)).
(* Input: (1) An agent type i for which the reservation type should be calculated   *)
(* Output: Returns agent type i's exact reservation type   *)

1. Base cases: If i is highest or lowest type agent, or upper index was already calculated then return(Calculate Q_i by Solving (22));

2. Heuristic: if i-1 type is known then FindUpper(i,agents[i-1].upper) and return(Calculate Q_i by Solving (22));

3. Use findSequence(n,i) to set q_{uppe} and q_{lower} as the two initial bounding arrays as in section 4.2.

4. First Segment: Set Agents[j].upper=n for every $j \geq q_{upper}[1]$;

5. Repeat
   a. *i* is in first segment: If ($q_{lower}[0] < i$) then set agents[i].upper=$q_{lower}[i]$ and return(Calculate Q_i by Solving (22));
   b. Both sequences collide: If $q_{lower}[j] = q_{upper}[j]$ for any $j \leq length(q_{lower})$, then:

  i.   Shorten both arrays so that q_{upper} will start with its
       member j, and q_{lower} with its member j+1;

 ii.   For any $q_{lower}[j] \le k < q_{lower}[j]$, FindUpper($k, q_{upper}[i]$);

 c. Adjacent members of sequences: If $(q_{upper}[j] - q_{lower}[j]) = 1$ then:

  i.   for any $q_{lower}[j+1] < k < q_{upper}[j+1]$ Set agents[k].upper=$q_{lower}[j]$;

 ii.   Shorten both arrays so q_{upper} and q_{lower} will start with their j+1
       member;

 d. i is in new first segment: If $((q_{lower}[0]) \le i)$ then

  i.   FindUpper($i, q_{upper}[0]$);

 ii.   Return (Calculate Q_i by Solving (22));

 e. $q = findSequence((q_{upper}[0] + q_{lower}[0])/2), q_{upper}[last]$;

 f. Update bounding sequences: If (q[last]=i) then
  i.   FindUpper(q[last],q[last-1]);
 ii.   Return (Calculate Q_i by Solving (22));

 g. Else if (q[last]>i) then $q_{upper} = q$;

 h. Else $q_{lower} = q$;

The function *CalculateReservation* returns the lowest agent type an agent i will accept in its equilibrium optimal strategy.

In the worst case, where each agent type's reservation quantity equals its own quantity, the algorithm will calculate a reservation quantity for all agents with a type higher than i (since we are considering discrete types and Q_i can be easily calculated using (22)). Using simulations, we tested the proposed algorithm performances when creating random agent types with random probabilities. For each simulation we set a random search cost, and used a typical price function[9] (according to (1) and (2)). Agent type distribution was created randomly for each simulation, and the discrete types (quantities) were randomly drawn for each simulation from the interval (1,10). We summarize the results of the simulations in Figure 3.

Figure 3 describes the average[10] extent of usage of equation (22), which is the most resource intensive calculation module in any algorithm within this problem's context. The horizontal axis represents the number of agent types used. The vertical axis represents the percentage of agent types for which we had to calculate a reservation quantity, out of the total number of agents with a higher type than the required one. In the absence of a heuristic, an agent is forced to calculate all reservation quantities for types greater than its own (represented as the one hundred percent line in the graph), thus the time required by our proposed heuristic is significantly lower than any straightforward algorithm. Notice that the algorithms performance improves as the environment (number of agent types) increases.

Finally, we present in Figure 4, an example of the agent's utility graph, in the context of a search (Recall that the lower the overall cost, the better the agent's

---

[9] We used a price function of type a-b*ln(c*X).

[10] Each graph point is the average of 5000 random simulations for calculating a reservation agent for a type outside the first (trivial) segment.

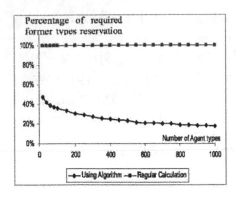

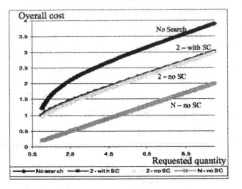

Fig. 3. Algorithms performance   **Fig. 4.** Utility Comparison

utility). Four scenarios were analyzed using direct calculation and simulation, where the agent types were drawn randomly from the interval [1,10]. Search cost was ~0.5 cents, and product cost $0.2+2/x-1/x^2$, where x is the required quantity. In the first scenario (represented by the most upper curve, marked as *no search* in the legend), agents did not engage in a search and purchased the product with a cost correlated to their required quantity. Secondly, we used the simulation to obtain the agent's costs when conducting a search in a costly environment (represented by the middle upper curve, marked as *2 – with Search Costs* in the legend). The reservation quantities were calculated for each agent according to the proposed algorithms. Then, an upper limit for the search benefits was set, by calculating the agent's cost when searching for partners in a non-costly environment (represented by the middle lower curve, marked as *2 – no Search Costs* in the legend). This is not the case of one united coalition but rather a solution where each agent forms a coalition with another agent of its own type[11] (a known result for the two-size costless model – see [1]).

A theoretical n-size coalition with no search costs is represented by the lower curve (marked as *N – no Search Costs*). Here all agents form together one big coalition, and buy the product with a price $P_{q \to \infty}$. This curve can be seen as a lower bound for cost of coalitions in the n-size scenario with search costs.

In Figure 4, all agents have an incentive to conduct a search. The case where agent's cost when buying directly the product is higher than when conducting a search, is well supported by the model, and this agent type will abandon the search in equilibrium. This was fully analyzed in section 3. Therefore in equilibrium, all agents engage in search will benefit more than the cost of buying directly the product.

Notice that in figure 4 the difference between the results obtained from the costly search and those belonging to the theoretical costless environment are significantly small. However, this is well correlated with search cost. An example of the effect the

---

[11] As if all buyers get together in one place and find pairs that belongs to the core.

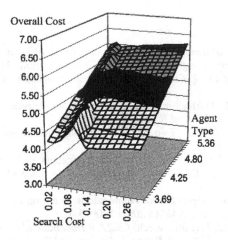

Fig. 5. Agent type and search cost effects

search cost has on the perceived utility for a given agent type is given in figure 5. As the overall search costs increase, two contrast effects occur: the agent becomes more attractive to higher type agents since the benefit of being selective decreases, and the agent's own payments for search increases. These two factors are the reason for the local maximum in figure 5.

5 Conclusions

In this paper we analyzed the model and equilibrium optimal strategies for agents engaged in costly searches for potential coalition partners. The incentive for cooperation is a volume discount and the search is characterized with a fixed cost for locating partners and variable costs for sub-coalition coordination towards the final coalition structures.

Understanding the characteristics of agent strategies in equilibrium is the main brick stone for any algorithm and heuristic to be used for solving the general case. We have shown a comprehensive analysis of two algorithms for solving specific variants of the problem where the coalition size is restricted to pair partnerships. We do see these algorithms as a basic infrastructure for suggesting further algorithms for the general n-size case. This is mainly because of the similar equilibrium structure (the continuum of agents engaged in a search) and the special characteristics of the agent's strategies as we proved in this paper (reservation vectors\values increase in type). The proposed tools for calculating the equilibrium strategies of agents when searching in pair coalitions can be used in several plausible applications and environments (Gnutella\Kazaa, VoIP service providers, etc.).

We plan to extend the research towards completing the algorithms to be used in the general case and simulations that can describe the evolution of steady-state agent types' distributions. Though we have focused on the non-transferable utility case, we see great importance in understanding the changes in such models when the agents can negotiate over the surplus of the partnership.

References

1. G. S. Becker. Theory of marriage: Part I, *Journal of Political Economy*, 81(4):813-846, 1973.
2. S. Breban, J. Vassileva. Long-term Coalitions for the Electronic Marketplace, *in B. Spencer (ed.) Proceedings of the E-Commerce Applications Workshop, Canadian AI Conference*, Ottawa, 2001.
3. C. H. Brooks, E.H. Durfee and A. Armstrong. An Introduction to Congregating in MultiAgent Systems. *In Proc. of ICMAS*, Boston, 2000.
4. K. Burdett and R. Wright. Two-sided search with nontransferable utility, *Review of Economic Dynamics*, 1:220–245, 1998.
5. A. R. Greenwald and J. O. Kephart. Shopbots and pricebots. *In Proc. of IJCAI*, 1999.
6. K. Lermann, O. Shehory. Coalition Formation for Large Scale Electronic Markets. *Proc. of ICMAS*. 2000.
7. C. Li and K. P. Sycara. Algorithm for combinatorial coalition formation and payoff division in an electronic marketplace. *AAMAS 2002*: 120015–127.
8. J. McMillan and M. Rothschild. Search, *Ch.27 of Handbook of Game Theory with Economic Applications*, Vol. 2, 905-927, ed. Robert J. Aumann and Sergiu Hart, Amsterdam, 1994.
9. P. Morgan. A Model of Search, Coordination, and Market Segmentation, *mimeo*, SUNY Buffalo, 1995.
10. T. Sandholm, K. Larson, M. Andersson, O.Shehory, F. Tohme. Coalition structure generation with worst-case guarantees. *Artificial Intelligence*. 111:209–238, 1999.
11. T. Sandholm and V. Lesser. Coalitions among computationally bounded agents. *Artificial Intelligence*, 94:99–137, 1997.
12. S. Sen and P.S. Dutta. Searching for optimal coalition structures. *In Proceedings of ICMAS*, 2000.
13. O. Shehory and S. Kraus. Methods for task allocation via agent coalition formation. *Artificial Intelligence*, 101:165–200, 1998.
14. L. Smith. The marriage model with search frictions. *Journal of Political Economy*, 2003 (To appear).
15. N. Tsvetovat, K. P. Sycara, Y. Chen and J. Ying. Customer Coalitions in Electronic Markets, *AMEC*, 2000.
16. J. Yamamoto and K. Sycara. A Stable and Efficient Buyer Coalition Formation Scheme for E-marketplaces. *Proceedings of Autonomous Agents*, 2001.

GraniteNights – A Multi-agent Visit Scheduler Utilising Semantic Web Technology

Gunnar AAstrand Grimnes, Stuart Chalmers, Pete Edwards, and Alun Preece

Dept. of Computing Science, University of Aberdeen
Aberdeen, AB24 5UE, Scotland.
{ggrimnes, schalmer, pedwards, apreece}@csd.abdn.ac.uk

Abstract. This paper describes a multi-agent system, GraniteNights, modelled on the Agentcities project "evening agent" scenario. GraniteNights allows a user to plan an evening's entertainment in the city of Aberdeen, Scotland. The application fuses agent and Web technology, being viewed as an agent-based Web service. In particular, Semantic Web standards are used to a great extent in delivering the service. The paper argues that, in fact, the Semantic Web standards are more important for this type of application than the agent standards. A key feature of the application is component re-use: GraniteNights attempts to reuse without modification existing ontologies wherever possible; it also is comprised of a number of generic and thus wholly-reusable agents, including a user profiling agent and a constraint-based scheduler. The system is open in the sense that most of the individual agents can be invoked directly by external agent platforms, without going through the Web interface.

1 Introduction

GraniteNights is a multi-agent application which allows a user to schedule an evening out in Aberdeen (aka the "Granite City"). Intended users of the GraniteNights application are visitors to Aberdeen or anyone else requiring assistance in identifying suitable dining and entertainment venues, as part of an evening schedule. The scenario is closely modelled on the Agentcities evening-planning agent scenario [7]. We view this type of application as a form of (intelligent) Web service, and have therefore employed Web standards wherever possible. In particular, we have committed to the Resource Description Framework [11] as the main content language in order to align our work as closely as possible with the Semantic Web [2]. The cost of creating RDF to describe the resources of interest in our application domain - restaurants, public houses, etc. is relatively low (a form-filling interface facilitates the process). Moreover, we are able to utilise for the most part existing ontologies represented in DAML+OIL [10], and we retain forward compatibility with the emerging OWL standard [12].

Agents within the application infrastructure are organised according to a series of predefined roles: information agents (wrappers for RDF resources - either static or dynamically generated from existing WWW sources); profile agent (manages user data, such as id, password and preferences); constraint-solver

M. Klusch et al. (Eds.): CIA 2003, LNAI 2782, pp. 137–151, 2003.
© Springer-Verlag Berlin Heidelberg 2003

agent (maps RDF data to finite domain constraints and produces valid instantiated schedules); evening-agent (receives user queries and controls invocation of
other agents to generate a solution); user-interface agent. The application has
been constructed using the Java Agent DEvelopment framework (JADE) agent
platform[1], SICStus Prolog (+ Jasper[2]) as well as BlueJADE [6] running under
the JBoss[3] J2EE application server.

The GraniteNights application was conceived as a vehicle for exploring a
number of issues: integration of agent and Semantic Web standards; utilisation
of off-the-shelf ontologies; re-use of components of information agent systems (at
a number of levels); use of constraint-based scheduling; semantic user profiling;
and not least the deployment of a real and substantial Agentcities application.
We believe that a number of novel contributions arise from this work. Firstly,
we assert that (at least for this type of information agents application) most
of the power comes from the content standards, specifically the Semantic Web
standards. Essentially all of the FIPA[4] standards employed in GraniteNights
could easily be replaced by Web services technology, for example SOAP and
WSDL [5]. Perhaps controversially, we discarded FIPA-SL altogether as we took
the view that it brought nothing to our type of application.

Secondly, we believe that GraniteNights demonstrates that currently available, relatively weak ontologies expressed for the most part simply in RDF
Schema, are the appropriate level of Semantic Web technology for useful applications. In fact, our view is that stronger ontologies would have been harder
to re-use, because they would have imposed overly-restrictive commitments on
their applicability. Thirdly, GraniteNights embodies several strategies for component reuse. Several of the agents are wholly general and would serve as useful
components of other agent systems — the information agents, the ProfileAgent,
and the SchedulerAgent (the latter *is* in fact already being used in another application). Moreover, within the various agents, there is considerable reuse of
code, notably in the information agents that all share the same "shell".

Finally, we aim to show in this paper that GraniteNights includes a number
of novel technologies, in particular its approach to semantic profiling (allowing
users to incrementally create profiles that are meaningful to them, and portable
across a variety of applications), and the RDF Query By Example language.

The remainder of this paper is organised as follows: Section 2 provides an
overview of the system architecture, and the relationships between the various
components; Section 3 describes the lowest level agents which manage a series of
information resources (encoded using RDF); Section 4 discusses the operation of
the scheduling component, including the constraint solver; Section 5 presents the
user-profile management aspects of GraniteNights; we conclude with a discussion
of lessons learned and related work in Section 6; and discuss suggested extensions
to the architecture in Section 7.

---

[1] http://sharon.cselt.it/projects/jade/
[2] http://www.sics.se/sicstus/docs/latest/html/sicstus.html/Jasper.html
[3] http://www.jboss.org
[4] Foundation for Intelligent Physical Agents, http://www.fipa.org

2   GraniteNights System Overview

The GraniteNights architecture is presented in Figure 1. The system consists of a collection of service providing agents, and a central agent which coordinates the process of delivering a plan, called the EveningAgent. The decomposition of services into the collection of agents shown (white ovals) aims to maximise the reusability of the components; where possible, each discrete independent sub-service is embodied in a separate agent.

The application can be accessed by another software agent via communication with the EveningAgent, or by a user directly through a Web interface. For space reasons we are unable to present full details of interactions with the EveningAgent here, but these are available from our Web site[5].

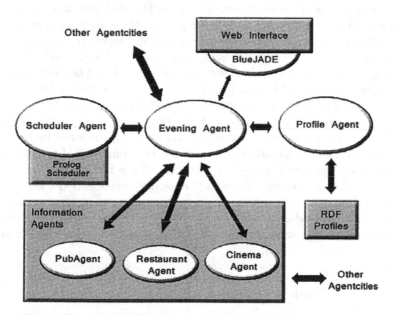

Fig. 1. GraniteNights - Architecture Diagram.

The EveningAgent receives a partially instantiated evening-plan containing a list of events, possibly including start times and durations. Each event is either a visit to a public house, a restaurant or a cinema, with optional constraints on that event. Example constraints include: *This Pub must serve Guinness*, or *I want to see the film "The Pianist"*. The EveningAgent queries the appropriate InformationAgent to get a list of possible events which match the given constraints. Once all the possible events have been assembled they are passed to the SchedulerAgent along with the partial plan. The SchedulerAgent then

---
[5] http://www.csd.abdn.ac.uk/research/AgentCities/GNInfo/

generates a set of possible complete plans for the evening, choosing times and events according to the user specified criteria. One finished plan will then be returned to the user, who has the option of accepting the plan or asking for the next solution. The EveningAgent uses a hard-coded collaboration strategy; it knows about the three information agents available, and makes no attempt at discovering new information sources. It also works closely with the ProfileAgent and SchedulerAgent, but is only tied to the external interfaces of these agents, which makes them pluggable modules of GraniteNights. It would thus be trivial to deploy a more sophisticated scheduler or profiling mechanism in the future.

The GraniteNights Web interface[6] is implemented using Java Server Pages (JSP), Java Servlets and BlueJADE. BlueJADE allows Web applications to send and receive agent messages through a *gateway agent*, which in turn allowed us to write an EveningAgent client that generates the RDF messages from simple Web forms completed by the user. Screenshots from the Web interface are presented in Figure 2. On the left hand side is the input interface, showing that a user has specified that (s)he wants to go to a public house that serves *Hoegaarden* at 18.00, followed by a visit to a cinema showing the film *The Pianist* and ending their evening with a meal in a restaurant serving Italian cuisine. The right hand side of Figure 2 shows one possible plan for their evening generated by GraniteNights. Note how the user has also specified that the cinema should be a 15 minute walk (or less) away from the pub, and the restaurant a 15 minute walk away from the cinema. These proximity constraints are implemented by positioning each venue available in GraniteNights within a two dimensional grid overlaid on a map of Aberdeen (see Figure 4 for a section of the full map). There are also some venues that are outside the map. Three different location constraints are available: 15 minutes walk, which means within an adjacent square; 30 minutes walk or a short cab-ride, meaning within two squares; and long taxi-ride which is everything else. The sections that follow deal with the various agents in more detail.

Table 1. Ontologies Used By GraniteNights.

Name	Developers	URI
Pubs	Aberdeen	http://www.csd.abdn.ac.uk/research/...
		... AgentCities/ontologies/pubs
Beer	Aberdeen	— " —/beer
Query By Example	Aberdeen	— " —/query
Eveningplan	Aberdeen	— " —/eveningplan
Restaurants v.4	Agentcities	— " —/restaurant-v4.daml
Shows v.2.7	Agentcities	— " —/shows-v27.daml
Address	Agentcities	http://sf.us.agentcities.net/ontologies/address.daml
Calendar	Agentcities	http://sf.us.agentcities.net/ontologies/calendar.daml
Price	Agentcities	http://sf.us.agentcities.net/ontologies/price.daml
Contact Details	Agentcities	http://sf.us.agentcities.net/ontologies/contact-details.daml

---

[6] http://www.csd.abdn.ac.uk/research/AgentCities/GraniteNights

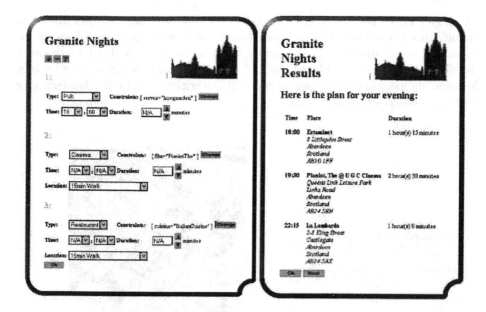

Fig. 2. GraniteNights – Web Interface.

3   Information Agents

GraniteNights uses three information agents, all of which act as simple wrappers for RDF data-sources. Each has a simple, consistent query interface based upon Query By Example[7] (QbEx), discussed in Section 3.2. The three agents facilitate access to information about public houses, cinemas and restaurants in Aberdeen. The PubAgent and RestaurantAgent both wrap static RDF files, while the CinemaAgent wraps RDF which is dynamically generated from a conventional Web page supplying up-to-date cinema listing information. Although the information agents form the basis of GraniteNights, their usefulness is not restricted to this application, as they are all externally accessible over the Agentcities network, and were designed with re-use in mind.

All the information agents run off the same code-base with configuration files used to specify the input source to wrap. As far as possible our information agents use standard Agentcities ontologies, such as the utility ontologies for addresses, contact details and calendar information (Table 1).

3.1   Static vs. Dynamic Information Agents

The static information agents facilitate access to RDF data that has been manually generated, containing information about public houses and restaurants in Aberdeen. Ontology support for the PubAgent is provided by pub and beer

---

[7] http://www.csd.abdn.ac.uk/research/AgentCities/QueryByExample

ontologies developed at Aberdeen (Table 1). The RestaurantAgent uses the Agentcities restaurant ontology. Examples of instances from these ontologies are presented in Figures 3 and 5. Instances contain information about the contact details and services available in each pub or restaurant; in addition they contain location information, expressed as coordinates within a map of Aberdeen city centre, as described in Section 2.

Fig. 4. Location Map Example.

```
<pub:EnglishPub rdf:ID="#estaminet">
 <pub:liveEntertainment
   rdf:resource="pubs#Sometimes"/>
 <pub:location>
   <add:Address rdf:ID="address">
     <add:publicPlaceName>Little John St.
       </add:publicPlaceName>
     <add:cityName>Aberdeen</add:cityName>
     <add:countryName>Scotland
       </add:countryName>
     <add:doorNumber>8</add:doorNumber>
     <add:zipCode>AB10 1FF</add:zipCode>
     <add:locationId> 7, 7
       </add:locationId>
   </add:Address>
 </pub:location>
 <pub:onLicense>true</pub:onLicense>
 <pub:pubName>Estaminet</pub:pubName>

 <pub:openingPeriods
   rdf:resource="times#sun_thu_midnight"/>
 <pub:openingPeriods
   rdf:resource="times#weekend_three"/>

 <pub:servesBeer
   rdf:resource="beer#budweiser"/>
 <pub:servesBeer
   rdf:resource="beer#leffeblonde"/>
 ...
 <pub:servesFood>on</pub:servesFood>
 <pub:telNumber>01224 622657
   </pub:telNumber>
</pub:EnglishPub>
```

```
<res:Restaurant rdf:about="#lalombarda">
 <res:name>La Lombarda</res:name>
 <res:averageMealDuration>2
   </res:averageMealDuration>
 <res:address>
   <add:Address rdf:about="rest#lombardaaddr"/>
 </res:address>
 <res:atmospheres rdf:resource="res#CasualAtmosphere"/>
 <res:atmospheres rdf:resource="res#RelaxedAtmosphere"/>
 <res:caterings rdf:resource="res#ALaCarte"/>
 <res:caterings rdf:resource="res#HomeDelivery"/>
 <res:facilities rdf:resource="res#SmokingFacility"/>
 <res:typeOfCuisine rdf:resource="res#ItalianCuisine"/>
</res:Restaurant>
```

Fig. 5. Example RDF Restaurant Instance.

Fig. 3. Example RDF Pub Instance.

GraniteNights also contains a dynamic information agent, which wraps a conventional HTML Web page giving information about films showing at cinemas in Aberdeen (Figure 6). This information is extracted and converted into RDF conforming to the Agentcities Shows ontology (Table 1). The extraction and conversion is done via simple regular expression pattern matching, and would need to be rewritten if the structure of the HTML source were to change. For performance reasons, the RDF is extracted once a day and cached locally.

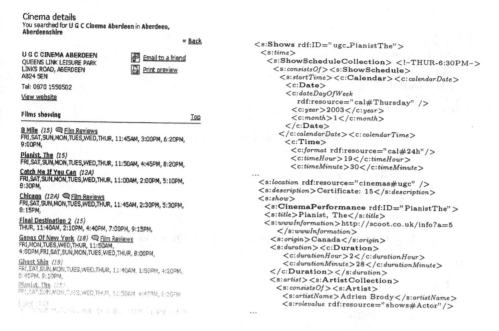

Original HTML Page.   Resulting RDF.

Fig. 6. Dynamic Information Agent Example.

3.2   RDF Query by Example

RDF Query By Example (QbEx) is the query language used throughout GraniteNights. It was developed by the authors to fulfil the need for a higher-level RDF query language than existing triple-based solutions such as RDQL [14], used in the Jena Semantic Web toolkit[8] and RDFStore[9]. We felt that RDQL, while a useful tool for the application developer, is not suitable for end-user queries, as constructing RDQL queries requires detailed insight into the workings of RDF and the RDF schemas used. Our solution is RDF Query By Example (QbEx) which allows the user to express queries in RDF, partially describing the RDF instance(s) to be returned. Figure 7 shows a simple example of a QbEx query, requesting that all pubs serving *Guinness* be returned. RDF statements can be constructed using either RDF literals or variables constrained using an RDF constraint language [9]. Internally the RDF QbEx structure is converted to RDQL (with automated RDF schema subclass inference). Figure 9 shows a more sophisticated example using a variable to return all restaurants open after 7 PM, while Figure 8 shows the same query when converted to RDQL by the QbEx engine.

---

[8] http://www.hpl.hp.com/semweb/jena.htm
[9] http://rdfstore.sourceforge.net/

```
<q:Query>
 <q:template>
  <p:EnglishPub>
   <p:servesBeer
     rdf:resource="beertypes#guinness"/>
  </p:EnglishPub>
 </q:template>
</q:Query>
```

Fig. 7. Simple QbEx Example.

SELECT ?x **WHERE** (?x, ?y, ?z),
  (?x, <r # open-time>, ?v_x),
  (?x, <rdf # type>, <r # *restaurant*>),
  (?x, <r # type>, <r # *Tandoori*>) **AND** (?v_x > 1900)

Fig. 8. RDQL Generated From the QbEx Query in Figure 9.

```
<q:Query>
 <q:template>
  <r:Restaurant>
   <r:type rdf:resource=?r#Tandoori" />
    <r:open-time>
     <cif:variable rdf:ID="x">
      <cif:varname>x</cif:varname>
     </cif:variable>
    </r:open-time>
  </r:Restaurant>
 </q:template>
 <q:constraints>
  <cif:comparison>
   <cif:comparison_operator>&gt;
    </cif:comparison_operator>
   <cif:comparison_op1>
    <cif:variable rdf:about="#x"/>
   </cif:comparison_op1>
   <cif:comparison_op2>
    <cif:integerconst>
     <cif:constant_value>1900
      </cif:constant_value> .. . .
```

Fig. 9. QbEx Example with Variables.

4   The Scheduling Agent

The purpose of the SchedulerAgent is to take information on available films, restaurants and pubs (provided by the EveningAgent), together with the preferences expressed by the user on type, time, duration and location (provided by the user through the Web interface) and create a set of valid schedules, showing the order, start time and duration of the events requested. To achieve this the agent implements a finite domain scheduling algorithm using the SICStus finite domain constraint library [4] to match the user requirements to the given information on the available venues, creating sets of valid schedules that satisfy the request.

The information given to the SchedulerAgent consists of a piece of RDF containing the possible venues for the evening (plus the information on those venues) together with the user requirements. On receipt of this the agent extracts the set of possible events, which are parsed and asserted as simple prolog facts. These are then matched with the schedule created from the user's request, with the requirements provided by the user constraining the items in the schedule.

```
<ep:EveningPlan>
  <ep:events>
   <rdf:Seq>
    <rdf:_1>
     <ep:Event>
      <ep:duration>
       <c:Duration>
        <c:durationHour>2</c:durationHour>
        <c:durationMinute>0</c:durationMinute>
       </c:Duration>
      </ep:duration>
      <ep:place>
       <rdf:Alt>
        <rdf:li><pub:EnglishPub rdf:about="pubs#estaminet" /></rdf:li>
        <rdf:li><pub:EnglishPub rdf:about="pubs#wildboar" /></rdf:li>
        <rdf:li><pub:EnglishPub rdf:about="pubs#eastneuk" /></rdf:li>
       </rdf:Alt>
      </ep:place>
    </rdf:_1><rdf:_2>
     <ep:Event>
      <ep:place>
       <rdf:Alt>
        <rdf:li><cin:Shows rdf:about="films#ugc_PianistThe" /></rdf:li>
        <rdf:li><cin:Shows rdf:about="films#lighthouse_PianistThe" /></rdf:li>
       </rdf:Alt>

...

% data(<name>,<type>,<open>,<close>,<location>).
data('ugc_PianistThe',movie,2020,2248,9,6).
data('lighthouse_PianistThe',movie,1815,2043,5,6).
data('estaminet',pub,1000,2700,7,7).
data('wildboar',pub,1000,2400,5,5).
data('eastneuk',pub,1000,2400,7,5).
```

Fig. 10. An RDF Fragment and its Equivalent Prolog Representation.

As an example, Figure 10 shows such an RDF fragment detailing two movies and three pubs, along with their equivalent prolog representation (the `data/6` constructs)[10]. In this example, suppose the user asks for a schedule containing three items: a pub, a movie and a restaurant (in that order). To represent these we begin by creating two finite domains, one for the start time of each

---

[10] Space does not permit us to show the full RDF representation, which also contains a number of restaurants

event requested and one for its duration. The example below shows the internal representation of the three events along with their respective domains:

```
% domain ( events, start-time, stop-time).
domain([START1,START2,START3],0,104),
domain([DUR1,DUR2,DUR3],4,24).
```

These predicates set up three tasks each with a start time between 0 and 26hrs (as some pubs are open till 2 AM) and durations of 1 to 6hrs[11]. Depending on the requirements set by the user, these domains are then constrained with the following information:

- Order & Location Constraints: The initial constraint on the schedule domains comes from the ordering of the events and their relative locations (described in Section 2). For example, if the three tasks mentioned were to be ordered as START1, START3, START2, all within 15 minutes walking distance of each other we would set the following constraints on the domains:

```
START1 + DUR1 + 1 #=< START3,
START3 + DUR3 + 1 #=< START2
```

- Time Constraints: These can be provided by the user or left unspecified. This constrains the time that the user wants to visit the venues, and the amount of time spent in each location. If specified then we make the START and DUR variables equal to the values given.

Once constrained, the remaining domain values are matched with the given possibilities (held in the data/6 format). From this we create a set of possible evening schedules. Figure 11 shows one such valid schedule. The scheduler creates as many of these schedules as required (or as many as is possible) and returns these as a set of possible evening plans (in RDF format).

5 Profile Agent

The ProfileAgent has two tasks within GraniteNights: The first is handling initial user registration and user authentication on return visits; registration simply involves setting up an account with a username and a password. The second task of the ProfileAgent is to keep track of the user's interests; the interest model is generated through analysis of previous interactions with the system, so there is no model available for new users. If a user's preferences are available, they will be included in the reply to a successful login request.

To generate the user interest model the ProfileAgent has access to the following information: the constraints specified for each event, the possible evening plans that were rejected, and the final evening plan that the user accepted. The

---

[11] The measurement scale shown means that the duration and start time can be measured at a granularity equivalent to 15 minute intervals.

EveningAgent informs the ProfileAgent of each of these every time a user visits GraniteNights. Note that there is no information available about why a user rejects a plan, although some information can be extracted by comparing the rejected plan(s) with the accepted version.

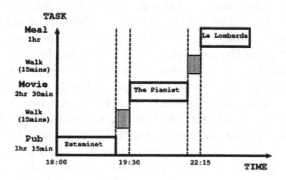

Fig. 11. An Example Schedule Created by the SchedulerAgent.

```
<ep:User>
  <ep:name>pedwards</ep:name>
  <ep:pword>gnes</ep:pword>
  <ep:preferences>
    <pub:EnglishPub pub:serves="beer#hobgoblin" />
  </ep:preferences>
  <ep:interactions>
    <rdf:Seq>
      <rdf:li>
        <ep:Interaction ep:date="20030315T164433" >
          <ep:pref>
            <pub:EnglishPub pub:serves="beer#hobgoblin" />
          </ep:pref>
        </ep:Interaction>
      </rdf:li>
      <rdf:li>
        <ep:Interaction ep:date="2003037T153710" >
          <ep:pref>
            <pub:EnglishPub pub:serves="beer#flowersale" />
          </ep:pref>
        </ep:Interaction>
      </rdf:li>
      <rdf:li>
        <ep:Interaction ep:date="2003032T121567" >
          <ep:pref>
            <pub:EnglishPub pub:serves="beer#hobgoblin" />
          </ep:pref>
        </ep:Interaction>
      </rdf:li>
    </rdf:Seq>
  </ep:interactions>
</ep:User>
```

Fig. 12. Example RDF Profile Instance.

For example, a user specifies that (s)he wants a single event for the evening, which should be a pub offering live entertainment. GraniteNights' first candidate plan suggests going to the pub *Estaminet* at 18.00. The user was in that pub recently, and would like to try something else, so (s)he asks for the next solution. GraniteNights suggests *The Blue Lamp* at 18.00 and the user accepts this plan. The ProfileAgent has now been informed of the user's constraint that the pub must have live entertainment, and also that (s)he accepted the second plan and rejected the first. By comparing the two the ProfileAgent could determine that it was the choice of venue that was incorrect, and not the time.

The architecture of GraniteNights was designed to abstract away the implementation details of the ProfileAgent, allowing us to experiment with different profiling techniques by simply writing new pluggable ProfileAgent modules. The current implementation of the ProfileAgent is basic, as it ignores all information about rejected or accepted plans, and simply caches user specified constraints for each available information event. Using this information, the most frequently cited constraint becomes the user's preference. For example, as shown in Figure 12, user *Pete* has used the system on three occasions, asking for pubs serving *Hobgoblin Ale* twice and *Flowers Ale* once, this means that Pete's current preference is for pubs serving *Hobgoblin*. The ProfileAgent stores the user profiles using RDF; an example profile is shown in Figure 12.

6   Discussion and Related Work

In this paper we have shown that RDF is a good alternative to SL as a content language for agent interaction. Agents communicating through RDF are not new, and are indeed central to the Semantic Web vision [17]. However, in the Agentcities project there has been a commitment to FIPA standards, and thus to FIPA-SL. Although FIPA-SL is more expressive than RDF (for example, it allows quantified variables), we feel that the much larger user-base of RDF, the variety of tools available, and the fact that it is based on XML, make it a better choice as content language for agent-based Web services. In addition, we feel that the current expressiveness of RDF is more than sufficient for a large range of applications. There are several RDF based solutions already being used within Agentcities, mainly DAML+OIL and OWL for describing ontologies and DAML-S for service description, but there are also projects committed to using RDF for content, for example in the Travel Agent Game in Agentcities (TAGA) [19].

Through developing GraniteNights we have also shown how re-use of components and ontologies facilitates construction of advanced composite services, such as the process of putting together an evening plan. In creating GraniteNights we have also attempted to supply the Agentcities network with a set of new reusable components, such as the information agents and their ontologies, in the hope that others will make use of these and combine them with other services in a new and interesting manner. This component re-use model is very much in the spirit of Agentcities and many projects are deploying simple component services suitable for integration into larger applications, for example Whitestein Technologies' CAMBIA service for currency exchange[12], and the agent-based medical services developed by GruSMA [16].

We have also demonstrated how multi-agent applications can be given a user-friendly Web interface which still remains a loosely coupled component of the system by using the gateway agent in BlueJADE. Many other Agentcities projects are also using BlueJADE, and there is currently significant effort going into improving integration between agent platforms and Enterprise Application Servers [3].

GraniteNights is also a first step towards user profiling using RDF for profile acquisition and representation: creating profiles which are meaningful to the user, and to a range of systems outside the originating application. Learning symbolic user profiles is a well researched field, for example in [15] where symbolic rules were learned for a user's meeting preferences. However, the interest in such profiling in a Semantic Web environment is only now slowly gaining momentum. For example, the Internet Content Rating Association has recently started a project to investigate "Customization and Personalization through RDF"[13]. Some work has also been done in representing user interest profiles with respect to a specified ontology and, by using RDF, deploying and keeping these profiles up to date in a different applications. [13].

7   Future Work

GraniteNights came together as a joint project between different members of the Aberdeen research community, each person bringing different technologies and different perspectives. We are all excited to see our work integrated into one application like GraniteNights, and we are all keen to improve the current implementations of each module.

In the current information layer of GraniteNights the information about public houses and restaurants is all hand generated by the project members, and while this has worked well, there are several short-comings in the current data. The PubAgent does not have information about drinks served beyond beers, and the RestaurantAgent does not know about individual dishes. We are currently exploring links with local goverment and other service providers with a view to accessing a number of available data-sources to replace some of the current information agents, and also for generation of new agents, such as an HotelAgent, CastleAgent and WhiskeyDistilleryAgent.

As mentioned above, the current ProfileAgent implementation is very simple. We plan to improve this module with a more sophisticated solution in several steps: Firstly we intend to explore the use of RDF inference to generalise better when generating user preferences. As shown in Figure 12, user *Pete* currently has the preference *a pub should serve Hobgoblin*, because that is the most frequent constraint he has specified. However, closer inspection of the ontology shows that

---

[12] http://zurich.agentcities.whitestein.ch/Services/CambiaService.doc
[13] http://www.icra.org/cprdf/

Hobgoblin and *Pete's* other preferred beer, *Flowers*, are in fact both sub-classes of the class *Real Ale*. A more intelligent ProfileAgent should be able exploit this relation, and generate the preference *Pete likes pubs serving Real Ales*. Secondly, we will look into the use of knowledge intensive Machine Learning algorithms for generating the profiles, in contrast to the current statistical approach. We have performed some preliminary work using the Inductive Logic Programming system Progol for learning from data marked up using RDF [8], and plan to explore the use of Case-Based Reasoning [1] and Explanation Based Generalisation [18], as these are also capable of learning from symbolic data. Thirdly we will explore further the advantages of expressing the user model as RDF, the re-usability of such a model will enable us to make a ProfileAgent that is not only usable within GraniteNights, but also within other projects, such as the upcoming Information Exchange[14] project in Aberdeen.

GraniteNights' current user-interaction model is based on the user sitting at home, having access to a computer, and planning their evening before they go out. While this is useful, a more common scenario is a group of people having been to the cinema, and only when the film has finished agreeing to extend their evening with a drink in a pub. Having GraniteNights accessible on their PDA just then would be very useful. Implementing this would also raise several interesting issues surrounding localised information delivery, for generating output such as "200m down Union St, on your right hand side, there is a pub serving *Director's Bitter*. The current modularised architecture makes writing another client-interface to work with mobile devices very easy, and we are current exploring mobile/wireless access to GraniteNights through a local wireless service provider.

References

1. A. Agnar and P. Enric. Case-based reasoning : Foundational issues, methodological variations,and system approaches. *AI Communications*, 7:39–59, 1994.
2. T. Berners-Lee, J. Hendler, and O. Lassila. The semantic web. *Scientific American*, May 2001.
3. S. Brantschen and T. Haas. Agents in a j2ee world. Technical report, Whitestein Technologies AG, 2002.
4. M. Carlsson, G. Ottosson, and B. Carlson. An open-ended finite domain constraint solver. In *Proc. Programming Languages: Implementations, Logics, and Programs*, 1997.
5. M. Champion, C. Ferris, E. Newcomer, and D. Orchard. Web services architecture. W3c working draft, World Wide Web Consortium, 2002.
6. Dick Cowan, Martin Griss, and Bernard Burg. Bluejade - a service for managing software agents. Technical report, Hewlett-Packard Labs, 2001.
7. J. Dale and L. Ceccaroni. Pizza and a movie: A case study in advanced web-services, 2002.
8. P. Edwards, G. A. Grimnes, and A. Preece. An empirical investigation of learning from the semantic web. In *ECML/PKDD, Semantic Web Mining Workshop*, 2002.

---

[14] http://www.csd.abdn.ac.uk/research/iexchange/

9. P. Gray, K. Hui, and A. Preece. An expressive constraint language for semantic web applications. In *E-Business and the Intelligent Web: Papers from the IJCAI-01 Workshop*, pages 46–53. AAAI Press, 2001.
10. J. Hendler and D. L. McGuinness. The darpa agent markup language. *IEEE Internet Computing*, 2000.
11. Ora Lassila and Ralph R. Swick. Resource description framework (rdf) model and syntax specification. W3c recommendation, World Wide Web Consortium, 1999.
12. D. L. McGuinness and F. van Harmelen. Web ontology language (owl): Overview. W3c working draft, World Wide Web Consortium, 2003.
13. S. Middleton, H. Alani, N. Shadbolt, and D. De Roure. Exploiting synergy between ontologies and recommender systems. In *11th International WWW Conference*, 2002.
14. L. Miller, A. Seaborne, and A. Reggiori. Three implementations of squishql, a simple rdf query language. Technical report, Hewlett-Packard Labs, 2002.
15. Tom M. Mitchell, Rich Caruana, Dayne Freitag, John McDermott, and David Zabowski. Experience with a learning personal assistant. *Communications of the ACM*, 37(7):80–91, 1994.
16. A. Moreno and D. Isem. Offering agent-based medical services within the agentc-ities project. In *Proceedings of Agents Applied in Health Care at 15th European Conference on Artificial Intelligence*, 2002.
17. T. R. Payne, R. Singh, and K. Sycara. Browsing schedules - an agent-based ap-proach to navigating the semantic web. In *Proceedings of The First International Semantic Web Conference (ISWC)*, 2002.
18. F. van Harmelen and A. Bundy. Explanation based generalisation = partial eval-uation. *AI*, 36:401–412, 1988.
19. M. P. Wellman and P. R. Wurman. A trading agent competition for the research community. In *IJCAI Workshop on Agent-Mediated Electronic Commerce*, 1999.

Send Fredo off to Do This, Send Fredo off to Do That*

Luís Botelho, Hugo Mendes, Pedro Figueiredo, and Rui Marinheiro

ADETTI/ISCTE Av. das Forças Armadas, Edifício ISCTE, 1600-082 Lisboa, Portugal
{Luis.Botelho, Hugo.Mendes, Pedro.Figueiredo,
Rui.Marinheiro}@iscte.pt; http://we-b-mind.org/

Abstract. Fredo is a generic domain-independent broker that creates value-added information taking into account the preferences specified by its clients. Fredo uses ontology services and yellow pages services to discover a set of agents that can provide information relevant to its clients' requests. Fredo uses an intelligent heuristic strategy based on a fuzzy evaluation mechanism to plan the queries it uses to gather relevant information for its clients' needs. In order to handle possible information overload, we have designed a special purpose interaction protocol, the paged information-request protocol, which is used to govern the interaction between Fredo and information providers. Fredo also uses a fuzzy inference engine to evaluate the gathered information with respect to the preferences specified by its clients. Fredo has been developed by and used in the Agentcities project. Fredo uses the FIPA ACL inter agent communication language with FIPA SL contents. It was implemented in JAVA and Prolog and runs on FIPA++, a FIPA compliant agent platform.

1 Introduction

In open agent systems such as that of the Agentcities project [17] it is important to have agents capable of dynamically creating value-added information for the user or for other agents. Further more, the process by which information is sought, integrated, and evaluated should be as independent as possible of the particular application domain so that it can be used in different domains, relying on different ontologies.

Fredo is a broker agent capable of searching information from various sources, pertaining diverse topics, integrating it in coherent ways and evaluating it according to specified preferences. Fredo uses absolutely general algorithms in the sense that they are totally independent of the application domain.

Fredo was built using some original proposals and ideas from several other authors and research groups. The main contributions to the state of the art of engineered software agents are the integration of several ideas put forth by other researchers in a

---

* The research described in this paper is partly supported by the EC project Agentcities.RTD, reference IST-2000-28385 and partly by UNIDE/ISCTE. The opinions expressed in this paper are those of the authors and are not necessarily those of the Agentcities.RTD partners. The authors are also indebted to all other members of the Agentcities ADETTI team.

M. Klusch et al. (Eds.): CIA 2003, LNAI 2782, pp. 152–159, 2003.

single implemented agent working in an open environment; the original proposal regarding the representation of preferences; the paged information-request protocol, a new interaction protocol used to handle possible information overload; and deploying all the above using the FIPA standardization framework (FIPA++ [8], a FIPA compliant agent platform; FIPA ACL agent communication language [11]; and FIPA SL content language [12][1]). Fredo also relies on the existence of FIPA compliant directory and ontology agents (DF [10] and OA [9]).

Fredo may be used in several scenarios, such as the one represented in Fig. 1. Fredo receives information requests from its clients. In general, it is impossible to satisfy the client's request consulting only a single information provider. The relevant agents are discovered by contacting Directory Facilitaror agents and Ontology agents, using the information contained in received requests.

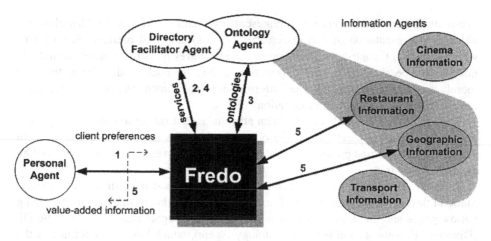

Fig. 1. Scenarios where Fredo may be used.

Section 2 describes Fredo and analyses the obtained results. Section 3 compares our approach with related work. Finally, section 4 presents conclusions and future work.

2   Fredo: An Information Broker Agent

In order to satisfy clients' requests, Fredo discovers information providers relevant for the received requests (Task 1 in Fig. 2); it plans queries to send to the discovered providers using a fuzzy heuristic rule (Task 2 in Fig. 2); and it integrates the information received from the providers, evaluates it using a fuzzy inference mechanism and sends it to its clients (Task 3 in Fig. 2). All these steps of Fredo's operation are absolutely general in the sense that Fredo does not hold any domain dependent information and it does not use any domain dependent algorithm.

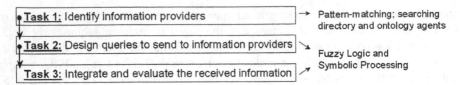

Fig. 2. Fredo's major tasks and used technology

Although Fredo uses fuzzy reasoning, it does not assume its clients or its providers to use fuzzy logic.

2.1 Technical Overview

We defined the class Preference to represent information preferences. This class enables the representation of soft preferences (**values**) and hard preferences (**cut-off**), which constrain the attributes specified in the **attributes** property. Soft constraints do not need to be satisfied by the information to be sent back to the client; they are merely used to evaluate the returned information. Hard constraints, on the other hand, must fulfilled by the returned information.

The Preferences class also contains an attribute called **target** to hold the target object of the specified preferences. The object hold by this attribute is evaluated with respect to the specified preferences. Table 1 shows a 0.7 weight preference for Italian cheap restaurants.

When Fredo receives a query with a set of preferences it must discover the information relevant for the preferences. For that purpose, Fredo consults agents providing yellow pages and ontology information services. In our application, these are the DF (Directory Facilitator) and the OA (Ontology Agent), which have been defined in the FIPA specifications.

Fredo asks the OA for ontologies containing the concepts mentioned in the received query. Then, Fredo asks the DF agent for information agents using the identified ontologies. Finally, Fredo sends queries to the identified information agents asking them for the relevant information for the received information request.

Table 1. Preference for cheap Italian restaurants.

```
(Preference
    :target <Restaurant> // specific object
    :targetClass Restaurant
    :attributes (sequence maxPrice foodType)
    :values (any   (sequence ?price ?type)
                   (and  (= ?type Italian)
                                  (<= ?price 10)))
    :cut-off (sequence
             (AttributeCutOff :similarity 0.8)
             (AttributeCutOff))
    :weight 0.7)
```

In order to discover information providers for the preference in Table 1, Fredo asks the OA for an ontology containing the class *Restaurant* with attributes *maxPrice* and *foodType*, among others. Assuming the OA returns the ontology identifier "Agentcities-Reastaurant-Ontology", Fredo asks the DF for information agents using that ontology.

After the DF sends Fredo the identifications of the necessary information providers, Fredo asks them for the relevant information. Since the soft constraints are not mandatory, the information to be returned by Fredo may not fulfill them. This means Fredo cannot use the softly constrained attributes to limit the amount of information that will be returned by each information provider, which may lead to the exchange to huge messages (e.g., messages containing 400 restaurants).

In order to avoid information overload, Fredo uses the hard constraints. Since hard constraints must be fulfilled by the returned information, Fredo uses them to limit the amount of information he asks the information providers. However, hard constraints are not mandatory therefore Fredo uses a fuzzy heuristic rule to create hard constraints whenever they are not specified in the received preferences.

The heuristic rule is based on the specified preference weight, which is mandatory. When the preference is very important (high weight), it means Fredo's client is willing to receive only information that is not too bad with respect to the preference. If the preference is not important (low weight), it means Fredo's client would not mind receiving information that is not highly rated with respect to the preference. Using this heuristic, Fredo computes a symbolic condition that constrains the asked information to those records that are as good as ¾ of the value of the preference weight. The quality of the record is evaluated using a fuzzy mechanism.

Even so, the returned information may be too much therefore Fredo uses a special purpose interaction protocol, called the paged-information-request protocol, that was created to ask information one page at a time (Fig. 3). Using this protocol, the agent my find answer for its problem in the first page and decided to cancel the interaction.

When the information asked from information providers is received, Fredo integrates and evaluates it and send it to its client. The evaluation of the received information with respect to the specified preferences is made by a fuzzy inference mechanism. Each preference is converted into a fuzzy proposition. The final evaluation is the average of the fuzzy values of each of the fuzzy propositions weighted by the preference weight.

2.2 Analysis of the Results

Fredo has been implemented and tested in several circumstances, including in the Agentcities audit in Barcelona in which it was used with agents (requesters, providers, directory and ontology agents) designed and developed by different teams. In one experiment Fredo integrates information from two main ontologies: restaurant ontology, and transportation ontology, which share the geographic information ontology. Different agents serve the information described in these ontologies, which means that Fredo is capable of interacting with different information providers.

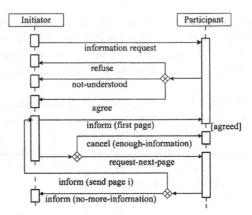

Fig. 3. Paged Information-Request Protocol.

With our approach, preferences representation is very expressive, allowing Fredo to integrate information from several ontologies provided by different agents, and supports a general domain-independent algorithm in all of its processing stages.

The same message may specify several preferences at the same time, about different classes and ontologies. Each preference may specify any logical combination of soft and hard constraints. The expressive power of the approach results not only of the proposed preferences representation but also of the flexibility of the used content language (FIPA SL [12]).

The process used by Fredo for discovering the relevant information providers relies upon the structure of the received information request whose content is completely expressed in FIPA SL. But it is possible only because Fredo can dynamically consult directory services and ontology services provided by FIPA agent platforms.

The use of cut-off values (whether explicitly specified within the received preferences or heuristically computed by the Fredo) greatly reduces the amount of information that is asked to information providers.

The use of the paged information-request protocol allows the agent to request the provider to stop sending information as soon as it becomes satisfied. This may happen because some *"satisficing"* criterion specified in the message is met or because the client does not want to receive more information. In some experiments, using our 600-restaurant database and a page length of 10 restaurants, the satisficing criterion is met by information contained in the first or in the second page sent by the provider. This means Fredo processes only 20 instead of 550 restaurants.

The choice of evaluating all received data with respect to the preferences, instead of considering only the data that totally satisfies all the preferences at once has shown appropriate in realistic applications. This is the case because, most of the times, it is impossible to find data that satisfies all preferences and also because the client prefers to receive imperfect solutions instead of no solutions at all.

3   Related Work

Brokers are intermediates who receive client requests, distribute the load to process those requests among several registered service providers and, in the end, return the obtained results. The design of these brokers may be tailored to a specific domain, like electronic commerce [2], be less domain dependent as in [3] and [14], where it is required a priory knowledge of the domain, or be domain independent as it is the case with [15] and Fredo.

The application scenario used in [14] is quite similar to Fredo's. However, their solution is quite rigid, since brokers have their own ontology with schema mappings to information providers' ontologies maintained locally. From those mappings it is then easy to distribute requests, but conversely we are constrained to the existence of those mappings. Fredo searching for providers is dynamic, since it does not hold domain ontology or mapping, it searches directory and ontology agents.

The search for providers may be supported by intermediates, like in [3], where a Jini-based directory and ontology service is used. Fredo works in a similar way, in the sense that it doesn't hold any registration regarding providers' domain information. Fredo has to use ontology agents and directory facilitator agents (yellow pages agents) to dynamically find providers, according to their ontologies and service types.

In order to distribute a request, one usually has to break it down and then search for the right information providers that satisfy the partial requests. This task can be done using previous acquired domain knowledge [3], or using existent mappings [14]. But Fredo's requests are decomposed using a domain independent process, relying on an analysis of specified preferences; domain information is just acquired from ontology agents, after receiving the request.

Domain knowledge may also be required to merge information from several providers [3]. Fredo does not have that limitation: value-added information is obtained using a generic process.

A more generic approach than [3] and [14] is used in [15] where domain knowledge about services is acquired only after receiving and analyzing requests. Those requests use hard-constraints, facilitating the finding and querying of providers. Fredo also uses preferences received in requests to better plan and distribute requests among providers, without previous domain knowledge. However, in [15], a simplistic approach is taken for preferences, by basically adding a new predicate. No weighted or fuzzy evaluation is used, as it is done in Fredo.

None of previously described approaches have used weights on preferences. However, soft-constraints considering weights in user queries, have been in use in several domains, such as information searching [5][7]. In [7] absolute weights, concerning individual terms, and relative weights, concerning a relation between terms, may be used. Fredo allows for both approaches, by permitting queries to cater for constraints on individual attributes, and constraints among attributes.

Soft-constraint fuzzy preferences are also used in several domains, like solving decision-making problems [4] [13], where it is necessary to satisfy multiple user preferences. Fuzzy searching and classification of information has also been in use in multimedia systems for some time [5] [6]. Fredo also uses a fuzzy approach to overcome the problem of possibly over restricted requests, poorly covered domains in providers or intrinsic vague definition of information in providers. Nevertheless, Fredo does not require that providers are aware of its fuzzy processing mechanism, where all queries sent by Fredo are tailored with hard constrains to retrieve the necessary results and to perform the fuzzy evaluation and merging the obtained results.

In [5], as in Fredo, fuzzy evaluation is associated with weighted preferences. These weights, assign different relevance to the required fuzzy conditions, in order to better adapt to user needs. But Fredo does more, by also considering hard-constraints (i.e., cut-offs) in client queries. This allows, at once, a better specification of user needs, and a better performance of the broker, since it is possible to considerably reduce exchanged information with providers, making the overall solution more scalable.

One can say that up to now no agent broker has considered all the techniques used by Fredo in one solution.

4   Conclusions and Future Work

We have proposed a flexible and expressive method for representing preferences that allows the specification of preferences about several attributes of an object. The representation provides for the specification of soft and hard constraints about individual attributes but also about relations among them.

The identification of the necessary information providers is an absolutely dynamic generic process. There is nothing that depends on a specific domain. Furthermore, the received set of preferences can refer to several ontologies possibly provided by several agents. Therefore, Fredo is a general agent (i.e., domain independent) that provides a value-added information service since it may integrate information services using several ontologies provided by different information providers.

We have also proposed a generic mechanism that is used to create the queries to send information providers in order to constrain the amount of returned information without discarding potentially interesting records. In addition, we have also designed an interaction protocol to be used when there is the risk that the answer to an information request may contain an exaggerated number of records.

Finally, we have designed a fuzzy mechanism that is used to evaluate gathered information from information providers with respect to the weighted preferences of the clients. This mechanism captures the fuzziness of human-like evaluation processes. Although Fredo uses a fuzzy evaluation mechanism, it does not assume other agents to also have fuzzy reasoning capabilities.

This set of proposals described in this paper makes up a general information brokering service that may be used in any domain without modification or recompilation.

References

1. Botelho, L.M.; Antunes, N.; Ebrahim, M.; and Ramos, P. 2002. "Greeks and Trojans Together". In Proc. of the Workshop "Ontologies in Agent Systems" of the AAMAS2002 Conference

2. Caughey, S.; Ingham, D.; and Watson P. 1998 "Metabroker: A Generic Broker for Electronic Commerce", Computer Networks and ISDN Systems, vol. 30, no. 1–7, pp. 619–620

3. Chakraborty, D.; Perich, F.; Joshi, A.; Finin, T.; and Yesha, Y. 2002. "Middleware for Mobile Information Access", 5th Int. Workshop on "Mobility in Databases and Distributed Systems", in conjunction with DEXA

4. Chiclana, F.; Herrera, F.; and Herrera-Viedma, E. 1998. "Integrating three representation models in fuzzy multiple propose decision making based on fuzzy preference relations", Fuzzy Sets and Systems, 97, 33–48

5. Ciaccia, P.; Montesi, D.; Penzo, W.; and Trombetta, A. 2000. "Imprecision and User Preferences in Multimedia Queries: A Generic Algebraic Approach", In Proc. of the 1st Int. Symposium on Foundations of Information and Knowledge Systems (FoIKS 2000)

6. Fagin, R. 1998. "Fuzzy Queries in Multimedia Database Systems", In Proc. of the 17th ACM SIGACT-SIGMOD-SIGART Symposium on Principles of Database Systems

7. Fagin, R.; and Maarek, Y.S. 2000. "Allowing users to weight search terms", Proc. Recherche d'Informations Assistee par Ordinateur RIAO '2000, pp. 682–700

8. FIPA++ Webpage, http://fipapp.page.vu

9. Foundation for Intelligent Physical Agents. 2001. FIPA Ontology Service Specification. Document 00086. http://www.fipa.org/specs/fipa00086/XC00086D.html

10. Foundation for Intelligent Physical Agents. 2002. FIPA Agent Management Specification. http://www.fipa.org/specs/fipa00023/SC00023J.html

11. Foundation for Intelligent Physical Agents. 2002. FIPA Communicative Act Library Specification, Document SC00037J. http://www.fipa.org/specs/fipa00037/SC00037J.html

12. Foundation for Intelligent Physical Agents. 2002. FIPA SL Content Language Specification. Document SC00008I. http://www.fipa.org/specs/fipa00008/SC00008I.html

13. Fuller, R.; and Carlsson, C. 1996. "Fuzzy multiple criteria decision making: Recent developments", Fuzzy Sets and Systems, 78, 139–15

14. Martin, D.; Oohama, H.; Moran, D.; and Cheyer, A. 1997. "Information brokering in an agent architecture". In Proc. of the 2nd Int. Conf. on the Practical Application of Intelligent Agents and Multi-Agent Technology

15. Mcllraith, S.A.; Son, T.C.; and Zeng, H. 2001. "Semantic Web Services", IEEE Intelligent Systems. Special Issue on the Semantic Web. 16(2): 46–53

16. Mota, L.; Botelho, L.M.; Mendes, H.; and Lopes, A. 2003. "O3F: An Object-Oriented Ontolgy Framework". Proc. 2nd Int. Joint Conf. on Autonomous Agents and MultiAgent Systems.

17. Willmott, S.; Dale, J.; Burg, B.; Charlton, P; and O'Brien, P. 2001. "Agentcities: a worldwide open agent network". Agentlink News, 8:13–15

Database Integration Using Mobile Agents

Philip S. Medcraft, Ulrich Schiel, and Cláudio S. Baptista

Departamento de Sistemas e Computação, Universidade Federal de Campina Grande
Av. Aprígio Veloso, 882, Campina Grande, PB Brazil
{philip, ulrich, baptista}@dsc.ufcg.edu.br

Abstract. The classic problem of information integration has been addressed for a long time. The Semantic Web project is aiming to define an infrastructure that enables machine understanding on the Web. This is a vision that tackles the problem of semantic heterogeneity by using ontologies for information sharing. Although designed to be used on the entire Web, the ideas behind the Semantic Web can be used in a federated database environment, in which the data sources are previously known and there is a global schema, described in an ontology, which enables data integration. Agents have an important role in this infrastructure. Based on ontologies, software agents will be capable of finding the correct data on the adequate sites of the federation, and achieve the integration process as soon as possible. In this paper we present a solution, known as DIA (Data Integration using Agents), for semantic integration of federated databases using mobile agents and ontologies. Also, we present an itinerary classification which aims to improve the data integration process.

1 Introduction

Information integration has been addressed for a long time. One of the main goals of an integrated system is to provide query location independence. Three database architectures have been proposed to solve the data integration problem: Federated databases, which enforces the virtual approach; data warehousing, which is based on the materialized approach; and mediators, which uses the virtual approach [1].

Recently, the Semantic Web vision is aiming to define an infrastructure that enables machine understanding of data on the Web. This is a vision that tackles the problem of semantic heterogeneity by using ontologies for information sharing [2]. Although designed to be used on the entire Web, the ideas behind the Semantic Web can be used in a federated database environment, in which data sources are previously known and there is a global schema, described using an ontology, enabling data integration.

The three database architectures previously mentioned undertake a considerable amount of data flow and the unnecessary visiting of data sources. Mobile agents represent an excellent option to solve these problems. Using an ontology, agents may do the data integration process.

In this paper we present a new solution, known as DIA (Data Integration using Agents), for semantic integration of a federated database using mobile agents and ontologies. The availability of an explicit ontology for the data sources is at the core of the integration process, as it represents the global schema of the federated database.

M. Klusch et al. (Eds.): CIA 2003, LNAI 2782, pp. 160–167, 2003.

Specifically we aim to design a data integration architecture using mobile agents; to develop a strategy in which agents can reduce the number of data sources to be visited, resulting in an optimized itinerary; to execute data integration in the data sources; and to produce agents that visit a minimum of data sources in order to obtain the desired information.

The rest of the paper is outlined as follows. Section 2 describes the DIA architecture. Section 3 focuses on design and implementation issues. Section 4 discusses related work and presents our main contributions. Finally, section 5 concludes the paper and discusses further work to be undertaken.

2   The DIA Architecture

Traditional information retrieval over the Internet employs the client-server architecture. The exchange of direct communication between the information request site and the information sources by mobile agents can reduce the overhead of the communication link, used to transmit the client requests and the server replies, by moving the know-how about the retrieval close to where the information resides.

The support for disconnected operations and the efficient execution of global queries are some of the many advantages in using mobile agents for this kind of application. The former is intrinsic to mobile agents and the latter can be greatly improved by having an ontology defining the global concepts and how they interconnect semantically with the schema in the distributed database.

The objective of our architecture is to provide a uniform interface to heterogeneous, pre-existing Relational Database Systems, in a way that users can formulate queries (global queries) that are transported between these different databases by a mobile agent to produce a single consolidated response. For this purpose, it is necessary to identify the objects in the databases that represent equivalent or similar concepts, that is, are semantically related. Heterogeneities among databases appear as semantic conflicts. They are detected and solved at the moment a new database enters the federation. Once identified the equivalent or similar concepts in the new database, they are defined as global concepts in the existing ontology.

There are several design patterns for agent-based applications. These patterns are usually divided into three classes: *traveling*, *task*, and *interaction* patterns [3]. In our architecture we propose the use of a *traveling* pattern and a *task* pattern only, but *interaction* patterns are also perfectly applicable in our context. Moreover, we propose the use of an extended *Itinerary* traveling pattern. A basic itinerary pattern maintains a list of destinations and always knows where to go next. It also defines special cases such as what to do if a destination is temporally unavailable. In the extended version the itinerary can be changed dynamically, i.e., the mobile agent is able to decide where to go depending on the result of its local task.

To enable a host to be part of the mobile agent destination list, every destination needs to have an agency running a local stationary agent, which cooperates with the mobile agent in the local query adaptation process.

The user triggers the process by preparing a global query, based on terms from an ontology. When the user submits the query, the application notifies a stationary agent running inside an agency. This stationary agent (master agent) creates a mobile agent (slave agent) for the migration through the databases. Applying the Itinerary pattern explained previously, before its creation, a list of destinations is set for the new mobile agent. With the query in hand and knowing its itinerary, the migration process starts.

As the mobile agent reaches a destination, it contacts the local stationary agent, passing it the global query. This agent knows the ontology on which the global query terms are based on, and also knows the local database schema. Therefore, with a local matching mechanism, it is able to convert the global query to a corresponding local one. The database query is performed and the result set presented to the visiting mobile agent in XML syntax.

In case the mobile agent is not at the first destination, before moving to the next node, the mobile agent performs an integration of the local result with the result collected previously. This reduces the size of the carried XML, and means that when the mobile agent returns to its origin, no extra result integration or analysis will be performed.

When the mobile agent completes its itinerary, it migrates back to its origin, returns the final result to its master agent and removes itself. The master agent presents the collected data to the user.

The interface was developed for web browsers. A tree is automatically built from the DAML+OIL ontology classes. Moreover, the fields for the input query are also built according to the ontology properties for each class. Figure 1 shows an example of the interface. The tree on the left side presents three classes: *Person*, *Employee* and *Customer*. The classes *Employee* and *Customer* are both subclasses of Person. In the example, the user has selected the class *Customer*. Therefore, its properties are shown on the right side of the interface, organized in an HTML form for the input query definition. The query defined in figure 1 means that we want the sum of all credits obtained by a specific customer.

The following operations can be used: *undefined*, which maintains the existing value; sum, which adds the value of column to the existing value; min, which takes the minimum of the two; max which takes the maximum of the two; and avg, which takes the average of the two.

Since we want to obtain the best itinerary for a given global query, several points are considered in order to avoid the visit of unnecessary hosts. First we distinguish between static and dynamic itineraries.

A static itinerary is an itinerary that can be established in advance by the stationary master agent. Depending on information available about the local databases, the master agent analyses the global query and selects those local databases that must be visited to process the query. In the simplest case, the itinerary is "visit all nodes".

In a dynamic itinerary, the mobile agent can decide, depending on the partial result it gets, if the query is already answered and it can return, or not. This dynamic capability depends on a previous classification of the global query. For instance, queries as "What is Philip's birthday?" or "Are Philip's credits more than 700?" allow a dynamic itinerary, whereas "Give me Philip's total credits" needs always a static itinerary. Therefore, the constructions of the itinerary (full or selected) and its classification (static or dynamic) is done by the master agent analyzing the SQL structure of the global query together with the local schemas.

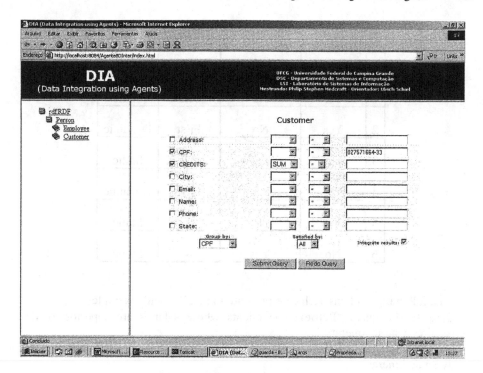

Fig. 1. Dia interface

When we analyze the types of queries that can be made to a database, we discover that they can divided into two categories: queries for which the agent always has to search all the local databases of the itinerary (static itinerary); and queries that may be answered in the middle of the mobile agent migration through the databases, and the agent can return earlier to its origin (dynamic itinerary).

In order to apply this division to improve the integration process, we created a query taxonomy. The classification of the itinerary permits the agent to decide when to return to its origin, no matter if all the targets in the itinerary have not been visited. The following table presents the query taxonomy.

After the user submits the data of the query, the master agent structures this data in a SQL query. Doing so the agent analyses the query structure and classifies it following the taxonomy described in table 1.

When we analyze the types of queries, we notice that the existence or not of conditions and of aggregation operations are determinant for classifying the itinerary as *static* or *dynamic*. For example, the fifth row in table 1 says that every query which has no conditions and no aggregation operation always requires a static itinerary.

We noticed that some queries have the same characteristics regarding the existence or not of conditions and of aggregation operations, however, may require both a static itinerary and a dynamic one. In this case, the master agent analyses the attribute *Satisfied* present in table 1. This characteristic depends strongly on the semantic of the query, and should be determined by the user while preparing the query.

Table 1. Query taxonomy

	Condition	Aggregation	Satisfied	Itinerary
1	Yes	No	All	Static
2	Yes	No	First	Dynamic
3	Yes	Yes	All	Static
4	Yes	Yes	First	Dynamic
5	No	No	--	Static
6	No	Yes	--	Static

The following explains each case presented in table 1 with examples:
- Case 1: The query "Retrieve the clients whose salaries are superior to 1000" requires a static itinerary.
- Case 2: The query "Is there a client whose salary is superior to 1000?" requires a dynamic itinerary.
- Case 3: The query "Give me the sum of the salaries of all clients whose credits are superior to 1000 and where enrolled after 01/01/2002" requires a static itinerary.
- Case 4: The query "Retrieve the sum of the debits of all clients that where enrolled after 01/02/2001, having that the sum of the debits cannot be higher than 10000", requires a dynamic itinerary.
- Case 5: The query "Retrieve the name of the clients" requires a static itinerary.
- Case 6: The query "Count the number of clients" requires a static itinerary.

3   Design and Implementation Issues

The system analysis and design were based upon a methodology for agent-based applications proposed by [4], producing   UML artifacts (Unified Modeling Language). The system was developed using the JAVA and Grasshopper platforms [5]. The former was used to construct the internal classes and interfaces of the system, and the latter was used as the system agent platform. We have also used some design patterns (Iterator, Observer, etc.) to improve the system design quality [6].

The class diagram of the system is shown in figure 2. We emphasize the RelationalWrapper class, which is responsible for the query local adaptation process. This class has three methods: the matchSchema() method translates the query terms to the appropriate terms of the local source; prepareSQL() structures the query before retrieving data from the local database; processXML_SQL() structures the query answer in XML syntax.

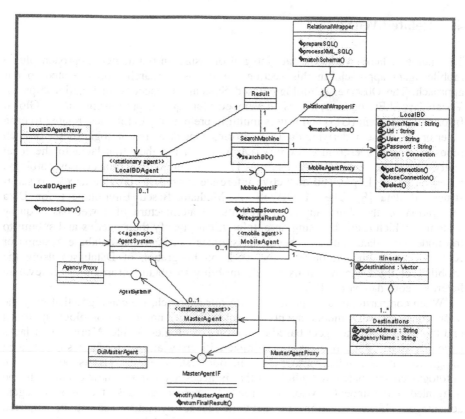

Fig. 2. DIA class diagram

The Grasshopper agent platform permits local communication as well as remote communication between its components (agents, agencies and regions) and external objects. A desired property of mobile agent systems is localization transparency. In other words, the entity that wants to communicate with a mobile agent does not need to worry about its localization. To be able to provide this characteristic the Grasshopper platform uses a communication pattern called Proxy. Proxy consists of an intermediary entity on the communication between a client and a server, being responsible for the connection establishment and for identifying the server localization. The class diagram on figure 2 presents three agent classes: MasterAgent, MobileAgent and LocalBDAgent. As shown in the figure, each class is associated to a correspondent proxy class, which will intermediate the communication to any external objects (agencies, other agents or external objects).

The MasterAgent is a stationary agent and is responsible for listening to the user. When the user submits a new query, this agent sets up the itinerary, creates the MobileAgent (slave agent), and delegates the realization task to it. The MobileAgent then migrates through its Itinerary and as it reaches each destination, it contacts the LocalBDAgent that is responsible for adapting the query locally, for retrieving data from the database, and for returning the local result to the MobileAgent. Then, it integrates the results and continues its itinerary.

4   Related Work

The literature lacks works on data integration using an ontological approach plus a mobile agent approach. In this section we discuss research works related to our approach. The Observer (Ontology Based System Enhanced with Relationships for Vocabulary hEterogeneity) was developed for query processing in a Global Information System (GIS) and it uses multiple pre-existing ontologies, related to each other or not, in the underlying data repositories. One or more ontologies describe each repository using Description Logics (DLs), which are then translated to the local query languages of the data repositories [7]. The Ontobroker project uses ontology, based on Frame Logic, and deductive inference systems to provide access to semi-structured data [8]. The MEDIWeb (A Mediator-Based Environment for Data Integration on the Web) approach presents an architecture of a web-based query system in which users, by using an ontology, can specify their queries and submit to the underlying data sources. These data sources can be either database systems or XML files [9]. Finally, there is the work on Integration of Databases using the Mobility of the Code which uses code mobility to obtain information retrieval in heterogeneous databases [10].

When comparing these approaches with our approach, we can argue that only the latest considers using mobile agents. However, it does not use an ontology approach and therefore lacks the agent-based computing ontologies enable. Moreover, it lacks code portability. DIA realizes an optimized itinerary and performs a sophisticated integration of its results. Furthermore, in our system, every class is portable. An ontology-schema matching table is all that is necessary to add a new database to the integrated environment. Also, the related approaches lack the mobile agent advantages, like: reduction in network load, dynamic adaptation, reduced communication costs, autonomous execution, and network latency overcoming.

5   Conclusion

We have presented a new solution for data integration, which uses a global ontology to inform the user what information is stored in the whole enterprise and helps the system where to get the results for a specific query. The processing of the query is realized by a mobile agent, which gets its job from a global stationary agent and runs the federation in order to request from local stationary agents the information needed. The result sets are joined pair wise and after each local processing the mobile agent decides if it is necessary to continue or he can return to the host. This circular letter strategy seems to be better than other approaches, such as mediator based ones, since it relieves network communication and its sensibility to the real information needs for a particular query, reduces unnecessary data flow. We have also presented an itinerary classification: static or dynamic, the order of the itinerary traversal could be significant. If the more "light" nodes are visited first, the amount of data the mobile agent takes along could be reduced. On the other hand, in a dynamic itinerary, the order could determine an earlier return to the origin agency. This ordering of the itinerary can only be performed if the origin agency has statistical information about the local databases.

References

1. Garcia-Molina, H., Ullman, J. and Widom, J., *Database Systems: The Complete Book*, Prentice Hall, 2002.
2. Berners-Lee, T., *Semantic Web on XML*, In: XML 2000 Conference, 2000.
3. Lange, D. and Oshima, M., Programming and Deploying Java Mobile Agents with Aglets, Addison-Wesley, 1998.
4. Guedes, F., A Model for Developing Agent-Based Applications, World Wide Web, 2001.
5. *Grasshopper Programmer's Guide*, Release 2.2, Germany. Available at: http://www.grasshopper.de
6. Gamma, E., Helm, R., Johnson, R. and Vlissides, J., *Design Patterns: Elements of Reusable Object-Oriented Software*, Addison-Wesley, 1995.
7. Mena, E., Kashyap, K., Sheth, A. and Illarramendi, A., OBSERVER: *An approach for Query Processing in Global Information Systems Based on Interoperation across Preexisting Ontologies*, in Proceedings of the First IFCIS International Conference on Cooperative Information Systems (CoopIS'96), 1996.
8. Erdmann, M. and Studer,R., *Ontologies as Conceptual Models for XML documents*, In: Proceedings of the 12th Workshop on Knowledge Acquisition, Modeling and Management (KAW'99), 1999.
9. Arruda, L., Baptista, C. S., Lima, C. A. *MEDIWeb (A Mediator-Based Environment for Data Integration on the Web*, In: ICEIS'2002, 4th International Conference on Enterprise Information Systems, ICEIS Press, 2002.
10. Claro, D. and Sobral, J., Integration of Databases using the Mobility of the Code, World Wide Web, 2001.

Adaptive Web Search Based on a Colony of Cooperative Distributed Agents

Fabio Gasparetti and Alessandro Micarelli

Dipartimento di Informatica e Automazione
Università degli Studi "Roma Tre"
Via della Vasca Navale, 79 I – 00146 Roma, Italy
{gaspare,micarel}@dia.uniroma3.it

Abstract. This work introduces an adaptive Web search system, based on a reactive agent architecture, which drew inspiration from the Ant System computational paradigm. This system aims at searching reactively and autonomously information about a particular topic, in huge hypertextual collections, such as the Web. The adaptivity allows it to be robust to environmental alterations and to user information need changes. Besides showing significant results on standard collections, this work widens further the range of intelligent search topic, towards theories and architectures of agent and multiagent systems.

1 Introduction

The Web search of interesting information is a hard target, because it presents peculiar features, in fact the Web is huge, complex and highly dynamic. Furthermore, due to mirroring and aliasing, the resources can occur many times. Even worse, the Web contains vast and unknown quantities of dark matter [2] due to Web page access restrictions, to the lack of connectivity in the link graph [6] and to the existence of automatic Web page generators.

The Information Retrieval (IR) research community has been attempting for long time to improve the algorithms used in large file collections. Most of these algorithms are based on the natural language statistical processing [28] of the user queries, of the document contents or other features that can be evidenced in one or more texts.

In the last years, the Internet and hypertextual document spreading led to innovative search techniques, which exploit the presence of the link structure between documents to try to unearth new information, and to learn to navigate the information space [4,12].

New theories, architectures and agent applications have also been taken into consideration to face this problem. The information agent systems enjoy a relevant attention, because they achieve benefits in many domains thanks to their peculiar properties, as: the autonomy, the reactivity, the proactiveness and the social ability [26]. The autonomy and the reactivity, in particular, allow the systems to survive in dynamic, heterogeneous and hardly-accessible environments, as in case of Internet.

M. Klusch et al. (Eds.): CIA 2003, LNAI 2782, pp. 168–183, 2003.

The system presented in this work falls under the last category. It is based on a reactive agent architecture, which draw inspiration from the Ant System computational paradigm [11]. From a representation of the user information needs, its purpose is to search information in domains represented by vast collections of hypertextual resources (e.g. HTML pages or XML documents) such as the Web.

The system is composed of agents which cooperate to adapt to the environment and to the user information needs, to reduce the response time due to the exploration, and to increase the quality of retrieved information. Briefly, the agents learn to choose from several information sources, assisting users in coping with information overload.

This adaptivity makes the system robust to its environment, to keep minor changes in the world from leading the system's behaviour to a total collapse. Furthermore, it is able to adapt itself to the possible slow changes of the user information needs, without starting new instances.

The next section provides a brief state of the art about the information discovery and the intelligent crawling on the Web. Then, the proposed adaptive system will be explained, beginning from the Ant System computation paradigm description up to the algorithm and related architecture discussions. The last section focuses on the testing and on the evaluation of a system implementation in the Web domain where the standard test collection results are presented and discussed.

2 Related Work

Many researches consider multiagent systems as a mean to decrease the human-computer interaction necessary to manage the vast quantity of online information, thanks to their ability to make automatic decisions on behalf of the user [18,13,17].

A great number of works about intelligent and focused crawling, i.e. the crawl focused to a specific topic, have been accomplished, with approaches that can often appear very dissimilar one another (see for example [9,7,28,1]). Even if these works are considered very important for those who want to have the greatest amount of available information up to date and personalized [15], currently a few of them regard agent systems and architectures.

InfoSpiders [20] is without doubt one of the most remarkable system. It is an evolving information agent ecosystem, where every population agent focuses on a small set of Web page features. During the exploration, the agent population adapts itself to the best representative features, by means of machine learning techniques, such as genetic algorithms. In other words, the agents die and reproduce in order to bias optimally the search.

Chen et al. [8] proposed a personal spider agent based on the best first search and on genetic algorithm techniques, whose purpose is to look for similar pages, compared to the page set, suggested by the user. As for the best first search algorithm, the first pages to be analysed are those similar to the start page set.

For the genetic algorithm, the crossover operator selects pages connected to multiple initial set ones, and the mutation operator gathers new references from the Yahoo's categories chosen by the user, to avoid trapping in local minimum. The gained pages, with the highest fitness, are stochastically selected and explored. The similarity measure and the fitness function favour the pages similar in links and in keywords to the ones in the initial set.

Other researches has been focused on the interaction between autonomous agents and users, and on the personal assistant concept, that is software executing tasks like finding, retrieving and organizing information on behalf of the user (see for example [16,17]), without discovering important algorithms able to explore and find autonomously interesting information.

3   The Adaptive Web Search System

The developed multiagent system derives from a reactive architecture that satisfies the fundamental properties, specified by intelligent agent theories, such as the autonomy, the reactivity and the social ability. It is not composed of a few agents with distinct and clearly defined functions, but rather by a large number of agents trying collectively to satisfy user requests. Practically, each agent moves online from document to document, making autonomous decisions about links to follow.

The system ability to reach its objective is not realized by explicit representations and abstract reasonings as symbolic AI proposes. It can be rather considered the results from the indirect cooperation among agents, mediated by the environments. This architecture has the quality to provide quick response to a complex and dynamic environment as the Web.

Before describing its relevant features in detail, the computational paradigm will be observed.

3.1   The Ant System Computation Paradigm

The system architecture, taken into consideration, is inspired by the Ant System computational paradigm [11,3]. This paradigm is based on a combinatorial optimization algorithm, derived from models of social insect collective behaviour. Its efficacy has been pointed out in several scopes, for instance: in telecommunications, for the load balancing in networks routing [24,10], or in robotics, to design cooperative transport algorithms [14]; characterized by difficulties that are unlikely to be well solvable, i.e. solvable by an amount of computational effort, which is bounded by a polynomial function of the size of the problem. In these cases, it is not possible to achieve the optimality, because the search for an optimum requires prohibitive amount of computation time (e.g. see optimal solution for Travelling Salesman Problem). One is forced to use approximation algorithms or heuristics which do not ensure that the solution found by the algorithm is optimal, but for which polynomial bounds on the computation time can be given.

The ant cooperative food retrieval is the social insect behaviour model. It is created by biologists and ethologists to understand how blind animals can find the shortest ways, from the ant nest to the feeding sources and back. This phenomenon can be explained because ants are able to release some pheromone on the ground to mark the path by a trail of this substance. Such a substance allows the ants, encountering a previously laid trail, to follow it, thus reinforcing the trail with its own pheromone. By intuition, the first ants returning to their nest from the food sources are those which have taken the shortest path, and they have done that twice (from the nest to the source and back), and for this reason they release twice the pheromone on the path. The following ants, leaving from the nest, are attracted by the chemical substances. Therefore, if they have to choose among different paths, they will prefer the ones were frequently covered by preceding ants, that is, those with high trail level. That is why they will direct themselves towards the shortest branch, which is the first to be marked.

Sometimes, it can occur that the shortest path is located only after having discovered a longer one. In this case, the first ants to leave the nest will follow the wrong way releasing new pheromone on the path, attracting in its turn other ants. To avoid this drawback, the pheromone decay must be taken into consideration. It simulates the evaporation of the substance released by the ants. In this way, it is more difficult to maintain stable pheromone trails on longer paths and, consequently, it is possible to avoid convergences towards not optimal solutions. Furthermore, the evaporation can also prevent the oscillatory and chaotic behaviour, where agents continuously move among resources without rationality.

Many adaptations have been accomplished to exploit the Ant System potentials in the hypertextual information search domain. These differences will be mentioned in detail later.

3.2   Description of the System

This work begins from the user behaviour analysis while they are looking for information in hypertextual environments. Starting from a little resource set, for instance: bookmarks, first results of a search engine or references in some categories of directory services (e.g. Yahoo!); the user selects interactively links which, in his opinion, have the potentiality to reach new interesting resources.

The link choice derives from different considerations; one of the most significant is the current context in which the user is [22] (it is not the same context meaning of word sense disambiguation or machine translation problems [19]). Often, a link represents the author's intention to connect the page in which it is located to another one concerning the same topic (phenomenon frequently called *linkage locality*). If a surfer is looking for resources on specific topic, and if the current page is related to the same one, he will probably look at the linked pages because they are seriously considered concerning the topic at issue. Nevertheless, a typical similarity measure analysis between the page's content and the query is not enough to achieve satisfactory results. This consideration is based on the phenomenon which frequently occurs: to reach the current page, Web page authors suppose that surfers have followed a special path and, consequently, visited and read certain pages too.

For instance, if a surfer needs to find a particular professor, he will probably look at his university homepage, and then his faculty, his department and people working for it. During the route, the surfer implicitly learns a particular context, based on the visited Web page content. Supposing this behaviour, the Web page author does not have to insert a complete description of the page. In the mentioned example, it can occur that, in the professor's homepage, detailed information about his university, his faculty or his research group is omitted. If the user based his search on this information, he would run the risk of not finding the homepage.

The choice of the route to follow, that is the link to visit, should not be founded only on the similarity between the current page content and the query, but also on the affinities of the visited pages that led to the one. In this way, it is possible to consider the content of these pages, too. If these affinities have a significant importance, even if the mentioned page is not so interesting, the current context, built from the visited pages, is related to the query, consequently, a certain chance to be visited is attributed to the link in the pages. These observations have been taken into consideration by the experimented agent architecture, and represent a peculiar element compared to the others suggested.

The architecture is composed of reactive agents living in a hypertextual environment, where it is possible to associate a similarity measure with the user query, to each resource. The agents do not have a representation of the world in the traditional sense (e.g. by means of: first-order predicate logic, frames, etc.), and their control is completely decentralized. Briefly, the system does not correspond to the traditional notion of intelligent central system, which operates as a symbolic information processor (see similarities with the Brooks's Intelligent system [5]).

Each agent corresponds to a virtual ant which has the ability to move from a hypertextual resource to another one, when a link joining the first to the second is present. The available information for the agent is: the matching result between the user query and the current resource, and the pheromone intensity values on paths corresponding to the outgoing links. Pheromone trails represent the mean that allows an ant to communicate the exploration results among the other ones. They are exploited to make better local decisions with limited local knowledge both on environment and group behaviour.

The system execution is divided into cycles; in each of them, the ants make a sequence of moves from a resource to another. The maximum number of movements per cycle depends proportionally on the value of the latter. At the end of a cycle, each ant updates the trail values of the followed path as a function of the retrieved resource scores.

So, increasing the cycles, the number of the movements raises, and, consequently, the visited resource set. In the first cycles, the trail values are not so meaningful due to the limited number of the visited resources, so the exploration is basically characterized by a random behaviour. After that, the paths that permit to find interesting resources will be privileged with a major intensity of released pheromone, therefore, a great number of ants will have the chance to follow them. As long as the paths bring new interesting resources, the respective trails will be reinforced and the ants will be more and more attracted. Briefly, the process is characterized by a positive feedback loop where, in every cycle, the probability that an ant follows a particular path depends on the number of the ones which followed it in the previous cycles.

It is possible to describe generically each ant-agent with these *task accomplishing behaviours*:

1. if I do not have any available information I move randomly;
2. if an ant trail exists, I decide to follow it with a probability which is function of the respective pheromone intensity.

These behaviours may be though as an individual action function of a reactive system, which continually takes perceptual input and maps it to an action to perform. The intelligent behaviour emerges from the interaction of these various simple behaviours, and from the interaction that agents establish with their environment.

This relative simplicity permits to decrease considerably the computational load due to the reasoning and, consequently, to achieve significant benefits in terms of reaction time. In other words, it is reduced the risk to spend too much time for the reasoning about complex choices which, when they will be carried out, could be considered inappropriate due to the high environment changeableness. Moreover, the presence of a certain number of autonomous computational elements makes the system more robust. If the behaviour of one of them is not suitable, there will be no risk that it can provoke the collapse of the whole system.

The ant exploration begins from a set $S = \{url_1, url_2, \ldots, url_n\}$ of initial references which, in the Web case, can be: bookmarks, first results of a search engine or references in some categories of directory services.

Each ant is located in a *virtual page o* where it is possible to reach every page in S. The ants can move autonomously, choosing paths according to the task accomplishing behaviours described before. At the end of each cycle the ants are repositioned in the virtual page o and the trails of the followed paths are updated according to the exploration results.

In particular, the generic ant in the url_i page, that has to make a move, will draw the transition probabilities values $p_{ij}(t)$ for each j that it exists a link from url_i towards url_j. According to these probabilities, it will choose the next resource to visit. The $p_{ij}(t)$ value is calculated by the following formula:

$$p_{ij}(t) = \frac{\tau_{ij}(t)}{\sum_k \tau_{ik}(t)}$$

where $\tau_{ij}(t)$ corresponds to the pheromone intensity on the path from url_i to url_j and the summation extends for all the resources url_j that can be reached from url_i. The t variable refers to the current cycle.

To keep the ants from following circular paths, and to encourage the new page exploration, each ant has a L list containing its visited url. The probability related to the path from url_i to url_j, in case url_j belongs to the L list, is equal to 0. At the end of each cycle, the list is emptied out.

Furthermore, another accomplishing behavior is added to the two previously-mentioned ones. It concerns the pheromone updating at the end of each cycle, afterwards every ant has reached the maximum number of moves at its disposal. This behaviour can be described as follows: every k-th ant draws the variation of pheromone trail from url_i to url_j:

$$\Delta\tau_{ij}^k = \frac{score(url_j)}{l_k}$$

where l_k is the ant k-th path length (i.e. the number of resource visited up to url_i), and $score(url_j)$ is the function that, for each resource url returns a value included in $[0,1]$ interval, corresponding to the similarity measure between query and resource content (where 1 is the maximum similarity). If the k-th ant has not followed the path from url_i to url_j, the corresponding $\Delta\tau_{ij}^k$ is equal to 0. The τ_{ij} trail intensity of a generic path from url_i to url_j at the $t+1$ cycle is updated from every ant, according to the previously value at the t cycle, in the following way:

$$\tau_{ij}(t+1) = \rho \cdot \tau_{ij}(t) + \sum_k \Delta\tau_{ij}^k$$

where ρ is the coefficient of trail evaporation that must be set to a positive value less than 1 to avoid unlimited accumulation of substance caused by the repeated and limitless positive feedback. The summation widens to all the ants in the system. The τ_{ij} trail value at the initial cycle is set to a small prefixed constant.

Supposing the movement number is proportional to the cycle number, the computation complexity of the algorithm is $O(c^2 \cdot m \cdot n)$, where c is the reached cycle number, m is the number of the ants and n is the average link number per page (i.e. the average out-degree of a page). To make it simpler, the n value is upper-bound limited and input data set independent, consequently, it can be replaced by a constant complexity value, while the other two parameters can be related to the number of the requested resources r, that is directly proportional to $c \cdot m$, gaining in this way a computational complexity equal to $O(r^2)$.

Many adaptations have been made to the original ant system computational paradigm, considered the starting point of the proposed reactive architecture and multiagent system. These adaptations are due to the kind of problem dealt with. Unlike the various scenarios the algorithm has already been applied, the one at issue refers to a basically unbounded environments (i.e. huge hypertextual environments, for instance the Web), where it is impossible to update the trails after completing the whole resource exploration. For this reason, the exploration is bounded, for the first execution cycles, to a limited number of movements and it gradually increases to exploit all the information retrieved.

The kind of environment modifies the trail updating rules, too. At the beginning of the execution all the τ_{ij} trails have a constant value. When this value is not interested by the ant transits, it decreases as a function of the evaporation rate. More the environment is vast, more the paths tend to have long lengths. Therefore, when the number of the cycles allows the ants to make long routes, they will analyse very small pheromone intensities. If an ant leaves its own trail after choosing a path, increasing significantly low pheromone intensities, there will be a risk that all the next ants will inevitably follow the path because the pheromone values on the other routes, have risible values and, consequently, the relative probabilities. To prevent this phenomenon, the initial pheromone value has been constantly maintained, i.e. without operating the evaporation process, until an ant decides to follow the corresponding path. When the ant updates the pheromone intensity at the end of the cycle, the trail evaporation process begins.

Another important modification regards the possibility of backtracking. Every time an ant is located on a hypertextual resource with no outgoing links, it will retrace its steps and so, at the next cycle, it could make a new movement starting from the previous resource. The reference of the no-link resource is added to the visited list and so, the ant cannot choose it any more.

The phenomenon about the lack of the complete context description in the hypertextual documents is held into consideration with the trails left by the ants in their routes. If an ant reaches an interesting resource, the ones judged negatively in the path, are not ignored or reduced in rank. The system has to explain the low query affinity as a possible lack of an explicit author's context. If these pages do not contain the query keywords, they have to be considered valid sources to find other resources which satisfy the query.

To carry out this intent, at the end of each cycle, every ant updates the trails it followed according to the scores of all the visited resources. As it was supposed, if interesting resources have been analysed during the path, the $\Delta\tau$ value (function of the score sum) results greater than 0. As a result, each τ_{ij} trail intensity of the followed path is increased by the pheromone updating process, even when to reach interesting resources it was necessary to analyse some of them with affinity close to 0.

The system aleatory behaviour, i.e. the $p_{ij}(t)$ probability, gives a further possibility to reach interesting resources beginning from paths of insignificant ones. In fact, if an ant is positioned in a particular hypertextual resource and it has to choose where to go, and, if during the past cycles the ants that have run through this resource have not found a better path than another, it will randomly decide its path. It is possible to find slight analogies with approaches used in other systems for the search and the analysis of the hypertextual information, such as the aleatory variable of the hybrid version of the simulated annealing algorithm proposed in [28], or the "random surfer" model applied to the crawling [4,9]. In the last case, a probability function considers the dumping factor, that is to say the probability of the event where the user stops following the links in the current page to start on another random page.

Information Representation. An information retrieval approach is used to represent the user queries and hypertextual documents. Instead of the boolean queries, it is used the more flexible coordinate matching model [25], which counts the number of the query terms that appear in each document. More terms appear, more the document is judge relevant.

In particular, the TFxIDF (term frequency inverse document frequency) method [23] is used for weighting the terms that occur in a document. To achieve this purpose it is necessary to draw the integer $f_{d,t}$ indicating how many times the term t appears in the document d, often called within-document frequency. Moreover the inverse document frequency value idf_t has to be held into consideration to reduce the term rank as a function of all the times it appears in a document collection, i.e. how it can be considered a common term. The two metrics, TF and IDF, are drawn from:

$$tf_{d,t} = \sqrt{f_{d,t}}$$

$$idf_t = 1 + \log_e \frac{N}{f_t + 1}$$

where N and f_t are respectively the number of documents in the collection and the document frequency containing the t term. The same weighting process is used on the query terms obtaining the $tf_{q,t}$ value. The *similarity measure* of the query Q with document D_d is the inner product of these two value sets, i.e. the sum of the products of the weights of the query and the corresponding document terms:

$$M(Q, D_d) = \sum_{t \in Q} \frac{tf_{q,t} \cdot idf_t}{\sqrt{\sum_{t \in Q}(tf_{q,t} \cdot idf_t)^2}} \cdot \frac{tf_{d,t} \cdot idf_t}{\sqrt{L_d}}$$

where L_d is the length of document d obtained by counting the number of the indexed terms. To reduce the effect that long documents are favoured over short ones, since they contain more terms and, therefore, the value of inner product increases, it is introduced a normalization factor corresponding to the two denominator elements of the equation. The terms to be analysed derive from the documents, ignoring the ones belonging to the formatting and to the common words by means of a stoplist.

The $M(Q, D_d)$ function correspond to the *score(url)* function previously used in the updating trail process, where *url* corresponds to the address of D_d document.

Unfortunately in the information exploration systems, as the one at issue, it is impossible to calculate the right value of the inverse document frequency measure, since there is no way to compute it over all the huge document collection, unless the system has explored it in advance. For this reason, IDF is dynamically computed each time new textual resources have been discovered, obtaining consequently a time-dependent IDF component.

3.3   The Adaptivity

The system shows two adaptivity forms: the first concerns the opportunity of the user to refine the query during the execution when the results are not so satisfactory or, more in general, the user does not know how to look for a query able to express what he wants. The second form regards the eventuality of analysed hypertextual resource changes due to the environment instability. These two types of adaptivity are possible because at every cycle the value of the pheromone intensities $\tau_{ij}(t)$ are updated according to the visited resource scores.

Once the query, or the content of the visited resources changes, the alteration of the similarity measure value affects the $\Delta\tau_{ij}(t)$ variation which influences, in its turn, $\tau_{ij}(t)$ (see the pheromone updating process). Moreover, as cycles go by, the current values of the pheromone intensities tend to become ideal (i.e. function of the current environmental status) with the pheromone evaporation effects.

For instance, given a particular path P, in case of a negative variation of the $\Delta\tau_{ij}^k(t)$ values (due to, for instance, a change of the user query), where the path from url_i to url_j belongs to P, the trails $\tau_{ij}(t+1)$ are subjected to a feedback which is reduced if it is compared to the one in the former cycles. For this reason, a smaller number of ants will be attracted, therefore, the $\Delta\tau_{ij}^k(t+2)$ increments are still further reduced, and so forth. In other words, each change in the environment causes a feedback modifying consequently the system behavior in order to adapt itself to the new conditions.

4   Testing and Evaluation

Analysing different types of experiments employed in the Web intelligent crawling systems, it is possible to observe several methodologies suggested for the evaluation measures and for the choice of the test collection.

As for the second point, almost all the systems were tested exploring directly the Web (see for instance [7,9,21]). This approach suffers from some defects, caused both for the very large domain, and for the high instability of the contents. The traditional measures of the information retrieval, like precision and recall [23], lose much of their sense, since both the query results and the corpus are basically open-ended. Moreover, the measures depend on the instance in which testing takes place and, therefore, it is not easy to reproduce and compare the results among several systems. In other words, it is assumed that the test collection is static but, in case of the Web, it results highly dynamic, with new documents which have been added, deleted, changed, and moved all the time.

For these reasons the .GOV, one of the Web collections suggested by the TREC[1], has been chosen. It is composed of a Web page corpus that, besides to permit the evaluation comparisons, can preserve and optimize some important properties, like: sufficient large and broadly representative of Web data, large set of representative Web queries and high degree of inter-server connectivity.

---

[1] http://trec.nist.gov

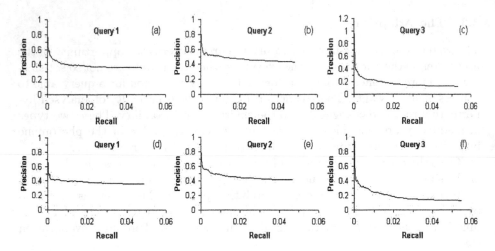

Fig. 1. Precision-recall curves, concerning the three queries: (a), (b) and (c) with initial Web pages chosen from those with highest similarity measure; (c), (d) and (e) with initial Web pages chosen at random.

The source data for the collection is .gov Web sites crawled in early 2002 by the Internet Archive digital library. The corpus is formed by 1.25 million of documents, nearly all HMTL pages, and its size roughly reaches 18.1Gbyte.

Table 1. Queries and the related number of relevant documents in the collection.

Query	Overall results
1 – *exchange office*	373712
2 – *education department*	445964
3 – *children foundation*	117036

Because of the finite size of the testing corpus, it was possible to employ the traditional IR evaluation measures, like: precision (the percentage of the relevant resources presented to the user) and recall (percentage of relevant resources that are retrieved). Unfortunately, the TREC does not still provide a standard set of queries and the respective relevance judgments of the documents. Therefore, to verify if a page is related to the query it will be necessary judge each page by the human inspection, but this is impracticable due to the large size of the collection. For this reason, a classical IR measure similarity is used as estimator, and, in particular, the same employed in the system. This issue does not induce any problem because this measure is located outside the system and, so, it is impossible that the system influences the weighing. In this evaluation, a resource is considered relevant if the corresponding similarity measure is greater than 0.

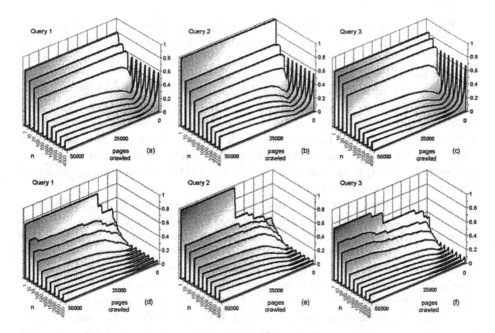

Fig. 2. Moving average curves of the n highest ranked pages retrieved, as a function of the number of pages crawled: (a), (b) and (c) with initial Web pages chosen from those with highest similarity measure; (c), (d) and (e) with initial Web pages chosen at random.

Each exploration is related to one of the three mentioned queries chosen in such a way as to select a suitable number of documents within the collection (see Table 1).

Table 2. Parameter descriptions and values

Parameter Description	Value
Ant colony size	25
Initial pheromone intensity trail	0.2
Trail evaporation rate ρ	0.8
Number of start urls	50
Increment of maximum moves per cycle	1
Resources to retrieve	50000

The initial Web pages, from which each exploration starts, were gathered by the query results in two ways: choosing the ones with the highest similarity measures, or making random choices from the set of resources with similarity greater than 0.

The testing evaluation is divided in a first part where the recall-precision curves (i.e. the precision is a function of the recall rather than of the rank) are compared, while in the second, the trends of the harvest ratio (the rate at which relevant pages are acquired) are analysed.

The latter is measured considering the moving average of the n highest ranked pages retrieved, where the n values are: 3, 10, 30, 100, 500, 1000, 1500, 2000, 3000 and 4000. Obviously, when the number of the retrieved pages n' is less than n, the average is limited to the n' values. These trends suggest how the system adapts itself to select information sources to retrieve in short time interesting information. The system shows a good behaviour if the moving average gets high after having crawled just a small set of pages.

The explorations were effectuated setting to 50000 the maximum number of the retrieved resources. The number of the cycles is set up in such a way as to reach the mentioned exploration limit. The other system parameters are given in Table 2.

It is possible to note how the recall-precision curves (see Figure 1) show the classical decreasing trend due to the high precision at low recall levels, and low at high recall levels. The absolute low level of the recall values are justified because of the kind of information system analysed. It is not considered a classical Information Retrieval system, where all the resources are indexed and it is possible to do a global filtering on them. In this case, the exploration, and consequently the filtering, affects all the documents which can be reached from the initial set and it is limited by the maximum number of retrieved resource setting.

The harvest ratios have an overall increasing tendency. This is an eloquent advice that the system can efficiently lead the exploration towards relevant pages, reducing at the same time the resources employed for the estimation of the irrelevant ones. An unfocused crawler would provide poor results after having visited just few hundreds of pages (see testing results in [7]).

Another observation is the low dependency between the exploration results and the initial document set from which the system begins the search. In fact, comparing the harvest ratios for the explorations starting from the best evaluated documents (see Figures 2a 2b and 2c), and the ones beginning from the documents randomly chosen (Figures 2d 2e and 2f), it is possible to verify that, after having visited few thousands of documents, the tendencies almost correspond. The same observation can be inferred considering the difference of the recall-precision curves due to same change in the initial document set.

5   Future Work

The proposed architecture is a reactive one, where the system rational behaviour emerges from the interaction and the cooperation of an agent population; therefore, it is necessarily to attempt to completely understand the relationship between local and global behaviour. In particular, it is useful to be aware of the changes of the global behaviour in function of some parameter variations, as the initial values and the decay of the pheromone intensities, or the number of agents employed. For this purpose, the agent behaviour has to be analysed, i.e. how agent chooses paths in function of interesting resource positions, to see if they behave properly under all the possible circumstances.

Besides spending much time in the tuning phase, it is also necessary to make testing evaluation on larger collections, like the 100Gbyte VLC2, where a higher degree of the inter-page connectivity is available, an indispensable information for all the systems based on the autonomous exploration.

6 Conclusion

In this work a particular agent architecture has been presented, from which an adaptive information search system for huge hypertextual collections has been implemented. The architecture has been inspired by the Ant System computation paradigm, derived from models of social insect collective behaviours which proved to be fruitful in several domains. The adaptivity permits to have a system robust to the environmental alterations and to the user information need changes.

The results obtained look like promising and suggest that the system can be suitable for autonomous search in hypertextual environments. It has been developed and evaluated in the Web domain, but it is also suitable to other ones, constituted by a vast collection of hypertextual documents.

Thanks to its relative simplicity, it does not need of heavy computational link analysis [12], neither of structured taxonomies classifier training [7]. The only needed constraint is a similarity measure between user query and hypertextual resources, therefore this architecture is particularly appropriate for classical Web information retrieval systems, like search engines, to obtain focused information search systems. It is also possible to use it in personal assistant instances which provide help in the process of finding and organizing information. The architecture, constituted by a set of computational autonomous component, leads to a natural concurrent implementation.

This work does not want to give exhaustive and definitive results on the intelligent search systems but, on the contrary, it wants to widen further the range of the intelligent search topic towards theories and architectures of agent and multiagent systems.

References

1. Aggarwal, C.C., Al-Garawi, F., Yu, P.S.: Intelligent Crawling on the World Wide Web with Arbitrary Predicates In Proc. of the WWW10 Conference (2001) 96–105.
2. Bailey, P., Craswell, N., Hawking, D.: Dark matter on the web. In Poster Proc. of the WWW9 Conference (2000).
3. Bonabeau, E., Dorigo, M., Theraulaz, G.: Inspiration for optimization from social insect behavior. Nature, Vol. 406 (2000) 39–42
4. Brin, S., Page, L.: The Anatomy of a Large-Scale Hypertextual Web Search Engine. Computer Networks and ISDN Systems, Vol. 30 (1998) 107–117.

5. Brooks, R.A.: Intelligence without representation. Artificial Intelligence 45 (1991), 139–159.
6. Broder, A., Kumar, R., Maghoul, F., Raghavan, P., Rajagopalan, S., Stata, R., Tomkins, A., Wiener, J.: Graph structure in the web. In Proc. of the WWW9 Conference (2000) 309–320.
7. Chakrabarti, S., Van Den Berg, M., Dom, B.. Focused Crawling: A New Approach to Topic-Specific Web Resource Discovery. In Proc. of the WWW8 Conference (1999) 1623–1640.
8. Chen, H., Chung, Y., Ramsey, M., Yang, C.C.: An Intelligent Personal Spider (Agent) for Dynamic Internet/Intranet Searching Decision Support Systems Vol. 23 No. 1 (1998) 41–58.
9. Cho, J., Garcia-Molina, H.G., Page, L.. Efficient Crawling Through URL Ordering. Computer Networks and ISDN Systems, Vol. 30, N. 1-7 (1998) 161–172.
10. Di Caro, G., Dorigo, M.: AntNet: Distributed stigmergetic control for communications networks. Journal of Artificial Intelligence Research, Vol. 9 (1998) 317–365.
11. Dorigo, M., Maniezzo, V., Colorni, A.: The Ant System: Optimization by a colony of coop-erating agents. IEEE Transactions on Systems, Man, and Cybernetics–Part B , Vol. 26, No. 2 (1996) 29–41
12. Kleinberg, J.M.: Authoritative Source in a Hyperlinked Environment. Journal of the ACM Vol. 46 No. 5 (1999) 604–632.
13. Klusch, M.: Information Agent Technology for the Internet: A Survey. Journal on Data and Knowledge Engineering, Vol. 36(3) (2001) 337–372.
14. Kube, C.R., Zhang, H.: Collective robotics: from social insects to robots. Adaptive Behavior, Vol. 2 (1993) 189–218.
15. Lawrence, S.: Context in Web Search. IEEE Data Engineering Bulletin, Vol. 23, No. 3 (2000) 25–32.
16. Lieberman, H.: Autonomous Interface Agents. In Proc. of ACM Conference on CHI-97, Atlanta, USA (1997)
17. Lieberman, H.: Personal Assistants for the Web: An MIT Perspective. In Matthias Klusch, editor, Intelligent Information Agents. Springer-Verlag, Berlin (1999) 272–292.
18. Maes, P.: Agents that Reduce Work and Information Overload. Communications of the ACM 37, No. 7 (1994) 31–40.
19. Manning, C.D., Schutze, H.: Foundations of Statitical Natural Language Processing. MIT Press (1999).
20. Menczer, F., Monge, A.E.: Scalable Web Search by Adaptive Online Agents: An InfoSpiders Case Study. In Matthias Klusch, editor, Intelligent Information Agents. Springer-Verlag, Berlin (1999) 323–340.
21. Menczer, F., Pant, G., Srinivasan, P., Ruiz, M.E.: Evaluating Topic-Driven Web Crawlers. In Proc. 24th Annual International ACM SIGIR Conference on Research and Development in Information Retrieval (2001) 241–249.
22. Mizuuchi, Y., Tajima, K.: Finding Context Paths for Web Pages. In Proc. of ACM Hypertext (1999) 13–22.
23. Salton, G., McGill, M.J.: Introduction to Modern Information Retrieval. McGraw-Hill (1983).
24. Schoonderwoerd, R., Holland, O., Bruten, J., Rothkrantz, L.: Ant-based load balancing in telecommunications networks. Adaptive Behavior, Vol. 5, No. 2 (1996) 169–207.
25. Witten, I.H., Moffat, A., Bell, T.C.: Managing Gigabytes: Compressing and Indexing Documents and Images. Morgan Kaufmann Publishing, San Francisco (1999).

26. Wooldridge, M., Jennings, N.R.: Intelligent Agents: Theory and Practice. Knowledge Engineering Review, 10(2) (1995) 115–152.
27. Wooldridge, M.: Intelligent Agents. In G. Weiss, editor, Multiagent Systems: A Modern Approach to Distributed Artificial Intelligence. The MIT Press, Cambridge, MA, USA (1999).
28. Yang, C.C., Yen, J., Chen, H.: Intelligent Internet searching agent based on hybrid simulated annealing. Decision Support Systems Vol. 28 (2000) 269–277.

Agents for Collaborative Filtering

Fabrício Enembreck and Jean-Paul Barthès

Université de Technologie de Compiègne, Centre de Recherches Royallieu,
60205 Compiègne, France
enembrec@hds.utc.fr
barthes@utc.fr

Abstract. This paper describes a new generic agent-based framework for collaborative filtering. Usually, collaborative filtering tools use large collaborative document databases to model users' preferences. Nevertheless, we believe that collaborative filtering can be accomplished with decentralized systems in which user's preferences are learned from small individual databases. Such a distributed approach gives more flexibility in adding and removing users, and distributes computational effort naturally, economizing computing resources. In addition, it facilitates a continuous evolution of the users' preferences. At the same time, agents are commonly used to decentralize generic systems, which leads us to adopt a Multi-Agent System for representing the collaborative environment. In particular, we propose Personal Assistants to communicate with the user and to acquire users' models. Then, a Decision Agent uses such models to decide who must receive the incoming documents.

1 Introduction

Internet is a large heterogeneous source of information. We are continuously publishing or to searching for new information in a variety of domains. Hence, millions of users increase the amount of data on the Internet often without paying any attention to how such information is organized. The result is a huge unstructured database in which the search becomes increasingly difficult. To address the problem, researchers on *information retrieval*, *machine learning*, *intelligent user interfaces*, and *intelligent agents* develop applications taking into account user profiles and user preferences to reduce the document search space and to retrieve useful and interesting information with a minimal human effort [15]. Thus, researchers on *text learning* [9] [14] combine machine learning and information retrieval techniques to produce intelligent interfaces [12].

In particular, agents are able to search for information intelligently [13]. In this work, we use some information retrieval techniques for classifying documents (i.e., distributing them to users), adapted to collaborative filtering. The problem consists of creating models for users and using them to decide which users are interested by new documents, looking for similar models. Such a problem concerns generally news serv-

M. Klusch et al. (Eds.): CIA 2003, LNAI 2782, pp. 184–191, 2003.

ers [8] [16] and e-mail filtering [17] [11], where the goal is to reduce the quantity of useless messages or of documents circulating in a network. Thus, only directed and personalized messages are transmitted, which saves computational resources and users' time. In the next sections we use the well known 20 news-group database of the UCI [1] for illustrating the technique.

The paper is organized as follow: Section 2 discusses the relationships between document classification and document filtering. Section 3 describes how we intend to accomplish collaborative filtering using agents. Section 4 discusses some questions related to collaborative filtering and in Section 5 we discuss related works. Finally Section 6 concludes the paper.

2 Document Classification and Document Filtering

In this paper, user models are assumed to be classes of documents. Most applications on collaborative learning do not consider large corporate environments where hundreds of users share some domain of interest. The main reason is that with traditional approaches, each user is considered to be a class in the system, and classification is very difficult in problems having many classes. Therefore, if we consider the problem as one of document classification, we need a method that works with a large number of classes containing little information.

Most works on document classification use a global document database for determining the classes. In a learning phase, a fixed set of features is chosen and the model of data is generated from such features. However, current learning algorithms are not able to produce classifiers for many classes for two main reasons: (i) as the number of classes increases the problem becomes more difficult. Indeed, in this case, the amount of training data is crucial, since each class needs a sufficient number of training instances, which is a constraint in collaborative filtering; (ii) the space dimension is directly proportional to the number of classes. To find class limits, machine-learning algorithms need a set of good features. In document classification problems each class is usually represented by a large number of features, say, 1000. So, for several classes, the dimension of the tuple space will make the classification a very hard problem.

In [7] a feature selection process is carried out to reduce the complexity of the data, allowing the application of machine learning algorithms. However, such an approach tends to be very slow. Instead, we work with each class individually. For each class, a small individual database of documents is used and a predefined number of features is chosen[1] as described in Section 3.1, using Personal Agents. We then try to find a good representation for the classes by selecting good features. Next, the centroid for each class is computed as defined in Equation 2. Finally, such centroids are transmitted to a Decision Agent that evaluates the discriminating power of the features and uses a quality measure to find the best classes for classifying a new document (Section 3.2). The next section describes our technique.

---

[1] We eliminate stop words and verbs with a dictionary. Stemming algorithms are not used.

3 Agents for Collaborative Filtering

In [5] we presented a new centroid-based classification paradigm where models are learned separately and thereafter combined to tackle classification. Here, we extend such a method to obtain a decentralized agent-based collaborative filtering approach. Personal Assistants (PAs) use a centroid-based classification and information retrieval techniques in order to learn the user's models considering the user's reference documents. Each user has an individual PA. In fact, the PA inspects the documents kept in the user's personal document database, and uses the documents marked as "interesting" for creating the model. Consequently, only "positive" documents are used to model the user. A user model is a centroid-vector of features, chosen according to well-known TFIDF criteria (Section 3.1). Next, a Decision Agent (DA) uses the users' models to decide who must receive the incoming documents.

The DA uses the classification approach proposed in [5]. Out of a set of user models DA computes the discriminating power for all terms. The discriminating power measure takes into account the importance of the terms for each user and gives a general degree of interest of the term for the set of models. Terms are weighted according to their discriminating power, using the gini index criterion [20] (Section 3.3). Finally, for classifying a document, models are ranked according to a similarity degree, using a simple weighted average multiplication between the document vector and the centroid vector (Section 3.4). DA uses the most similar models to identify target users. Fig. 1 shows the general architecture of the proposed system. In Fig. 1, the DA decides to send a given document only to agent B. Thus, the DA must compute feature weights and classify documents using a given similarity measure.

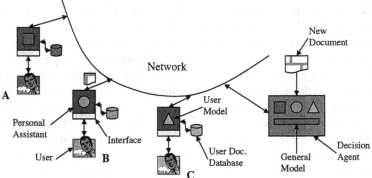

Fig. 1. Multi-Agent System Architecture.

The method described in the previous paragraph can handle an unlimited number of classes (users), because users' models are learned separately. Furthermore, each model needs only a small number of documents.

3.1 Learning User Profile with Personal Assistant

In this work PAs are used to learn users' models. PAs offer the users an interface for storing documents. PAs are integrated into a collaborative tool serving as a document database. The user tells his PA what are the most interesting documents and when the assistant must update his profile based on such documents. In order to model the user, we use document classification and information retrieval techniques.

Documents are represented as vectors of important terms for a class. A common measure of quality for terms is the TF-IDF[2] measure [18]. TF-IDF gives the relevance of a given term in relation to a collection of documents. The idea is the following: if a term appears frequently in a small number of documents, then it is important. TF is the simple frequency of the term in the document collection. IDF is the inverse document frequency of the term. It is given by $\log(N/DF_{term})$ where N is the total number of documents and DF_{term} is the number of documents having *term* in their content. So the TF-IDF measure of a term i is given by Equation (1).

$$TFIDF(i)=TF_i \times \log\left(\frac{N}{DF_i}\right)$$

(1)

A given document d is represented by a vector $\mathbf{d} = \{TF_1*\log(N/DF_1), TF_2*\log(N/DF_2), ..., TF_m*\log(N/DF_m)\}$.

To learn the class model, machine-learning algorithms (decision trees, naïve Bayes, neural networks, nearest-neighbor, etc.) can be applied to the data. Here, we use a centroid-based approach. In a centroid approach an averaged vector represents a class. So, given a collection S of documents of the class c Equation (2) gives the centroid vector for c.

$$\mathbf{c} = \frac{1}{|S|} \times \sum_{d \in S} \mathbf{d}$$

(2)

3.2 Weighted Centroid Approach and Decision Agent

In this work, Decision Agents (DA) implement the classification process. A DA combines several user models to locate users having similar interests and classifies documents accordingly. In our case, the classification phase consists in identifying the most similar centroid vectors and returning the respective classes (users). In the centroid approach the classification reduces to a comparison between two vectors. The comparison can be performed using several techniques like computing the cosine or the Euclidian distance. However, we cannot use such techniques directly because we start the learning phase individually for each class and because each class models has different dimensions (features). We later discuss how DAs use the class models received from PAs.

---

[2] Term-frequency – inverse document frequency

PAs supply a DA with users' models (individual centroids). The result from this phase is a set of centroid vectors with equal size but different features. Obviously, vectors can present common features depending on the similarity in the contents of the documents. For instance, the classes "religion" and "atheism" will probably have similar features. Thus, the PA can check the different features of each class, but does not know how to use them. In particular, important class composition features can be very poor at discriminating. For instance, in a given document database, we found that the term "article" was important for most classes. Thus, such a term is not a good discriminating term.

To combine and normalize the different class representations, we produce a generic model composed by feature weights (details in Section 3.3). The weights of the features represent the General Model that can be seen Fig. 1. They are used in the next step for classifying documents (Section 3.4).

3.3 Feature Discriminating Power

To measure the discriminating power of the features, we use the *gini* index technique. Let $\{C_1, C_2,..., C_m\}$ be the set of centroids computed according to Equation (1) and T_w the vector derived from the relevance of the term w in all the classes — $T_w = \{C_{1w}, C_{2w},..., C_{mw}\}$. T'_w is the vector T_w normalized with the one-norm — $T'_w = \{C_{1w} / \| T_w \|_1, C_{2w} / \| T_w \|_1, ..., C_{mw} / \| T_w \|_1\}$ the discriminating power of w — P_w — is given by Equation (3).

$$P_w = \sum_{j=1}^{m} T_{jw}^2 \tag{3}$$

P_w is equal to the square length of the T'_w vector. So P_w is always in the range $[1/m, 1]$. P_w has the smallest value when $T'_{w1} = T'_{w2} = ... = T'_{wm}$, whereas the highest value of P_w occurs when only one class has the term w.

The weight in the features acts as a normalizing parameter, allowing centroid vectors with different features to be compared. All the features belonging to all the centroids are weighted. Such weights are used in a classification phase described in Section 3.4.

3.4 Document Classification

To classify a given document, a set S of valid terms (nouns) and their frequency (TF) is extracted. For each class c, we create a specific vector d for representing the document. For each term i in c, di is $TF_i IDF_i$ (on c). Next the centroid vector c is scored with a degree of similarity using d and the weights of the terms, according to Equation (4). In Equation (4) c is the centroid vector, d is the document vector and w is the feature weight vector. Hence, in Equation (4) we compute the average quality of the terms inside the document, taking into account the discriminating power of each feature.

$$score(c,d,w)=\frac{\sum_{i=1}^{|d|}c_i\times d_i\times w_i}{|d|} \tag{4}$$

To increase the system performance we can use only "good" discriminating features. So, we introduce an empirical threshold to avoid the influence of poor discriminating features, considering features having a weight greater or equal than 0.3, otherwise we arbitrarily set the weight to 0.

4 Considerations on Collaborative Filtering

In collaborative filtering performance is not a crucial factor. The main objective is to decrease the number of messages (mails, documents, etc.) transmitted through a network, delivering messages only for supposedly interested people. Hence, if a mistake is done, two cases can occur: (i) a user receives an uninteresting document, or (ii) a user does not receive an interesting document. The second case is much more serious than the first one. Hence, we try to minimize mainly the second type of error. Another question is the multi-class nature of the documents, since a given document can be of interest to several users. Observing the experiments, we could perceive that close classes are generally at the top of the priority queue. For instance, classes as "talk.religion.misc," "alt.atheism" and "soc.religion.Christian" are generally clustered because they use the same vocabulary. A threshold computed from the top class can be used to select a group of classes. Such a simple technique can be used in collaborative filtering, because several users will have similar needs. In this case we increase the errors of type (i) but decrease the errors of type (ii).

5 Related Works and Contribution

In applications including collaborative filtering [4] [19], information about the users can be maintained in generic databases or in individual databases. When an instance-based algorithm like nearest neighbor, is used for classifying new items, a single generic database contains information about all the users. Because each user can present a lot of transactions or items, such a database tends to become large, requiring much computation resources for the learning algorithms. Thus, the performance of such algorithms depends on the number of users and of items. This is the well-known *scalability* problem. A solution to this problem consists in using individual databases. When each user has a separate database, the items need to be classified as "interesting" or "not interesting," which assumes that the system must get the user's feedback for building a good training database. In [4], for instance, the user tells the system which documents are interesting when analyzing the results of a search for web pages.

Such documents are classified as "positive." The addresses deleted from the book-mark, misclassified bookmarks, or refused bookmarks are classified as "negative" examples. We believe that such a user's feedback induces a high workload. Therefore, a better and more general technique must be found. The technique presented in this paper uses individual user's databases, but does not require "negative" examples, saving user's time. In addition, our technique presents a high *scalability* tolerance. Because only individual databases are considered in the learning phase, and because each assistant learns the users' models in parallel, the system does not depend so much on the number of items. Since each user is represented by a single vector of terms within the decision agent, we ensure a slow linear growth in terms of complexity when updating the general model.

Agents are often used in distributed information retrieval, e.g., by Clark [3]. In such systems a major problem is how to merge the results from distributed sources. Kretser and coworkers [10] and Callan [2] discuss this problem. Kretser concludes that dis-tributed approaches are fast and effective, but are not efficient. However, preliminary experiments made on the 20 newsgroup of the UCI show that the technique introduced in this paper can outperform the Rocchio algorithm when many features are used.

6   Conclusions

In this work we have introduced a new agent-based framework for collaborative fil-tering. The work uses the document classification method introduced in [5]. Such a technique allows the construction of flexible collaborative tools. Personal Assistants are responsible for learning user's models. Secondly, a Decision Agent combines users' models to decide who must receive a new incoming document. Most of the document classification approaches use a global database to discriminate all the classes (users). Instead we work with each class separately. Within each PA, an equal number of features is chosen in order to model the master. We try to maximize the intra-cluster cohesion choosing good features using the TFIDF measure. Next, the centroid for the class is computed. To maximize the inter-cluster distance, the DA uses weights in the features. To classify a given document, the DA scores the users models and the top users' models win. The method presented here distributes the processing in collaborative environments naturally, using agents, and allows the input, output and update of an individual user profile without changing the models of other users. In such a case, only the feature weights must be recomputed. Future work includes an application of the method to an actual collaborative environment.

Acknowledgements. This research was financed by Région Picardie in France. We thank Indira Thouvenin, Marie-Hélène Abel, Bruno Ramond, Philipe Trigano, and Cesar Tacla for their help with important remarks and discussions.

References

1. Blake, C.L.; Merz, C.J., *UCI Repository of machine learning databases* [http://www.ics.uci.edu/~mlearn/MLRepository.html]. Irvine, CA: University of California, Department of Information and Computer Science, 1998.
2. Callan, J., *Distributed information retrieval.* In W.B. Croft (ed.), *Advances in information retrieval*, chapter 5, pages 127–150. Kluwer Academic Publishers, 2000.
3. Clark, K. L.; Lazarou, V. S., 1997. *A Multi-Agent System for Distributed Information Retrieval on the World Wide Web.* In WETICE97, Collaborative Agents in Distributed Web Applications, IEEE Computer Society Press, 1997.
4. Delgado, J.; Ishii, N.; Ura, T., *Intelligent Collaborative Information Retrieval*, IBERAMIA, pp 170-182, 1998. http://citeseer.nj.nec.com/delgado98intelligent.html
5. Enembreck, F.; Barthès, J-P., *Classification in Many-Classes Environments*, The International Symposium on Document Technologies STD, Brazil, São Paulo, 17–19 September, 2002.
6. FIPA, *Foundations for Intelligent Physical Agents*, http://wwwfipa.org
7. Goller, C.; Löning J.; Will, T.; Wolf, W., *Automatic Document Classification: A thorough Evaluation of various Methods*, IEEE Intelligent Systems, n° 14, vol 1, pp. 75–87, 2000.
8. Joachims, T. *A probabilistic analysis of the Rocchio algorithm with TFIDF for text categorization*, Proceedings of ICML-97, 14th International Conference on Machine Learning, Morgan Kaufmann Publishers, (ed. Douglas H. Fisher) San Francisco, US, pp. 143–151, 1997.
9. Kosala, R.; Blockeel, H., *Web Mining Research: A Survey*, ACM SIGKDD Explorations, vol. 2, ed. 1, pp. 1–15, July 2000.
10. De Kretser, O.; Moffat, A.; Shimmin, T.; Zobel, J., Methodologies for Distributed Information Retrieval, Int. Conf. on Distributed Computing Systems, pg. 66–73, 1998. http://citeseer.nj.nec.com/dekretser98methodologies.html
11. Lashakari, Y.; Metral, M.; Maes, P., *Collaborative Interface Agents*, Proceedings of the Twelfth National Conf. on AI, AAAI Press, vol 1, Seattle, WA, 1994.
12. Lieberman, H. *Autonomous Interface Agents*, In Proceedings of the ACM Conference on Computer and Human Interface. Atlanta, Georgia, March 1997.
13. Lieberman, H; Dyke, N. van; Vivacqua, A. *Let's browse: a collaborative browsing agent*, Knowledge Based Systems, Elsevier Science B. V., n° 12, 1999. pp. 427–431.
14. Mather, L. A.; Note, J., *Discovering Encyclopedic Structure and Topics in Text*, KDD-2000 Text Mining Workshop, Boston MA, USA, August 20, 2000.
15. Mladenic, D., *Text-Learning and Related Intelligent Agents: A Survey*, IEEE Intelligent Systems, July/August, 1999. pp 44–51.
16. Pannu, A. S.; Sycara, K., A *Learning Personal Agent for Text Filtering and Notification*, Proc. of the International Conference on Knowledge Based Systems, 1996.
17. Rennie, J. D. M., *ifile : An Application of Machine Learning to E-mail Filtering*, KDD-2000 Text Mining Workshop, Boston MA, USA, August 20, 2000.
18. Salton, G., *Automatic Text Processing: The Transformations*, Analysis, and Retrieval of Information by Computer, Addison-Wesley, 1989.
19. Sarwar, B. M.; Karypis, G.; Konstan, J. A.; Reidl, J., *Item-based collaborative filtering recommendation algorithms*, In. World Wide Web, pp. 285–295, 2001.
20. Shankar, S.; Karypis, G., *A Feature Weight Adjustment Algorithm for Document Categorization*, KDD-2000 Workshop on Text Mining, Boston, USA, August 2000.

Emergence and Stability of Collaborations Among Rational Agents

Sandip Sen[1], Partha Sarathi Dutta[2], and Sabyasachi Saha[1]

[1] University of Tulsa, Tulsa, OKlahoma, USA
{sandip,sahasa}@ens.utulsa.edu,
http://www.mcs.utulsa.edu/~sandip
[2] University of Southampton, UK
psa01r@ecs.soton.ac.uk

Abstract. Autonomous agents interacting in an open world can be considered to be primarily driven by self interests. In this paper, we evaluate the hypotheses that self-interested agents with complementary expertise can learn to recognize cooperation possibilities and develop stable, mutually beneficial coalitions that is resistant to exploitation by malevolent agents. Previous work in this area has prescribed a strategy of reciprocal behavior for promoting and sustaining cooperation among self-interested agents. That work have considered only the task completion time as the cost metric. To represent more realistic domains, we expand the cost metric by using both the time of delivery and quality of work. In contrast to the previous work, we use heterogeneous agents with varying expertise for different job types. This necessitates the incorporation of the novel aspect of learning about other's capabilities within the reciprocity framework. We also present a new mechanism where agents base their decisions both on historical data as well as on future interaction expectations. A decision mechanism is presented that compares current helping cost with expected future savings from interaction with the agent requesting help.

1 Introduction

Agent-based systems are important aspects of real world applications like electronic commerce, recommender systems and personal assistants. Agents deployed in these applications often interact in an open environment with other agents or humans [1,2,3,4]. The interactions involve cooperation, collaboration or competition for resources to achieve the specified goals of these agents. With increase in the complexity of agent interactions, the behavioral characteristics of agents acting in a group should be studied in detail and suitable interaction strategies developed that optimize system performance.

We have been interested in agent strategies for interactions with other agents that can promote cooperation in groups of self-interested agents. Our approach is different from other researchers who have designed effective social laws that can be imposed on agents [5]. We assume that typical real-world environments

M. Klusch et al. (Eds.): CIA 2003, LNAI 2782, pp. 192–205, 2003.

abound in *cooperation possibilities*: situations where one agent can help another agent by sharing work such that the helping cost of the helper is less than the cost saved by the helped agent. As agent system designers we can define rules of interactions to increase the likelihood of cooperation possibilities. We prescribe reciprocative behavior as a stable sustainable strategy that creates cooperative groups in the society. This behavior not only sustains group formation in a homogeneous society of self-interested agents, but also helps to ward off exploitative tendencies of selfish agents in the society [6]. This strategy of reciprocal behavior becomes more stable if the helping agent takes into account the opinion of all other agents before extending any favor [7].

A restriction of the previous work on reciprocity was the incorporation of only a single cost metric, time, used by the agents. In real-life scenarios multiple objectives like time, quality, dependability, etc. will be involved when an agent evaluates the benefit of interacting with another agent. As a first step to handling such a scenario, we expand on the set of cost metrics by including both time and quality in an agent's evaluation scheme. The measures of *time* and *quality* of a work need clarification. The *time* attribute refers to the absolute time units required for completing a particular task, and the *quality* attribute is a measure of the effectiveness of executing a task. These values will depend on the expertise level of agents on different task various task types.

A second restriction in the previous work was the explicit assumption that all agents had the same capabilities i.e. agents were homogeneous in task expertise. We assumed this to focus on the help-giving behaviors of the agents. Having established a basic competence of probabilistic reciprocity based agents in recognizing mutually cooperative relationships and effectively neutralizing exploitative behavior [7], we now turn our attention to the interesting and practical aspect of variance in agent expertise. We assume that different agents have different skill sets which make them more effective in accomplishing some tasks compared to others. We require agents to learn the capabilities of themselves and others through repeated task performance and interaction.

The goal of this work is to evaluate whether self-interested agents can learn to recognize agents with complementary expertise and develop a self-sustaining relationship through exchange of help. This can be described as an augmentation of the basic probabilistic reciprocity model with the concept of *selecting a partner*. Additionally, such help exchange inclinations must be resistant to exploitation by malevolent agents who do not reciprocate help-giving actions. Our hypothesis is that when combined with an appropriate learning scheme, probabilistic reciprocity based strategies will enable the development of stable, mutually beneficial coalitions of self-interested agents with complementary skill sets.

In this paper, we also introduce a new expected utility based decision mechanism used by reciprocative agents to incorporate an outlook for the future. We endow our agents with an expectation on the future behavior of the task arrival pattern and the ability to adapt to expertise changes of other agents. An agent bases the decision of helping another agent on the expected utility of its action by using expectations of future interactions with the help-seeking agent. We posit that such expected utility based decision mechanism is effective in generating significant cost savings under time varying task arrival distributions. It will also enable the agents to identify others' expertise and form stable, mutually beneficial groups with agents having complementary capabilities.

2   Reciprocity

Our probability-based reciprocal behavior is designed to enable an agent make decisions about agreeing to or refusing a request for help from another agent. The probability that agent k, having task l, will help agent i to do task j is given by

$$Pr(i,k,j,l) = \frac{1}{1 + \exp^{-\frac{C_{ij}^k + OP_i - \beta * C_{avg}^k - B_{ki}}{\tau}}},$$

where C_{avg}^k is the average cost of tasks performed by agent k; B_{ki} is the net balance that agent k has with i, due to the previous helps given to and received from agent i; OP_i is the balance that agent i has with other agents excluding agent k; C_{ij}^k is the cost of agent k to do the task j of agent i; β and τ are the only two constant parameters used in the function, where β is used to set the cost an agent is ready to incur to help an unknown agent with the hope of initiating a long-term cooperative relationship and τ is used to set the shape of the probability curve. This is a sigmoidal probability function where the probability of helping increases as the balance increases and is more for less costly tasks. We include the C_{avg} term because while calculating the probability of helping, relative cost should be more important than absolute cost.

In this paper we aim at extending the basic probabilistic reciprocity framework. We evaluate the importance of "quality of performance" as another cost metric and the applicability of learning other agents' capabilities in developing stable, cooperative coalitions among self-interested agents.

We also like to introduce expected utility based reciprocity mechanism, which makes agents enable respond to the future interaction possibilities. We will discuss this mechanism later in the Section 5.

3   Problem Domain

We evaluate our hypothesis using simulations in a job completion problem domain. In this domain each of N agents are assigned T jobs. There are K job types and each agent has expertise in exactly one of these K job types. An agent who is an "expert" in a particular job type can do the job in less time and with higher quality than other job types. We draw the time and quality of performance from a normal distribution with a set mean and a standard deviation. We have two different values of the mean - "high" and "low". For a task type in which an agent is expert, the time required to complete the task is computed from the distribution using the "low" mean value (the agent completes the task in which it is an expert, in less time). We draw the quality of performance of an expert using the "high" mean value (experts complete with high quality). For performance measure of a non-expert, however, we use the "high" and "low" mean values for computing the time and quality respectively. The standard deviation chosen is the same for both experts and non-experts. The jobs can be finished at any one of F different machines. Each agent is assigned the same number of jobs at the start of the simulation. At this point the agents ask for help from one another. When help is given, the agent who is helped updates its estimate of the helper agent's expertise, i.e., the time and quality of performance of the helper agent. With more interactions, therefore, agents develop better models of each other. This biases their help asking behavior - for a given task type, an agent is more likely to ask help from those agents who are expected to produce higher quality results in less time. The simulation ends when every agent has finished all of their assigned jobs.

3.1   Partner Selection and Coalition Formation

We have incorporated simple reinforcement learning schemes to update agent performance estimates. Agents also have estimates of their own abilities to do the different job types. Estimates are of two types: *time estimate*, which reflects the possible time of completion of the job, and *quality estimate*, which reflects the possible performance level of an agent to do that job. Agents also keep estimates of every other agents' abilities.

The time and quality estimates are used by the agents to compute the cost of a particular task delivery. In the current formulation, the cost of completing a task is directly proportional to the time and inversely proportional to the quality of performance. For a given task type, an expert takes less time to produce higher quality work than a non-expert. Hence, the design of the cost function in the above manner ensures that the cost of completing a task of a certain type is less for an expert in that type and compared to a non-expert. When asking for help, agents compute the cost $C1$, incurred by itself to do that task. The estimated cost $C2$ that the prospective helping agent incurs for that work is also computed. Help is obtained only if $C2 < C1$. This condition corresponds to a "cooperation possibility".

Initially, agents have neutral estimates about their own abilities and that of other agents. To obtain accurate estimates about their own abilities, agents must themselves perform jobs of different types. When an agent performs a task, it requires a certain time and achieves a certain quality of performance. These values are used by the agents to measure their performance. When an agent helps another, the helped agent updates its estimate of the helper using the time and quality of performance values that the helper agent requires to complete the particular type of job. The simple reinforcement that we use to update the time and quality estimates is given below:

$$t_{ij}^{n+1} \leftarrow (1 - \alpha)t_{ij}^n + t_{ij}, \text{ where } t_{ij}^n \text{ is the time taken by agent } i \text{ to do task } j \text{ on}$$
$$\text{the } n^{th} \text{ time instance.}$$

We use a similar update policy for the quality of performance (q_{ij}). More interactions between the same pair of agents provide each with the opportunity of developing more accurate models of one another. This information is used to select an agent for asking help. As a consequence of developing the reinforced model of others' abilities, an agent i who specializes in job type T_1 when given a job of type T_2, will decide in favor of asking help from an agent j specializing in job type T_2, rather than agents who specialize in other job types. The knowledge that agent j is capable of delivering the job with lesser time and with higher quality comes from the reinforced models that the asking agent has developed over time. As a consequence, agents with complementary expertise interact with each other more often than agents with similar expertise. Thus, given sufficient interaction opportunities and cooperation possibilities, agent coalitions develop where self-interested agents have complementary skill sets.

3.2   Agent Types

The behavior of reciprocative agents is determined by the level of available information to the agents about other agents. We mentioned that agent A can receive help from agent B only if the cost incurred by A to do that task is more than incurred by B for helping A. However, in deciding whether to help or not to help, the reciprocative agents can ask *some* other agents for their *opinion* about the agent asking help. The agents from whom a help-giving agent x, asks for opinion are only those with whom x has a favorable balance of help. This is a reasonable policy, to believe in those who have *earned trust* by their interactions. The opinion received by x from another agent y is the cumulative balance that y has with the agent seeking help. An agent who has a "good" record of help giving behavior is more likely to be helped. Reciprocative agents who decide to help or not based on such collaborative opinion are called *earned trust based reciprocative agents*.

Selfish agents by definition do not extend help under any circumstances. The selfish agents that we use in our simulations are characterized by the additional property of *lying* when they are asked for their opinion. They lie about the balance they hold at any time with the agent who is currently waiting to receive help. If agent x is asking agent y whether or not to help agent z, then y reports a negated balance with z if y is a liar. This means that liars "bad-mouth" helpful agents.

4   Experimental Results

To examine our claim that the ability to estimate other agents' expertise enhance the performance of agents and boost coalition formation among agents with complementary expertise, we present the following experimental results. In our experimental setups we have used 3 different task types, i.e., each agent having one of 3 possible expertise levels. The "high" and "low" mean values used to define the distributions from which we draw time an quality of performance

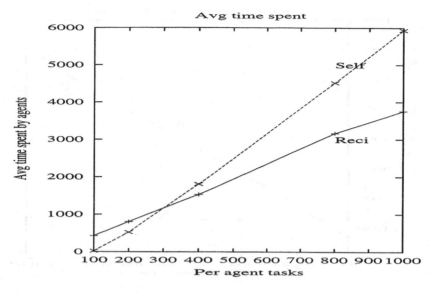

Fig. 1. Average time spent by agents.

of experts and non-experts are fixed at 10.0 and 1.0 respectively, the standard deviation being 0.05.

We have considered two task cost metrics, time of completion and quality of performance. Our first experimental setup focuses on examining the relative performances of the reciprocative and selfish agents on those two cost metrics. We record the average time taken and the average quality of performance of the reciprocative and selfish agents for completing all tasks. We ran experiments taking a total of 100 agents with equal number of reciprocatives and selfish agents. The tasks per agent was set at 100, 200, 400, 800 and 1000. The average time to complete and the average quality of performance to complete all tasks for each agent type were recorded. Figures 1 and 2 show the results.

Figure 1 shows the relative performance of individual lying selfish and earned-trust based reciprocative agents in terms of the average time spent in performing all tasks. We see from the graphs that selfish agents outperform reciprocatives (take lesser time to complete tasks) until the per agent task reaches a value of 300. As the task value is increased, reciprocatives prove to dominate the performance of selfish agents. As noted earlier, the increase in the number of tasks allow the reciprocatives to have more interactions with other agents. This, in turn, helps in their learning process of identifying potential helpful partners, and in particular, those with non-selfish behavior and having complementary expertise and detect the exploiters. This, when coupled with the strategy of earned trust that the reciprocatives employ, i.e., rely on the opinion of only those agents who have been helpful in the past, leads to dominating performances in most cases.

Figure 2 shows the quality of performance of "individual lying" selfish and "earned trust based" reciprocatives. The graphs follow a pattern similar to that

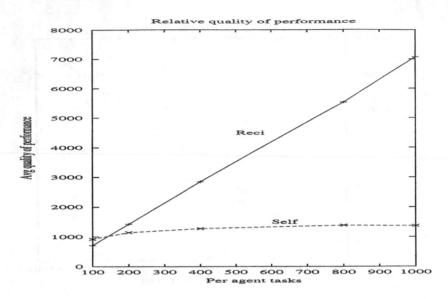

Fig. 2. Average quality of performance of agents.

in figure 1. Reciprocatives, initially fail to extract the advantage by learning other agents' models since the number of tasks is not large enough for learning to produce good models and using them to form fruitful partnerships. With increasing tasks, agents interact with agents more often which help them better identify others' expertise and learn more robust models of other agents. Hence, with increasing tasks reciprocatives can get their tasks completed at a higher quality by obtaining help from partners of complementary expertise in emerging coalitions.

In the results presented so far we have attempted to verify our claim that agents do learn to identify partners with complementary expertise by examining and explaining the consequences or external effects of the strategies. In our next experimental setup, we show the results that fully establishes the fact. We present, in this experimental setup, information regarding the group/coalition formation among agents. Stability of a coalition is determined by the frequency of interaction and the net savings earned by such coalitions.

Table 1 shows the number of helps (interaction frequency) and total savings generated by the different groups or coalitions of agents of different expertise in a population of size 30 of learned trust based reciprocatives with 2000 tasks per agent. The interaction frequency of a "group" (like $(1, 1)$) is defined as the total number of interactions between all agents with expertise in task type 1. Since there are 3 task types, there can be a total of 6 groups that are enumerated in the table. The "savings" of such a group is the total savings earned over the interactions that define the group size. From table 1, we find that both the interaction frequencies and savings earned by the groups of agents having complementary expertise are larger than the corresponding values of groups of similar agents.

This corroborates our hypothesis that when agents are endowed with the ability to learn others' expertise, they develop mutually beneficial coalitions with agents of complementary expertise. The benefit is particularly obtained in groups of heterogeneous agents.

Table 1. Group interaction information of earned trust based reciprocative

Group	Number of helps	Saving
(1,1)	4470	2987.03
(2,2)	4409	3023.38
(3,3)	4584	3560.69
(1,2)	12946	130703.34
(1,3)	12744	128684.23
(2,3)	12976	135528.07

In the previous sets of experiments we have shown that reciprocatives perform better on both the dimensions, time and quality, that define task cost. Savings earned by an agent gives in a nutshell how well it performed in accomplishing its assigned tasks. So, in our last set of experiments we studied the variations in average savings earned by both selfish and reciprocative agents after each agent has completed all of its jobs. We used a mix of individual lying selfish and learned-trust based reciprocative agents. Figures 3 and 4 show the results obtained by varying the percentage of selfish agents in the population under two different values of "tasks per agent", 20 and 40 respectively. The percentage of selfish agents in the population was varied from 50 to 80% in steps of 10%. In both the figures we find reciprocative agents outperform selfish agents, because the average savings earned by the reciprocative agents are more than those of the selfish agents for all selfish percentages in the population. In both cases the savings earned by reciprocatives decrease with increase in the percentage of selfish population. For the same percentage of selfish population, however, the savings earned by the reciprocatives are higher when the per-agent tasks are higher. From these observations, we can conclude that, reciprocative agents learn to identify potential helpful agents and their expertise which enables them to enter into mutually beneficial coalitions. Savings earned, reflect the effectiveness and stability of agent coalitions. Lower values of savings earned by the selfish agents indicate that the reciprocative agents have effectively shunned the exploitative selfish agents. The performance of reciprocative agents, however, decreases with increase in the number of the selfish agents. This is due to the fewer reciprocative agents with which stable mutually beneficial coalitions can be formed. With increase in the task level, however, the savings of reciprocative agents for the same number of selfishes in the population are more because a higher number of per agent tasks allows agents to receive help from few reciprocative agents for a much longer time.

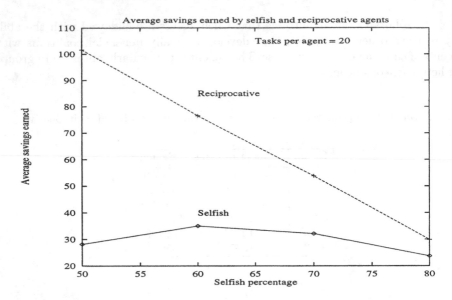

Fig. 3. Average savings of agents with 20 tasks per agent.

5   Expected Utility Based Helping Decisions

In this paper, we introduce an expected utility based decision mechanism used by the reciprocative agents to decide whether or not to honor a request for help from another agent. When requested for help, an agent, using this decision mechanism, estimates the utility of agreeing to the request by evaluating its chance of obtaining help from the asking agent in future. An agent, being self-interested, has the objective of earning more savings by receiving help than cost incurred by helping others in the long run. When an agent using this strategy decides whether or not to provide help, it uses a statistical summary of its past interactions with the requesting agent as a metric for evaluating its expected interaction pattern with the latter in future. Using this information, it evaluates the difference between the expected benefit and the expected cost it might incur for that agent by helping it in the future.

We assume a set of $\mathcal{A}$ agents executing tasks from a set Υ. Let $\mathcal{H}$ denote the interaction histories of the agents. $\mathcal{H}$ is an ordered list of tuples where each tuple is of the form $\langle i, j, x, t, c_i, c_j, help \rangle$ where the components are respectively the agent requesting help for a task, the agent being asked for help, the task type, the time instance, the cost of performing the task to the requesting agent, the cost of performing the task to the agent being asked for help, and whether or not j helped i. Let $\mathcal{H}_{i,j} \subseteq \mathcal{H}$ be the part of the history that contains interactions between agents i and j only. Let H denote the space of all possible histories. Our goal is to derive a decision procedure $\mathcal{F} : \mathcal{A} \times \mathcal{A} \times \Upsilon \times H \to Yes/No$ that maps a request from an agent to another agent to a boolean decision based on the task type involved and the interaction history of these two agents.

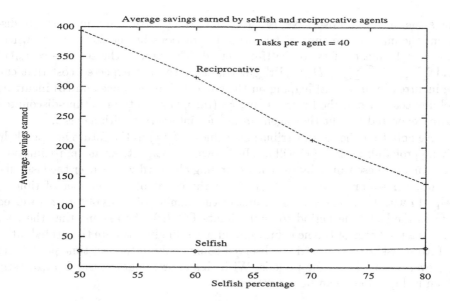

Fig. 4. Average savings of agents with 40 tasks per agent.

In the following, we present the expected utility based decision mechanism that agent m uses to evaluate a help request by another agent o for helping with task type τ. The expected utility of agent m for interacting with agent o at time $\mathcal{T}$ and future time steps, $E_{\mathcal{T}}(m, o, \tau)$, is defined as:

$$E_{\mathcal{T}}(m, o, \tau) =$$

$$\sum_{t=\mathcal{T}}^{\infty} \gamma^{t-\mathcal{T}} [\sum_{x \in \Upsilon} (D_m^t(x) \mathrm{Pr}_{m,o}^t(x) cost_m(x)) -$$

$$\sum_{x \in \Upsilon} (D_m^t(x) \mathrm{Pr}_{o,m}^t(x) cost_m(x))] - cost_m(\tau), \qquad (1)$$

where $cost_i(x)$ is the expected cost that i incurs doing a task of type x, $cost_m(\tau)$ is the cost to be incurred by agent m to help agent o in the current time instance, γ is the time discount, and Υ is the set of different task types. We assume that an agent is expert in only one of the possible task types. The evaluation of the expected utility of agent m helping agent o considers all possible interactions in future and for all task types. In equation 1, $D_m^t(x)$ is the expected future distribution of task types that agent m will receive at time instance t. We define $\mathrm{Pr}_{i,j}^t(x)$ as the probability that agent i will receive help from agent j at time step t, given it has a task of type x.

The term $\sum_{t=\mathcal{T}}^{\infty} \gamma^{t-\mathcal{T}} \sum_{x \in \Upsilon} D_m^t(x) \mathrm{Pr}_{m,o}^t(x) cost_m(x)$ represents the time discounted (with discount factor γ) expected savings of m by receiving helps from o in future. We assume that when an agent is helped by another agent, the helped agent incurs no cost for the task. Hence, when an agent m is helped with task type x, its savings is $cost_m(x)$, the cost it would have incurred to complete the same task on its own. We use an infinite time horizon and increasingly discount the impact of estimates for future interactions by the factor $\gamma^{t-\mathcal{T}}$, where $0 < \gamma < 1$, and t refers to the time period. The sum of the terms $-cost_m(\tau)$ and $\sum_{t=\mathcal{T}}^{\infty} \gamma^{t-\mathcal{T}} \sum_{x \in \Upsilon} D_m^t(x) \Pr_{o,m}^t cost_m(x)$ is the net expected cost that can be incurred by m for (a) helping on the current time instance and (b) incurring helping cost for o in the future. Thus, $E_{\mathcal{T}}(m, o, \tau)$ gives the net time-discounted future expected benefit that agent m has for interacting with agent o.

We note that the task distributions values, $D_m^t(x)$ in the future and the help giving probabilities $\Pr_{i,j}^t(x)$ will not be known to an agent. As an approximation, we estimate these values by the corresponding observed values over the last time period. For example, we use the ratio of the count of the number of times j helped i with task type x to the count of the number of tasks of type x received by i in the last time period to approximate $\Pr_{i,j}^t(x)$. We assume that the near past is a predictor of the near future, and accordingly estimate the probabilities of future task arrivals based on observed counts only in the last time period and not over all previous time periods. With this approximation, the $E(m, o)$ term given in Equation 1 can be rewritten as:

$$
\begin{aligned}
E_{\mathcal{T}}(m, o, \tau) = \\
\sum_{t=\mathcal{T}}^{\infty} \gamma^{t-\mathcal{T}} [\sum_{x \in \Upsilon} (D_m^{\mathcal{T}}(x) \Pr_{m,o}(x) cost_m(x)) - \\
\sum_{x \in \Upsilon} (D_m^{\mathcal{T}}(x) \Pr_{o,m}(x) cost_m(x))] - cost_m(\tau).
\end{aligned}
\tag{2}
$$

Our suggested decision mechanism $\mathcal{F}$ will evaluate a help request from agent o to agent m for a task x_0 of type τ at time $\mathcal{T}$ given the history of interactions, $\mathcal{H}_{m,o}^{\mathcal{T}}$ and $\mathcal{H}_{o,m}^{\mathcal{T}}$, between these two agents. The history is used to first calculate $\Pr_{m,o}(x)$ and $\Pr_{o,m}(x)$ values and the distribution of task arrivals. It then calculates the expected utility of agent m for interacting with agent o in the current and future time steps, $E_{\mathcal{T}}(m, o.tau)$. Our prescription is for agent m to help agent o in the current time if $E(m, o)$ is greater than the expected cost of an agent processing its next assigned task without receiving help from others, i.e.,

$$
\mathcal{F}(o, m, \tau, \mathcal{H}_{m,o}^{\mathcal{T}} \cup \mathcal{H}_{o,m}^{\mathcal{T}}) = \text{Yes, if}
$$
$$
E_{\mathcal{T}}(m, o, \tau) + \sum_{x \in \Upsilon} D_m(x) cost_m(x) > 0,
$$
$$
= \text{No, otherwise,}
\tag{3}
$$

where the summation term is the expected cost of agent m for doing a task in the next time instance. This summation term represents the initial bias or willingness for an agent m to help another agent o incurring a risk of not being reciprocated. As initial probability values are all zero, the agent will not help another without this initial bias.

6   Related Work

Using agent coalitions is an interesting and much explored approach to solve complex, distributed tasks. Assigning groups of agents to do a task or multiple tasks has the advantage of complementary individual agent expertise being used to complete different parts of the global problem.

However, work in the area of coalition formation in agent societies has focused on cooperative agents [8]. A related work on coalitions in agent societies takes self-interested agents into account [9]. But it does not consider the possible heterogeneity in performance of a task between different agents. Our work is different from these because it takes into consideration self-interested agents that have different performance levels for different task types. We also have a learning parameter in our agents which is used to identify other's capabilities. This, in turn, favors those with complementary expertise when asking for help. Mutual understanding of capabilities evolve cooperative groups in the society of self-interested agents. Learning of cooperative behavior has also been addressed in [10]. However, there the learning uses an off-line learning module which generates situation-action pairs using GA. To determine the fitness of the evolved situation-action pairs during off-line learning an agent-model is required. Our work uses only online learning and agents do not have to store a priori models of other agents. However, in an attempt to learn behaviors of all other agents, our approach can become time consuming in situations where number of agents increase exponentially. A concept of using "congregations" to determine who to interact with in an agent society is addressed in [11]. However, determining the right congregation again suffers from the time issue when number of agents increase exponentially.

A fair number of approaches have been developed that use reasoning mechanisms that consider exchange of help or social reputations in deciding how to interact with other agents. Our own work has concentrated on the use of a probabilistic decision mechanism for deciding to help based on past balance with the requesting agent [12]. Castelfranchi, Conte, and Paolucci use normative reputation [13] to enhance the performance of agents that comply with social norms. In the SPIRE framework developed by Grosz and collaborators [14,15], performance in a group is improved when agents reason about the effects of withdrawing from social commitments on their reputation.

Our approach of using expected utility based decision mechanism is different from recent work on utility based strategies for sharing information [16] because we take into consideration dynamically changing environments and endow our agents with the ability to maintain future expectations of such dynamics to adaptively alter group behaviors.

7   Conclusions and Future Directions

Adoption of reciprocal behavior in a society of self-interested agents generates incentives that promote cooperative behavior. In this paper we hypothesized that in an agent society where agents differ in their expertise, incorporation of a learning component will help generate cooperative groups of agents with complementary expertise. Our simulations confirmed this hypotheses. These groups are mutually beneficial to the agents because they save more time by giving the tasks to other agents who have the required expertise and accomplish their jobs with better quality. Such cooperative group formation is stable since the exploitative agents are effectively shunned.

We also hypothesize that cooperative behavior based on future expected utility is a robust decision mechanism for agents to develop stable, mutually beneficial groups containing agents with complementary capabilities. This type of decision mechanism benefits agents by allowing them to quickly respond to changing behaviors of other agents and the environmental conditions. We have presented an expected utility based forward-looking decision mechanism that considers future benefits of interacting with other agents. The future projection of experience from the near past allows these reciprocative agents to be adaptive and responsive to both changing environmental demands, agent behaviors and group composition.

One assumption in this work has been that agents have fixed behaviors. A more realistic scenario would be for an agent to have the freedom of changing its behavior when it deems appropriate. Such behavior adoption leads to an evolutionary process with a dynamically changing composition of agent group behaviors. We plan to investigate whether such evolving agent behavior might create a society of agents with the same behavior, which could be the optimal behavior to adopt.

In the expected utility framework, we are working to introduce other competitive decision mechanisms to determine the relative effectiveness of different agent interaction strategies under dynamic agent behavioral and environmental settings. We also plan to investigate the effects of task failures and performance variation on the stability and strength of the relationship between agents of complementary expertise.

Acknowledgments. This work has been supported in part by an NSF CAREER award IIS-9702672 and IIS-029208.

References

1. Bradshaw, J.M.: Software Agents. AAAI Press/The MIT Press, Menlo Park, CA (1997)
2. —, Communications of the ACM, july 1994, volume 37, number 7 (1994) Special Issue on Intelligent Agents.
3. —, Communications of the ACM, march 1999, volume 42, number 3 (1999) Special Issue on Multiagent Systems on the Net and Agents in E-commerce.
4. Huhns, M.N., Singh, M.P.: Readings in Agents. Morgan Kaufmann, San Francisco, CA (1997)

5. Shoham, Y., Tennenholtz, M.: On the synthesis of useful social laws for artificial agent societies (preliminary report). In: Proceedings of the National Conference on Artificial Intelligence, San Jose, California (1992) 276–281
6. Biswas, A., Sen, S., Debnath, S.: Limiting deception in groups of social agents. Applied Artificial Intelligence, Special Issue on Deception, Fraud, and Trust in Agent Societies 14 (2000) 785–797
7. Sen, S., Biswas, A., Debnath, S.: Believing others: Pros and cons. In: Proceedings of the Fourth International Conference on Multiagent Systems, Los Alamitos, CA, IEEE Computer Society (2000) 279–285
8. Shehory, O., Kraus, S.: Methods for task allocation via agent coalition formation. Artificial Intelligence Journal 101 (1998) 165–200
9. Lerman, K., Shehory, O.: Coalition formation for large-scale electronic markets. In: Proceedings of the Fourth International Conference on Multi-Agent Systems. (2000) 167–174
10. Denzinger, J., Kordt, M.: Evolutionary on-line learning of cooperative behavior with situation-action-pairs. In: Proceedings of Fourth International Conference on MultiAgent Systems, ICMAS 2000, Los Alamitos, CA, IEEE Computer Society (2000) 103–110
11. Brooks, C.H., Durfee, E.H., Armstrong, A.: An introduction to congregation in multiagent systems. In: Proceedings of the Fourth International Conference on Multi-Agent Systems. (2000) 79–86
12. Sen, S.: Believing others: Pros and cons. Artificial Intelligence 142 (2002) 179–203
13. Castelfranchi, C., Conte, R., Paolucci, M.: Normative reputation and the costs of compliance. Journal of Artificial Societies and Social Simulation 1 (1998)
14. Glass, A., Grosz, B.: Socially conscious decision-making. In: Proceedings of the Fourth International Conference on Autonomous Agents, New York, NY, ACM Press (2000) 217–224
15. Sullivan, D.G., Grosz, B., Kraus, S.: Intention reconciliation by collaborative agents. In: Proceedings of the Fourth International Conference on Multiagent Systems, Los Alamitos, CA, IEEE Computer Society (2000) 293–300
16. Azoulay-Schwartz, R., Kraus, S.: Stable strategies for sharing information among agents. In: Proceedings of the Seventeenth International Joint Conference on Artificial Intelligence. (2001) 1128–1134

A Framework for the Social Description of Resources in Open Environments*

Matthias Nickles and Gerhard Weiß

Department of Computer Science, Technical University of Munich
85748 Garching bei München, Germany, {nickles,weissg}@cs.tum.edu

Abstract. The description of public resources such as web site contents, web services or data files in open peer-to-peer networks using some formal framework like RDF usually reflects solely the subjective requirements, opinion and preferences of the resource provider. In some sense, such resource descriptions appear "antisocial" as they do not reflect the social impact of the respective resource and therefore might not provide impartial, reliable assessments. E.g., commercial web sites do not contain any relationship to the information, service and product offers of competing sites, and the assessment of the site by customers, experts or competitors is unknown to users and information agents also. We introduce an open multiagent system framework which derives multidimensional resource descriptions from the possibly conflicting opinions of interacting description agents, which act as representatives for individual, organizational or institutional clients, and compete in the assertion of individual opinions against others to provide a "socially enhanced" solution for this problem. In contrast to the results of majority voting based recommender systems, the obtained social resource descriptions reflect social structures such as norms and roles which emerge from communication processes.

Keywords: Semantic Web, Information Agents, Web Ontologies, Recommender Systems, Multidimensional Rating

1 Introduction

In the context of the World Wide Web and large, open and heterogenous peer-to-peer networks like Gnutella [19], FastTrack [20] or eDonkey [18], a well-known problem is constituted through the notorious lack of reliable, impartial descriptions of publicly accessible resources such as web sites (or the content they provide, respectively), shared files or web services. If a resource description (RD) is available, in most cases the description is provided by the original resource provider, which at least for commercial supplies restricts its trustworthiness and might makes it as useless as any other kind of advertisement. In contrast, recommender systems [3] based on the evaluation of access statistics, voting or resource content analysis try to ascertain the "objective" value of resources. E.g., collaborative filtering recommender systems provide filter criteria for site classification, that classify the rated site in terms of "appropriate/inappropriate" or "interesting/uninteresting", based on the surfing behavior of a more or less homogenous

---

* This work is supported by DFG under contracts no. Br609/11-2 and MA759/4-2.

M. Klusch et al. (Eds.): CIA 2003, LNAI 2782, pp. 206–221, 2003.

group of users with a common interest profile (user community) or implicit majority voting processes like Google's *PageRank* technology [16], which count the number of hyperlinks referring to the rated site. As a supplement or as a competing approach, content-based filtering recommender systems try to analyze the content of web resources (usually by means of keyword counting and bayesian classification) and compare the results with the interest profiles of the web surfers [2]. The main drawback of such filtering systems is their limitation to one-dimensional descriptions (amounting to something like *"you like/dislike..."* or *"...suits your needs"*) based on presumed predilections. This approach does not provide much help for the process of interest forming, which should precede any recommendation and filtering. Likewise, systems based upon trust networks (e.g., PeopleNet [11]), which are expected to be especially important for the identification of trustworthy web services, can't do much if there is no trust yet related to a specific rater, topic or object, or the potential truster is anonymous. Another problem is the apparent black-box character of many (commercial) recommender systems, which on the one hand provides some protection against manipulation, but on the other hand seriously restricts their trustability. For these reasons, transparent, balanced descriptions which are in addition reliable and semantically rich can currently only be provided by humans, for example journalists and experts, or through discussion forums (e.g., newsgroups and threaded message boards like *Slashdot* [17]), with well-known shortcomings like the absence of a machine readable encoding, which makes it almost impossible for information agents like web spiders to analyze these descriptions. Although the Semantic Web effort addresses the problem of missing machine-understandability of web site descriptions, it currently focusses primarily on the specification of languages and tools for the representation of consistent semantics and ontologies, not on the process of information gathering and rating itself, and it is just beginning to take into consideration phenomena like social RD impact [12], conflicting opinions, information biasing by commercial interests, and inconsistent or intentionally incorrect information. In contrast to traditional approaches, our goal is to provide *social* resource descriptions, which are obtained from the contribution of multiple, conflicting opinions represented by interacting information agents (so-called *(resource) description agents*), and which are *rich* (i.e., with unrestricted multidimensional description criteria [1], multiple levels of generalization and unveiled information about the social relationship of their contributors) - somewhat comparable to a computational résumé of a human discussion. Aiming at this, this work proposes a framework for the derivation of formal *social expectation structures* from observed agent communications [6,7], and describes how the social description of web resources can be seen as a special case of such structures. To allow for the embedding of our framework into open environments like the Semantic Web, its architecture is *open*, i.e., it assumes a heterogeneous, unrestricted and fluctuating set of autonomous agents, and does make almost no assumptions about special agent capabilities and agent architectures, except agent rationality and ability to communicate.

The reminder of this paper is structured as follows: The next section specifies the general objectives and requirements for a multiagent system for social descriptions. In section 3, we introduce the overall architecture of the framework. Section 4 describes how social structures can be represented and generated from observed communications, and section 5 outlines how social descriptions can be obtained from social structures. With a short discussion of open problems and directions for further research in section 6 the paper concludes.

2   Terms and Requirements

In terms of the RDF standard (the XML-based *Resource Description Framework* [9], a successor of the internet description language PICS [14], which aimed at the rating of controversial web content), the description of a certain (web) resource is a finite set of statements (*elementary (resource) descriptions*) together with a description vocabulary. Each statement describes the properties of the respective resource (which can be virtually any kind of object like web site attributes, documents or web services, but also other statements) by means of meta data, according to a vocabulary of property types or classes (sometimes called an "ontology" or "schema"). Technically, such an elementary description is defined as a proposition of the form $(resource, propertyType, value)$, in which $resource$ denotes an object with an unique identifier (i.e., a Uniform Resource Identifier (URI) or a P2P-resource locator like ed2k://|file|filename.mp3). $propertyType$ is the described attribute of the resource (an element of the given description vocabulary), and $value$ is its assigned value. $value$ can be a resource by itself, and thus the description vocabulary can form a hierarchy of property types (e.g., $Author$ and $Credibility$ in (www.somesite.com, $Author, John$), $(John, Credibility, high)$) Elementary descriptions can be expressed through a formal description language, for example RDF or DAML [13]. An example for a description with boolean property type is (www.SomeCompany.com, $MinorOrientation, True$). Beside such simple statements, description languages like RDF can of course express more complex RDs, but their basics are always as described, so we don't deal with technically more complicated cases. We talk about a *competitive RD* if the elementary description is pro-actively supported by a description agent in competition with inconsistent descriptions represented by other agents, with his goal to make some supra-individual social description (e.g., the public opinion) consistent with his individual descriptions. A *social RD* is a probably inconsistent RD together with a social weighing of each of its elements, i.e., a more or less abstract description of the degree of social assent and of the supporters or opponents of the respective elementary description. A well known example for such a social description would be the result of an opinion poll: "10% of the questioned individuals do support opinion A, 90% do support opinion B". The percentages here are supposed to describe the social acceptance of each opinion obtained from a majority voting, which also underlies most web site recommender systems, although these systems usually unveil only the winner of the poll. Additionally, usual recommender systems are limited to a single property type that is assumed to be appropriate with regard to the presumed interests of certain users. While our approach can lead to similar results given certain circumstances, our descriptions are derived from an active competition process among description agents, they are multidimensional, allowing to asses multiple criteria at the same time, and, most important, they are able to reflect social structures and conditions. Therefore, our approach is settled on the knowledge-gathering and inference layer of the Semantic Web, preceding recommendation and filtering. For the human part of the web there already exist social structures with a strong influence on the provision of shared content. In our opinion, an objective of the Semantic Web effort should be to make these latent structures technically explicit to web users and information gathering agents by means of formal, socially rich descriptions which unveil who advocates a certain opinion, by which criteria and under what circumstances. In a larger scenario, the social descriptions for a significant part of the internet could be a step towards a "Social Semantic Web".

The characteristics and objectives for an approach towards this goal can be summarized as follows:

Recognition of controversies. A high amount of RDs are subjectively biased quality judgements with a high conflict potential. Competitive descriptions, represented by software agents, shall *enable* such controversies, and social descriptions shall make them *explicit* and available to information agents. In general, it is unavoidable that the contributors of the Semantic Web or other hybrid open systems (i.e., open systems where humans interact with machines) will generate intentionally inconsistent information. In absence of a omniscient, normative instance, knowledge inference mechanisms for the Semantic Web will have to acknowledge inconsistencies.

Pro-active opinion representation. The competitive descriptions which contribute to social descriptions are no single "passive" statements like votes for an opinion poll, but shall instead continuously be represented by intelligent, social agents which support them actively in a dynamic social process, e.g. by means of argumentation, negotiation, distributed reasoning and conflictive behavior.

Complexity and hybridity. Due to the size, the heterogeneity and the openness of the World Wide Web and public peer-to-peer networks, the agent-supported description of resources is a highly complex task. Social descriptions increase the complexity of hybrid information-rich environments because they make human sociality "behind" the technical infrastructure visible. Nevertheless, to overcome the idea of a semantic web consisting of unrelated (or only syntactically related) information pieces, the enabling of computational social structures is inalienable in our opinion.

Unveiling of social interests. Even an individual description does not only assert the rated resource, but makes an implicit statement about the actor which is responsible for that description [12]. The presence of social descriptions is supposed to strengthen this exhibition of subjective preferences and opinions.

3 Architecture

As an approach to the described issues, we outline a multiagent system that consists of the following components:

1. Formal languages for competitive descriptions and the (presumably indefinite) social descriptions to enable the utterance of individual descriptions by agents and the representation of inconsistent contributions from different opinion sources. The

emphasis should be on opinion announcement rather than on usual objectives like cooperation and consensus finding, and these languages should be compatible with current standards for agent communication languages (ACLs) like FIPA-ACL [8] and WWW-oriented description languages like RDF or DAML [13].

2. Intelligent *resource description agents* which are able to deliberatively rate resources in accordance with the opinions, criteria and interests of their private/public/ commercial etc. clients, and to represent their individual descriptions in a social discourse with other description agents.

3. A technical instance (*social resource description system*) for the technical facilitation of description agents communication and for the derivation of social descriptions from these communication.

Description agents act either as representatives for existing RDs (therefore in some sense the pro-active "incarnations" of RDF documents), peers, user communities, source creators (e.g., web sites owners or multimedia providers), or private and public organizations. Every description agent supports a certain opinion and announces, asserts and defends it in an open discussion forum which is assigned to the rated resource (usually a web site) or a peer-to-peer client (e.g., a file sharing application). Every forum is part of the Social Resource Description System (SRDS), a software application (within the Semantic Web knowledge inference infrastructure) which observes the forums and continuously derives from the forum communication so-called *social expectation structures* [6,7]. These structures are distilled to social descriptions. Together with the rated web site, the social descriptions are presented to the user (e.g. to the web surfer through a special HTML frame within the browser window or via some user agent), and to information agents, for example the web spiders of internet search machines like Google or Altavista. The description agents will of course also obtain these information, since social knowledge is of high importance for the agents to allow them to intentionally avoid or achieve oppositional or conformist behavior in respect to other agents and social norms, and to find appropriate allies and opponents.

Figure 1 shows the proposed framework. For simplicity, the figure consists only of a few description agents, a single web site and the central rating system, and an attached recommender system (cf. below).

3.1   Resource Description Agents

In figure 1, the ovals in the top left part symbolize description agents (gray color) and their clients (white color) - users, organizations and institutions (i.e., governmental organizations). Every description agent should be able to obtain individual descriptions conforming to the preferences of his client, to keep these descriptions up-to-date with respect to changes of the resource content and the opinion and needs of his client, and to represent the descriptions in the forum. The latter means, that the agent tries to influence the social descriptions with the goal to make them *consistent* with his subjective descriptions. To achieve this goal (which induces a goal conflict with

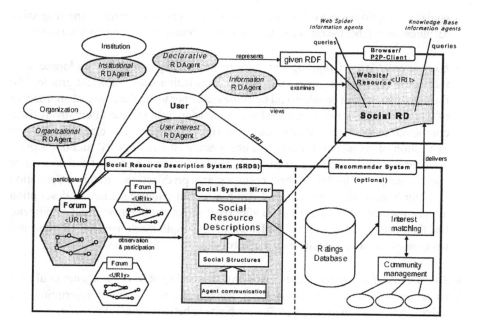

Fig. 1. Architecture of the framework

competing description agents), the agent must have adequate technical, mental and social capabilities (for example the capability to cooperate with other agents in the assertion of some common opinion). Since social descriptions are derived solely from the forum communications, the agent must be able to participate in the forum (e.g., as a mobile agent which is executable on the forum server), know the description communication language and the algorithms the SRDS uses to derive social descriptions to obtain a reasonable argumentation strategy. In addition, description agents should idealistically not only be able to propagate some predefined description, but also to gather new information about the respective resource, other comparable resources, and in particular the descriptions, knowledge and strategies of other description agents.

The following set of description agent types is presumably useful for large, information rich environments like the World Wide Web:

– *Organizational description agents* represent private or public organizations (including companies). Their purpose is to propagate interests and evaluation criteria of almost any kind (commercial, legal, scientific, ethical, political...).

– *Institutional description agents* are supposed to have a strong influence on other agents and the social descriptions, because as a particular sort of organizational agents they represent governmental authorities. Their description criteria and opinions are thus supposed to be base on law. Such description agents can participate in the SRDS to inform the web surfers (as far as they are able to influence the social descriptions) and other agents about the legal assessment of the respective resource, or to label the rated resource, e.g. for a minor-protecting filtering software.

– *User-interest description agents* rate resources regarding the preferences of individual web surfers, peers and communities with a similar interest profile. The finding of an interest profile could be achieved either using the classical approaches of content- or collaborative-based recommender systems, or alternatively in a combined process of simultaneous description obtainment (e.g., through the evaluation of social descriptions and observation of other agents) and description announcements. It would also be conceivable to evaluate parts of the content of user home pages to derive their opinions and predilections, if this information is publicly accessible and encoded using a formal language. Like all description agents, user description agents are supposed to act deliberatively and intelligent, but they could just as well be implemented as simple machinery which translates user intentions into a machine readable format.

– *Declarative description agents* represent an existing RD. Such agents could act as advertisers, or they compare their descriptions with another description and calculate their difference (e.g., "This web site is better/worse/... than ...").

– *Content analyzing description agents* analyze resources and feed the obtained information into the forum as asserted descriptions. The information acquisition could be done via statistical keyword analysis, for example. Therefore, content analyzing description agents act as service agents which help other agents to complete their own descriptions. Obviously, the purpose of this type of agent might overlap with the objectives of other description agent, for example user-interest description agents which form a description by means of a comparison of the results of content analysis and interest profiles of their clients.

Figure 2 shows an description agent in the context of our framework.

3.2   Social Resource Description System

For each web site, the description system accommodates a *forum* which has the respective resource as its communication topic (corresponding to a specific ontology that can be used with the RD language). The forum serves as a public whiteboard, on which the agents put their messages addressed to other agents and receive responses - very much like people do in Usenet newsgroups and web-based message boards. Every forum has its own description vocabulary which could be assembled by the agents themselves via some ontology negotiation technique. Besides the syntax of the RD language and the communication protocols that may accompanying this language, the common vocabulary causes the only constraint for the agent's social behavior. Forums are *open* - every agent which is able to communicate using the RD language can participate at any time (even in multiple forums simultaneously), as long as he identifies himself and his clients to the

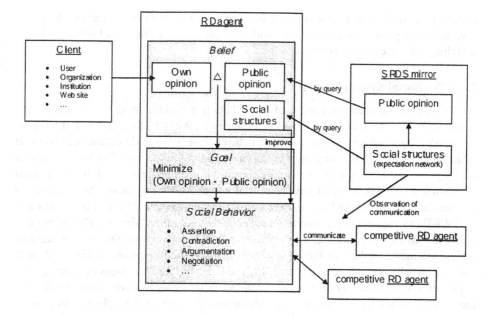

Fig. 2. Generic resource description agent

SRDS and therefore to the system users[1]. As the central part of the SRDS, a so called Social System *Mirror* (or "Mirror" for short) [5,6] continuously observes each forum, analyzes observed communications and derives the social structures which emerge from the communications. In a second step, for each forum (and therefore each resource) the Mirror generates social RDs corresponding to the obtained social structures. The generation of social RDs is carried out either continuously for each newly observed communication (similar to the examination and moderation of a newsgroup or a message board), or on request.

Social descriptions are not only communicated to the description agents, but primarily to the users and to information gathering agents. Doing so, the SRDS act very similar to a newspaper. Because of this, it is of course recommended to place the SRDS on "neutral ground", e.g. as a service of a web search engine which returns social descriptions for web sites, or through a web service or a proxy server that delivers social descriptions to the browser or peer clients together or prior with/to the requested resources[2].

A straightforward extension of our framework would be to implement a recommendation system as part of the SRDS, which stores the social descriptions generated from the SRDS Mirror in a descriptions database. Instead of requesting directly the social descriptions, the user in this scenario forwards a personal interest profile to the recommendation

---

[1] For obvious reasons, the identity of the client should be authenticated by means of a trusted security certificate.

[2] Instead of just publishing the descriptions, it would of course be feasible to use them for filtering mechanisms which hide resources with a someway "bad rating" to the user, although this would be very much in contrast to the intention behind our approach.

system (e.g. in form of a desired social description). The recommendation system then compares this profile with each of the collected social descriptions and returns a list of matching resource identifiers back to the user.

3.3   The Social System Mirror

The Mirror as the core component of the SRDS is a middle agent which models the social system of the focussed forum(s)[3]. Technically, it can be thought as an intelligent knowledge base which derives social structures from observed communications and makes them available for the participating agents and human users. The Mirror has two major purposes: First, the monitoring of communication processes and the continuous derivation of emergent social structures and social RDs from these observations (to inform the users of the SRDS), and second, the announcement of social structures and social RDs to the agents (the so-called *reflection* effect of the Mirror). The agents can query the Mirror very much like a database and deliberatively use the social structures which are made explicit to them as a guideline for their decision making and their interaction behavior, i.e., to assess their own social status and the status of other agents, to prevent (or intentionally not to prevent) the violation of social norms, and to influence the current social RDs. If the agents deliberatively adopt to the reflected structures, these structures become "stronger", otherwise "weaker" (cf. next section). By means of this the Mirror reflects a realistic model of a social system to the agents and thus influences them (similar to mass media in human societies). Doing so, it never restricts agent autonomy - its influence is solely by means of information and not through the imposition of constraints.

4   Social Expectation Structures

To derive social descriptions from competitive RDs, we need a means for the derivation and representation of social structures, in particular the relationships among competitive RDs. In our framework, this is achieved by the Mirror component within the SRDS, which models each forum as a *communication system* [7] consisting of communications (with competitive RDs as messages content) and their relationships. The assumption underlying this approach (influenced by sociological *Systems Theory* [4]) is that all relevant aspects of sociality are eventually revealed through communication, and that empirically obtained expectations regarding communications are the most general way to model sociality if no a-priory assumptions about agent behavior or mental properties of agents can be made, as it is surely the case in an open environment like the internet.

The data structure a Mirror operates on to represent social structures is called *expectation network* [6,7]. An expectation network is a graphical data structure (not necessarily coherent), which consists of *elementary expectations* regarding the future communicational behavior of a set of observed agents (obtained from a temporal generalization of observed communication trajectories)[4]. Its basic constituents are

---

[3] The Mirror is also a general design concept and a coordination medium for open multiagent systems and therefore not restricted to our kind of application.

[4] *Trust*, which is used by e.g. [11] to achieve reliability, is a special case of expectation.

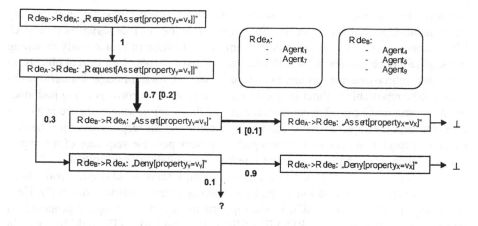

Fig. 3. An expectation network

event nodes which represent expected utterances, and probabilistically weighted *edges* connecting event nodes, which represent significant correlations of the respective utterances. Expectation networks always represent dynamic belief, i.e., belief that is constantly under revision according to the evolution of social structures as they show up in each forum. For lack of space, we cannot introduce the formal framework and the stochastic approach behind communication systems and expectation networks here (cf. [7,5]). Instead, with figure 3 we provide an example of an expectation network that represents the structure of a discourse among description agents[5]. Presumably, it is possible to use other formal structures to model the social expectation structures of an SRDS (e.g., belief networks or stochastic automata).

Nodes (squares) are labelled with message templates (in a formal RD agent communication language) and the special symbols "⊥" (denoting the end of a conversation) and "?" (denoting an unknown continuation). Nodes are connected by edges (arrows) labelled with numerical *expectabilities*, which denote the probability that the respective message(s) occur subsequently. These probabilities are derived from observed frequencies of the respective message sequences in the past. The thickness of edges represents the *normativity* of the respective expectability and the numerical value in square brackets denotes its *deviancy*. An edge with high normativeness (thick arrow) represents an expectation which has proved itself as empirically stable in the long term, which is a typical property of expectations obtained from laws and other social norms. The deviancy is the difference of long-term and short-term expectability, corresponding to the expectability of agent behavior which deviates from a social norm. Substitution lists appear in rounded boxes. A substitution list denotes a social *role* the listed agents can impersonate. For this purpose, the message templates contain role variables ($Role_A$ and $Role_B$) that can be bounded to each of the list entries, provided this bounding is done in a consistent way along the respective path. An expectation network can be *generalized* in

---

[5] We use a graphical notation that is slightly simpler than the notation introduced in [6,7,5].

two ways: First, a single expectation network might describe the expectations regarding multiple message sequences due to different instantiations of role variables (the MAS Mirror obtains these roles automatically from the unification of syntactically matching message sequences observed for different agents) and variables for external objects, in our case resource descriptions and their values. Second, each message sequence is expected to be repeatable without precondition if the root of the corresponding path does not have incoming edges. The numerical expectabilities correspond to the frequency of observed message trajectories that unify syntactically with the respective paths. Theoretically, an expectation network contains paths for every possible sequence of messages, but in practice, edges with a very low (or unknown) probability are omitted.

The message templates attached to the nodes do only serve as examples, formalized in a pseudo speech-act notation ("Sender$\rightarrowtail$Addressee:Performative[Content]"). Generally, any speech-act based ACL which supports the assertion of logical propositions (corresponding to elementary RDs) like FIPA-ACL or KQML/KIF could be used. In addition, the description agents shall be able to query the current social descriptions (cf. next section) and the current expectation network (or parts of it) to improve their social behavior.

5 Social Resource Descriptions

Now that we've introduced social expectation structures derived from observed communications, it is straightforward to derive social descriptions: Social descriptions based on the underlying model of social expectations are sets of social expectations regarding the utterance of elementary RDs. Each element of a social description is therefore the expectation of a *reply* to a question regarding the *agreement* with an elementary description, directed to agents (or social roles) which currently participate in the observed forum. The calculation of social descriptions regarding resource properties from expectations regarding communications makes use of the fact that an elementary RD is equivalent to a set of meta descriptions, i.e. descriptions of descriptions with a common property type "*Assent*": From a multi-dimensional description $(resource, propertyType, value)$ as in RDF we can generate meta-descriptions in the form of

$$(propertyType = value, Assent, degree\ of\ assent),$$

where the first element of this tuple is the content (logical proposition) of an assertive ACL message, the second element denotes the property type corresponding to the ACL message performative "*Assert*"[6]. The omitted resource $resource$ is provided implicitly through the forum topic. The social amount of agreement or dissent, respectively, can then simply be measured as the probability that a certain agent or a role subsuming a set of agents utters the message

$$"Actor_1 \rightarrowtail Actor_2 :' Assert[propertyType = value]'".$$

---

[6] or what ever performative the ACL provides to signal consent.

For example, a query regarding the assessment of the SomeCompany web site directed to a set of agents A would look like

$$(\texttt{www.SomeCompany.com}, MinorOrientation, ?x)$$

(where $?x$ is an existentially quantified variable with instances v_i), which could for example be transformed into the speech-acts

"$B \rightarrowtail A :' Query[MinorOrientation =?v]'$ or

"$B \rightarrowtail A :' Request[Assert[MinorOrientation = v_i]]'$.

The social description is then a set of expectabilities of the potential reactions to such a request, together with the respective values for expectation normativity and deviancy. For example, the resulting values for answers asserting

$$(\texttt{www.SomeCompany.com}, MinorOrientation, True(= v_1)) \text{ might be}$$

$$strength = 0.9, normativity = 0.7, deviancy = 0.1$$

and for

$$(\texttt{www.SomeCompany.com}, MinorOrientation, False(= v_2))$$

$strength = 0.1, normativity = 0.7, deviancy = 0.1^7$ (i.e., these agents believe in a quite normative way that SomeCompany is highly minor-oriented).

This result could have been obtained from expectation network Fig. 3, on condition that $MinorOrientation$ is a valid instance of variable $property_x$, and $v_x = True$, because according to this graph, the probability that $Agent_1$ or $Agent_7$ (via $Role_A$) asserts that $MinorOrientation = True$ is 0.7, and the probability that $Agent_4$, $Agent_5$ or $Agent_9$ would assert this is implicitly 1, so the average probability that any agent asserts $MinorOrientation = True$ is approximately 0.9.

Of course, this particular result would not provide much more value than the result obtained from a usual recommender system, as it likewise aggregates the opinions of multiple agents to a single "vote", but our example network would (with more detailed queries, see below) not only reveal collaborating sets of agents or roles, but also that $Agent_1$ and $Agent_7$ support opinion $MinorOrientation = True$ just because they want to reward other agents ($Role_B$) for their support of $property_y = v_y$, i.e. for "commercial reasons" and not because of the strong conviction that SomeCompany is indeed suited for children.

We denote (unconditioned) social descriptions as sets of terms having the form

---

[7] Uttered using a "$Deny$" performative, for example.

$Actor : (resource, propertyType, (value, expectability, normativity, deviancy)),$

where *Actor* can denote an agent or a social role.

The query results are obtained from the expectation network, either directly if the expectation network already contains paths which correspond to the focussed $Query/Request[...] \rightarrow Assert/Agree/Deny[...]$ sequences, or by means of an SRDS query on the forum directed to the agents. In the latter case, the SRDS communication introduces the required expectation network paths, and then it observes the subsequent agent communications to obtain significant expectabilities which reflect the agent opinions along this paths[8]. Besides this example, expectation networks allow for the obtainment of a large variety of other kinds of social descriptions. The usefulness of the following patterns for social RD of course depends on the particular interests of the SRDS user.

- *Single agent RD*, obtained from
  "$B \rightarrowtail SingleAgent :' Query[PropertyType =?v]'$" $\rightarrow$
  "$SingleAgent \rightarrowtail B :' Assert[PropertyType = v_i]'$"

- *Social role RD*[9], obtained from
  "$B \rightarrowtail Role :' Query[PropertyType =?v]'$" $\rightarrow$
  "$Role \rightarrowtail B :' Assert[PropertyType = v_i]'$"

- *Public opinion RD* (provided that the substitution list for role *All* contains every agent within the forum), obtained from
  "$B \rightarrowtail All :' Query[PropertyType =?v]'$" $\rightarrow$
  "$All \rightarrowtail B :' Assert[PropertyType = v_i]'$"

- *Conditioned social RD*, obtained from
  $Prefix \rightsquigarrow$ "$B \rightarrowtail A :' Query[PropertyType =?v]'$" $\rightarrow$
  "$A \rightarrowtail B :' Assert[PropertyType = v_i]'$"
  Here, "*Prefix* $\rightsquigarrow$" denotes a sequence of messages (or message templates) which has to precede the Query/Answer pattern. For example, an agent might commit himself to a certain RD that has been requested from another agent only if the other agent agrees with a certain RD by himself (as in figure 3).
  Since an expectation network can model virtually any kind of interaction pattern, *Prefix* could denote highly complex conditions, e.g. auctions for the selling of web site ratings for the purpose of commercial advertising (i.e., the agents commit themselves to agree with the opinion of the auction winner).

---

[8] In the case that A is a singleton (and therefore the SRDS does not need to generalize upon multiple agents by means of social roles), the SRDS could simply ask agent A for his opinion regarding SomeCompany.

[9] Although social roles usually group similarly behaving agents, in our formal framework [7], a single role can generalize different inconsistent opinions.

5.1   Embedding Social Descriptions within RDF Documents

Social RDs have to be communicated to information gathering agents in some standard language. In addition, it is expected to be useful to store a set of often-requested social RDs with the respective resource (very much like RDF is used) instead of calculating them on demand.

To provide a machine-readable format for (simple) social descriptions taking the form $\{Actor : (resource, propertyType, (value, expectability, normativity, deviancy))\}$, it seems reasonable to extend a well-established XML-based RD language like the RDF. This can basically be done by means of a replacement of the description parts of statements with lists of probabilistically annotated propositions. The description vocabulary for the following example is implicitly given as an XML namespace "V" , provided by some organization "description.org", and through a "Social Resource Description Rating Meta Language" namespace called SRDML.

```
<rdf:Description about='http://www.SomeCompany.com'
xmlns:s='http://description.org/schema'>
     <V:MinorOrientation>
          <SRDML:disjunctive>
               <SRDML:boolean strength=0.9 normativity=0.7 deviancy=0
                    agent='Entertainment industry'>True</SRDML:boolean>
               <SRDML:boolean strength=0.1 normativity=0.7 deviancy=0
                    agent='Entertainment industry'>False</SRDML:boolean>
               <SRDML:boolean strength=0.3 normativity=0.7 deviancy=0.6
                    agent='User community 6'>True</SRDML:boolean>
               <SRDML:boolean strength=0.7 normativity=0.7 deviancy=0.6
                    agent='User community 6'>False</SRDML:boolean>
          </SRDML:disjunctive>
     </V:MinorOrientation>
</rdf:Description>
```

An alternative approach would be the usage of higher-order statements (i.e. statements about statements) already provided by RDF. Here, we treat the elementary descriptions as subjective statements, as in:

```
<rdf:Description>>
     <rdf:subject resource'http://www.SomeCompany.com'/>
     <rdf:predicate resource='http://description.org/schemaMinorOrientation'/>
     <rdf:object>True</rdf:object>
     <rdf:type resource='http://w3.org/TR/1999/PR-rdf-syntax-19990105Statement'/>
     <a:attributedTo>Entertainment industry
          <SRDML:expectationAttr strength=0.9 normativity=0.7 deviancy=0/>
     </a:attributedTo>
</rdf:Description>
```

6 Conclusions

We have introduced a framework for social RDs as a contribution to the emerging Semantic Web, and to provide a novel approach to collaborative resource rating. In contrast to traditional approaches, we've focussed on the unveiling of social structures obtained from communications and on multidimensional descriptions instead of interest-driven filtering criteria. To achieve this, we've used social expectation structures emerging from observed communication trajectories and have outlined how social RDs can be derived from social expectations. Currently, we are implementing a prototypical version of a SRDS for website ratings to evaluate the framework. For future research, we consider it as a very important objective to extend our approach towards the social semantics of large net societies ("Social Semantic Web"), whereas this paper focussed on demarcated agent interaction systems (forums). In addition, to enable complex communication processes like *trading with RDs*, we are investigating a RD communication language that is enhanced with interaction protocols for scenarios like information trading platforms and auctions, and language performatives corresponding to so-called Symbolically Generalized Communication Media [4] like "Money". Since social RDs are calculated from expectation networks which consist of expected action event sequences, virtually any kind of protocol can be used as a pattern for social RDs, but it would be necessary to create an RDF extension with support for complex social RDs beyond the examples in section 5.1. Another issue which deserves attention is the fact that search engines like Google or Altavista are flooded with fake web sites and linkages for the purpose to increase the ranking of some advertised content. Because the SRDS Mirror calculates expectation structures on the basis of stochastical frequency analysis, it will probably be affected by this problem too.

References

1. R. Burkey. Semantic Ratings and Heuristic Similarity for Collaborative Filtering. Department of Information and Computer Science, University of California, Irvine, 2000.
2. J. Delgado, N. Ishii, T. Ura. Content-based Collaborative Information Filtering: Actively Learning to Classify and Recommend Documents. In M. Klusch, G. Weiss (Eds.). Cooperative Information Agents II. Learn- ing, Mobility and Electronic Commerce for Information Discovery on the Internet. Lecture Notes in Artificial Intelligence Series No. 1435. Springer-Verlag, 1998.
3. J. Delgado. Agent-based Recommender Systems and Information Filter- ing on the Internet. PhD. Thesis. Nagoya Institute of Technology, 2000.
4. N. Luhmann. *Social Systems*. Stanford University Press, Palo Alto, CA, 1995.
5. M. Nickles and G. Weiß. Multiagent Systems without Agents – Mirror-Holons for the Compilation and Enactment of Communication Structures. In K. Fischer, M. Florian: Socionics: Its Contributions to the Scalability of Complex Social Systems. Springer Verlag, 2003. To appear
6. W. Brauer, M. Nickles, M. Rovatsos, G. Weiß, and K. F. Lorentzen. Expectation-Oriented Analysis and Design. Proceedings AOSE-2001, Springer Verlag, 2001.
7. M. Nickles, M. Rovatsos, W. Brauer, and G. Weiß. Communication Systems: A Unified Model of Socially Intelligent Systems. In K. Fischer, M. Florian: Socionics: Its Contributions to the Scalability of Complex Social Systems. Springer Verlag, 2003. To appear

8. FIPA, Foundation for Intelligent Agents, http://www.fipa.org.
9. http://www.w3.org/RDF/
10. P. Resnick et.al. GroupLens: an open architecture for collaborative filtering of netnews. Proceedings of the conference on Computer supported cooperative work, 1994.
11. http://peoplenet.stanford.edu
12. http://www.w3.org/2001/sw/meetings/tech-200303/social-meaning/
13. http://www.daml.org/
14. http://www.w3.org/PICS/
15. http://www.w3.org/2000/01/sw/
16. http://www.google.com
17. http://www.slashdot.org
18. http://www.edonkey2000.com/
19. http://www.gnutella.com/
20. http://www.fasttrack.nu/

A Coordination Framework for a Community of Over-Helping Agents

Franck Gaultier

Ecole des Mines de Saint-Etienne, France
gaultier@emse.fr

Abstract. We consider a community of heterogeneous agents that interact by handling objects in shared repositories. Such situations may for instance arise in groupware applications. Agents involved in such systems may be humans or software agents encapsulating specific tools, interfacing with users, assisting the groupware activities etc. Over-help is an important issue in those systems, since users may have incomplete knowledge on how to solve their specific tasks, or even incomplete knowledge on what they need. We introduce in this article our approach for achieving over-help in our target class of multi-agent system and propose a new coordination framework to tackle specific issues related to this approach.

1 Introduction

We consider a community of heterogeneous agents that interact by handling objects in shared repositories (by handling we mean the creation, use and deletion of objects). Such situations may for instance arise in groupware applications and more specifically in those groupware applications that are centered around production spaces. Agents involved in such systems may be humans or software agents encapsulating specific tools, interfacing with users or assisting the groupware activities. Over-help is an important issue in those systems, since users may have incomplete knowledge on how to solve their specific tasks, or even incomplete knowledge on what they need. This fact besides has been noticed in [3], *A demand in fact is just a possibly wrong or limited expression of the underlying need.* In the following, we thus introduce our approach for achieving over-help in our target class of multi-agent system. However, as we'll see, letting agents take pro-active initiatives implies to solve specific coordination issues, otherwise the community of agents may quickly degenerate into a collection of chaotic, incohesive individuals.

In the next section, we explain our approach for achieving over-help and the requirements that are implied by such a solution. In the third section, we describe a proposal that complies with the coordination requirement. In section 4, the Shared Spaces, a coordination medium and its associated primitives are described and compared with related work. Finally, in section 5 we conclude and describe the issues that we plan on investigating in the near future.

M. Klusch et al. (Eds.): CIA 2003, LNAI 2782, pp. 222–237, 2003.

2 How to Over-Help ?

In situations where users of a MAS have incomplete knowledge on how to solve their tasks or even incomplete knowledge on what they need, over-helping abilities may be a crucial feature for agents in the system. Over-helping agents [2] have to take care of users' interests and objective needs not only of users' explicit goals. On figure 1 we sketch the situation of "classical" (literal-help) systems of information agents. Users'demands partially meet their needs, because the formulated demands are either a wrong expression of the needs or are not achievable by the agents. In the classical situation, agents' activities are all rational consequences of their commitment to fulfill (or at least to try to fulfill) the demands.

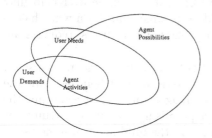

Fig. 1. Literal-help

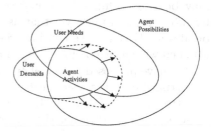

Fig. 2. Over-help, abstracting from demands

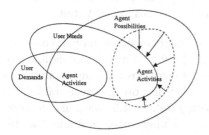

Fig. 3. Over-help, sticking to the needs

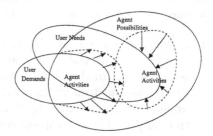

Fig. 4. Over-help, combined-approach

We distinguish two main approaches to let agents take pro-active initiatives (see figure 2 and 3), that is to design over-helping agents :

- On the one hand, agents could abstract from demands the presumed real (i.e. the perceived subjective) needs in order to achieve them (figure 2). Consider for instance the following scenario : *The user requests of an agent encapsulating an ID3 induction tree tool to generate a classifier on a given data. Another agent, the one encapsulating a C4.5 induction tree tool, decides then to construct a classifier from the same data, because this agent makes the assumption that the user is first of all interested in getting a decision tree from the given data, not in getting an ID3 decision tree.*

– On the other hand, agents could try to guess what users need by making trials (that is creating unrequested objects) and then adopting the pragmatic point of view that those objects (or informations) that are useful, are not necessarily those that users demand but more probably those that they will actually use (figure 3).

Consider for example the following scenario : *The agent encapsulating a binning filter has cleaned the 2001 weather data, but no one has used them since. These cleaned data sources are presumably of no utility, they will also be removed from the repository.*

We have in contrast to [3] chosen to consider solely simple over-help and not what the author calls *critical over-help* and *tutorial over-help* (in both cases, the user's request may not be satisfied and something else may be performed). Both may be also useful, but we believe that in our context simple over-help may be sufficient, and moreover that users should keep some control on what has to be absolutely done. We consider therefore only cases where users' requests are satisfied whenever possible (see 2 3 and 4).

We have proposed to model our community of over-helping agents as a set of opportunistic agents, where each commits itself to do what it believes to be the best (the most useful) for it. In other words, each agent pursues at each time the most promising (or rather the perceived most promising) action opportunity at that time. It might believe the best is to engage in the fulfillment of some user's demand, or to perform some action independently of users' demands but nether that inaction is. For such a community to actually achieve the above combined over-helping approach (see figure 4), we claim it requires at least that :

1. Agents have a domain-dependent and context-sensitive model (possibly evolving but inevitably partially inaccurate) that relates demands and potential needs. In the above scenario, for instance, the C4.5 agent abstracts from a specific demand the need for a tree classifier on the given data. This implies the agent's knowing that ID3 trees, just as C4.5 trees, are decision trees and that in the current context the user may not care about the difference.

2. Agents have a (inevitably evolving and partially inaccurate) context-sensitive utility function for their actions. An action is useful only if it corresponds to an agent's or user's need, and the utility function must help to choose among useful actions.

3. Users have some intelligent retrieval interface to their disposal, that helps them to check if a peculiar object does not already lie in repositories or that helps them to review unrequested objects in search of potentially useful ones.

4. Some coordination mechanism maintains over time the global coherence of the system; that is a mechanism ensuring that firstly the nominal activities (those which are rational consequences of the demands, see fig. 1) will be achieved and not disturbed (because of the resources usage of opportunistic activities), and secondly the repositories will not be flooded with useless or redundant objects.

Without the last requirement the community of opportunistic agents may quickly degenerate into a set of chaotic and incohesive entities. In this paper we will consider issues related to the first three requirements only succinctly and will instead focus on the last one. The next section is indeed dedicated to the presentation of a coordination model for a community of opportunistic agents. The model we have coined *opportunity-based coordination*, is then showed to be suitable for maintaining the coherence of our agent community.

3 Opportunity-Based Coordination

The objective of this section is to firstly outline the main features of the coordination model. We shall therefore begin with some definitions of opportunities and opportunistic agents. We will then describe the basic principles of opportunity-based coordination.

Opportunities and opportunistic behaviors have been described in results stemming from the cognitive science research [9]; from these results we derived the following simple definition of opportunity.

An opportunity for a given agent, is a partial state of its environment that enables it to pursue some suspended goals that it believes to be of potential utility.

Suspended goals [9] are goals that cannot be pursued in the current context and that are postponed. The concept of opportunity has been also discussed and formalized in [1] but in a MAS specification perspective. We are in contrast interested in opportunities as internal structures available to the decision processes of agents. We now move on to our definition of an opportunistic agent.

An opportunistic agent, is an agent that systematically pursues the most promising opportunity.

Opportunistic behavior hence is a memory-based utility-driven behavior [9]. From a point of view of the agent architecture, this means that the agent stores its set of suspended goals and it scans the events from its environment in the search of those enabling factors (consider for instance the C4.5 agent waiting for an ID3 tree induction request, see also requirement 1) that will help it to pursue some of its suspended goals. The selection of suspended goals and their adoption as current goals, eventually in place of others, has to be done by a utility-driven reasoning module (see requirement 2).

When trying to coordinate a community of such agents, one see easily that controlling the opportunities (i.e. favor or on the contrary prohibit the occurrence of specific opportunities, restrict or increase the overall amount of opportunities in the system) is a reasonable way of achieving it. This is also the approach we choose and our model of coordination hence follows the twofold strategy below to control opportunities:

- Locally first: When pursuing its goals each agent can provide others with new opportunities that are likely to encourage them to help it, or it can on the contrary prohibit some potential opportunities by using specific action-restriction mechanisms if these opportunities would disturb the achievement of the agent's goals. The process is not necessarily intentional: the user, for instance, requesting of the ID3 agent to induce a tree may not be aware that he has also provided the C4.5 agent with a new opportunity. Put another way: coordination at this level is not necessarily intentional because the production space has a non empty intersection with the coordination space.

– Globally then: Agent produce consume resources (time, space, user attention) whose overall amount may be intentionally limited so as to limit the overall amount of potential opportunities. Each agent has thus to manage the set of the objects it has already produced so that its total resource usage does not exceed some specific limitation.

Our model of coordination is a mixture of objective and subjective coordination. Objective coordination models ([16,13]) are mostly based on the concept of mediated interaction, in such models interactions occur through a coordination medium whose behavior is determined by coordination rules and that in turn constraints the behavior of the coordinated entities. The main advantage of such approaches is the clean separation between coordinated and coordination activities they promote. In contrast, subjective coordination ([6]) is *the process by which an agent reasons about its local action and the (anticipated) actions of others to try and ensure the community acts in a coherent manner.* When the two types of coordination coexist they are never independent because subjective coordination is based on and supposes the existence of the second [16]. In [13] the authors propose a unifying view of the two types of coordination: the subjective coordination is considered as the process by which agents forge in the coordination medium the coordination rules (by producing coordination artifacts) that will objectively coordinate the activities. This is also the best view to understand the link between the objective and subjective part of our coordination model.

Within our model, the subjective coordination may be either explicit or implicit. In the first case, agents reason about their local goals, the available resources and the potential opportunities of others to determine the dependencies between them all and to design the coordination artifacts that will help them (the agents) to achieve their respective goals (by favoring or on the contrary prohibiting specific opportunities). Agents then incorporate the designed coordination artifacts into the coordination medium. In the second case, agents produce also coordination artifacts but no more as a result of a dependencies management stage; the specific tasks agents are involved in may also result in the production of coordination artifacts (for instance whenever new objects are put in the repositories). This last kind of coordination is often named *stigmergic coordination* [16]. Explicit subjective coordination is highly related with agent architecture issues; we have designed a model of opportunistic agents as an extension of the operational model of [10] with explicit notions of suspended goals and abilities and we are thus at present working on defining a resource management module, a social reasoning module (for reasoning on opportunistic agents and their opportunities) and on grounding the coordination primitives (defined later in the objective coordination model) in the agent model.

According to previous results on (objective) coordination models [16,12], we present now the three elements that define a general coordination model.

- *What is being coordinated ?*
  The coordinable entities are usually actively computing entities, that is the agents. However since agents behavior is strongly affected by occurring opportunities, one could consider that the coordination of agents is actually achieved by coordinating the occurrence of opportunities in the community.
- *What are the media for coordination ?*
  Traditional coordination models in MAS assume a simple communication infrastructure with ports, channels and primitives like send and receive. We adopt, in contrast a *generative* [16] communication infrastructure: coordination is accomplished via a shared data space in which agents generate data in order to communicate. The main advantages of such an approach is the potential spatial and temporal uncoupling of interactions. This is an important feature, because it seems not feasible in our context to require agents to necessarily know whom they are providing with a new opportunity, or even to require opportunity creation to be synchronous.
- *What are the protocols and rules used for coordination ?*
  These are the laws that rule the relationship between the coordinables and the coordination media. In our model, they are expressed in an operational way by a set of coordination primitives which may be used by agents to access and alter the shared data space.

We now move on to the presentation of a key element, namely the objective part of our coordination model also called the Shared Spaces below.

4   The Shared Spaces

Ideas on shared spaces were partly inspired by considerations on workspaces stemming from the groupware research. It was suggested that it should be possible to dynamically structure workspaces into independent workspaces and sub-workspaces to support the organization of groupware activities, and that it should also be possible to define for participants access policies that rule access to the different parts of the above structure according to the part the participant plays in the organization. Basically, each workspace is a collaboration environment dedicated to the achievement of a particular sub-task; each workspace contains all necessary initial, intermediate and final objects that will be used or produced during the achievement of the task; each workspace is accessible to the very set of participants that take part to the achievement of the task.

We now move on to the presentation of the architecture of the shared spaces. We expose then the primitives associated to this coordination medium, and distinguish between those that do alter the medium, and those that do not. Then, we conclude this section with a comparison of our shared spaces with Linda-like coordination media and primitives.

4.1 Architecture

The architecture of our coordination medium is rooted on the notions of *common workspace, personal workspace* and *object space* (or simply *object*). Each of these spaces can be created or deleted dynamically. A common workspace is the kind of workspace outlined above : it is a local collaboration space that can contain other spaces (common, personal, or object). Each common workspace also is a kind of agora where data structures can be exchanged associatively almost as in the Linda coordination language. A personal workspace is at one and the same time a data repository (that is, it may contain object spaces) accessible to a unique agent (also called the *owner*) and the unique interface for agents with the coordination medium. Agents can own several personal workspaces, personal workspaces can move from one common workspace to another. An object space is a kind of proxy that hide a real object and make its use *observable* to agents.

Our coordination medium consists of a collection of common workspaces, each being therefore the root of a tree of sub-spaces. Every space is denoted by a globally unique identifier and is characterized by a fixed set of properties. Common workspaces and object spaces have also access rights attached to them: the right to enter, leave or destroy them. We will see in a later section how these access rights constraint the use of coordination primitives. Access rights are useful since they allow agents to locally prohibit specific opportunities by denying access to specific workspaces or objects. In figure 5, we propose a possible configuration for our coordination medium. We adopt two different perspectives for the same configuration. On the one hand, we show the logical structure of the medium : a tree of spaces and sub-spaces. On the other hand, we give a possible physical structure that is compatible with the former perspective; it is here emphasized that spaces are independent, distributed and last point to notice, that personnal workspaces are the unique entry points for agents to the coordination medium. A common workspace named CWS_1 contains two common workspaces (CWS_2 and CWS_3), one personal workspace (PWS1) and two objects (O_1 and O_2). Figure 5 indicates also typical properties by space category: Object spaces are characterized by an identifier (as each space), an agent identifier (the agent that added the object to the medium), a type (the type of the object) and a list of object identifiers representing the list of objects that were used to create the real object. Personal workspaces are characterized by a globally unique identifier, and an agent identifier (the agent this workspace belongs to). Common workspaces are characterized by a globally unique identifier, an agent identifier, and a purpose formulae describing the kind of task this common workspace serves the achievement. Properties but also informations about movements inside the shared spaces are very useful since they provide the necessary means for agents to inform (intentionally or not) about new opportunities.

The interactions of agents through the coordination medium alter its tree structure and reciprocally the structure of the coordination medium constraints the way agents can interact. We have formalized the shared workspaces using the ambient calculus [7,8,5], because it is suited for representing tree structures of computations spaces and their evolution, but also access rights to these spaces and asynchronous anonymous communication. This formalization provides a strong formal basis to our framework, and it is also used for the implementation of the shared spaces since it relies on an interpreter for the ambient calculus. The ambient calculus is a formalism for describing processes and mobility; it is well-known from the distributed and mobile computing community. An ambient represents basically a place where computation may happen (in our case workspaces), it is a named cluster of running processes and nested sub-ambients. Each computation state has a spatial structure, the tree induced by the nesting of ambients. Mobility is abstractly represented by re-arrangement of this tree: an ambient can move inside or outside other ambients. Capabilities control movement, that is a process (in our case an agent) can't trigger the moving of an ambient if it (the process) does not possess the capability of doing it. Capabilities can also be communicated between processes. To conclude on this issue we add that we also gave the coordination primitives (which will be introduced in a later section) a denotational semantics in terms of ambient processes.

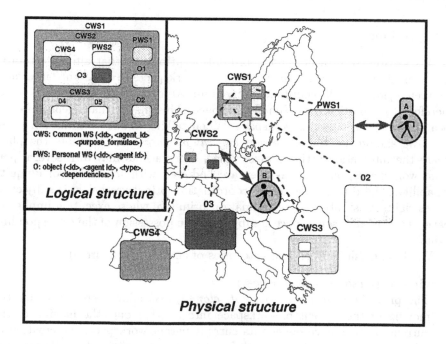

Fig. 5. An example Shared Spaces configuration

The last but not least component of our architecture is a resource information manager. The resource information manager makes informations on *space* resource usage available to agents. This includes the amount of resource currently taken by a particular object or the maximum amount of resource that may possibly be taken by a particular object (basically the use of a given object decreases that object's current resource usage, the maximum resource usage of a given object corresponds to its usage when the object is not currently used). Those informations can then be used by agents to manage their resources. Resource management is an important issue in our coordination model since the use of certain coordination primitives (see section below) may require specific resource amounts. For instance, the creation of spaces by agents consumes resources, the destruction in contrast frees resources, the use of an object frees a part of the resources its creation has consumed. The rationale for using and managing resources explicitly is to avoid the explosion of interactions and to preserve the results of useful interactions (useful objects are those that are used and therefore those that take less resources, on the other hand useless objects take the maximum amount of resource they can).

However the query of the resource information manager remains transparent in our coordination model and we do not assume any particular implementation strategie for it, we only assume that it exists and that agents make use of it. This is an issue we plan on investigating in the near future.

4.2   Actions

In this section we present those coordination primitives that alter the coordination medium. As stated above, personal workspaces are the only interfaces between agents and the coordination medium. All coordination primitives relate therefore to a particular personal workspace. This means that agents interact locally to a given personal workspace. When talking about coordination primitives we should use the expression *current p. workspace* to denote the place where the interaction actually takes place. Since agents may own several personal workspaces, one can say they are endowed with some kind of ubiquity capability. The use of some of the coordination primitives below is subject to access rights; basically every coordination primitive whose execution implies to leave, enter or solve some space is subject to the possession of the corresponding rights.

We distinguish between four categories of actions (see figure 6):

Moving of personal workspaces :
> The primitives *move_in*, *move_out*, *clone*, *finish* allow respectively for the moving of the current p. workspace into another one, the moving of the current p. workspace outside its current parent workspace, the creation of a brand new personal workspace for the current agent and the destruction of the current p. workspace (the objects eventually contained in the current p. workspace at the deletion time are simply released in the surrounding workspace). Moving inside or outside a given workspace requires the apropriate capacity (that is the right to enter in the first case, or to leave in the second case). It requires moreover that the target workspace is currently accessible (that is, the target workspace is a neihgbor workspace in the first case, the target workspace is the surrounding workspace in the second case);

hence coordination primitives only allow for local movings. The capacities are granted at creation time by the medium to the owners of workspaces and may be granted by agents to others using the *grant* coordination primitive.

Creation and deletion of spaces :

The primitives *create, open, delete, release* allow respectively for the creation of a new common workspace or object space (in the first case the space appears outside the current p. workspace, but in the second it remains inside the current p. workspace), the dissolution of some common workspace boundaries (that is all spaces and messages eventually contained in the workspace at the deletion time are simply released in the surrounding workspace), the deletion of an object space and the transfer of an object contained in the current p. workspace abroad.

Using an object for the construction of another one requires the right to enter and to leave the proxy representing the object. The deletion of an existing object or common workspace requires of course the appropriate destruction right.

Exchanges for workspace identifiers :

The primitives *say* and *ask* allow respectively to put a tuple containing a workspace identifier and a description of that particular workspace (for example the description could tell whether the workspace is an object or a common workspace, the kind of objects it uses and so on), and to retrieve in an associative way via a pattern matching mechanism a workspace identifier that matches a given description.

Exchanges for access rights :

The primitives *grant* and *request* allow for the exchange of access rights. The involved mechanism is the same as above except that descriptions refer to right types. The current implementation of these primitives ensures moreover that access rights cannot be communicated in another way, that is, using a communication channel not belonging to the shared spaces. For example figure 5, agents a and b cannot exchange access rights in another way as through the shared spaces. Without this restriction some hypothesis with regard to the formalization of the shared spaces do not hold anymore and we are no more authorized to reason about the system properites.

The use of coordination primitives may have an impact on resources or may be affected by the amount of available resources. The creation of any space using either *create* or *clone* requires indeed that the invoking agent as engouh resources. In contrast *open, delete* and *finish* free resources. The use of an object (for the construction of another one) results in a resource exchange between the owner of the object and the user. The exchange may be temporary since it lasts only as long as the new object exists. The way resources are consumed (what consumes an object space creation, is it some fixed amount or some fixed percentage of the object real size ?) freed or exchanged is a matter of the resource information manager and an application specific issue, hence we should not go on in greater detail about this issue here.

Coordination primitives may be blocking: The *open, move_in, move_out* and *delete* are all blocking operations, that is if for instance a given workspace is not actually accessible any of the previous operation will block until it becomes accessible. This does not mean that agents will block in such cases, since agents are not limited to run a single thread.

Of course, we have given to this action language a denotational semantic that relates the primitives to the changes they produce in a given environment (see section 5 for a simplified presentation of the semantics). Each primitive is associated to a process in the ambient calculus and the execution of this process in a given ambient structure leads to a new ambient structure reflecting the expected changes.

$$
\begin{aligned}
\text{Action} ::= \ &create\text{"("(obj\_id(, obj\_id)}^*)? : \text{obj\_type")"} \\
&create\text{"("purpose")"} \\
&move\_in\text{"("ws\_id, Cap")"} \\
&move\_out\text{"("ws\_id, Cap")"} \\
&open\text{"("ws\_id, Cap")"} \\
&delete\text{"("obj\_id, Cap")" | } release\text{"("obj\_id")"} \\
&clone \mid finish \\
&say\text{"("id","ws\_pattern (: agent\_id)?")"} \\
&ask\text{"("ws\_pattern (: agent\_id)?")"} \\
&grant\text{"("Cap (: agent\_id)?")"} \\
&request\text{"("cap\_pattern (: agent\_id)?")"}
\end{aligned}
$$

Cap   :moving capabilities

id   ::= ws_id | obj_id

Fig. 6. Syntax of primitives

4.3   Observation

We present in this section the observation primitive *obs*, the only one that do not alter the coordination medium (just like the *read* primitive in the Linda coordination model). Just as actions (see section above), the observation primitive relates to a personal workspace: in other words agents can only observe locally the interaction places where they currently are. Since agents possess some kind of ubiquity capabilities, they can observe in different locations at the same time nevertheless.

There are two kinds of things an agent should be able to observe:

- Firslty, it should be able to observe the static properties of its local environment. Static properties are those properties that characterize shared spaces (see fig. 5), for instance the owner of a workspace, the type of an object space, the objects used by another one and so on. Such properties do not change of course over time.
- Secondly, it should be able to observe the dynamic properties of its local environment, that is the spatial configuration of the shared spaces. Since spaces can be created, deleted or simply move from one place to another, spatial properties are indeed dynamic.

The primitive *obs* when called by an agent through a given p. workspace returns a set containing the properties set (see figure 5) of each neighbor space sharing (that is contained in the same surrounding workspace). The result of the primitive call contains therefore static informations on neighbor workspaces but also spatial informations too since properties entail workspaces identifiers it is also possible to know the local spatial configuration at query time. Consider for instance, agent a figure 5, using the primitive *obs*, it may deduce the following spatial configuration 7 *(i)*.

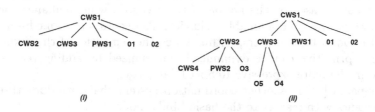

Fig. 7. Local vs. global observation

One can see that the correct spatial configuration of the shared spaces is actually 7 *(ii)*. However agent a is not in position to reconstruct the correct representation as long as it does not own personal workspaces in each common sub-workspace (that is in CWS_2 and CWS_2).

It is quite straightforward to see that an agent may also construct a representation of local evolutions, using sequences of local observations. On the other hand, the construction of a sound representation of global evolutions is more difficult. Agent activities in the system result in changes in the tree structure of the coordination medium, the ability to reconstruct sound representations of those changes is an important requirement if we wish the agent to be able to detect complexe patterns of activity. That's why we have also, as a complement of our coordination medium, developped a framework for the construction of coherent representations of sets of local observations sequences. The basic idea is to construct incrementally a petri-net to organize in a coherent manner local observations (basically, there's one place for each observation; successive observations at the same location are linked by transitions; joint transitions are used to represents a shared event between different locations). The petri-net can then be used by the agent to detect a peculiar pattern of activity (we use actually a fragment of the ambient logic [7] to represent these patterns and a model-checking algorithm to check the petri-net against a given formulae of the logic).

4.4   Related Works

The objective part of our coordination model has many connections with Linda and Linda-based coordination models. In these models, agents interact by exchanging tuples through a tuple space and more precisely by storing, reading and consuming tuples in an associative way. The semantics on the manipulation of tuples, the structure of the coordination medium, the programmability of the medium are among the main features that differentiate these different models [15].

The Linda coordination model, for instance, allows for the insertion and associative retrieval of tuples, its coordination medium is constituted by a single data space, and the semantics of its coordination primitives cannot be customized.

TuCSoN and Luce [14,4] are coordination systems that implement a coordination model based on the notion of tuple center, which enhance the one of tuple space with a programmable behavior. The coordination medium is made of a collection of tuple centers, within which the semantics of the linda-like coordination primitive can be dynamically customized by adding reaction rules specified in the quite expressive ReSpecT language.

JavaSpaces [11] is another coordination system that introduce three main enhancements with respect to the basic Linda model:

- Multiple operations across multiple tuple spaces can be grouped into a bundle that acts as a single atomic action.
- Each tuple is associated with a lease time that refers to the maximum length of time it can stay in the space.
- The writing of a given tuple can be notified to agents that have registered their interest on this event.

Our coordination model defines a medium constituted by multiple nested tuple spaces (the common workspaces). Tuples spaces are first class objects in the model, agents can manipulate them just as tuples. The model allow indeed for the insertion, reading, deletion and moving of complexe tuples (that is, object spaces, workspaces and personnal workspaces). The model allow also for the insertion and associative retrieval of specialized tuples (tuples describing either spaces or access rights to spaces). This latter set of operations is related to the former since operations on complexe tuples make use of the tuple (space) identifiers and rights. The model does not define a language to programme the data spaces, but the semantics of the coordination primitives (on complexe tuples) may be dynamically configured by resource availability and access rights.

Since ReSpecT has been proven to be fully expressive (in terms of SIM computations [18]), it works as a sort of assembly language for coordination, and it is natural to ask ourselves about the consequences of implementing our coordination model on a TuCSoN infrastructure. This work is still in progress, the first attempts to give a mapping of our coordination model upon ReSpecT have shown to couple unnecessarily coordination activities that are not otherwise related.

5   Conclusion and Future Work

We have described our approach to over-help in a production-centered community of agents. The approach relies on letting agents behave opportunistically (that is to act every time they have the opportunity to do so) and no more only as the answer of some user requests. The solution makes also four assumptions :

- Agents are somehow able to relate user demands and user needs.
- Agents have at least a primitive model of the a-priori utility for their actions.
- Users spare some time exploring unrequested objects (possibly using dedicated tools) in search of potentially useful objects.
- Some coordination mechanism prevents the system from degenerating and flooding the repositories with useless objects.

We have proposed a coordination framework suitable to coordinate such over-helping agents, and we have shown how the framework relates to other works. However, we still need to further investigate several other issues. Following [12], we have also defined an abstract machine for our coordination model and we expect that this common semantic framework will help us to build soon a deeper understanding of what the different tuple-based coordination models have in common and how they differ. Another unifying framework for comparing coordination models that we will also consider is the recent work in [17].

We plan then on investigating issues related to the subjective part of our coordination model and issues specific to the resource information manager.

References

1. J. Meyer B. Van Linder, W. van der Hoek. Formalising abilities and opportunities of agents. *Fundamenta Informaticae*, 34:53–101, 1998.
2. R. Falcone C. Castelfranchi. Delegation conflicts. In W. Van de Velde M. Boman, editor, *Multi-Agent Rationality*, number 1237 in Lecture Note in Artificial Intelligence, pages 234–254. Springer Verlag, 1997.
3. Cristiano Castelfranchi. Information agents: The social nature of information and the role of trust. In Franco Zambonelli Matthias Klusch, editor, *Proceedings of the Fifth International Workshop on Cooperative Information Agent (CIA 2001)*, Lecture Note in Artificial, pages 208–210, Modena, Italy, September 2001. Springer.
4. Enrico Denti and Andrea Omicini. Engineering multi-agent systems in luce. In Stephen Rochefort, Fariba Sadri, and Francesca Toni, editors, *Proceedings of the ICLP'99 International Workshop on Multi-Agent Systems in Loggic Programming (MAS'99)*, 1999.

5. Franck Gaultier and Philippe Beaune. An interaction model based on the observation of shared spaces. In *To appear in, Secondes Journées Francophones, Modèles Formels de l'Interaction*, Lille, France, May 2003.

6. N. Jennings. *foundations of Distributed Artificial Intelligence*, chapter Coordination techniques for distributed artificial intelligence, pages 187–210. Wiley, 1996.

7. Andrew D. Gordon Luca Cardelli. Anytime, anywhere. modal logics for mobile ambients. In *Proceedings of the 27th ACM Symposium on Principles of Programming Languages*, pages 365–377, 2000.

8. Andrew D. Gordon Luca Cardelli. Mobile ambients. In D. Le métayer, editor, *Theoretical Computer Science, Special Issue on Coordination*, pages 177–213, June 2000.

9. Janet L. Kolodner Marin D. Simina. Opportunistic reasoning a design perspective. In *Proc. of the seventeenth annual Cognitive Science conference*, 1995.

10. Mickael Winikoff, Lin Padghan, James Harland, John Thangarajah. Declarative and procedural goal in intelligent agent systems. In *Proceedings of the Eighth International Conference on Principles of Knowledge Representation and Reasoning*, 200.

11. Sun Microsystems. Javaspaces^{tm} specification. White paper, January 1999.

12. N. Busi, P. Ciancarini, R. Gorrieri, G. Zavattaro. *Coordination for Internet Agents: Models, Technologies, and Applications*, chapter Models for Coordinating Agents: a Guided Tour, pages 6–24. Springer-Verlag, 2001.

13. Andrea Omicini and Sascha Ossowski. Objective versus subjective coordination in the engineering of agent systems. In Matthias Klusch, Sonia Bergamaschi, Peter Edwards, and Paolo Petta, editors, *Intelligent Information Agents: An AgentLink Perspective*, volume 2586 of *LNAI: State-of-the-Art Survey*, pages 179–202. Springer-Verlag, March 2003.

14. Andrea Omicini and Franco Zambonelli. Coordination of mobile information agents in tucson. *Internet Research: Electronic Networking Applications*, 8(5):400–413, 1998.

15. Davide Rossi, Giacomo Cabri, and Enrico Denti. Tuple-based technologies for coordination. In Andrea Omicini, Franco Zambonelli, Matthias Klusch, and Robert Tolksdorf, editors, *Coordination of Internet Agents: Models, Technologies, and Applications*, chapter 4, pages 83–109. Springer-Verlag, March 2001.

16. Mickael Schumacher. *Objective Coordination in Multi-Agent System Engineering - Design and Implementation*, volume 2039 of *Lecture Note in Artificial Intelligence*. Springer-Verlag, April 2001.

17. Mirko Viroli and Andrea Omicini. Coordination as a service: Ontological and formal foundation. In Antonio Brogi and Jean-Marie Jacquet, editors, *FOCLASA 2002 - Foundations of Coordination Languages and Software Architecture*, volume 68(3) of *Electronic Notes in Theoretical Computer Science*. Elsevier Science B. V., March 2003. CONCUR 2002 Satellite Workshop, Brno, Czech Republic, 19 August 2002. Proceedings.

18. Peter Wegner. Why interaction is more powerful than computing. *Communications of the ACM*, 40(5), 1997.

Annexe

$$[\![_n[P]]\!] \quad\triangleq\quad _n[[\![P]\!]_n]$$

$$[\![P \mid Q]\!]_n \quad\triangleq\quad [\![P]\!]_n \mid [\![Q]\!]_n$$

$$[\![say\ m]\!]_n \quad\triangleq\quad _{io}[out\ n\ \cdot\ in\ COM\ \cdot\ \langle m\rangle]$$

$$[\![say\ m\ to\ l]\!]_n \quad\triangleq\quad _{io}[out\ n\ \cdot\ in\ l\ \cdot\ _n[\langle m\rangle]]$$

$$[\![grant(in\ m)]\!]_n \quad\triangleq\quad _{cap}[out\ n\ \cdot\ in\ CAP\ \cdot\ \langle in\ m\rangle]$$

$$[\![grant(in\ m)\ to\ l]\!]_n \quad\triangleq\quad _{cap}[out\ n\ \cdot\ in\ l\ \cdot\ _n[\langle in\ m\rangle]]$$

$$[\![ask\ x\ \cdot\ P]\!]_n \quad\triangleq\quad (\nu\ r)\ _{io}[out\ n\ \cdot\ in\ COM\ \cdot\ (x)\ \cdot\ _r[out\ COM\ \cdot\ in\ n\ \cdot\ \langle x\rangle]]$$
$$\mid\ open\ r\ \cdot\ [\![P]\!]_n$$

$$[\![ask\ x\ to\ l]\!]_n \quad\triangleq\quad open\ io\ \cdot\ open\ l\ \cdot\ (x)\ \cdot\ [\![P]\!]_n$$

$$[\![request\ x\ \cdot\ P]\!]_n \quad\triangleq\quad (\nu\ r)\ _{cap}[out\ n\ \cdot\ in\ CAP\ \cdot\ (x)\ \cdot\ _r[out\ CAP\ \cdot\ in\ n\ \cdot\ \langle x\rangle]$$
$$\mid\ open\ r\ \cdot\ [\![P]\!]_n]$$

$$[\![clone(Q)\ \cdot\ P]\!]_n \quad\triangleq\quad _n[out\ n\ \cdot\ Q]\mid [\![P]\!]_n$$

$$[\![release\ o\ \cdot\ P]\!]_n \quad\triangleq\quad (\nu\ r)_{rel}[in\ o\ \cdot\ out\ n\ \cdot\ _r[out\ o\ \cdot\ in\ n]]$$
$$\mid\ open\ r\ \cdot\ [\![P]\!]_n$$

$$[\![new\ o(o_1,\ldots,o_k)\ \cdot\ P]\!]_n \triangleq\ (\nu\ r_1,\ldots,r_k)$$
$$USE[out\ n\ \cdot\ in\ o_1\ \cdot\ _{r_1}[out\ o_1\ \cdot\ in\ n]]\mid$$
$$\ldots$$
$$USE[out\ n\ \cdot\ in\ o_k\ \cdot\ _{r_k}[out\ o_k\ \cdot\ in\ n]]\mid$$
$$open\ r_1\ldots open\ r_k\ \cdot\ (\nu o\ rel)(_o[open\ rel.open\ USE]\mid [\![P]\!]_n)$$

$$[\![new\ pc\ \cdot\ P]\!]_n \quad\triangleq\quad (\nu pc,r)\ _{pc}[out\ n\ \cdot\ _r[out\ pc\ \cdot\ in\ n]\mid open\ DEL]\mid open\ r\ \cdot\ [\![P]\!]_n$$

$$[\![delete\ o\ \cdot\ P]\!]_n \quad\triangleq\quad (\nu r)\ _{DEL}[out\ n\ \cdot\ open\ o\ \cdot\ _r[in\ n]]\mid open\ r\ \cdot\ [\![P]\!]_n$$

Fig. 8. Denotational semantics

Trust Networks on the Semantic Web

Jennifer Golbeck, Bijan Parsia, and James Hendler

University of Maryland, College Park
A. V. Williams Building
College Park, Maryland 20742
{golbeck,hendler}@cs.umd.edu, bparsia@isr.umd.edu

Abstract. The so-called "Web of Trust" is one of the ultimate goals of the Semantic Web. Research on the topic of trust in this domain has focused largely on digital signatures, certificates, and authentication. At the same time, there is a wealth of research into trust and social networks in the physical world. In this paper, we describe an approach for integrating the two to build a web of trust in a more social respect. This paper describes the applicability of social network analysis to the semantic web, particularly discussing the multi-dimensional networks that evolve from ontological trust specifications. As a demonstration of algorithms used to infer trust relationships, we present several tools that allow users to take advantage of trust metrics that use the network.

1 Introduction

"Trust" is a word that has come to have several very specific definitions on the Semantic Web. Much research has focused on authentication of resources, including work on digital signatures and public keys. Confidence in the source or author of a document is important, but trust, in this sense, ignores many important points.

Just because a person can confirm the source of documents does not have any explicit implication about trusting the content of those documents. This project addresses "trust" as credibility or reliability in a much more human sense. It opens up the door for questions like "how much credence should I give to what this person says about a given topic," and "based on what my friends say, how much should I trust this new person?"

In this paper, we will discuss the application of a social network to the semantic web. Section 2 discusses how to build a meaningful social network from the architecture of the semantic web, and how it conveys meaning about the structure of the world. Section 3 will describe the implementation of such a network. We describe a sample ontology, an algorithm for computing trust in a network, and present tools that use this network to provide users with information about the reputation of others.

1.1 Related Work
This paper uses techniques developed in the field of social network analysis, and applies that to the issue of trust on the semantic web. This section describes the most relevant works from each area.

M. Klusch et al. (Eds.): CIA 2003, LNAI 2782, pp. 238–249, 2003.

1.1.1 Social Networks

Social networks have a long history of study in a wide range of disciplines. The more mathematical of the studies have appeared in the "Small World" literature. The work on Small Worlds, also commonly known as "Six Degrees of Separation" originated out of Stanley Milgram's work in the 1960s. His original studies indicated that any two people in the world were separated by only a small number acquaintances (theorized to be six in the original work) [18]. Since then, studies have shown that many complex networks share the common features of the small-world phenomenon: small average distance between nodes, and a high connectance, or clustering coefficient [21].

Small world networks have been studied in relation to random graphs [29]. For social systems, both models have been used to describe phenomena such as scientific collaboration networks [20], and models of game theory [29]. The propagation of effects through these types of networks has been studied, particularly with respect to the spread of disease [19, 7]. The web itself has shown the patterns of a small world network, in clustering and diameter [4, 1].

Viewing the current web as a graph, where each page represents a node, and the hyperlinks translate to directed edges between nodes, has produced some interesting results. The main focus of this research has been to improve the quality of search [7,6,5,8,14,26]. Other work has used this structure for classification [9] and community discovery [15].

1.1.2 Trust on the Semantic Web

Yolanda Gil and Varun Ratnakar addressed the issue of trusting content and information sources [12]. They describe an approach to derive assessments about information sources based on individual feedback about the sources. As users add annotations, they can include measures of Credibility and Reliability about a statement, which are later averaged and presented to the viewer. Using the TRELLIS system, users can view information, annotations (including averages of credibility, reliability, and other ratings), and then make an analysis.

Calculating trust automatically for an individual in a network on the web is partially addressed in Raph Levin's Advogato project [17]. His trust metric uses group assertions for determining membership within a group. The Advogato [3] website, for example, certifies users at three levels. Access to post and edit website information is controlled by these certifications. On any network, the Advogato trust metric is extremely attack resistant. By identifying individual nodes as "bad" and finding any nodes that certify the "bad" nodes, the metric cuts out an unreliable portion of the network. Calculations are based primarily on the good nodes, so the network as a whole remains secure.

2   Networks on the Semantic Web

Studying the structure of the hypertext web can be used to find community structure in a limited way. A set of pages clustered by hyperlinks may indicate a common topic among the pages, but it does not show more than a generic relationship among the pages. Furthermore, pages with fewer outgoing links are less likely to show up in a cluster at all because their connectance is obviously lower. These two facts make it difficult for a person to actually see any relationship among specific concepts on the web as it currently stands – classification is not specific enough, and it relies on heavy hyperlinking that may not be present.

The Semantic Web changes this. Since the semantic data is machine-understandable, there is no need to use heuristics to relate pages. Concepts in semantically marked up pages are automatically linked, relating both pages and concepts across a distributed web.

By it's nature, the semantic web is one large graph. Resources (and literals) are connected by predicates. Throughout the rest of this paper, we will refer to resources as objects, and predicates as properties. Mapping objects to nodes and properties to labeled edges in a graph yields the power to use the algorithms and methods of analysis that have been developed for other manifestations of graphs.

While the graph of the entire Semantic Web itself is interesting, a subgraph generated by restricting the properties, and thus edges, to a subset of interest allows us to see the relationships among distributed data. Applications in this space are vast. Semantic markup means that retrieving instances of specific classes and the set of properties required for a particular project, becomes easy. Furthermore, merging data collected from many different places on the web is trivial.

Generating social networks on the semantic web is a similar task with useful results. Information about individuals in a network is maintained in distributed sources. Individuals can manage data about themselves and their friends. Security measures, like digital signatures of files, go some way toward preventing false information from propagating through the network.   This security measure builds trust about the authenticity or data contained within the network, but does not describe trust between people in the network.

There are many measures of "trust" within a social network. It is common in a network that trust is based simply on knowing someone. By treating a "Person" as a node, and the "knows" relationship as an edge, an undirected graph emerges (Figure 1 shows the graph of acquaintances used in this study). If A does not know B, but some of A's friends know B, A is "close" to knowing B in some sense. Many existing networks take this measure of closeness into account. We may, for example, reasonably trust a person with a small Erdos number to have a stronger knowledge of graph theory than someone with a large or infinite number.

Techniques developed to study naturally occurring social networks apply to these networks derived from the semantic web. Small world models describe a number of algorithms for understanding relationships between nodes. The same algorithms that model the spread of disease [19, 7] in physical social networks, can be used to track the spread of viruses via email.

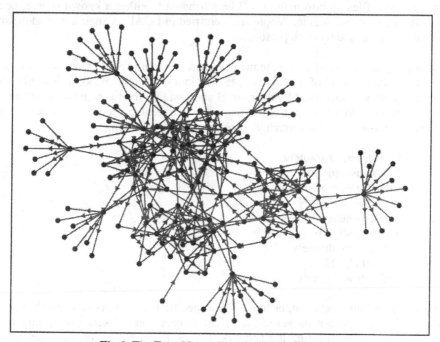

Fig.1. The Trust Network generated for this paper

For trust, however, there are several other factors to consider. Edges in a trust network are directed. A may trust B, but B may not trust A back. Edges are also weighted with some measure of the trust between two people. By building such a network, it is possible to infer how much A should trust an unknown individual based on how much A's friends and friends-of-friends trust that person. Using the edges that exist in the graph, we can infer an estimation of the weight of a non-existent edge. In the next section, we describe one method for making such inferences in the context of two implementations.

3 Implementation

The semantic web of trust requires that users describe their beliefs about others. Once a person has a file that lists who they know and how much they trust them, social information can be automatically compiled and processed.

3.1 Base Ontology

Friend-Of-A-Friend (FOAF) [10] is one project that allows users to create and interlink statements about who they know, building a web of acquaintances. The

FOAF schema [24] is an RDF vocabulary that a web user can use to describe information about himself, such as name, email address, and homepage, as well as information about people he knows. In line with the security mentioned before, users can sign these files so information will be attributed to either a known source, or an explicitly anonymous source. People are identified in FOAF by their email addresses, since they are unique for each person.

In this project, we introduce a schema, designed to extend foaf:Person, which allows users to indicate a level of trust for people they know [28]. Since FOAF is used as the base, users are still identified by their email address. Our trust schema adds properties with a domain of foaf:Person. Each of these new properties specifies one level of trust on a scale of 1-9. The levels roughly correspond to the following:

1. Distrusts absolutely
2. Distrusts highly
3. Distrusts moderately
4. Distrusts slightly
5. Trusts neutrally
6. Trusts slightly
7. Trusts moderately
8. Trusts highly
9. Trusts absolutely

Trust can be given in general, or limited to a specific topic. Users can specify several trust levels for a person on several different subject areas. Users can specify topic specific trust levels to refine the network. For example, Bob may trust Dan highly regarding research topics, but distrust him absolutely when it comes to repairing cars.

Using the trust ontology, the different trust ratings (i.e. "distrustsAbsolutely," "trustsModerately," etc.) are properties of the "Person" class, with a range of another "Person". These properties are used for general trust, and are encoded as follows:

```
<Person rdf:ID="Joe">
 <mbox rdf:resource="mailto:bob@example.com"/>
 <trustsHighly rdf:resource="#Sue"/>
</Person>
```

Another set of properties are defined for trust in a specific area. They correspond to the nine values above, but are indicated as trust regarding a specific topic (i.e. "distrustsAbsolutelyRe," "trustsModeratelyRe," etc). The range of these topic specific properties is the "TrustsRegarding" class, which has been defined to group a Person and a subject of trust together. The "TrustsRegarding" class has two properties: "trustsPerson" indicates the person being trusted, and "trustsOnSubject" indicates the subject that the trust is about. There are no range restrictions on this latter property, which leaves it to the user to specify any subject from any ontology. Consider the following example, that shows syntax for trusting one person relative to several different topics:

```
<Person rdf:ID="Bob">

  <mbox rdf:resource="mailto:joe@example.com"/>

  <trustsHighlyRe>
      <TrustsRegarding>
          <trustsPerson rdf:resource="#Dan"/>
          <trustsOnSubject
          rdf:resource="http://example.com/ont#Research"/>
      </TrustsRegarding>
    </trustsHighlyRe>

    <distrustsAbsolutelyRe>
      <TrustsRegarding>
          <trustsPerson rdf:resource="#Dan"/>
          <trustsOnSubject
          rdf:resource="http://example.com/ont#AutoRepair"/>
      </TrustsRegarding>
    </distrustsAbsolutelyRe>

</Person>
```

With topic-specific information provided, queries can ask for trust levels on a given subject and the network is then trimmed down to include only the relevant edges.

Large networks form when users link from their FOAF file to other FOAF files. In the example above, the can include a reference to the trust file for "Dan". Spidering along these links allow a few seeds to produce a large graph. Many interesting projects have emerged from these FOAF networks, including the Co-depiction project [25], SVG image annotation [2], and FoafNaut [11], an IRC bot that provides FOAF data about anyone in its network [10].

Having specified trust levels as described above, the network that emerges becomes much more useful and interesting. A directed, weighted graph is generated, where an edge from A to B indicates that A has some trust relationship with B. The weight of that edge reflects the specified trust level.

3.2 Computing Trust

Direct edges between individual nodes in this graph contain an explicitly expressed trust value. Beyond knowing that a given user explicitly trusts another, the graph can be used to infer the trust that one user should have for individuals to whom they are not directly connected.

Several basic calculations are made over the network.
- Maximum and minimum capacity paths: In the algorithms used in this research, trust follows the standard rules of network capacity – on any given path, the maximum amount of trust that the source can give to the sink is limited to be no

larger than the smallest edge weight along that path. The maximum and minimum capacity path functions identify the trust capacity of the paths with the highest and lowest capacity respectively. This is useful in identifying the range of trust given by neighbors of X to Y.

- Maximum and minimum length paths: In addition to knowing the varying weights of paths from X to Y, it is useful to know how many steps it takes to reach Y from X. These path length functions return full the chains of weighted edges that make up the maximum and minimum length paths.

- Weighted average: In the algorithm described below, this value represents a recommended trust level for X to Y.

The weighted average is designed to give a calculated recommendation on how much the source should trust the sink. The average, according to the formula (1), is the default trust metric used in all applications querying this network. It is designed to be a very simple metric, and it is reasonable that different users would want to use different metrics In our metric, the maximum capacity of each path is used as the trust value for that path. There is no diminution for long path lengths. Users may want a lower trust rating for someone many links away as opposed to a direct neighbor. Another issue deals with "trust" and "distrust." The maximum capacity calculation does not assign any external value to the trust ratings; they are considered simply as real values. Since there is a social relevance to those numbers, variants of the single path trust value calculation may be desirable. For example, if A distrusts B regarding a specific subject and in turn, B distrusts C on that subject, it is possible that A will want to give C a relatively *higher* rating. That is, if A and B hold opposite views, as do B and C, it may mean that A and C are actually close to one another. Alternately, A may want to distrust C even *more* that A distrusts B, the logic being if A distrusts B, and B cannot even trust C, then C must be especially untrustworthy.

The variants on the trust metric make a long list, and it is unrealistic to provide different functions for each variant. Instead, we have designed an interface where users can create and user their own metrics. This process is described in section 3.3.

By default, trust is calculated according to the following simple function. Using the maximum capacity of each path to the sink, a simple recursive algorithm is applied to calculate the average. For any node that has a direct edge to the sink, we ignore paths and use the weight of that edge as its value. For any node that is not directly connected to the sink, the value is determined by a weighted average of the values for each of its neighbors who have a path to the sink. The calculated trust t from node i to node s is given by the following function:

$$t_{is} = \frac{\displaystyle\sum_{j=0}^{n} \begin{cases} (t_{js} * t_{ij}) & \text{if } t_{ij} >= t_{js} \\ (t_{ij}^2) & \text{if } t_{ij} < t_{js} \end{cases}}{\displaystyle\sum_{j=0}^{n} t_{ij}} \tag{1}$$

where i has n neighbors with paths to s. In calculating the average, this formula also ensures that we do not trust someone down the line more than we trust any intermediary.

Though in the current implementation, our metric searches the entire graph, a simple modification could easily limit the number of paths searched from each node. Since this is a social network that follows the small world pattern, the average distance across the network increases only logarithmically with the number of nodes. Thus, with a limit on the number of paths searched, the algorithm will scale well.

3.3 Trust Web Service

A web service is a function or collection of functions that can be accessed over the web. Access to the trust network is available as a web service. Web users can provide two email addresses, and the weighted average trust value, calculated as described above is returned. The benefit of a web service is its accessibility. It can be composed with other web services or used as a component of another application. This also makes access to trust values available for agents to use as components in intelligent web applications.

The web service interface also allows users to supply their own algorithms for calculating trust. We provide access to a Java API for querying the trust graph. This includes functions such as retrieving a list of neighbors, getting the trust rating for a given edge, detecting the presence or absence of paths between two individuals, and finding path length. With this information, users can write small Java programs to calculate trust based to their own algorithms. The corresponding class file for this user-defined Java code is passed as an argument to our Trust Web Service, along with the source and sink email addresses, and our service will implement the user defined function.

4 Applications

4.1 TrustBot

TrustBot is an IRC bot that has implemented algorithms to make trust recommendations to users based on the trust network it builds. It allows users to transparently interact with the graph by making a simple series of queries.

At runtime, and before joining an IRC network, TrustBot builds an internal representation of the trust network from a collection of distributed sources. Users can add their own URIs to the bot at any time, and incorporate the data into the graph. The bot keeps a collection of these URIs that are spidered when the bot is launched or called upon to reload the graph. From an IRC channel, the bot can be queried to provide the weighted average, as well as maximum and minimum path lengths, and maximum and minimum capacity paths. The TrustBot is currently running on icr.freenode.net, and can be queried under the nick 'TrustBot'.

4.2 TrustMail

TrustMail is an email client, developed on top of Mozilla Messenger, that provides an inline trust rating for each email message. Since our graph uses email address as a unique identifier, it is a natural application to use the trust graph to rank email. As with TrustBot, users can configure TrustMail to show trust levels for the mail sender either on a general level or with respect to a certain topic.

To generate ratings, TrustMail makes a call to the web service, passing in the email address of the sender and the address of the mailbox to where the message was delivered. It is necessary to use the mailbox email address instead of the "to" address on the email to prevent a lack of data because of cc-ed, bcc-ed, and mailing list messages. Figure 2 shows a sample inbox and message with trust ratings.

There are two points to note about the figure below. First is that trust ratings are calculated with respect to the topic of email (using the TrustsRegarding framework described above). If a user has a trust rating with respect to email, that value is used. If there is no trust rating specifically with respect to email, but a general trust rating is available, the latter value is used.

Consider the case of two research groups working on a project together. The professors that head each group know one another, and each professor knows the students in her own group. However, neither is familiar with the students from the other group. If, as part of the project, a student sends an email to the other group's professor, how will the professor know that the message is from someone worth paying attention to? Since the name is unfamiliar, the message is not distinguishable from other, not-so-important mail in the inbox. This scenario is exactly the type of situation that TrustMail improves upon. The professors need only to rate their own students and the other professor. Since the trust algorithms looks for *paths* in the graph (and not just direct edges), there will be a path from professor to professor to student. Thus, even though the student and professor have never met or exchanged correspondence, the student gets a high rating because of the intermediate relationship. If it turns out that one of the students is sending junk type messages, but the network is producing a high rating, the professor can simply add a direct rating for that sender, downgrading the trust level. That will not override anyone else's direct ratings, but will be factored into ratings where the professor is an intermediate step in the path.

The ratings alongside messages are useful, not only for their value, but because they basically replicate the way trust relationships, and awareness thereof, work in social settings. For example, today, it would sensible and polite for our student from above to start of the unsolicited email with some indication of the relationships between the student and the two professors, e.g., "My advisor has collaborated with you on this topic in the past and she suggested I contact you." Upon receiving such a note, the professor might check with her colleague that the student's claims were correct, or just take those claims at face value, extending trust and attention to the student on the basis of the presumed relationship. The effort needed to verify the student by phone, email, or even walking down the hall weighed against the possible harm of taking the

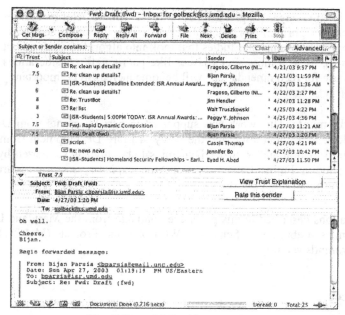

Fig. 2. Trust Mail with trust ratings

student seriously tends to make extending trust blindly worthwhile. TrustMail lowers the cost of sharing trust judgments even in across widely dispersed and rarely interacting groups of people, at least in the context of email. It does so by gathering machine readably encoded assertions about people and their trustworthiness, reasoning about those assertions, and then presenting those augmented assertions in an end user friendly way.

Extending this partial automation of trust judgments to other contexts can be as simple as altering the end user interface appropriate, as we did in earlier work where we presented the trust service as Internet Relay Chat "bot"[30]. However, one might expect other situations to demand different inference procedures (which our service supports), or even different networks of relations. In the current Web, the latter would be difficult to achieve as there is only one sort of link. On the Semantic Web, we can overlay many different patterns of trust relation over the same set of nodes simple by altering the predicate we focus on.

5   Conclusions and Future Work

This paper illustrates a method for creating a trust network on the semantic web. By introducing an ontology, an algorithm for finding trust from the resulting network, and different methods for accessing the network through a web service or applications, this is a first step for showing how non-security based efforts can become part of the foundation of the web of trust.

As work in this area progresses, developers should consider more in depth investigation of algorithms for calculating trust. The algorithm here was designed to be a simple proof-of-concept. Studies that look into algorithmic complexity (as graph size increases), as well more social issues like path length considerations and which averages to use for recommendations will become increasingly important.

Acknowledgements. This work was supported in part by grants from DARPA, the Air Force Research Laboratory, and the Navy Warfare Development Command. The Maryland Information and Network Dynamics Laboratory is supported by Industrial Affiliates including Fujitsu Laboratories of America, NTT, Lockheed Martin, and the Aerospace Corporation.

The applications described in this paper are available from the Maryland Information and Dynamics Laboratory, Semantic Web Agents Project (MIND SWAP) at http://www.mindswap.org.

References

1.   Adamic, L., "The Small World Web". *Proceedings of ECDL*, pages 443–452, 1999.
2.   Adding SVG Paths to Co-Depiction RDF, http://Jibbering.com/svg/codepiction.html
3.   The Advogato Website: http://www.advogato.org
4.   Albert, R., Jeong, H. AND Barabasi, A.-L. "Diameter of the world-wide web." *Nature* 401, 130–131, 1999
5.   Bharat, K and M.R. Henzinger. "Improved algorithms for topic distillation in a hyperlinked environment," *Proc. ACM SIGIR*, 1998.
6.   Brin, S and L. Page, "The anatomy of a large-scale hypertextual Web search engine," *Proc. 7th WWW Conf.*, 1998.
7.   Broder, R Kumar, F. Maghoul, P. Raghavan, S. Rajagopalan, R. Stata, A. Tomkins, and J. Wiener. "Graph structure in the web. " *Proc. 9th International World Wide Web Conference,* 2000.
8.   Carriere, J and R. Kazman, "WebQuery: Searching and visualizing the Web through connectivity," *Proc. 6th WWW Conf.*, 1997.
9.   Chakrabarti, S, B. Dom, D. Gibson, J. Kleinberg, P. Raghavan, and S. Rajagopalan, "Automatic resource compilation by analyzing hyperlink structure and associated text," *Proc. 7th WWW Conf.,* 1998.
10. Dumbill, Ed, "XML Watch: Finding friends with XML and RDF." IBM Developer Works, http://www-106.ibm.com/developerworks/xml/library/x-foaf.html, June 2002.
11. FOAFNaut: http://foafnaut.org/
12. Gil, Yolanda and Varun Ratnakar, "Trusting Information Sources One Citizen at a Time," *Proceedings of the First International Semantic Web Conference (ISWC)*, Sardinia, Italy, June 2002.
13. Kleczkowski, A. and Grenfell, B. T. "Mean-fieldtype equations for spread of epidemics: The 'small-world' model." *Physica A* 274, 355–360, 1999.
14. Kleinberg, J, "Authoritative sources in a hyperlinked environment," *Journal of the ACM,* 1999.
15. Kumar, Ravi, Prabhakar Raghavan, Sridhar Rajagopalan, D. Sivakumar, Andrew Tomkins, and Eli Upfal. "The web as a graph". *Proceedings of the Nineteenth ACM SIGMOD-SIGACT-SIGART Symposium on Principles of Database Systems*, May 15–17, 2000.

16. Labalme, Fen, Kevin Burton, "Enhancing the Internet with Reputations: An Openprivacy Whitepaper," http://www.openprivacy.org/papers/200103-white.html, March 2001.
17. Levien, Raph and Alexander Aiken. "Attack resistant trust metrics for public key certification." *7th USENIX Security Symposium*, San Antonio, Texas, January 1998.
18. Milgram, S. "The small world problem." *Psychology Today* 2, 60–67, 1967.
19. Moore, C. and Newman, M. E. J. "Epidemics and percolation in small-world networks." *Physical Review* E 61, 5678–5682, 2000.
20. Newman, Mark, "The structure of scientific collaboration networks," *Proc. Natl. Acad. Sci. USA* 98, 404–409 (2001).
21. Newman, Mark, "Models of the small world", *J. Stat. Phys.* 101, 819–841 (2000).
22. Open Privacy Initiative: http://www.openprivacy.org/
23. Mutton, Paul and Jennifer Golbeck, "Visualization of Semantic Metadata and Ontologies, " *Proceedings of Information Visualization 2003*, London, England, July 2003.
24. RDFWeb: FOAF: 'the friend of a friend vocabulary', http://rdfweb.org/foaf/
25. RDFWeb: Co-depiction Photo Meta Data: http://rdfweb.org/2002/01/photo/
26. Spertus, E, "ParaSite: Mining structural information on the Web," *Proc. 6th WWW Conf.*, 1997.
27. Szalay, A. S. 2001, "Astronomical Data Analysis Software and Systems X," in *ASP Conf. Ser., Vol.* 238, eds. F. R. Harnden, Jr., F. A. Primini, & H. E. Payne (San Francisco: ASP), 3.
28. The Trust Ontology: http://www.mindswap.org/~golbeck/web/trust.daml
29. Watts, D. and S. H. Strogatz. "Collective Dynamics of Small-World' Networks", *Nature* 393:440-442 (1998).

Exchanging Advice and Learning to Trust

Luís Nunes[1,2] and Eugénio Oliveira[2]

[1] ISCTE, Av. Forças Armadas, 1649-026 Lisbon, Portugal, `Luis.Nunes@iscte.pt`
[2] LIACC/FEUP, Av. Dr. Roberto Frias, 4200-465, Porto, Portugal, `eco@fe.up.pt`

Abstract. One of the most important features of "intelligent behaviour" is the ability to learn from experience. The introduction of
Multiagent Systems brings new challenges to the research in Machine
Learning. New difficulties, but also new advantages, appear when learning takes place in an environment in which agents can communicate
and cooperate. The main question that drives this work is "How can
agents benefit from communication with their peers during the learning
process to improve their individual and global performances?" We are
particularly interested in environments where speed and band-width limitations do not allow highly structured communication, and where learning agents may use different algorithms. The concept of *advice-exchange*,
which started out as mixture of reinforced and supervised learning procedures, is developing into a meta-learning architecture that allows learning
agents to improve their learning skills by exchanging information with
their peers. This paper reports the latest experiments and results in this
subject.

1 Introduction

The field of Multiagent Systems (MAS) deals with software products (agents)
that have some specific characteristics. The full list of these characteristics is
still not consensual, but some are pointed out by most authors: the parts of the
system (agents) may be distributed through several physical or logical environments; Each part has a certain degree of autonomy; Agents interact with each
other. When an agent faces a problem that requires learning capabilities the
above mentioned characteristics add some complexity to the learning task, but
they may also provide new ways to deal with the problems. The main objective
of the current work is to create an integrated set of techniques that enables
learning agents to profit from these special characteristics of MAS. The most
obvious way to have learning agents (hereafter referred to as agents for the sake
of simplicity) profit from communication with their peers is to exchange information concerning their experience in the problem. This may sound simple, but
a closer analysis brings up several questions:

- What type of information to exchange when an agent is not aware of the
  type of learning algorithm their peers are using?
- How does an agent select the best source of information?

M. Klusch et al. (Eds.): CIA 2003, LNAI 2782, pp. 250–265, 2003.

- How much information can be exchanged to produce good results without over-using the (possibly limited) band-width?
- How can an agent be sure that its peer is solving a similar problem, and that the information it produces is useful?
- How should an agent decide when to explore individually and when to request information?
- How does an agent incorporate the information in its current hypothesis?

In the course of this work several tentative answers to these questions were developed. Some assumptions were made regarding the agents and the environment in which they act: it is assumed that agents will help their peers to the best of their knowledge at all times; The only feedback the environment can provide is a qualitative measure of the agent's performance and not the desired action that it should have performed; Agents have simple communication skills and are not aware of what type of algorithm their peers use; Agents are solving problems with similar structure but possibly different dynamics, i.e. the meaning and order of the variables that compose both the environment's state and the agent's actions are the same in all situations, but the environment may respond differently to the same action when executed by different agents or at different times.

The most obvious way to exchange knowledge consists in sending an agent the entire set of parameters that form a solution according to a certain learning algorithm. Given the above restrictions this is not possible, both because agents are not aware of which algorithm their peers are using and because an agent's solution may not be appropriate to another agent, if the dynamics of its environment are different. Notice that, even when in the same environment, agents may experience different dynamics due to local interaction with different peers, or localized differences in the dynamics of the environment.

Since internal solution parameters cannot be exchanged we must turn to other types of information. The simplest type of information that is already understood by all agents is the one generated by the environment, i.e. observed states, actions and quality measures. Other types of information may be used, such as "trust agent X". The use of this information requires either that there is a previous agreement on the meaning of the messages or that an ontology for this domain is available. Because ontologies are, currently, not the main concern of this work we have adopted the first option, allowing a small number of predefined messages to be exchanged.

In the following section the reader can find an explanation of the concept of *advice-exchange*. The experimental setup is explained in section 3, followed by the presentation and discussion of the results in section 4. Section 5 is dedicated to related work and section 6 contains the concluding remarks as well a preview of the future work.

2   Advice-Exchange

Advice-Exchange, first introduced in [1], consists on giving agents the capability of requesting information to their peers and learn from it as well as from the environment's feedback.

During the learning process agents acquire information from the environment and formulate hypothesis for the resolution of the problem they face. The key questions lie on how to select, incorporate, and benefit-from all the available information without re-processing all the data gathered by each of an agent's peers (which is time and band-width consuming). The objective is to gain knowledge based on the synthesis that was done by others without exchanging the entire solution and adopting it blindly.

In the next sections the reader can find a description of the several parts that compose the *advice-exchange* process, but before that we must define a few concepts.

An *advice* is the action that an agent (the *advisor*) would select, for a given state, based on the parameters that achieved the highest average reward in a previous epoch. The *advisee* is the agent that is actually experiencing the, above mentioned, state, and requests the advice. In some situations an *advice* comprises, both the advised action and the state which it refers to. An *epoch* is a measure of time, at the end of which a set of parameters is updated. For simplicity reasons we often relate the end of an epoch to an agent or to the environment. In this case it is possible because the learning epochs of all agents are synchronized, as well as the update of the environment's quality statistics. Nevertheless all the procedures described bellow can be equally applied in asynchronous agents. An epoch is divided in *turns*. In each turn all agents are given the opportunity to act.

When we refer to an agent's *performance* (p_n), the actual measure we are referring to is defined by:

$$p_n = \alpha r_n + (1 - \alpha)p_{n-1}, \tag{1}$$

where n is the epoch number, r_n is the *average reward* given to the agent in epoch n and $\alpha \in]0, 1[$ is a *discount parameter*. Performance measures as well as rewards are always positive values. An agent's *best performance* at epoch n is defined as:

$$b_n = \max(\beta b_{n-1}, r_n), \tag{2}$$

where $\beta \in [0.9, 1[$ is a *decay rate*. When the need arises to refer to the *absolute best performance* this will be mentioned explicitly and it will refer to the highest average reward, measured over a full epoch, that was achieved up the current moment. When it is informally mentioned that some event depends on the performance of an agent (i) being *similar to the a given agent's performance* (k), the exact definition of such a condition is:

$$p_{i,n} > \gamma p_{k,n}, \tag{3}$$

where $p_{i,n}$ is the performance of agent i in epoch n and $\gamma \in]0,1[$ (usually close 1.0, depending on how "similar" the performance must be). A *decaying parameter* (d) is one that is updated every d_{sched} epochs (or turns, depending on the use of the parameter), according to:

$$d_n = \max(\lambda d_{n-d_{sched}}, d_{min}), \qquad (4)$$

where λ is the *decay rate* and d_{min} the minimum value parameter d can reach. A *variable parameter v* is one that is updated according to:

$$v_n = \begin{cases} \min(v_{up} * v_{n-v_{sched}}, v_{max}) & : & C1 \\ \max(v_{down} * v_{n-v_{sched}}, v_{min}) & : & C2 \\ v_{n-v_{sched}} & : & \neg C1 \wedge \neg C2. \end{cases} \qquad (5)$$

where C1 and C2 are the conditions for increase and decrease of parameter v, respectively; $v_{down} \in]0,1[$, $v_{up} \in]1,2[$; v_{min} and v_{max} are the minimum and maximum values parameter v is allowed to reach.

2.1   Learning Stages

When humans work in a team and learn from their peers, we can observe several stages. First they explore solutions individually until someone finds a way to solve the problem, then others observe how the problem was solved and try to mimic the solving behaviour. As this phase progresses the "students" gain a growing degree of autonomy. The "students" tend, first, to ask for a complete demonstration and, afterwards, to ask only for small pieces of information to clear the doubts concerning a particular aspect of the solution. After they have mastered the current solution the members of the group regain their autonomy and try, each individually, to improve the previous solution, or find a better one. When one succeeds the process goes back to one of the previous phases and most of the members of the group start, once again, to learn this new solution by imitation of the "teacher's" behaviour.

This process was transposed to the domain of learning agents, by the introduction of four different learning stages:

1. Individual Exploration: Agents do not exchange information with their peers and act individually. This stage is ended at a predefined time or, optionally, when the performance of the agent stabilizes. Previous tests [1] allowed to conclude that the use of advice-exchange at an early stage will often lead all agents to explore the same area of the search-space, diminishing the exploration capabilities of the system as a whole.
2. Beginner Advisee: At this stage an agent will ask for advice for all its actions and use the same advisor for a full epoch. Agents, in this stage, have a performance that is considerably lower than the best of its peer's.
3. Advanced Advisee: When an agent achieves a performance that is close enough to that of its advisor it becomes an Advanced Advisee and will only request advice when the choice of the next action is unclear. This is more efficient than requesting advice for all actions, providing that the agent has already reached a reasonable performance.

4. Expert: This is the stage attributed to the agent(s) with best performance(s). They may request advice in the same situation as the Advanced Advisee's, but most of the time they are engaged in individual exploration and in trying to improve the current hypothesis by their own means.

Agents evaluate the conditions to transit from one stage to the other at the end of each epoch. An agent can transit one level down in each epoch or as many levels up as it can by meeting the appropriate conditions. A similar approach was taken in [2].

2.2   Deciding to Request Advice

When an agent is prompted to act it should choose the best action according to the quality measure it is learning to maximize. In classical Machine Learning an agent uses a learning algorithm to accumulate experience in a compact and generalizable format. This will allow it to improve its performance by choosing better actions. In MAS an agent has other options, such as requesting advice to its peers as to what is the best action to take for a given state of the environment. Advice-exchanging agents make this decision whenever they are prompted to act. The decision is based on one of two conditions: a comparison of its own performance with those of its peers, or a measure of the certainty an agent has in a given course of action. A Beginner Advisee will request advice whenever its performance is relatively low when compared to that of its peers. Other agents, that are not in the Individual Exploration stage, only request advice when they are uncertain concerning what action to take next.

When comparing its own performance with that of its peers an agent will use a *variable parameter*, labelled *self-confidence*, as a weight term to underrate or over-rate its own performance, depending if the value of this parameter is lower or higher than 1.0. The introduction of this term, as well as the use of performance measures that incorporate information from several epochs, was found useful in dealing with dynamic environments, where there may be a high variance in the reward values from one epoch to the other even when policies are stable. The *self-confidence* parameter is increased whenever the agent's performance is increases or when it is similar to the best agent's performance, and decreased otherwise.

The second condition, which concerns the (un)certainty the agent has in its choice of action, is computed differently depending on the learning algorithm used and type of problem. Most learning algorithms produce an estimate of the appropriateness of each action available at a given stage. The certainty an agent has on the action to take next can be computed based on the variance of these estimates. In this case we have selected a number of the best rated options and, if the difference between each of these and the best option is lower than a given threshold, the agent is said to be uncertain regarding the next action to take. A similar technique was used in [3].

2.3 Deciding on the Source of Information

After having decided that it needs advice, the agent must choose the best source of information. In previous experiments (reported in [4,5]) it was clear that the best advisor was not always the agent with the best performance. This can happen for several reasons, but the most common of these is that advisor's and advisee's local environments have different dynamics and respond differently to the same actions. In partially observable environments, or when the agent is not aware of other agent's presence, as is the case of the environments studied so far, this situation is common. In this case an agent needs to learn which of its peers it can *trust*, or who has the most useful solution for a given state.

The decision of which peer an agent (i) should request advice to, when the observed state is s, is the selection of an agent (k), where:

$$k = argmax_j(trust_{ij} * e_j(s)), \tag{6}$$

for all agents j, where $trust_{ij}$ is a *variable parameter* that represents the level of trust an agent (i) has in peer j and $e_j(s)$ is the estimated performance agent j can achieve when the environment is in state s. The $trust_{ij}$ parameter is increased for all advisors that contributed to the decisions of agent i during an epoch when the average reward is higher than the current performance, and decreased otherwise. To compute the estimated performance of an agent for a given state all agents perform an *unsupervised learning* algorithm based on the states they observe. The algorithm that was used is a simple from of *competitive learning*. This allows the agent to define clusters of states and compute the estimated performance achieved for states in a given cluster. These values are accessible to its peers upon request.

Trust in a given peer can also be influenced by another agent. When an agent issues a message of "trust agent X" the receiving agent will update the trust on agent X in the same way as if it had been an advisor for a successful epoch, thus, increasing the trust on this advisor. A similar procedure could be applied to a "distrust" message, but this was not used in the experiments.

This is an important mechanism that allows a group of agents to synchronize the requests of advice to another group in a flexible way. When it is possible to define groups of agents that are engaged in solving the same task in the same environment (i.e. are partners), it is important for unsuccessful groups, that need to learn from more successful ones, to synchronize their advice requests, so that each member of an advisee-group will request advice to a different member of the advisor-group. This way, the roles that each agent is playing in the cooperative solution can be successfully learned. When an agent issues a message to its own partners that will bias them to trust its advisor's partners it is contributing to the synchronization of the requests. The lack of such a mechanism leads all agents to request advice to the most successful member of the advisor group, which prevents the advisee-group from learning joint strategies [5]. The difference between influencing a partner to trust others and forcing global synchronization in a team is mainly that the latter is less flexible, demands a synchronized protocol and a team-leader or a referee. The process used here allows the composition of solutions using advice from members of different successful groups when this proves efficient enough to overcome the bias towards getting advice from one group. Nevertheless, the possibility of adopting the team-synchronization is not discarded and may payoff when extra knowledge about the roles of each member of the team are known in advance.

2.4   Incorporating Advice

The process of incorporating advice depends on the learning structures used. Most learning structures (such as Artificial Neural Networks or Reinforcement Learning Quality Tables) allow some form of *supervised learning*. The details of how this is conjugated with the main learning algorithms (based on reinforcement feedback) will be explained in section 3.1.

3   Experimental Setup

This section starts with a summarized description of the learning algorithms used in the experiments. This description is focused on the variations from their standard form that were introduced in this work. For details on the standard versions of these algorithms, omitted here due to space constraints, the reader should consult the referred bibliography or [6], where a more detailed explanation of the standard algorithms and the variants used in these experiments can be found. After this first part follows a description of the experimental scenarios.

3.1   Learning Algorithms

Competitive Learning (CL) [7] is an unsupervised clustering algorithm. In this case we use simple Euclidean distance between state vectors to verify to which class a certain state belongs. During training the class representative of each observed state is moved slightly closer to that state, so that the representative will converge asymptotically to the center of mass of the set it represents. Each class representative is also associated with the estimated reward that is achieved by a given agent when acting from a state that belongs to that class. The estimated reward is updated in a similar way to the performance of an agent (equation 1). The objective is to have an estimate of how good is the performance of each advisor for a given state (or set of states).

Backpropagation (BP) [8] is a well known *supervised learning* algorithm, commonly used with networks of differentiable non-linear units connected by weights (Artificial Neural Networks, ANNs). In this work we use classical, online, *backpropagation* with a momentum term, to integrate the information received by *advice-exchange* in agents whose main learning algorithm is also based on ANNs.

Q-Learning (QL) [9] is the most commonly used learning algorithm in the class of *Reinforcement Learning*. Its most simple form (one-level Q-learning), is based on a table that stores the estimated quality $Q(s, a)$ of performing action

a at state s for every possible state-action pair. When a reward r_t is received, at time t, the value of $Q(s, a)$ is updated as follows:

$$Q_{t+1}(s, a) = (1 - \alpha)Q_t(s, a) + \alpha(r_t + \beta Q_{max}(s')), \qquad (7)$$

where s' is the state of the environment after performing action a at state s, α is the learning rate and $\beta \in]0, 1[$ a discount factor applied to the estimated quality of the next state $(Q_{max}(s'))$, which is given by:

$$Q_{max}(s') = \max_a(Q(s', a)), \qquad (8)$$

for all possible actions a when the system is in state s'.

To incorporate the advice from other agents, a form of *supervised learning* is employed in the update of the quality values. When an agent is advised to use action a as response to state s it will sum a positive value (b_{up}) to $Q(s, a)$ and a negative value (b_{down}) to all other actions available at state s (in the current experiments $b_{up} \approx na|b_{down}|$, where na is the number of actions available for the current state). A similar technique, labelled *Biasing-Binary* uses the same absolute quantity both for positive and negative feedback is reported in [10].

Evolutionary Algorithms (EAs) [11,12] are a well known learning technique, with biological inspiration. The solution parameters are interpreted as a specimen (or phenotype), and its performance in a given problem as its fitness. After the evaluation of all the specimens the ones with best fitness are selected for breeding. The selected specimens are then mutated and crossed-over to generate a new population.

The variant of EAs used in these experiments is based on the work presented in [13], and its main characteristics are:

- The genotype is the set of real-valued matrixes that correspond to the weights an ANN of fixed size.
- Each specimen is evaluated during a certain number of epochs (3 in this case). In the first epoch of evaluation *advice-exchange* is inhibited.
- The selection strategy is elitist (keeps a number of the best specimens in the next generation).
- Contrary to [13] this variant does not use tournament selection.
- Mutation is done by disturbing all the values of the parameters with random noise with null average, and normal distribution. The variance of the mutation rate is controlled by a *decaying parameter*.
- The crossover strategy consists on choosing two parents from the selected pool and copying each node of the ANN (along with the weights of all incoming connections) from a randomly chosen parent.

Each agent contains a population of specimens. To incorporate information given by advice an agent will use backpropagation with the advised action for the current state as desired response. The selection process will work on the specimens after they have been changed by the *backpropagation* algorithm, which can be interpreted as *Lamarckian learning*. It was observed that this process took a considerable amount time to produce noticeable effects. To overcome this problem it was necessary to store the advice and replay it before the beginning of a training epoch. The advice is stored after being used. When the storage-space is filled, incoming advice will replace the oldest advice stored. The advisors are evaluated by their *trust-quality product*, defined by: $trust_{ij} * p_{i,n}$. At the beginning of an epoch, if the last advisor still has a high trust-quality product and the agent still requires advice, the stored advice is replayed. If the last advisor has lost the trust of the advisee, or its quality has diminished, the stored advice is thrown away and the next time an advisor is chosen the specimen that receives advice is re-initialized before replaying the advice.

Although advice-replay allows to incorporate knowledge gathered by advice more rapidly, is still under study because it is computationally heavy and it may reduce the diversity of the specimens.

3.2   The Pursuit Problem

The experiments were conducted in the Pursuit Problem (often referred to as Predator-Prey Problem). This problem was first introduced in [14]. This version was inspired on several variations of this environment presented in [15] and [16]. The problem faced by the predator consists in learning to catch a prey in a grid world. A predator is said to have caught the prey if at the end of a given turn it occupies the same position as the prey. The grid-world (arena) is spherical (although it is usually represented in its planar form), and contains two agents (predators) and one prey. The predators in the same arena will be referred to as *partners*. The agents receive the relative position of the prey based on their own position on the grid. The spherical shape of the grid is taken into account when computing the relative position of the prey as well as when moving. Distances are measured in the planar representation of the arena, but predators and prey can see and move across borders to the opposite sides of the arena.

The accuracy of the state received by the predator depends on its visual range. The predator perceives the correct position of the prey up to a limit defined by the visual range parameter (the value of this parameter in these experiments was 3). If the prey is at a distance greater than the visual range its relative position is disturbed (by Gaussian noise with null average) proportionally to the distance between predator and prey. The further the prey is from the limit of the visual range, the higher is the random noise added to the prey's position.

Each predator has to choose between nine possible actions in each turn, i.e. it chooses either to move in one of the eight possible directions (four orthogonal, and four diagonal), or to remain in its current position. Each predator moves one step in one direction in each turn. Any two units can occupy the same cell simultaneously at any time.

The prey, moves before the predators. To decide in which direction to move, the prey detects the presence the closest predator and moves in the opposite direction. If there is more than one predator at the same distance, one of the predators is picked randomly and the prey moves away from it regardless if it is approaching the other predator(s). The prey moves only nine out of each ten turns.

At the end of each turn predators are given a reward, which as an individual and a global component. The individual component is based on the predator's distance to the prey (d). This part of the reward is equal to 1.0, if the predator has captured the prey, or $(1.0 - d/d_{max})/10.0$ otherwise. The constant d_{max} represents the maximum distance between any two positions in the grid world and depends only on the grid dimensions. The global component of the reward is calculated by multiplying the partner's reward by a given number g, with $g < 1$. In these experiments we used $g = 0.25$. After a successful catch the predator that caught the prey is randomly relocated in the grid-world.

This version of the predator-prey problem does not involve either explicit co-operation or competition between the predators, although emergent cooperative behaviour has been detected in some experiments, substantiating the claims re-ported in [17]. Predators do not sense their partner or exchange any information except for the one necessary to perform *advice-exchange*.

The predator-agents use either *Q-Learning* (QL-agents) or *Evolutionary Algorithms* (EA-agents) to learn this task. In one scenario there are also *Heuristic agents* (H-agents). H-agents are pre-coded, and perform an optimal policy for solving this problem individually, i.e. always choose the movement that will take them closer to the prey.

The scenarios used in these experiments are the following:

1. *Individual*: Four arenas, each with two predators and one prey. In each arena all predators use the same learning algorithm and they do not exchange advice. Two arenas have EA-agents, the other two have QL-agents.
2. *Social Heterogeneous*: Same as previous, except that agents may request advice to any of its seven peers in the same or other arenas.
3. *Social Heuristic*: Same as previous but with an extra arena where two H-agents are performing the same task and may also be chosen as advisors.
4. *Social Homogeneous (2 scenarios)*: Same as the *Social Heterogeneous* sce-nario, except that all agents use the same learning algorithm (either QL or EA).

For each of the above scenarios 11 trials were made (x4, or x8, agents of each type), each with different random seeds. Each trial ran for 20000 epochs and each epoch has 150 turns. The *Individual Exploration* stage ends at epoch 5000. For each trial there is a corresponding test which runs for 1000 epochs without learning or exchange of advice. Each agent, in the beginning of the test, loads the parameters that the corresponding agent saved during training when it achieved the best absolute score. Partnerships were kept unchanged by this procedure.

Two sets of experiments were conducted, differing only in the dimension of the grid. In the first set the grid was 10x10, and in the second 20x20.

Table 1. Test results in Experiments 10x10 for each scenario-algorithm pair

Scenario	Alg	Best 10x10	Team 10x10	Avg 10x10
Social Heu.	Heu.	0.1762(+/-0.0196)	0.3425(+/-0.0258)	0.1730(+/-0.0055)
Social Heu.	QL	0.2062(+/-0.0167)	0.4124(+/-0.0235)	0.1942(+/-0.0027)
Social Heu.	EA	0.2059(+/-0.0158)	0.4024(+/-0.0212)	0.1883(+/-0.0046)
Social Het.	QL	0.2079(+/-0.0161)	0.4024(+/-0.0224)	0.1891(+/-0.0037)
Social Het.	EA	0.2060(+/-0.0157)	0.4098(+/-0.0208)	0.1885(+/-0.0035)
Social Hom.	QL	0.2067(+/-0.0160)	0.4048(+/-0.0234)	0.1843(+/-0.0022)
Social Hom.	EA	0.1649(+/-0.0175)	0.3255(+/-0.0224)	0.1466(+/-0.0024)
Individual	QL	0.2111(+/-0.0239)	0.4025(+/-0.0226)	0.1908(+/-0.0034)
Individual	EA	0.1617(+/-0.0150)	0.3234(+/-0.0205)	0.1429(+/-0.0041)

4 Results and Discussion

The results presented in tables 1 and 2 refer to the average performance achieved in the best test (labelled Best), the average performance of the best team (labelled Team) and the average of all the (average) performances in test (labelled Avg). Each measure has the correspondent standard deviation. The measures were taken for each experiment (10x10 and 20x20), scenario (Individual, Social Homogeneous, Social Heterogeneous and Social Heuristic) and learning algorithm (QL and EA).

Concerning the main assumptions, it is important to notice that the algorithm contains the basic tools necessary to relax most of them, with the exception of exchanging advice in problems with different structures, which does not seem to be profitable unless there is some knowledge concerning the possibility of applying similar solutions to these different problems. In this case a mapping, to translate the structure of one problem to the other, would be necessary.

The assumption that agents will always help each other can be erased, possibly at the expense of slower convergence, because the agents can learn to distrust the peers that do not reply or give malicious advice, and a time-out may be introduced to deal with the lack of response of uncooperative peers. Another implicit assumption: that the epochs of all agents are synchronized; is simply a practical solution to make the epoch evaluation equivalent for all agents (they all have the same number of moves in each epoch). The underlying problem, of having untrustworthy, or noisy, evaluations from the environment, is one of the main concerns that caused the introduction of different ways to evaluate an agent's performance, thus it is being addressed.

Before we start an analysis of the results in tables 1 and 2, it is important to notice that QL and EA-agents have quite different behaviours in these two problems. In the 10x10 experiment QL-agents are clearly superior to both EA-agents and H-agents. This is achieved by learning joint strategies in which predators push the prey towards each other.

In the 20x20 experiment joint strategies are harder to develop, and the best result is achieved by H-agents (the best learning agents are EA-agents). As can

Table 2. Test results in Experiments 20x20 for each scenario-algorithm pair

Scenario	Alg	Best 20x20	Team 20x20	Avg 20x20
Social Heu.	Heu.	0.1222(+/-0.0123)	0.2427(+/-0.0169)	0.1216(+/-0.0034)
Social Heu.	QL	0.1203(+/-0.0118)	0.2377(+/-0.0159)	0.1177(+/-0.0029)
Social Heu.	EA	0.1213(+/-0.0119)	0.2425(+/-0.0163)	0.1179(+/-0.0030)
Social Het.	QL	0.1150(+/-0.0102)	0.2298(+/-0.0140)	0.1110(+/-0.0026)
Social Het.	EA	0.1154(+/-0.0100)	0.2308(+/-0.0134)	0.1122(+/-0.0027)
Social Hom.	QL	0.1095(+/-0.0102)	0.2190(+/-0.0142)	0.0874(+/-0.0012)
Social Hom.	EA	0.1154(+/-0.0106)	0.2308(+/-0.0146)	0.1118(+/-0.0020)
Individual	QL	0.1024(+/-0.0075)	0.1960(+/-0.0110)	0.0860(+/-0.0012)
Individual	EA	0.1319(+/-0.0158)	0.2294(+/-0.0152)	0.1071(+/-0.0026)

be noticed by the disparity between the average and best results for Individual
EA-agents, the best individual result is uncommon. In fact there was only one
agent (in 44 trials) that produced a result that was better than the H-agent's
best. This has not occurred in other experiments where the best result of EA-
agents, for this problem, was always slightly inferior to those of H-agents. The
difference in performance of EA versus QL-agents, in these two experiments,
was one of the main reasons for the choice of these variants of the problem as
representatives of a more extensive set of experiments.

In the column labelled Best 10x10, in table 1, we can observe that the best
result in the 10x10 experiment was achieved by Individual QL-agents (although
the standard deviation is high) and the worst by Individual EA-agents. All agents
trained in Social scenarios have managed to achieve a best score above 0.205,
except EA-agents in Homogeneous scenarios. EA-agents clearly benefit from the
advice of their QL and Heuristic peers. The average results (in column Avg
10x10) are slightly different. The best average in test was achieved by QL-agents
in Social Heuristic scenarios. This is particularly interesting because H-agents
cannot be responsible for teaching good joint strategies to QL-agents, since their
performance is much lower and they are pre-programmed to work individually.
This is a case were it seems that the exchange of information during learning can
improve the average performance of agents working in a group *beyond the capabilities of the best of its members*. Another conclusion that can be drawn from
these values is that *advice-exchange* seems to hurt (slightly) the performance of
the best agents, although, in average, it is beneficial (this holds true also in the
20x20 experiment). This is related to the exploration-exploitation trade-off. This
trade-off is present in the decision to request advice to a peer that has a slightly
better solution (and be biased to explore the same search area), or explore individually, which can result in discovering an interesting area of the search-space
that was not discovered by its peers. We believe that further development of the
concept of *learning stages*, along with different types of conditions to make this
decision, can lead to further improvements.

In the 20x20 experiment the best result was achieved by Individual EA-
agents, although, as mentioned above, this is an unusual result. The worst result

is that of Individual QL-agents. The Best results column shows that QL-agents benefit from advice, having better results in all Social environments than those achieved individually. In the last column, showing the average performance results for experiment 20x20, we can observe several interesting facts: the results of Individual agents are worse than any of the results in Social scenarios by the same type of agents. Also, and more important, the results in Social Heterogeneous environment for both QL and EA-agents are considerably better than the average results of their individual counterparts. Again, we have a situation were the exchange of information leads to better average results than each of the members of the team could achieve individually. Learning from H-agents leads to the best average results. This is not surprising given that H-agents have a stable behaviour and a slightly higher performance than any of the other agent's, with the exception of the single EA-agent that achieved the best overall performance.

The results in Social Homogeneous environments are, with one exception, worse than those of the same type of agents in Heterogeneous scenarios. This gives credit to the initial assumption that heterogeneity is advantageous. These results also seem to indicate that, in most situations, the advisees have slightly lower scores than their advisors. In some cases the advisors can be disturbed by the process, possibly because they also take advice in some situations where individual exploration would be preferable in the long term.

5   Related Work

The work on exchange of information between QL-agents started in the early nineties. Whitehead [10] created a cooperative learning architecture labelled *Learning By Watching* (LBW), in which an agent learns by watching its peers' behaviour (this is equivalent to sharing series of state, action, quality triplets). In LBW an agent will use other agents' episodes as if they were its own. This work proves that the complexity of the search mechanisms of LBW is inferior to that of standard *Q-Learning* for an important class of state-spaces.

In [18], Lin uses an expert trainer to teach lessons to a QL-agent that is starting its own training. Lin experimented with several architectures, the most interesting for the current subject is: QCON-T (*Connectionist Q-Learning with Teaching*). This architecture records and replays both "taught" and "learned lessons", i.e. sequences of actions that lead to a success. Some of these sequences (the "taught lessons") are given by an expert trainer (human or automatic), while others recorded by the student agent as it explores the problem (the "learned lessons"). The most interesting conclusion is that *"advantages of teaching should become more significant as the learning task gets more difficult", (section 6.4)*.

Tan [15] addressed the problem of exchanging information between QL-agents during the learning process. This work reports the results of sharing several types of information among agents that are working in the pursuit problem. Experiments were conducted in which QL-agents shared policies (internal solution parameters), episodes (series of state, action, quality triplets), and sensation (observed states). Tan concludes that *"sharing learned policies or episodes among agents speeds up learning at the cost of communication"* and *"for joint tasks, agents engaging in partnership can significantly outperform independent agents",* (in *Abstract*).

In [3], Clouse reports the results of a strategy labelled *Ask for Help* (AH), in which QL-agents learn by asking other agents of the same type for suggestions and perform the suggested actions. This was labelled *learning from a teacher*. Clouse proposes two different approaches for the problem of deciding when to ask for help: in the first approach the advisee asks for help for a given percentage of the actions it has to take; in a second approach the agent asks for help only when it is "confused" about what action to take next. Confusion is defined has having similar quality estimates for all possible actions that the agent can perform at a given stage. Clouse concludes that the integration of *learning from a teacher*, with QL achieves better results than each of its constituents separately.

Recently, quite a few researchers have focused on the problem of exchanging/sharing information during learning from several points of view [19,20,21, 22,23,24,25]. The most important of these is the work of Price and Boutilier [24, 26] in which novice QL-agents learn by *implicit imitation* of pre-trained expert-agents. This work has some very interesting characteristics: the student agent has no knowledge of the actions done by the expert, it can only observe its state transitions; there is no explicit communication between the expert and the student; the goals and actions of both agents can be different. The student agent uses an augmented Bellman equation to calculate the utility of each state. The extra term in the Bellman equation incorporates information regarding the state transitions made by the expert. This technique has been tested in several maze problems with very good results.

6   Conclusions and Future Work

Advice-exchange has evolved over the past year, starting from simply sharing experiences with other agents, to the draft of an architecture that enables cooperation between heterogeneous groups of agents. Along the way, problems such as: disturbances in the learning process (caused by conflicting advice), learning of joint strategies from more successful groups, spurious results that caused agents to trust the "wrong" advisor, and many others, have been dealt with by introducing new concepts, mostly inspired in the human process of group learning. The initial objective was to create a process by which agents could improve their learning skills through communication with other agents. The results presented here show that this can be achieved, even though the experiments are still limited to a single problem.

Tests in more demanding problems, such as traffic-control, are being prepared, both to verify to what extent the particularities of this problem influence the process and to measure the scalability of this approach.

The, recently introduced, concept of learning stages may also be used to control the learning parameters of the agent, enabling it to vary its learning and exploration rates according to its current needs.

Other improvements, based on combination of advice from different sources, rendering unsolicited advice and the use of other learning algorithms, are also scheduled for future work.

References

1. Nunes, L., Oliveira, E.: On learning by exchanging advice. In: Proc. of the First Symposium on Adaptive Agents and Multi-Agent Systems (AAMAS/AISB'02). (2002) 29–40
2. Dorigo, M., Colombetti, M.: The role of the trainer in reinforcement learning. In et al., S.M., ed.: Proc. of MLC-COLT '94, Workshop on Robot Learning. (1994) 37–45
3. Clouse, J.A.: On integrating apprentice learning and reinforcement learning. PhD thesis, University of Massachusetts, Department of Computer Science (1997)
4. Nunes, L., Oliveira, E.: Advice-exchange in heterogeneous groups of learning agents. Technical Report 1 12/02, FEUP/LIACC (2002)
5. Nunes, L., Oliveira, E.: Advice exchange between evolutionary algorithms and reinforcement learning agents: Experimental results in the pursuit domain. In: Proc. of the Second Symposium on Adaptive Agents and Multi-Agent Systems (AAMAS/AISB'03). (2003)
6. Nunes, L., Oliveira, E.: Advice exchange architecture. Technical Report 3 04/03, FEUP/LIACC (2003)
7. Rumelhart, D.E., Zipser, D.: Feature discovery by competitive learning. Cognitive Science **9** (1985)
8. Rumelhart, D.E., Hinton, G.E., Williams, R.J.: Learning internal representations by error propagation. Parallel Distributed Processing: Exploration in the Microstructure of Cognition **1** (1986) 318–362
9. Watkins, C.J.C.H., Dayan, P.D.: Technical note: Q-learning. Machine Learning **8** (1992) 279–292
10. Whitehead, S.D.: A complexity analisys of cooperative mechanisms in reinforcement learning. In: Proc. of the 9th National Conf. on AI (AAAI-91). (1991) 607–613
11. Holland, J.H.: Adaptation in Natural and Artificial Systems. University of Michigan Press (1975)
12. Koza, J.R.: Genetic programming: On the Programming of Computers by Means of Natural Selection. MIT Press, Cambridge MA (1992)
13. Glickman, M., Sycara, K.: Evolution of goal-directed behavior using limited information in a complex environment. In: Proc. of the Genetic and Evolutionary Computation Conference, (GECCO-99). (1999)
14. Benda, M., Jagannathan, V., Dodhiawalla, R.: On optimal cooperation of knowledge resources. Technical Report BCS G-2012-28, Boeing AI Center, Boeing Computer Services, Bellevue, WA (1985)
15. Tan, M.: Multi-agent reinforcement learning: Independent vs. cooperative agents. In: Proc. of the Tenth Int. Conf. on Machine Learning. (1993) 330–337
16. Haynes, T., Wainwright, R., Sen, S., Schoenfeld, D.: Strongly typed genetic programming in evolving cooperation strategies. In: Proc. of the Sixth Int. Conf. on Genetic Algorithms. (1995) 271–278
17. Sen, S., Sekaran, M., Hale, J.: Lerning to coordinate without sharing information. In: Proc. of the National Conf. on AI. (1994) 426–431

18. Lin, L.J.: Self-improving reactive agents based on reinforcement learning, planning and teaching. Machine Learning **8** (1992) 293–321
19. Littman, M.L.: Markov games as a framework for multi-agent reinforcement learning. In: Proc. of the Eleventh International Conference on Machine Learning. (1994) 157–163
20. Thrun, S., Mitchell, T.: Lifelong robot learning. Robotics and Autonomous Systems **15** (1995) 25–46
21. Maclin, R., Shavlik, J.: Creating advicetaking reinforcement learners. Machine Learning **22** (1996) 251–281
22. Matarić, M.J.: Using communication to reduce locality in distributed multi-agent learning. Computer Science Technical Report CS-96-190, Brandeis University (1996)
23. Claus, C., Boutilier, C.: The dynamics of reinforcement learning in cooperative multiagent systems. In: Proc. of the Fifteenth National Conference on Artificial Intelligence. (1998) 746–752 Madison, WI.
24. Price, B., Boutilier, C.: Implicit imitation in multiagent reinforcement learning. In: Proc. of the Sixteenth Int. Conf. on Machine Learning. (1999) 325–334
25. Berenji, H.R., Vengerov, D.: Advantages of cooperation between reinforcement learning agents in difficult stochastic problems. In: Proc. of the Nineth IEEE International Conference on Fuzzy Systems (FUZZ-IEEE '00). (2000)
26. Price, B., Boutilier, C.: Imitation and reinforcement learning in agents with heterogeneous actions. In: Proc. of the Seventeenth Int. Conf. on Machine Learning (ICML2000). (2000)

A Component-Based Approach for Interoperability across FIPA-Compliant Platforms*

Mercedes Amor, Lidia Fuentes, and José Mª. Troya

Dpto. Lenguajes y Ciencias de la Computación
Universidad de Málaga. Campus de Teatinos, s/n
29071 Málaga, Spain
{pinilla,lff,troya}@lcc.uma.es

Abstract. Software Agents are becoming one of the most important approaches for developing open distributed systems. Interoperability is a critical issue to develop open and flexible agent-based applications, as it would make reusability possible across heterogeneous agent systems. Agent interoperability can be achieved through the use of FIPA standardized specifications. Although most major FIPA-compliant platforms have reached a consensus on the different alternative specifications to interoperate, for other platforms this would remain an open issue. For the latter cases FIPA suggests the use of gateways, but sometimes it is not possible to extend or provide the basic gateway for all cases. This paper presents an approach for developing heterogeneous agent-based systems regardless of the FIPA-compliant agent platforms involved. The basis of our proposal is the use of component technology for the development of adaptive software agents. Our compositional software agent separates the distribution of messages according to different transport services, which reduces platform dependency on the agent coordinated behaviour. This agent capability allows using these agents as gateways between agent platforms, providing an immediate solution to interoperability.

1 Introduction

Software agents are becoming one of the most important approaches for developing open distributed systems. Some research and development efforts in this field are beginning to embrace the concept of software agents and multi-agent systems (MAS). More than other technologies, agents seem to have the necessary characteristics to support the development of open and flexible distributed systems. Particularly, we identify two agent characteristics that seem to be most significant from this point of view: autonomy and interoperability. Autonomy is necessary to deal with dynamic environments since it enables the agent to adapt to unexpected communication protocols, and interoperability is a critical condition for the implementation of open systems [1].

Concretely, the construction of heterogeneous MAS is based on the interoperation across agent platforms. It is desirable that different agent platforms interoperate to support reusability across agent systems. One way to achieve interoperability is

---

* This research was funded in part by the CICYT under grant TIC: 2002-04309-C02-02.

M. Klusch et al. (Eds.): CIA 2003, LNAI 2782, pp. 266–280, 2003.

through the use of standards approved by an international committee. The Foundation for Intelligent Physical Agents (FIPA)[2] produces software standards for heterogeneous and interacting agents and agent-based systems. FIPA specifications represent a collection of standards that promote the interoperation of heterogeneous agents. These standards mainly comprise agent infrastructure and agent applications. FIPA specifications are being realized by a wide range of organizations offering different platform implementations. New releases of the most well known FIPA-compliant platforms, such as FIPA-OS [3], JADE [4] and ZEUS [5], already offer a totally interoperable configuration. This made it possible to create the Agenticities network [6], where agents from different FIPA platforms –deployed according to some consensual agreements- interoperate.

However, interoperability is not always possible, especially in those platforms that did not make the effort to offer a configuration compatible to Agentcities platforms. As a matter of fact, since the architecture of the FIPA specifications is explicitly intended to allow choice, the operation between different platform realizations might be unsuccessful even if FIPA specifications are used. For these cases FIPA also establishes the use of gateways to provide access across different transport services. This solution can be adopted by those agent platforms that are not involved in initiatives such as Agentcities. But providing these gateways is the responsibility of the platform vendor, which sometimes is not interested in doing so due to competitive issues concerning other vendors.

We propose an intermediate solution to provide interoperation between agent platforms by defining proxy agents that work as gateways to communicate agents inside a running agent-based application. The basis of this proposal is an agent architecture that endows software agents with sufficient flexibility to operate in different FIPA-compliant platforms simultaneously. We solve the interoperability issue as part of the agent architecture, which gives the agent developer more control to adapt the agent to operate through any agent platform regardless of the gateways provided by a platform vendor.

Originally this proposal was mainly motivated by the complexity of extending current agent architectures to support new capabilities, which is not straightforward and depends on programmer expertise regarding certain agent architecture. More flexible agent architectures may allow software agents to cope with the evolution and emergence of new technologies, e.g. new transport services, message encoding, etc. Instead of providing just another agent platform, our proposal was intended to provide a component-based agent architecture capable of being adapted to use any agent platform. In other words, the idea is to "write your agent once, run it on almost any platform".

It is widely recognized that Component-Based Software Engineering (CBSE) provides advanced techniques that can be applied to the design and development of complex systems such as software agents. The benefits of component-oriented systems arise from their increased flexibility, since a system built from reusable components is easier to recompose for addressing new requirements [7]. We propose a component-based model for the development of flexible and adaptive agents. Many benefits can be obtained from decomposing agent functionality, coordination and message distribution into independent components, since agent behaviour can be dynamically tailored to support new negotiation protocols and new functionality on different agent platforms. In our model, software agents include a high-level mechanism for their runtime adaptation, enabling them to participate in any interaction regardless of the protocols supported [8]. This benefit can also be applied to add new functionality provided by external components, such as Web services or COTS (Commercial-Off-The-Shelf) components [9]. This means that agent behaviour is given by different plug-in components that can be added, updated or replaced without affecting the system. Furthermore, platform-specific features like message service transport are separated from those that are application-specific, i.e. agent domain functionality. With this approach we encourage application developers to easily extend our architecture without depending on new platform releases. Since we endow our agents with the capability of interoperating across any FIPA-compliant platform, they can be used to provide a rapid solution to interconnect incompatible agent platforms and to communicate heterogeneous agents in an agent-based system.

The solution is to avoid hard coding deployment information (e.g. the message transport service) inside the agent or not to depend on the different message transport services provided by the platform provider. Instead, this information should be given as customisable deployment documents in XML. In consequence, our software agents will be able to exist simultaneously in different FIPA-compliant platforms, and can be used by these platforms as proxy agents to interoperate. One of the main benefits of this approach is that we encourage the reuse of software agents in heterogeneous MAS without worrying about their implementation platforms. The aim of this proposal is to avoid the development of new software agents from scratch; instead we (re)use and cooperate with already built agents that offer the desired functionality.

The structure of this paper is organized as follows: Section 2 gives a brief overview of the FIPA reference model and introduces a discussion about how to deal with interoperability in FIPA-compliant implementations. Section 3 presents our component-based agent architecture, and describes the main entities of our model. Section 4 illustrates a typical scenario in which it is profitable to apply our approach. Finally some concluding remarks are made in Section 5.

2   A Comparison of FIPA-Compliant Platforms

The main goal of FIPA is to support interoperable agent applications by specifying an agent architecture that can accommodate a wide range of commonly used mechanisms, such as various transport protocols or directory services. Agent systems built according to this architecture should be able to fully interoperate through transport gateways, because the FIPA Abstract Architecture [10] permits the creation of multiple concrete realizations, and provides transformations for message transports, encoding schemas, and locating agents and services via directory services. However, the architecture of FIPA specifications is specifically intended to allow choice. Since there are some decisions to be made and certain aspects are not fully specified, interoperation across agent platforms is not a straightforward issue.

2.1   The FIPA Reference Model

A FIPA agent platform is defined as software that implements the set of FIPA specifications. To be considered FIPA-compliant, an agent platform implementation must at least implement Agent Management [11] and Agent Communication

Language [12] specifications. FIPA Agent Management specifications deal with the control and management of agents within and across agent platforms. FIPA Agent Communication specifications deal with the Agent Communication Language (ACL) of messages, the message exchange interaction protocols, the speech act theory-based communicative acts and content language representations.

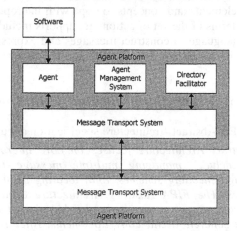

Fig. 1. Agent Management Reference Model (Extracted from [11])

The goal of agent management specifications is to provide a standard framework where FIPA agents exist and operate, establishing a logical reference model for the creation, registration, location, communication, migration and retirement of agents. The agent management reference model consists of a set of entities (shown in Fig. 1) providing different services. These entities are:

- A software agent, which is a computational process that implements the autonomous, communicating functionality of an application, providing one or more services. Agents communicate using an ACL. An agent must have at least one owner, and one Agent Identifier (AID), which labels it uniquely. Furthermore, an agent may be registered at a number of transport addresses where it can be contacted. In a concrete instantiation of the FIPA Abstract Architecture, an agent may be realized in a variety of ways, for example as a Java component or a CORBA object.
- A Directory Facilitator (DF) implements a yellow page service for other agents. Any agent may register its services inside the DF or query it to look up agents according to their services. Multiple DFs may exist within an agent platform, and may be federated.
- An Agent Management System (AMS) controls access to and use of the agent platform. Only one AMS can exist in a single agent platform, which is in charge of generating valid AIDs, and it provides a look-up service for agent addresses.
- A Message Transport Service (MTS) is the default communication method between agents and deals with message transportation between interoperating agents. For this component, FIPA specifies a reference model to allow interoperability between different message formats.

- An Agent Platform (AP) provides the physical infrastructure in which agents can be deployed. The AP consists of agent support software, the FIPA agent management components (DF, AMS and MTS) and the agents.
- A Software entity is used to describe all non-agent software systems accessible through an agent, for example COTS components and Web services.

Other important elements and concepts to cope with interoperability are: a service, which is defined in terms of the set of actions it supports included in an ontology; the ACL, which is the language to construct messages and express communicative acts; and the AID, which identifies an agent, including social names, nick names, and roles.

2.2 Incompatibilities between FIPA-Compliant Agent Platforms

According to the FIPA Abstract Architecture specification document:

"The FIPA Abstract Architecture focuses on core interoperability between agents. These include: managing multiple message transport schemes, managing message encoding schemes, and, locating agents and services via directory services. The FIPA Abstract Architecture explicitly avoids issues internal to the structure of an agent. It also largely defers details of agent services to more concrete architecture documents. After reading through the FIPA Abstract Architecture, many readers may feel that it lacks a number of elements they would have expected to be included. Examples include the notion of an "agent-platform", "gateways" between agent systems, bootstrapping of agent systems and agent configuration and coordination. These elements are not included in the FIPA Abstract Architecture because they are inherently coupled with specific implementations of the architecture, rather than across all possible implementations."[10]

In consequence, FIPA specifications do not cope with every issue related to the development of concrete agent platform implementations. Any realization of an agent platform must specify the set of transports that are supported, how new transports are added, and how effective interoperability can be achieved regarding any other issue. Consequently, agent platform vendors make their own assumptions about those concerns that are left open or undefined by FIPA, as a result of which some dissimilarity may arise. The following are some examples related to platform interoperability:

- There are a wide variety of transport services that may be used to convey a message from one agent to another. The FIPA Abstract Architecture is neutral with respect to this variety. But in practice, for two agents to communicate at least the MTS on a common transport protocol has to be shared, e.g. HTTP MTP. In order to interoperate, it is desirable that the shared MTP be one specified by FIPA, e.g. IIOP MTP or HTTP MTP. In this way, since FIPA does not provide a specification for using Java RMI as transport protocol, a Jade agent and a FIPA-OS agent, both using Java RMI as message transport protocol, cannot communicate.
- On top of the MTP, the envelope encoding must also be shared. Two platforms sharing the same MTP should also share the same envelope encoding, e.g. XML. But notice that there is no FIPA specification stating a concrete envelope encoding for each MTP. Although each MTP suggests a natural encoding (e.g. a CORBA

IDL envelope for a IIOP MTP) an XML or either a Bit-Efficient representation can be used for a HTTP MTP.

- Realizing that having multiple choices could postpone interoperation, FIPA proposes the development of gateways to bypass this problem. Since the abstract agent transport architecture supports the use of different transports, encodings, and infrastructure elements appropriate to the application domain, platform developers must consider the development of gateways that can provide full or limited interoperability. Such gateways may relay messages between incompatible transports, may translate messages from one encoding to another, and may also provide QoS features supported by one party but not by another. However, gateways, which are the responsibility of platform developers, are not always provided, despite the fact that they are sometimes needed.
- When multiple MTP implementations are provided, the platform may need some extra configuration for effective interoperation. For a non-expert user who is not aware of the possibility of having multiple MTP, reaching an interoperable configuration is sometimes annoying, and this is not desirable.
- The evolution and improvement of an agent platform to support new specifications depend on its development team. First versions did not provide a wide range of services and facilities specified by FIPA, but efforts as Agentcities lead towards establishing conformance points for interoperability.

Since the list of MTP is always open-ended, agent platforms should provide a way of easily adding new MTPs without depending on the gateways provided by platform vendors. These examples illustrate that interoperability can now be achieved, but that it requires some effort and a common agreement amongst platform developers. This section briefly showed why interoperability might not be achieved and the motivation of the intermediate solution presented here.

3 Compositional Agent Model

In this section we describe a compositional model for software agents. Software agents are systems that perform actions or tasks autonomously to reach a set of goals. The agent model is an abstraction that corresponds to functional and extra-functional aspects of these tasks and goals. Therefore, agent computational models should allow a high degree of adaptability to consider the agent as a reusable piece of software. Since FIPA does not propose any standard regarding internal agent structure, current implementations mainly use their own object-oriented design. But the agent design of current platforms is not flexible enough to meet the former requirements.

Our model encapsulates agent functionality in software components. Modelling agent functionality as components, we found out that a software agent should contain components for storing data (e.g. to store its internal goals, facts, etc.), for providing application domain functionality (e.g. buy, bid, search), and a special kind of component that coordinates internal and external agent execution.

Usually both the functional and the coordination code are entangled inside the component implementation, complicating its reuse. The goal of our agent compositional model is to encourage the agent designer to define interaction protocol templates to be free to modify the internal processing part of the agent components.

We thus improve functional agent decomposition, applying the principle of "separation of concerns" [13][14]. Specifically, we separate the *coordination aspect* into an entity called connector. This entity controls the interaction between internal agent components and/or external agents. Thus connectors, for instance, model negotiation protocols. In a previous work we successfully applied this paradigm [15] to component-based Web applications. In our case, the separation of the coordination aspect facilitates the reuse of agent behaviour across different interaction protocols and the dynamic adaptation of agents to new coordination patterns [8].

Since connectors also send messages, all of them need to make reference to the transport protocol of outgoing messages that depends, for example, on the target agent. So we see that deciding how to form a message regarding different target agent platforms cuts across all connectors. In consequence, we decided to model this *distribution concern* separately as a software aspect.

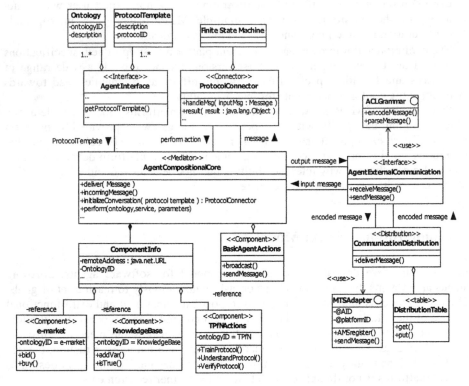

Fig. 2. Compositional Architecture for Software Agents

Fig. 2 shows the UML class diagram of the proposed compositional architecture of a software agent based mainly on components and connectors. We use UML stereotypes for modelling the principal entities of our model, which are <<Connector>>, <<Component>>, <<Interface>>, <<Mediator>>, and <<Distribution>>.

Connectors coordinate the different interactions or conversations in which the agent is involved. An agent can participate in more than one interaction or conversation simultaneously, and a protocol connector controls each conversation. Connectors coordinate dialogues according to a specific protocol (e.g. English Auction Negotiation Protocol). Instantiated connectors differ only in the coordinated protocol, given by a template filled with specific rules, transitions and constraints. Thus, an agent is able to encompass a new protocol only by uploading the corresponding template through the TPfN (Training Protocol for Negotiation) protocol [8].

Components encapsulate data and behaviour. Some behavioural components are always present in the architecture providing the generic agent functionality (*BasicAgentActions* and *TpfNActions* components), such as sending a message, or storing the general data (*KnowledgeBase* component). Domain specific behaviour is also provided by components (e.g. e-market component). For instance, the *e-market* component offers functionality to perform e-commerce tasks, such as generating a bid or making an on-line payment. These components may be plugged into agent functionality on demand, and are easily changeable over the lifetime of the agent, guaranteeing software agent evolution.

Interface components manage an agent's external interactions. The component *AgentInterface* contains the public agent interface, which is an extension of the traditional public interface of software components. For instance, the *AgentInterface* includes, in addition to the provided services, the public negotiation protocols, etc., (the agent interface description is beyond the scope of this paper). With respect to this paper, this component mainly stores the templates of the supported protocols and the ontology descriptions used by the agent protocols.

The *AgentExternalCommunication* (*AEC*) component allows the agent to communicate by means of different ACL representations. It parses the input messages to an independent representation format and encodes output messages in a concrete ACL representation. Incoming messages are first processed by this component, and it may discard messages that are not syntactically well formed. This component hides representation dependencies defining a high-level interface to send and receive messages in different ACL representations. For every ACL representation, the corresponding representation grammar rules are encapsulated in a class that realizes the interface *ACLGrammar* (shown in Fig. 2), which also supports the parsing and encoding of a message in a concrete ACL representation, such as XML, String or BitEfficient encoding formats.

The *CommunicationDistribution* aspect allows the agent to communicate by means of different agent platforms providing different MTSs. It receives the incoming messages and delivers outgoing messages to an agent platform. This aspect hides platform dependencies defining a high-level interface to send and receive messages to and from different platforms. For every agent platform the agent can access this component is in charge of instantiating the corresponding platform-dependent functionality (since FIPA do not define a unique and mandatory mechanism for bootstrapping), which is encapsulated in a component that realizes the interface *MTSAdapter* (shown in Fig. 2).

Separating specific-platform code into different components reduces the complexity of managing communication with multiple agent platforms, one of the goals of this work. The *MTSAdapter* components implement the mechanisms needed to send and receive legal messages from a concrete agent platform using the provided

MTS. After it is created, an *MTSAdapter* gets a valid ID and registers the agent in the corresponding agent platform. These components are not responsible for enclosing the encoded ACL message in the appropriate envelope format, since they make use of the agent platform's MTS. The *CommunicationDistribution* component knows which adapter class is responsible for sending a message and delegates it to the appropriate *MTSAdapter* instance. This component separates the distribution of messages to different agent platforms from the other internal agent components. When the agent needs to send a message, the distribution aspect must resolve that target agent's platform. So this aspect maintains a distribution table with pairs (AID, platform identifier). This table will be filled as messages come from different platforms. As soon as the agent receives a message the *CommunicationDistribution* component intercepts it and adds a new row to the distribution table with the pair (AID, adapter identifier). When the agent sends a message, and there is no information in the distribution table, the *CommunicationDistribution* component resolves the appropriate platform seeking out the target agent in the AMSs. This table is initialised with the addresses of target agents involved in the interactions where the agent participates as initiator.

The mediator component *AgentCompositionalCore* *(ACC)* mainly performs the dynamic composition of components and connectors. This component promotes loose coupling by keeping components and connectors from referring to each other explicitly, by plugging components into connectors dynamically. For instance, the ACC will link an auction connector to the *e-market* actions component, but notice that this will be done at runtime. The *ACC* receives input messages from the *AEC* component, dispatching them to the appropriate conversation according to the conversation identifier contained in the message. In addition, this component launches a connector encapsulating a specific protocol as a new interaction is initiated. Since inside connectors components are referred to by a role name, the ACC component is able to plug a new component implementation into the agent dynamically, achieving the upgrade of this compositional agent without replacing it.

An XML deployment document specifies the initial configuration of the agent behaviour, the initial coordination protocols and the communication capabilities by means of the ACL representation formats accepted and the distribution platforms. Fig. 3 shows the relevant elements of this document. This deployment information consists of: a list of agent platform identifiers and the related implementation class of the adapter; a list of ACL representation formats and the related implementation class of the parser; a list of references to XML documents that describe coordination protocols in DAML-S; and a list of URIs that identifies the components that will be initially registered as functionality providers.

4   Our Approach to Meeting Agent Interoperability

We are going to show how we resolve an agent platform interoperability incompatibility through a Marketplace example. Our goal is to make communication among market counterparts possible regardless of the agent platform they belong to. This example illustrates the situation of two FIPA-compliant platforms that do not share the MTP and in which neither one provides a gateway between the two.

```
<deployment>
  <distribution>
    <platform ID="FIPAVendor1">
      <adapter>FIPAVendor1Adapter.class</adapter>
    </platform>
    ...
  </distribution>
  <ACLrepresentation>
    <format ID="XML">
      <parser>XMLACLEncoding.class</parser>
    </format>
    ...
  </ACLrepresentation>
  <coordination>
    <protocol ID="FIPA-propose" href = "http://map/FIPA-proposeMarket.damls"/>
    ...
  </coordination>
  <behaviour>
    <component ID="e-market" URI = "emarket.class"/>
    ...
  </behaviour>
</deployment>
```

Fig. 3. XML deployment document

4.1 The Marketplace Description

The following is a simple but instructive Marketplace application. Every transaction in the Market is established by a Broker agent, which brings together buyers and sellers and simplifies the task of interaction in the Marketplace.

In this market, an agent called Provider, which is attempting to sell its products in this market, represents a seller. For example, if a Provider has to sell oranges, it subscribes to the Broker that publishes its offer (interaction 1 in Fig. 4). In this application, buyers are represented by the Trader agent, a representative of a supermarket that is in charge of buying products for stock. When this agent needs to buy a product, for example oranges, it queries the Broker agent for a supplier of oranges (interaction 2 in Fig. 4). The Broker agent tries to match its subscriptions with the requirements of the query, and returns the name of the Provider agent that offers oranges. After that, the Provider and the Trader negotiate by themselves the price of the oranges (interaction 3 in Fig. 4).

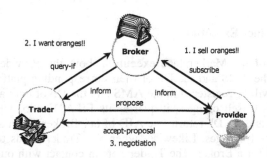

Fig. 4. Marketplace interaction schema

4.2 The Marketplace Implementation

Now we have to deal with the implementation of these agents. In analysing agents' functionality we find out that two existing agents fulfil Provider and Trader requirements so they can be (re)used. The Trader agent is a FIPA1Vendor agent, and the Provider is a FIPA2Vendor agent. However both platforms are not interoperable because one of them only provides an IIOP MTS and the other one is HTTP MTS. Though both platforms are FIPA-compliant, the agents will not be able to communicate. Now, the Broker agent has to attend to Provider subscriptions and Trader queries from both platforms. In addition, we will need a Proxy agent to circumvent the interoperability problems that arise when the Trader and the Provider need to negotiate. As a result of this, we are going to develop the Broker and the Proxy agents with our model.

Both the Broker and the Proxy agents have the architecture presented in the last section. They only differ in the service they provide to other agents. In fact, to implement both agents we only have to write two different deployment documents describing concrete agent requirements for distribution, coordination and behaviour patterns. The Broker agent deployment document needs to include FIPA1Vendor and FIPA2Vendor as distribution platforms, and references to the FIPA subscribe, query-if and inform interaction protocols. In the same way, the Proxy agent deployment document also has to include access to FIPA1Vendor and FIPA2Vendor platforms and a reference to a protocol description to deal with the proxy service. Once the Proxy agent is informed about a new service, it works as follows: when the Proxy agent receives the messages sent by the Provider through the FIPA2Vendor MTS, it solves the corresponding incompatibilities and retransmits them to the Trader through the FIPA1Vendor MTS. On the contrary, when the Proxy agent receives the messages from the Trader through the FIPA1Vendor MTS, it sends the same messages to the Provider through the FIPA2Vendor MTS.

Moreover, the *ACLParser* realization to parse the encoded message in XML is specified in the deployment document. We do not have to worry about different message representations, and the parser only has to be included for the ACL representations used in each platform, because they are parsed separately regarding the platform and the interaction. In other words, the messages interchanged in the same interaction do not have to share the ACL representation.

4.3 The Marketplace Execution

At the beginning of the Marketplace execution, both the Provider and the Trader agents register at the AMS and the DF of their corresponding platforms. Our Broker and Proxy agents will be registered in the AMS and the DF of both agent platforms. If the Provider wants to sell oranges, it queries its FIPA2Vendor DF for a Broker to subscribe its offer, and the DF returns the AID of our Broker. Then the Provider sends a subscription to sell oranges. Likewise, when the Trader needs to buy oranges, it searches in the DF for a Broker. The Trader gets in contact with our Broker to query about orange providers. The Broker probably returns the Provider agent's AID, and the FIPA1Vendor Trader and the FIPA2Vendor Provider start to negotiate about oranges.

Now we are going to deal with the problem of having the Trader and Provider belong to different agent platforms. Actually they are not able to communicate, but they are not aware of this problem. As the Broker is conscious of this incompatibility, it is responsible for searching in the DF for the appropriate Proxy agent. The Broker informs the Proxy about the required service and the name of the agents involved in the interaction. After that, the Broker returns the Proxy FIPA1Vendor AID to the Trader instead of the FIPA2Vendor Provider name. In this way, the Provider agent addresses the messages to the Proxy agent FIPA2Vendor AID, and the Trader agent sends the messages to the Proxy agent FIPA1Vendor AID.

When our agents are created, they instantiate the *FIPA1VendorAdapter* and *FIPA2VendorAdapter* classes specified in their deployment document. At this point we want to remark that an agent is able to add new *MTSAdapters* at runtime. As soon as a *FIPA2VendorAdapter* class for the FIPA2Vendor platform is instantiated (see Fig. 5), it obtains a valid AID and registers the agent in the FIPA2Vendor AMS. In this case, the agent is named proxy@FIPA2Vendor.map.es. With this identifier, it registers in the FIPA2Vendor DF to be subscribed as a proxy agent. The *FIPA1VendorAdapter* follows the same process: it gets proxy@FIPA1Vendor.map.es as AID in the FIPA1Vendor platform, and registers the agent in the corresponding DF. Once the agent is created, it is ready to attend service requests.

In addition, they instantiate the *XMLParser* class (inside the *AEC* component in Fig. 5) as the ACL representation parser included in the deployment document. Notice that the ACL representation of the message is independent from the platform sending or receiving it. This means that different *MTSAdapters* do not have to be developed depending on the ACL representation format used. Instead, the ACL parser is shared across the messages of different platforms. In addition, the agent is able to add new parsers at runtime.

As part of its service, before receiving the first message from the Trader the Proxy agent needs to know who the other participant in the interaction is. Hence the Broker agent previously informs the Proxy agent about the identity of the two agents participating in the interaction, in this case the Provider provider@FIPA2Vendor.map.es and the Trader trader@FIPA1Vendor.map.es. This pair of AIDs is stored in the *KnowledgeDatabase* component. As soon as the Trader's first message is received, a new connector is launched with the proxy protocol template. We want to point out that following our approach, programming a new agent interaction protocol entails defining an XML document in DAML-S. In consequence, nobody needs to be an expert programmer or a specialist in any agent application framework. Moreover, the compile and runtime errors are drastically reduced. During protocol execution, the internal agent components coordinate as shown in Fig. 5.

Both FIPA2Vendor and FIPA1Vendor adapters receive incoming messages enclosed in an envelope. From the transport message they extract the encoded message that is passed to *AEC* component for parsing (*receiveMessage* message in Fig. 5). The distribution table was previously checked to update the distribution information. The *AEC* component delegates message parsing to the corresponding ACL parser that generates data independent of the ACL representation format. This data is forwarded to the *ACC* component (*incomingMessage* message in Fig. 5) that delivers it to the appropriate connector looking up the *conversationID* field of the message. Every connector is identified by the conversation identifier (enclosed in all the messages interchanged inside the interaction). In this case the connector receives a message from one of the partners (method *handleMessage* in Fig. 5), and it has to produce the same message to the other paired agent, which is obtained from the *KnowledgeDatabase* component (method *getVar* in Fig. 5). The connector does not directly perform the action. Instead, it makes a request to perform the service described in an ontology (*perform(ontology,service,..)* call in Fig. 5) that is intercepted by the *ACC* component. In some way this component works as a service broker inside the agent. The *Mediator* entity forwards the service request to the component that provides the service and will send the result back to the connector.

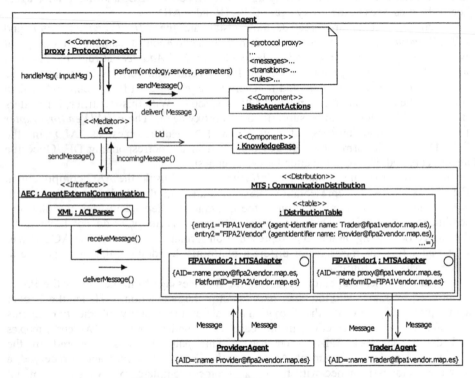

Fig. 5. Proxy Agent Collaboration Diagram

The action "to send a message" is first delegated to the *BasicAgentActions* component, which fills the empty fields of the message. This is necessary if the protocol template does not specify a message field, or if its content depends on the execution context. Then, the message is sent again to the *ACC* component (action *deliver(Message)* in Fig. 5) that forwards it to the *AEC* component, which encodes the message in XML. Finally, the *CommunicationDistribution* component (*deliverMessage* in Fig. 5) seeks the appropriate platform to deliver the message. If the message is addressed to the Provider agent, by way of the FIPA2Vendor adapter, the outgoing message is enclosed in an envelope and is delivered. If there is no distribution information for the target agent, it tries to determine the platform of the target agent querying the AMS service of both platforms.

5 Conclusions

The aim of FIPA is to produce specifications that lead to the interoperation of heterogeneous software agents. However since FIPA does not specify unique, mandatory and fully specifications, providing various specifications in practice allows for choice. Leaving FIPA specifications open has two consequences: first, new technologies can be easily adopted by FIPA and consequently by agent platforms; and second, this openness could hamper FIPA adoption process and cause platform developers to put too much effort in following FIPA guidelines. Different choices and different interpretations or assumptions about FIPA compliance points could put off the interoperation of different agent-based implementations that drastically reduce the (re)use of agents from different platforms.

In this paper, we propose an approach to resolve the particular interoperability problems on the basis of FIPA specifications using software agents that are able to communicate on top of different platforms simultaneously. The basis of this proposal is a component-based agent architecture that combines component orientation and separation of concerns. The flexibility provided by component orientation enables the software agent to be easily programmed to support new protocols and behaviour, but it also provides a weak coupling between the internal agent components and the components that provide access to the concrete MTS realizations. In other agent models, agent architecture consists of a set of coupled components with dependencies, which makes it difficult to adapt it to support, for instance, another ACL representation, or to change its communication protocol. We avoid these dependencies by separating into different components the distribution of messages to platforms, the coordination of interaction protocols, and the mere agent functionality, which is provided by plug-in components. In this paper we present the advantages of modelling separately the distribution aspect for interoperability purposes.

To situate our proposal in a concrete scenario we have described a situation where it is necessary to achieve interoperability. Although the approach involves the creation of two agents, we have illustrated that these agents are easy to program. It is only necessary to describe the interaction protocols, including the actions that have to be performed during its execution, in an XML document; and to write a deployment document specifying communication, coordination and functional requirements.

Our agents can be designed regardless of implementation features such as agent platform or message encoding. These details are particularized by the deployment information, and it can be updated at runtime to address new requirements. Thus we are not suggesting just another agent platform, but instead, propose a model to design component-based agents that can be reused on top of the existing platforms and can be easily adapted to new requirements that affect agent coordination and/or functionality even at runtime.

Currently our prototype implemented in Java works on top of Jade, FIPA-OS and Zeus as agent platforms.

Acknowledgements. The authors are very grateful to the reviewers for their insightful comments and suggestions that greatly helped improving the contents and readability of this paper.

References

1. F. Bergenti and A. Poggi "A development Toolkit to Realize Autonomous and Interoperable Agents". Proceedings of Agents'01, Canada, June 2001.
2. Foundation for Intelligent Physical Agents. http://www.fipa.org/
3. Emorphia, FIPA-OS. http://fipa-os.sourceforge.net/
4. TILAB, Java Agent Development Framework. http://jade.cselt.it
5. BtexaCT, The Zeus Agent Building Toolkit. http://193.113.209.147/projects/agents/zeus
6. Agentcities Network Services. http://www.agentcities.net/
7. G.T. Heineman, W.T. Councill., "Component-Based Software Engineering: Putting the Pieces Together", Addison Wesley, 2001.
8. M. Amor, L. Fuentes, J.M. Troya, "Training Compositional Agents in Negotiation Protocols". Next publication in the Integrated Computer-Aided Engineering International Journal.
9. M. Amor, L. Fuentes, J.M. Troya, "Putting Together Web Services and Compositional Software Agents". Next publication in Third International Conference on Web Engineering, 2003.
10. Foundation for Intelligent Physical Agents, FIPA Abstract Architecture Specification. 2000. http://www.fipa.org/specs/fipa00001/
11. Foundation for Intelligent Physical Agents, FIPA Agent Management Specification. 2000. http://www.fipa.org/specs/fipa00023/http://www.fipa.org/specs/fipa00023/
12. Foundation for Intelligent Physical Agents, FIPA Agent Communication Language. 2000. http://www.fipa.org/repository/aclspecs.html
13. G. Kiczales et al. "Aspect-Oriented Programming", Proceedings of ECOOP'97, LNCS 1241, Springer-Verlag, 1998.
14. Aspect-Oriented Software Development. http://www.aosd.net
15. L. Fuentes, J.M. Troya, "Coordinating Distributed Components on the Web: An Integrated Development Environment", Software Practice & Experience, 31(3), March 2001.

Logic Programming for Evolving Agents

Jose J. Alferes[1], Antonio Brogi[2], Joao A. Leite[1], and Luis M. Pereira[1]

[1] CENTRIA, Universidade Nova de Lisboa, Portugal
[2] Dipartimento di Informatica, Università di Pisa, Italy

Abstract. Logic programming has often been considered less than adequate for modelling the dynamics of knowledge changing over time. In this paper we describe Evolving Logic Programs (EVOLP), a simple though quite powerful extension of logic programming, which allows for modelling the dynamics of knowledge bases expressed by programs, and illustrate its usage in modelling agents whose specifications may dynamically change. From the syntactical point of view, evolving programs are just generalized logic programs (i.e. normal LPs plus default negation in rule heads too), extended with (possibly nested) assertions, whether in heads or bodies of rules. From the semantical point of view, a model-theoretic characterization is offered of the possible evolutions of such programs. These evolutions arise both from self (i.e. internal to the agent) updating, and from concomitant external updating originating in the environment. To illustrate the usage and power of EVOLP, and its ability to model agents' specifications, we elaborate on variations in the modelling of a Personal Assistant Agent for e-mail management.

1 Introduction

The agent paradigm, commonly implemented by means of imperative languages mainly for reasons of efficiency, has recently increased its influence in the research and development of computational logic based systems (see e.g. [15]).

Since efficiency is not always the crucial issue, but clear specification and correctness are, *Logic Programming* and *Non-monotonic Reasoning* have been brought back into the spotlight. Indeed, the *Logic Programming (LP)* paradigm provides a well-defined, general, integrative, encompassing, and rigorous framework for systematically studying computation, be it syntax, semantics, procedures, or attending implementations, environments, tools, and standards. Furthermore, *LP* approaches problems, and provides solutions, at a sufficient level of abstraction so that they generalize from problem domain to problem domain. This is afforded by the very nature of its foundations in logic, both in substance and method, and constitutes one of its major assets. To this accrues the recent significant improvements in the efficiency of *Logic Programming* implementations for *Non-monotonic Reasoning* [12,13,16].

While *LP* can be seen as a good representation language for static knowledge, if we are to move to a more open and dynamic environment, typical of the agency paradigm, we must consider ways and means of representing and integrating knowledge updates from external sources, but also inner source knowledge

M. Klusch et al. (Eds.): CIA 2003, LNAI 2782, pp. 281–297, 2003.

updates (or self updates). In fact, an agent not only comprises knowledge about each state, but also knowledge about the transitions between states. The latter may represent the agent's knowledge about the environment's evolution, coupled to its own behaviour and evolution.

To address this concern, the authors, with others, first introduced *Dynamic Logic Programming (DLP)* [2]. There, they studied and defined the declarative and operational semantics of sequences of logic programs (or dynamic logic programs). [6] addressed similar concerns. According to DLP, knowledge is conveyed by a sequence of theories (encoded as generalized logic programs) representing different states of the world. Each of the states may contain mutually contradictory and overlapping information. The role of DLP is to take into account the mutual relationships extant between different states to precisely determine the declarative and the procedural semantics of the combined theory comprised of all individual theories and the way they relate.

Now, since logic programs can describe well knowledge states and, we have just mentioned above, also sequences of updating knowledge states, it's only fit that logic programs be utilized to describe the transitions between knowledge states as well. This can be achieved by associating with each state a set of transition rules to obtain the next state. However, till recently, *LP* had sometimes been considered less than adequate for modelling the dynamics of knowledge change over time. To overcome this limitation, languages like LUPS [3], EPI [5] and KABUL [9] were defined. But both these languages, a bit against the spirit of *LP* (whose pure programs have no keywords), are too verbose, and that makes them complex and difficult to prove properties of their programs. Moreover, each keyword encodes a high-level behaviour for the addition of rules, this constituting a problem in case one wants to describe a different, unforeseen, high-level behaviour.

In a previous work [1] we took the opposite approach towards the design of a new language, EVOLP. There, we analyze what was basic in the aforementioned languages, what they did offer that was new compared to classical *LP*, and then opted to start anew, and only minimally add constructs to *LP* so as to account for the newly required abilities needed for evolution through external updating and internal self updating. EVOLP provides a simpler and at once more general formulation of logic program updating, and runs closer to traditional LP doctrine. And it does so in a precise way, with a well-defined semantics of possible program evolutions through updates. We now move to show how EVOLP can be utilized to model the specification of evolving agents.

Indeed, EVOLP generalizes *LP* to allow specification of a program's own evolution, in a single unified way, by permitting rules to indicate assertive conclusions in the form of program rules. Such assertions, whenever they belong to a model of the program *P*, can be employed to generate an updated version of *P*. This process can then be iterated on the basis of the new program. Whenever the program semantics affords several possible program models, evolution branching will occur, and several evolution sequences are made possible. This branching can be used to specify incomplete information about a situation. Moreover, the ability of EVOLP to nest rule assertions within assertions allows rule updates to be themselves updated down the line, conditional on each evolution strand. The ability to include assertive literals in rule bodies allows for looking ahead on some program changes and acting on that knowledge before the changes occur.

In all, EVOLP can adequately express the semantics resulting from successive updates to logic programs, considered as incremental specifications of agents, and whose effect can be contextual. In contradistinction to other approaches, it automatically and appropriately deals, via its update semantics, with the possible contradictions arising from successive specification changes and refinements. Furthermore, the EVOLP language can express self-modifications triggered by the evolution context itself, present or future. Additionally, foreseen updates not yet executed can automatically trigger other updates, and moreover updates can be nested, so as to determine change both in the next state and in other states further down an evolution strand.

It is the goal of this paper to show that the attending formulation of EVOLP provides a good firm formal basis in which to express, implement, and reason about dynamic knowledge bases of evolving agents, and to show that it goes beyond some of the limitations of other approaches. To do this, in the ensuing section we present, with motivating examples, the formal syntax and semantics of EVOLP. Immediately afterwards we make our case by presenting a detailed and protracted application example of EVOLP usage, employing it to define an e-mail Personal Assistant Agent, whose executable specification evolves by means of external and of internal dynamic updates, both of which can be made contingent on the evolution context in which they occur. We end with a section comprising discussion, comparisons with related application work, open issues, and themes of future developments.

2 Evolving Logic Programs

2.1 Language

As mentioned in the Introduction, we are interested in a logic programming language, EVOLP, that caters for the evolution of an agent's knowledge, be it caused by external events, or by internal requirements for change. Above all, we desire to do so by adding as few new constructs to traditional logic programming as possible.

What is required to let logic programs evolve? For a start, one needs some mechanism for letting older rules be supervened by more recent ones. That is, we must include a mechanism for deletion of previous knowledge along the agent's knowledge evolution. This can be achieved by permitting negation not just in rule bodies, as in normal logic programming, but in rule heads as well[1].

Moreover, one needs a means to state that, under some conditions, some new rule or other is to be added to the program. We do so in EVOLP simply by

---

[1] A well known extension to normal logic programs [10].

augmenting the language with a reserved predicate $assert/1$, whose sole argument is itself a full-blown rule, so that arbitrary nesting becomes possible. This predicate can appear both as rule head (to impose internal assertions of rules) as well as in rule bodies (to test for assertion of rules). Formally:

Definition 1. *Let $\mathcal{L}$ be any propositional language (not containing the predicate $assert/1$). The extended language $\mathcal{L}_{assert}$ is defined inductively as follows: – All propositional atoms in $\mathcal{L}$ are propositional atoms in $\mathcal{L}_{assert}$; – If each of $L_0, \ldots, L_n$ is a literal in $\mathcal{L}_{assert}$ (i.e. a propositional atom A or its default negation not A), then $L_0 \leftarrow L_1, \ldots, L_n$ is a generalized logic program rule over $\mathcal{L}_{assert}$; – If R is a rule over $\mathcal{L}_{assert}$ then $assert(R)$ is a propositional atom of $\mathcal{L}_{assert}$; – Nothing else is a propositional atom in $\mathcal{L}_{assert}$.*

An evolving logic program *over a language $\mathcal{L}$ is a (possibly infinite) set of generalized logic program rules over $\mathcal{L}_{assert}$.*

Example 1. Examples of EVOLP rules are:

$$assert(not\,a \leftarrow b) \leftarrow not\,c. \qquad a \leftarrow assert(b \leftarrow).$$
$$assert(assert(a \leftarrow) \leftarrow assert(b \leftarrow not\,c), d) \leftarrow not\,e.$$

Intuitively, the first rule states that, if c is false, then the rule $not\,a \leftarrow b$ must be asserted in the agent's knowledge base; the 2nd that, if the fact $b \leftarrow$ is going to be asserted in the agent's knowledge base, then a is true; the last states that, if e is false, then a rule must be asserted stating that, if d is true and the rule $b \leftarrow not\,c$ is going to be asserted then the fact $a \leftarrow$ must be asserted.

This language alone is enough to model the agent's knowledge base, and to cater within it for internal updating actions changing it. But self-evolution of a knowledge base is not enough for our purposes. We also want the agent to be aware of events that happen outside itself, and desire the possibility too of giving the agent update "commands" for changing its specification. In other words, we wish a language that allows for influence from the outside, where this influence may be: observation of facts (or rules) that are perceived at some state; assertion commands directly imparting the assertion of new rules on the evolving program. Both can be represented as EVOLP rules: the former by rules without the assert predicate in the head, and the latter by rules with it. Consequently, we shall represent outside influence as a sequence of EVOLP rules:

Definition 2. *Let P be an evolving program over the language $\mathcal{L}$. An* event sequence *over P is a sequence of evolving programs over $\mathcal{L}$.*

2.2   Semantics

In general, we have an EVOLP program describing an agent's initial knowledge base. This knowledge base may already contain rules (with asserts in heads) that describe some forms of its own evolution. Besides this, we consider sequences of events representing observation and commands arising from the outside. Each of these events in the sequence are themselves sets of EVOLP rules, i.e. EVOLP programs. The semantics issue is thus that of, given an initial EVOLP program and a sequence of EVOLP programs as events, to determine what is true and what is false after each of those events.

More precisely, the meaning of a sequence of EVOLP programs is given by a set of *evolution stable models*, each of which is a sequence of interpretations or states. The basic idea is that each evolution stable model describes some possible evolution of one initial program after a given number n of evolution steps, given the events in the sequence. Each evolution is represented by a sequence of programs, each program corresponding to a knowledg state.

The primordial intuitions for the construction of these program sequences are as follows: regarding head asserts, whenever the atom $assert(Rule)$ belongs to an interpretation in a sequence, i.e. belongs to a model according to the stable model semantics of the current program, then $Rule$ must belong to the program in the next state; asserts in bodies are treated as any other predicate literals.

The sequences of programs are then treated as in DLP, where the most recent rules are set in force, and previous rules are valid (by inertia) insofar as possible, i.e. they are kept for as long as they do not conflict with more recent ones. In DLP, default negation is treated as in stable models of normal [7] and generalized programs [10]. Formally, a *dynamic logic program* is a sequence $P_1 \oplus \cdots \oplus P_n$ (also denoted $\bigoplus P$, where P is a set of generalized logic programs indexed by $1, \ldots, n$), and its semantic is determined by[2]:

Definition 3. *Let $\bigoplus \{P_i : i \in S\}$ be a dynamic logic program over language $\mathcal{L}$, let $s \in S$, and let M be a set of propositional atoms of $\mathcal{L}$. Then:*

$$Default_s(M) = \{not\, A \leftarrow . \mid \nexists A \leftarrow B \in P_i(1 \leq i \leq s) : M \models B\}$$
$$Reject_s(M) = \{L_0 \leftarrow B \in P_i \mid \exists\, not\, L_0 \leftarrow B' \in P_j, i < j \leq s \wedge M \models B'\}$$

where A is an atom, $not\, L_0$ denotes the complement w.r.t. default negation of the literal L_0, and both B and B' are conjunctions of literals.

Definition 4. *Let $P = \bigoplus \{P_i : i \in S\}$ be a dynamic logic program over language $\mathcal{L}$. A set M of propositional atoms of $\mathcal{L}$ is a stable model of P at state $s \in S$ iff:*

$$M' = least \left(\left[\bigcup_{i \leq s} P_i - Reject_s(M) \right] \cup Default_s(M) \right)$$

where $M' = M \cup \{not\_A \mid A \notin M\}$, and $least(.)$ denotes the least model of the definite program obtained from the argument program by replacing every default negated literal $not\, A$ by a new atom not_A.

Before presenting the definitions that formalize the above intuitions, let us show some illustrative examples.

Example 2. Consider an initial program P, and that all the events are empty EVOLP programs:

a. $assert(b \leftarrow a) \leftarrow not\, c.$ $c \leftarrow assert(not\, a \leftarrow).$ $assert(not\, a \leftarrow) \leftarrow b.$

---

[2] For more details, the reader is referred to [2].

The (only) stable model of P is $I = \{a, assert(b \leftarrow a)\}$ and it conveys the information that program P is ready to evolve into a new program $P \oplus P_2$ by adding rule $(b \leftarrow a)$ at the next step, i.e. in P_2. In the only stable model I_2 of the new program $P \oplus P_2$, atom b is true as well as atom $assert(not\, a \leftarrow)$ and also c, meaning that $P \oplus P_2$ is ready to evolve into a new program $P \oplus P_2 \oplus P_3$ by adding rule $(not\, a \leftarrow)$ at the next step, i.e. in P_3. Now, the (negative) fact in P_3 conflicts with the fact in P, and so this older fact is rejected. The rule added in P_2 remains valid, but is no longer useful to conclude b, since a is no longer valid. So, $assert(not\, a \leftarrow)$ and c are also no longer true. In the only stable model of the last sequence both a, b, and c are false.

This examples simplifies the problem of defining the semantics in that it does not consider the influence of events from the outside. In fact, as stated above, all those events are empty. How to treat outside events? The idea is very simple: add the rules that came in the i-th event to the program of state i, and calculate as in the example above.

Example 3. In the example above, suppose that at state 2 there is an event from the outside with the rules, r_1 and r_2, $assert(d \leftarrow b) \leftarrow a$ and $e \leftarrow$. Since the only stable model of P is $I = \{a, assert(b \leftarrow a)\}$ and there is an outside event at state 2 with r_1 and r_2, the program should evolve into the new program obtained by updating P not only with the rule $b \leftarrow a$ but also with those rules, i.e. $P \oplus \{b \leftarrow a;\ assert(d \leftarrow b) \leftarrow a;\ e \leftarrow\}$. The only stable model I_2 of this program is now $\{b, assert(not\, a \leftarrow), assert(d \leftarrow b), e\}$.

If we keep with the evolution of this program (e.g. via some additional subsequent empty events), in the definition of the semantics we will have to decide what we want to do, in these subsequent states, about the event received at state 2. Intuitively, we want the rules coming from the outside, be they observations or assertion commands, to be understood as events given at a state, but which are not to persist by inertia. I.e. if R belongs to some set S_i of an event sequence, this means that R was perceived or given after $i - 1$ evolution steps of the program, and that this perception event is not to be assumed by inertia from then onward. In the example, it means that if we have perceived e at state 2, then e and all its possible consequences should be true at that state. But the truth of e should not persist into the subsequent state (unless e is yet again perceived from the outside, of course). In other words, when constructing subsequent states, the rules coming from events in state 2 should no longer be available and considered.

Definition 5. *An* evolution interpretation *of length n of an evolving program P over $\mathcal{L}$ is a finite sequence $\mathcal{I} = \langle I_1, I_2, \ldots, I_n \rangle$ of sets of propositional atoms of $\mathcal{L}_{assert}$. The* evolution trace *associated with an evolution interpretation $\mathcal{I}$ is the sequence of programs $\langle P_1, P_2, \ldots, P_n \rangle$ where:*

$$P_1 = P \text{ and } P_i = \{R \mid assert(R) \in I_{i-1}\} \quad \text{for each } 2 \leq i \leq n.$$

Definition 6. *An* evolution interpretation *of length n, $\langle I_1, I_2, \ldots, I_n \rangle$, with evolution trace $\langle P_1, P_2, \ldots, P_n \rangle$, is an* evolution stable model *of P given*

$\langle E_1, E_2, ..., E_k \rangle$, with $n \leq k$, iff for every i $(1 \leq i \leq n)$, I_i is a stable model at state i of $P_1 \oplus P_2 \cdots \oplus (P_i \cup E_i)$.

Notice that the rules coming from the outside indeed do not persist by inertia. At any given step i, the rules from E_i are added and the (possibly various) I_i obtained. This determines the programs P_{i+1} of the trace, which are then added to E_{i+1} to determine the models I_{i+1}.

The definition assumes the whole sequence of events given a priori. In fact this need not be so because the events at any given step n only influence the models in the evolution interpretation from n onward:

Proposition 1. Let $M = \langle I_1, \ldots, I_n \rangle$ be an evolution stable model of P given an event sequence $\langle E_1, \ldots, E_n \rangle$. Then, for any $m > n$ and any sets of events $E_{n+1}, \ldots, E_m$, M is also an evolution stable model of P given an event sequence $\langle E_1, \ldots, E_n, E_{n+1}, \ldots, E_m \rangle$.

Being based on stable models, it is clear that EVOLP programs may have various evolution models of a given length, as well as no evolution stable models at all:

Example 4. Consider P, and 3 empty events:

$$assert(a \leftarrow) \leftarrow not\, assert(b \leftarrow), not\, b. \quad assert(b \leftarrow) \leftarrow not\, assert(a \leftarrow), not\, a.$$

The reader can check that there are 2 evolution stable models of length 3, each representing one possible evolution of the program after those empty events:

$$\langle \{assert(a \leftarrow)\}, \{a, assert(a \leftarrow)\}, \{a, assert(a \leftarrow)\} \rangle$$
$$\langle \{assert(b \leftarrow)\}, \{b, assert(b \leftarrow)\}, \{b, assert(b \leftarrow)\} \rangle$$

Since various evolutions may exist for a given length, evolution stable models alone do not determine a truth relation. But one such truth relation can be defined, as usual, based on the intersection of models:

Definition 7. Let P be an EVOLP program and $\mathcal{E}$ be an event sequence of length n, both over the language $\mathcal{L}$. A set of propositional atoms M over $\mathcal{L}_{assert}$ is a Stable Model of P given $\mathcal{E}$ iff there exists an evolution stable model of P given $\mathcal{E}$ with length n, where the last interpretation is M.

We say that propositional atom A of $\mathcal{L}$ is: true given $\mathcal{E}$ iff all stable models of P given $\mathcal{E}$ have A; false given $\mathcal{E}$ iff no stable model of P given $\mathcal{E}$ has A; unknown given $\mathcal{E}$ otherwise.

With this definition of stable models given event sequences, we can now state that the semantics of EVOLP is, in fact, a proper generalization of the stable models semantics of normal and generalized logic programs, in the following sense:

Proposition 2. Let P be a generalized logic program (without predicate $assert/1$) over a language $\mathcal{L}$, and $\mathcal{E}$ be any sequence with $n \geq 0$ of empty EVOLP programs. Then, M is a stable model of P given $\mathcal{E}$ iff the restriction of M to $\mathcal{L}$ is a stable model of P (in the sense of [7,10]).

The possibility of having various stable models after an event sequence is of special interest for using EVOLP as a language for reasoning about possible evolutions of an agent's knowledge base. However, as we shall better discuss later, to implement agents that execute actions it might be important to guarantee that, for any given event sequence, no "branching" occurs, i.e. a single stable model exists.

Definition 8. *An EVOLP program P is* deterministic *given event sequence $\mathcal{E}$ iff there exists only one stable model of P given $\mathcal{E}$.*

The definition of conditions over programs and sequences to guarantee determinism is beyond the scope of this paper. Also beyond the scope is the issue of how to implement EVOLP, though an implementation already exists, available from http://centria.fct.unl.pt/~jja/updates/

3   E-mail Agent

Forthwith, EVOLP is employed to specify several features of a Personal Assistant agent for e-mail management, able to perform a few basic actions such as sending, receiving, and deleting messages, as well as moving them between folders, and to perform tasks such as filtering spam messages, storing messages in the appropriate folders, sending automatic replies, notifying the user and/or automatically forwarding specific messages, all of which dependant on user specified criteria. Some existing commercial systems already provide basic mechanisms to specify such tasks (e.g.[14,8,11]). If we expect the user to specify once and for all a consistent set of policies that trigger those actions then, such commercial systems would be all that is needed. But reality tells us otherwise: one observes that the user, every now and then, will discover new conditions under which incoming messages should be deleted, and under which messages now being deleted should not. If we allow the user to specify both the positive instances of such policies (e.g. *should be deleted*) and negative ones (e.g. *should not be deleted*), soon the union of all such rules becomes inconsistent, and we cannot expect the user to debug the set of rules so as to invalidate all the old rules that should no longer be used due to more recent ones that contravene them. We should allow the user to simply state whatever new is to be done, and let the agent automatically determine which of the old rules may persist and which not. We are not presupposing the user is contradictory, but just that he has updated his profile, something reasonable. For example, suppose he is tired of receiving spam messages advertising credit and tells the agent to delete all incoming messages whose subject contains the word *credit*. Later he finds out that important messages from his accountant are being deleted because the subject mentions *credit*. He should simply tell the agent not to delete such incoming messages from his accountant, and the agent should automatically determine that such messages are not to be deleted, in spite of the previous rule. But if we just evaluate the union of all specified policies, we obtain a contradiction. Next we show how EVOLP deals with these contradictions and automatically solves them with clear and precise semantics.

It would be important for the personal e-mail assistant agent to allow the user to specify tasks not as simple as just performing actions whenever some conditions are met. Suppose one is organizing a conference and wants to automate part of the communication with referees and authors. Basic tasks include automatic replies to authors whenever abstracts are submitted, etc. But more complex tasks can be conceived that we wish the agent to take care of, such as: waiting for messages from referees accepting to review a paper and, once the message arrives, forwarding to him a message with the paper if it has arrived, otherwise waiting till it arrives and forwarding it then; having different policies to deal with papers before and after the deadline; permitting the specification of extensions to the deadline on a case by case manner, and dealing with each of those papers differently; updating the initial specification for those policies; etc.

Throughout the remainder of this Section, we illustrate some features of EVOLP for these tasks. Instead of exploring all the basic features of the agent, many of which can be found in agents of the kind in the literature, we concentrate on those features directly concerned with the evolving specification of the agent, namely the representation of the dynamic user profile, and of the dynamic specification of its actions and their effects. The way to specify other common simple tasks can easily be inferred from the exposition. We also abstract from the way actions are actually executed. Often we address some of the issues in what does not seem like the most natural way, solely with the purpose of illustrating features of EVOLP, because it is difficult to show all of its capabilities in a single example. For lack of space, we do not show wholly the stable models, but rather single out their main characteristics for our purposes.

We start with a program that contains the initial specification of our agent. It consists of the rules r_1 through r_{10}, i.e. $P = \{\langle r_1 \rangle, \langle r_2 \rangle, \ldots, \langle r_{10} \rangle\}$.

$r_1 : time\,(1) \leftarrow \qquad r_2 : assert\,(time\,(T+1)) \leftarrow time\,(T)$

$r_3 : assert\,(not\,time\,(T)) \leftarrow time\,(T)$

$r_4 : assert\,(msg\,(M,F,S,B,T)) \leftarrow newmsg\,(M,F,S,B)\,, time\,(T)\,, not\,delete\,(M)$

$r_5 : assert\,(in\,(M,inbox)) \leftarrow newmsg\,(M,\_,\_,\_)\,, not\,move\,(M,F)\,, not\,delete\,(M)$

$r_6 : assert\,(in\,(M,F_{to})) \leftarrow newmsg\,(M,\_,\_,\_)\,, move\,(M,F_{to})$

$r_7 : assert\,(in\,(M,F_{to})) \leftarrow move\,(M,F_{from},F_{to})\,, in\,(M,F_{from})$

$r_8 : assert\,(not\,in\,(M,F_{from})) \leftarrow move\,(M,F_{from},F_{to})\,, not\,in\,(M,F_{to})$

$r_9 : assert\,(not\,in\,(M,F)) \leftarrow delete\,(M)\,, in\,(M,F)$

$r_{10} : assert\,(sent\,(To,S,B,T)) \leftarrow send\,(To,S,B)\,, time(T)$

The first three encode a clock which for now will be used to time-stamp all incoming messages. Note such time-stamping is not really required, but we thought it useful to show how a clock can be encoded in EVOLP. Rule r_4 specifies that all incoming messages, represented by atom $newmsg\,(MsgId, From, Subject, Body)$, if not specified to be deleted, represented by literal $not\,delete\,(MsgId)$, should be time-stamped and asserted as a fact $msg\,(MsgId, From, Subject, Body, Time)$. Rule r_5 specifies that all incoming messages, if not specified to be deleted, and not specified to be moved to a specific folder represented by $not\,move\,(MsgId, Folder)$, should be stored in the folder inbox. We use $in\,(MsgId, Folder)$ to represent that the message

$MsgId$ is in folder $Folder$. Rule r_6 specifies the effect of moving an incoming message to a specific folder. Rule r_7 and r_8 encode the effect of moving a message between folders, represented by $move\,(MsgId, Folder_{from}, Folder_{to})$. Note no problem exists with specifying that a message is to be moved between the same folder. Rule r_9 specifies the effect of the action delete, represented by $delete\,(MsgId)$. This action causes the message to be removed from its current folder. Finally, rule r_{10} encodes that sending a message, represented by the atom $send\,(To, Sbject, Body)$, causes the message to be sent, hereby represented by the assertion of the fact $sent\,(To, Subject, Body, Time)$.

At this initial state, the stable model only contains $time\,(1)$. With this initial specification, since we do not yet have any rules to specify which incoming messages are to be deleted and which are to be moved, every message received is moved to folder $inbox$. Also, at every state transition, the clock increases its value. Suppose we receive an update containing three messages i.e. an event E_1 with the facts:

$$newmsg\,(1, \text{``a@a''}, \text{``credit''}, \text{``some spam text''})$$
$$newmsg\,(2, \text{``accountant@c''}, \text{``hello''}, \text{``some text''})$$
$$newmsg\,(3, \text{``b@d''}, \text{``free credit''}, \text{``more spam''})$$

After this update, the stable model contains:

$assert\,(msg\,(1, \text{``a@a''}, \text{``credit''}, \text{``some spam text''}, 1)), assert\,(in\,(1, inbox))$
$assert\,(msg\,(2, \text{``accountant@c''}, \text{``hello''}, \text{``some text''}, 1)), assert\,(in\,(2, inbox))$
$assert\,(msg\,(3, \text{``b@d''}, \text{``free credit''}, \text{``more spam''}, 1)), assert\,(in\,(3, inbox))$
$time\,(1), assert\,(not\,time\,(1)), assert\,(time\,(2))$

With this, we construct P_2 containing the facts:

$msg\,(1, \text{``a@a''}, \text{``credit''}, \text{``some spam text''}, 1), in\,(1, inbox), not\,time\,(1)$
$msg\,(2, \text{``accountant@c''}, \text{``hello''}, \text{``some text''}, 1), in\,(2, inbox)$
$msg\,(3, \text{``b@d''}, \text{``free credit''}, \text{``more spam''}, 1), in\,(3, inbox), time\,(2)$

indicating that the agent's knowledge base has been updated so as to store all messages, properly time-stamped, in folder $inbox$. Moreover the clock was updated to its new value.

At this point, the user becomes upset with all the spam messages being received and decides to start deleting them on arrival. For this he updates the agent by asserting a general rule specifying that spam messages should be deleted, encoded as the assertion of rule r_{11}, and he also updates the agent with a definition of what should be considered a spam message, in this case those whose subject contains the word "credit", encoded by the assertion of rule r_{12}.

$$r_{11} : delete\,(M) \leftarrow newmsg\,(M, F, S, B), spam\,(F, S, B)$$
$$r_{12} : spam\,(F, S, B) \leftarrow contains\,(S, \text{``credit''})$$

Throughout, consider the literal $contains\,(S, T)$ true whenever T is contained in S, whose specification we omit for brevity. The assertion of these two rules, together with an update so as to delete messages 1 and 3, constitutes event E_2:

$$E_2 = \{assert\left(\langle r_{11}\rangle\right), assert\left(\langle r_{12}\rangle\right), delete\left(1\right), delete\left(3\right)\}$$

After this update, the stable model contains:

$assert\left(\langle r_{11}\rangle\right), assert\left(\langle r_{12}\rangle\right), delete\left(1\right), delete\left(3\right), assert\left(not\, in\left(1, inbox\right)\right)$
$assert\left(not\, in\left(3, inbox\right)\right), assert\left(time\left(3\right)\right), assert\left(not\, time\left(2\right)\right)$

together with those propositions of the form $msg/5$, $time/1$, $in/2$, representing the existing messages, their locations, and the current internal time[3].

From this model we construct program P_3, which contains r_{11}, r_{12}, together with the facts $time\left(3\right)$, $not\, time\left(2\right)$, $not\, in\left(1, inbox\right)$ and $not\, in\left(3, inbox\right)$.

Suppose we receive an update containing three messages, i.e. an event E_3 with the facts:

$newmsg\left(4, \text{``d@a''}, \text{``free credit card''}, \text{``spam spam spam''}\right)$
$newmsg\left(5, \text{``accountant@c''}, \text{``credit''}, \text{``got your credit''}\right)$
$newmsg\left(6, \text{``girlfriend@d''}, \text{``hi''}, \text{``theater tonight?''}\right)$

After this update, the stable model contains:

$spam\left(F, \text{``free credit card''}, B\right), spam\left(F, \text{``credit''}, B\right), delete\left(4\right), delete\left(5\right),$
$assert\left(msg\left(6, \text{``girlfriend@d''}, \text{``hi''}, \text{``theater tonight?''}, 3\right)\right), assert\left(in\left(3, inbox\right)\right)$

Since messages 4 and 5 are considered spam messages, they are both set for deletion and thus are not asserted. Only message 6 is asserted. From this model we construct the program P_4 which contains facts $not\, time\left(3\right)$, $in\left(6, inbox\right)$, $time\left(4\right)$, and $msg\left(6, \text{``girlfriend@d''}, \text{``hi''}, \text{``theater tonight?''}, 3\right)$.

Next we receive an update containing a single message i.e. an event E_4 with the fact[4]:

$newmsg\left(7, \text{``accountant@c''}, \text{``are you there?''}, \text{``...''}\right)$

This message made the user aware that previous messages from his accountant had been deleted as spam. The user then decides to update the definition of spam, stating that messages from his accountant are not spam. He does this by asserting rule r_{13} (below). Note this rule is contradictory with rule r_{12}, for messages from the accountant with subject containing the word "credit". But EVOLP automatically detects such contradictions and removes them by taking the newer rule to be an update of any previously existing ones, and we thus expect such messages not to be deleted. Now the user is appointed conference chair and decides to program the agent to perform some attending tasks. Henceforth, messages with the subject "abstract" should be moved to folder $abstracts$, encoded by rule r_{14}, those containing the word "cfp" in their subjects should be moved to folder cfp (r_{15}). Furthermore, as the user is accustomed to only looking at his inbox folder, he wishes to be notified whenever an incoming message is

---

[3] From now on, we omit all those propositions and assertions concerning the clock, unless relevant for the presentation.
[4] At this state we omit the model and update.

immediately stored at a folder other than *inbox*. This is accomplished with rule r_{16}, which renders *notify* (M) true in such cases. Mark that *notify*/1 represents an action with no internal effect on the agent's knowledge base. The agent must also send a message acknowledging receipt of every abstract (r_{17}). And since the user will be away from his computer, he decides to forward urgent mail to his new temporary address. This could be accomplished by simply stating that those messages should be sent to his new address. But he decides to create a new internal action, represented by *forward* $(MsgId, To)$, whose effect is to forward the newly incoming message $MsgId$ to the address To, thus making it easier to specify future forwarding options. The specification of this action is achieved by asserting rule r_{18}. Then, based on this action, he can specify that all urgent messages be forwarded to his new address, by asserting rule r_{29}. Finally, the user realizes that the messages that have been deleted are not being effectively deleted, but rather only removed from their folders, i.e. *msg* (M, F, S, B, T) is still true, except that there is no *in* $(M, \_)$ that is true. He then decides to create another internal action, *purge*, whose effect is that of making false all those messages that have been previously removed from all folders by the action *delete*. The specification of this action is obtained by asserting rule r_{20}.

$r_{13} :$ *not spam* $(F, S, B) \leftarrow$ *contains* $(F,$ "accountant"$)$

$r_{14} :$ *move* $(M, abstracts) \leftarrow$ *newmsg* (M, F, S, B) , *contains* $(S,$ "abstract"$)$

$r_{15} :$ *move* $(M, cfp) \leftarrow$ *newmsg* (M, F, S, B) , *contains* $(S,$ "cfp"$)$

$r_{16} :$ *notify* $(M) \leftarrow$ *newmsg* (M, F, S, B) , *not assert* $(in (M, inbox))$,

$\qquad\qquad\qquad\qquad\qquad\qquad\qquad\qquad$ *assert* $(in (M, Fldr))$

$r_{17} :$ *send* $(From, S,$ "Thanks"$) \leftarrow$ *newmsg* (M, F, S, B) , *contains* $(S,$ "abstract"$)$

$r_{18} :$ *send* $(To, S, B) \leftarrow$ *forward* (M, To) , *newmsg* (M, F, S, B)

$r_{19} :$ *forward* $(M,$ "b@domain"$) \leftarrow$ *newmsg* $(M, \_,$ "urgent"$, \_)$

$r_{20} :$ *assert* $(not\, msg\, (M, F, S, B, T)) \leftarrow$ *purge*, *msg* (M, F, S, B, T) , *not in* $(M, \_)$

The assertion of all these rules is event $E_5 = \{assert (\langle r_{13} \rangle),\ assert (\langle r_{14} \rangle),$ $assert (\langle r_{15} \rangle),\quad assert (\langle r_{16} \rangle),\quad assert (\langle r_{17} \rangle),\quad assert (\langle r_{18} \rangle),\quad assert (\langle r_{19} \rangle),$ $assert (\langle r_{20} \rangle)\}$

At the subsequent update the agent receives more messages, performs a *purge*, moves message 6 to the private folder, and deletes message 6, encoded by the following facts belonging to E_6:

newmsg $(9,$ "a2@e"$,$ "abstract"$,$ "abs..."$)$, *newmsg* $(10,$ "a3@e"$,$ "abstract"$,$ "abs..."$)$
newmsg $(13,$ "accountant@c"$,$ "fwd:credit"$,$ "..."$)$, *newmsg* $(11,$ "x@d"$,$ "urgent"$,$ "..."$)$
move $(6, inbox, private)$, *delete* (6) , *purge*, *newmsg* $(8,$ "a1@e"$,$ "abstract"$,$ "abs..."$)$
newmsg $(12,$ "accountant@c"$,$ "fwd:credit"$,$ "..."$)$

After this update, the stable model contains, for messages 1 and 3, as a result of the *purge*, *assert* $(not\, msg\, (M, F, S, B, T))$; *assert* $(in (M, abstracts))$ for messages 8, 9 and 10, *forward* $(11,$ "b@domain"$)$ and the corresponding send action, i.e. *send* $($"b@domain"$,$ "urgent"$,$ "..."$)$, and, concerning message 6, the stable model contains *assert* $(in (6, private))$ and *delete* (6). There are also notifications for messages 8, 9, 10 and 14. Next the user decides that whenever a message is both deleted and moved, the deletion action prevails, i.e. it should not be asserted into the folder specified by the move action. This is encoded by the assertion of rule r_{21} (below). Furthermore, the user decides to update his spam rules to avoid all the spam his accountant has been forwarding to him (r_{22}). Finally, because he wants the agent to deal with communication with the referees, he sets up the assignments between referees and submitted papers $(r_{23} - r_{28})$. The rules and event E_7 are:

$$r_{21} : not\, assert\, (in\, (M, F_{to})) \leftarrow move\, (M, F_{from}, F_{to}), delete\, (M)$$
$$r_{22} : spam\, (F, S, B) \leftarrow contains\, (S, \text{``credit''}), contains\, (S, \text{``Fwd''})$$
$$r_{23} : assign\, (\text{``paper1''}, \text{``ref2@b''}) \qquad r_{24} : assign\, (\text{``paper2''}, \text{``ref2@b''})$$
$$r_{25} : assign\, (\text{``paper2''}, \text{``ref3@c''}) \qquad r_{26} : assign\, (\text{``paper3''}, \text{``ref3@c''})$$
$$r_{27} : assign\, (\text{``paper3''}, \text{``ref1@a''}) \qquad r_{28} : assign\, (\text{``paper1''}, \text{``ref1@a''})$$

$$E_7 = \left\{ \begin{array}{l} assert\, (\langle r_{21} \rangle), assert\, (\langle r_{22} \rangle), assert\, (\langle r_{23} \rangle), assert\, (\langle r_{24} \rangle) \\ assert\, (\langle r_{25} \rangle), assert\, (\langle r_{26} \rangle), assert\, (\langle r_{27} \rangle), assert\, (\langle r_{28} \rangle) \end{array} \right\}$$

After all these rules have been asserted, and at the subsequent update, the agent receives a spam message from the accountant, performs a move and a delete of message 12 to test if the new rule is working, and sends messages to the referees inviting them to review the corresponding papers, encoded by the following facts and rules that belong to E_8:

$$newmsg\, (15, \text{``accountant@c''}, \text{``fwd:credit''}, \text{``...''}), move\, (12, inbox, folder1)$$
$$delete\, (12) \qquad send\, (R, PId, \text{``invitation to review''}) \leftarrow assign\, (PId, R)$$

At this point, we invite the reader to check that message 15 was rejected, and that message 12 was indeed deleted. It is important to note that the messages to the referees are only sent once. This is so because the rule belonging to E_8 is not an assertion and thus never becomes part of the agent's knowledge base. It is only used to determine the stable model at this state, and never used again.

Subsequently the user decides to specify the way the agent should deal with communication with authors and reviewers. Forthwith, we show how some of these tasks could be programmed. Upon receipt of a message from a reviewer accepting to review a given paper, the paper should be sent to the referee once it arrives. This could be specified by rule r_{29} (below) which specifies the assertion of a rule that sends the paper to the referee, but this assertion should only take place after the referee accepts the task. If the paper has already been received when the reviewer accepts the task, then it should be sent immediately (r_{30}). Of course, if papers are received after some deadline, and unless some extension was given for a particular paper, then they should be rejected and the author so notified. This is encoded by rules r_{31} and r_{32} which are asserted when the deadline is reached, even though it has not been set yet. Rule r_{31} sends a message to the author while rule r_{32} prevents the paper from being sent to the referee. Finally, the user asserts two rules to deal with deadline extensions on a paper by paper basis. Whenever the user includes an event of the form $dline\, (PId, Dur)$ in an update, he is giving an extension of the deadline concerning paper PId and with duration *Dur*. This immediately causes *ext* (PId) to be asserted, preventing the paper from being rejected. Concurrently, by means of rule r_{34}, a rule is asserted that will render *ext* (PId) false once the deadline plus the extension is reached, after which the paper is rejected.

$$r_{29} : assert\,(send\,(R, S, B) \leftarrow newmsg\,(M, F, S, B)\,, contains\,(S, PId)\,,$$
$$assign\,(PId, R)) \leftarrow newmsg\,(M, R, PId, B)\,, contains\,(B, \text{``accept''})$$

$$r_{30} : send\,(R, PId, B) \leftarrow newmsg\,(M, R, PId, B_1)\,, contains\,(B_1, \text{``accept''})\,,$$
$$msg\,(M_1, F, PId, B, T)$$
$$r_{31} : assert\,(send\,(F, S, \text{``too late''}) \leftarrow newmsg\,(M, F, S, B)\,, contains\,(S, PId)\,,$$
$$not\,ext\,(PId)) \leftarrow time\,(T)\,, deadline\,(T)$$
$$r_{32} : assert\,(not\,send\,(Referee, S, B) \leftarrow newmsg\,(M, F, S, B)\,, contains\,(S, PId)\,,$$
$$not\,ext\,(PId)) \leftarrow time\,(T)\,, deadline\,(T)$$
$$r_{33} : assert\,(ext\,(PId)) \leftarrow dline\,(PId, D)$$
$$r_{34} : assert\,(assert\,(not\,ext\,(PId)) \leftarrow time\,(D + T)\,, deadline\,(T))\,, dline\,(PId, D) \leftarrow$$

The event that encodes this update is: $E_9 = \{assert\,(\langle r_{29}\rangle),\ assert\,(\langle r_{30}\rangle),$ $assert\,(\langle r_{31}\rangle),\ assert\,(\langle r_{32}\rangle),\ assert\,(\langle r_{33}\rangle),\ assert\,(\langle r_{34}\rangle)\}$

Subsequently the user sets the deadline by asserting the fact *deadline* (14)[5], i.e. the event E_{10} contains the fact *assert* $(deadline\,(14))$.

The remainder of the story goes as follows: at event E_{11} the agent receives both acceptance messages from referee 1; at event E_{12} it receives paper 2; the user grants deadline extensions of two time units to papers 1 and 3, encoded in event E_{13}; at event E_{14} it receives the acceptance messages from referee 2; at event E_{15}, i.e. after the deadline but before the extension, it receives paper 1; at event E_{16} it receives the acceptance messages from referee 3; at event E_{17}, i.e. after the extension has expired, it receives paper 3. Lack of space prevents us from elaborating further on what happens after all these events, but we invite the reader to check that: after event E_{14} paper 2 is sent to referee 2; after event E_{15} paper 1 is sent both to referees 1 and 2; after event E_{16} paper 2 is sent to referee 3; since paper 3 arrives after the deadline extension it is rejected, a message is sent to the author, and the paper is not sent to any referee.

$E_{11} = \{newmsg(16, \text{``refl@a''}, \text{``paper1''}, \text{``accept''}), newmsg(17, \text{``refl@a''}, \text{``paper3''},$ $\text{``accept''})\}$;

$E_{12} = \{newmsg(18, \text{``a2@e''}, \text{``paper2''}, \text{``the paper''})\}$;

$E_{13} = \{dline(\text{``paper3''}, 2), dline(\text{``paper1''}, 2)\}$;

$E_{14} = \{newmsg(19, \text{``ref2@b''}, \text{``paper1''}, \text{``accept''}), newmsg(20, \text{``ref2@b''}, \text{``paper2''},$ $\text{``accept''})\}$;

$E_{15} = \{newmsg(21, \text{``a1@e''}, \text{``paper1''}, \text{``the paper''})\}$;

$E_{16} = \{newmsg(22, \text{``ref3@c''}, \text{``paper2''}, \text{``accept''}), newmsg(23, \text{``ref3@c''}, \text{``paper3''},$ $\text{``accept''})\}$;

$E_{17} = \{newmsg(24, \text{``a3@e''}, \text{``paper3''}, \text{``the paper''})\}$.

---

[5] Dealing with the synchronisation of external and internal times is outside the scope of this paper. Here, the deadline refers to the agent's internal time.

4   Discussion and Conclusions

Though permitted by EVOLP, the example does not involve any branching of evolutions, i.e. there is always a single stable model of the program, given any of the example's events. In fact, that program given those events is deterministic (in the sense of Definition 8). Non-stratified rules for assertions (as in Example 4) can be used to model alternative updates to the agent's knowledge base, e.g. for stating that, under certain conditions, either move a message to a folder or delete it, but not both. Non-stratification can also be used to model uncertainty in the external observations. In both these cases, EVOLP semantics provides several evolution stable models, upon which reasoning can be made, concerning what happens in case one or other action is chosen. On the other hand, by having various models, EVOLP can no longer be used to actually perform the actions, unless some mechanism for selecting models is introduced. For (static) logic programs, this issue of selecting among stable models has already been extensively studied: either by defining more skeptical semantic that always provide a unique model or by preferring among stable models based on some priority ordering on rules. The introduction of such mechanisms in EVOLP too is the subject of current and future work by the authors.

Another issue, not illustrated in the example, and not (yet) addressed by EVOLP, is that of synchronisation of external and internal times. In the example, this problem does not even appear, until the moment where we want to set the deadline. For expressing the deadline in terms of the internal time we can assume, for example, that an event is given to the agent (albeit empty) after every fixed amount of external time (say 5 minutes). This way, we could express the external time and date of the deadline as the time-stamp of an internal state. Another possibility would be to assume that every event comes with a fact $etime(T)$ stating at which moment T (in term of external time) the event occurred, and then compare the last T with the deadline. For this example, both these solutions would be enough, since synchronisation is not a crucial issue. But in general, synchronisation is an issue that deserves further attention, and is the subject of future work by the authors.

A large number of software products is nowadays available to perform email monitoring and filtering. One example is Spam Agent [14], a recently deployed email monitoring and filtering tool which features a comprehensive set of filters (over 1500) to block spam and unwanted emails. Email monitoring and filtering rules can be defined in terms of message sender, recipient, subject, body, and arbitrary combinations of them. The SpreadMsg software email filtering and forwarding agent [8] provides unattended data capture, scanning, and extraction from a wide variety of data. User rule sets are applied to data and, when criteria are met, data are further parsed and turned into messages that can be delivered to email addresses, text pagers, digital cellular or GSM mobile phones, laptops, PDA's etc.. The SuperScout Email Filter [11], besides supporting similar capabilities to the previousy mentioned agents, features a Virtual Learning Agent (VLA). The VLA is a content development tool that can be trained to understand and recognise specific proprietary content in order to protect confidential and business critical information from the security risks arising from accidental or malicious leakage. Widely used commercial email filtering systems provide SPAM filters and, in some cases, a more general set of email handling rules. Outlook, Netscape, and Hotmail, for instance, all provide means to define email filtering rules. Some systems require the user to write the filtering rules, while others employ learning algorithms or try to extract patterns from examples. An interesting, very recent proposal is the Personal Email Assistant (PEA) [4], which is intended to provide a customizable, machine learning based environment to support email processing. An aspect of PEA is that it relies on combining available open source components for information retrieval, machine learning, and agents.

Lack of space prevents us from mentioning other (out of many) email monitoring and filtering agents available. It is worth observing however that, to the best of our knowledge, none of the available agents enjoys the ability of autonomously and dynamically updating its own filtering policies in a way as general as the EVOLP specifications illustrated in the present work.

We began this article by extolling the virtue and promise of Logic Programming, for adumbrating the issues and solutions relative to the (internally and externally) updatable executable specification of agents, and to the study of their evolution by means of a precisely defined declarative semantics with well-defined properties. We have shown, in an example, how EVOLP can be used, not only to specify the agent's policies, but also to dynamically change that specification, and make those changes dependent on some external conditions or events.

References

1. J. J. Alferes, A. Brogi, J. A. Leite, and L. M. Pereira. Evolving logic programs. In *JELIA'02*, volume 2424 of *LNAI*. Springer, 2002.
2. J. J. Alferes, J. A. Leite, L. M. Pereira, H. Przymusinska, and T. Przymusinski. Dynamic updates of non-monotonic knowledge bases. *Journal of Logic Programming*, 45(1–3), 2000.
3. J. J. Alferes, L. M. Pereira, H. Przymusinska, and T. Przymusinski. LUPS : A language for updating logic programs. *Artificial Intelligence*, 138(1–2), 2002.
4. R. Bergman, M. Griss, and C. Staelin. A personal email assistant. Technical Report HPL-2002-236, HP Labs Palo Alto, 2002.
5. T. Eiter, M. Fink, G. Sabbatini, and H Tompits. A framework for declarative update specifications in logic programs. In *IJCAI'01*. Morgan-Kaufmann, 2001.
6. T. Eiter, M. Fink, G. Sabbatini, and H. Tompits. On properties of update sequences based on causal rejection. *Theory and Practice of Logic Programming*, 2(6), 2002.
7. M. Gelfond and V. Lifschitz. The stable semantics for logic programs. In *ICLP'88*. MIT Press, 1988.
8. Compuquest Inc. Spreadmsg. www.compuquestinc.com.
9. J. A. Leite. *Evolving Knowledge Bases*. IOS Press, 2003.
10. V. Lifschitz and T. Woo. Answer sets in general non-monotonic reasoning (preliminary report). In *KR'92*. Morgan-Kaufmann, 1992.
11. Caudex Services Ltd. Superscout email filter. www.caudexservices.co.uk.

12. I. Niemelä and P. Simons. Smodels: An implementation of the stable and well-founded semantics for normal LP. In *LPNMR'97*, volume 1265 of *LNAI*. Springer, 1997.
13. D. De Schreye, M. Hermenegildo, and L. M. Pereira. Paving the roadmaps: Enabling and integration technologies, 2000. Available from www.compulog.org.
14. Spam-Filtering-Software.com. Spam agent. www.spam-filtering-software.com.
15. V. S. Subrahmanian, Piero Bonatti, Jürgen Dix, Thomas Eiter, Sarit Kraus, Fatma Ozcan, and Robert Ross. *Heterogeneous Agent Systems*. MIT Press, 2000.
16. XSB-Prolog. The XSB logic programming system, version 2.0, 1999. www.cs.sunysb.edu/ sbprolog.

Temporal and Spatial Analysis to Personalise an Agent's Dynamic Belief, Desire, and Intention Profiles

Catholijn M. Jonker[1], Vagan Terziyan[2], and Jan Treur[1]

[1]Department of Artificial Intelligence, Vrije Universiteit Amsterdam
De Boelelaan 1081a, 1081 HV Amsterdam, The Netherlands
{jonker, treur}@cs.vu.nl, http://www.cs.vu.nl/{~jonker, ~treur}

[2]Department of Mathematical Information Technology, University of Jyvaskyla
P.O.Box 35 (Agora), FIN-40014 Jyvaskyla, Finland
vagan@it.jyu.fi, http://www.cs.jyu.fi/ai/vagan

Abstract. The paper addresses the dynamic belief, desire and intention profiles that can be made of an agent following a particular route, for example through a city. It assumes that location of an agent has effects on his beliefs desires and intentions and that the history of agent's mobility and observed states in different locations can be used to predict his future states if the location is being permanently observed. A formal spatial route language is introduced. Formal relationships between the intentional notions, and the spatial behaviour of an agent are defined. As an application an information agent architecture for reasoning about the intentions of the customers of a mobile location-based service is described.

1 Introduction

The simulation of social interactions in a complex natural environment by integrating intelligent agents and geographic information systems (GIS) have shown potential for improving resource management decision-making [1], [4], [6], [7], [8], [12], [13]. Spatial effect on a human or artificial agent's behavior (beliefs, desires, intentions, etc.) is also known to be quite essential. Laboratory experiments [6] gathered survey data on the connection between goals, intentions, conflicts and actions and landscape content information provided by the GIS. The survey gathered over a thousand responses over a ten-month period to be used as a basis to develop beliefs, goals, intentions, and plans of actions for recreation groups using the area. Subsequent analysis is being undertaken to aggregate these responses into defined classes of agents characterised by goals, intentions, beliefs, perceived conflicts and then derive appropriate plans of action. Knowing what landscape features are preferred in terms of human recreation behaviour from the both lab experiments and on-site surveys, and knowing what these agents are viewing, where they are in the landscape, which settings are important to satisfying their recreational experience, and knowing

M. Klusch et al. (Eds.): CIA 2003, LNAI 2782, pp. 298–315, 2003.

cognitive goals, desires and intentions, behavioural rules can be derived and utilised for calibrating a set of artificial agents.

As agent behaviour often goes beyond purely reactive behaviour and nontrivial means are needed to describe and predict it. An attractive feature of intentional notions (cf. [5], [10], [11]) to describe agent behaviour is that these notions offer a high level of abstraction and have intuitive connotations.

It may be also very helpful to have capabilities to predict in which places of the environment certain inappropriate desires or intentions are likely to arise, either to avoid the arising of these intentions by preventing the occurrence of circumstances that are likely to lead to them, or, if these circumstances cannot be avoided, by anticipating consequences of the intentions.

An agent is assumed to decide to act and communicate based on its beliefs about its environment and its desires and intentions. These decisions, and the intentional notions by which they can be explained and predicted, generally depend on circumstances in the environment, and, in particular, on the information on where these circumstances just acquired by observations and communication, but also on information acquired in the other places. To be able to analyse the occurrence of intentional notions in the behaviour of an observed agent in a certain place of the environment, the observable behavioural patterns over different places in the environment, which the agent has already visited, form an empirical basis.

Received information (observed or communicated), and decisions to perform specific actions (or communications), constitute the input and output interface states of an agent to the environment in which the agent functions. Externally observed mobility of the agent are formalised as spatial sequences of the world states. A spatial route language is used to express properties on mobility behaviour.

In Section 2 the formal languages used in this paper are introduced. In Section 3, the assumptions made on the notions belief, desire and intention, and the way they interact with each other and with external notions are discussed and formalised: formal relationships between the intentional notions, and the external behaviour of an agent are defined. As an application, Section 4 describes an agent architecture for reasoning about the intentions of the customers of a mobile location-based service. Section 5 concludes.

2   Basic Concepts Used

In Sections 2 and 3 the temporal approach described in [9] is adopted as a starting point, and later on extended with elements referring to spatial aspects. A basic assumption on the ontologies, describing properties of world states, is that for each agent that is distinguished within the world, specific (sub)sets of ontologies of basic (atomic) world properties can be identified, according to properties that concern world state aspects *internal* to the agent, world state aspects *external* to the agent, or *interaction* aspects (input or output of the agent). On the basis of this assumption, ontologies for the agent's input, output and internal state are used, and for the state of the world external to the agent. It is assumed that state properties based on these ontologies describe the world state.

In the formalisation, for simplicity, we use predicate logic to specify both ontologies and properties. Ontology is specified as a finite set of sorts, constants (names) within these sorts, and relations and functions over these sorts (sometimes also called a signature). The union of two ontologies is also ontology. For a given state ontology, state properties are the (ground) propositions that can be expressed using the concepts of ontology. A state property is called atomic if no propositional connectives (i.e., *and, or, implies, not*) are used to express it.

The text below can be read without involving the formal details. To this end the formal details have been put aside in boxes, to be read only by readers interested in all technical details. For more conceptually interested readers, the text without the boxes should be readable as an independent conceptual text.

2.1 State Language

First, a language is used to represent facts concerning the actual state of the external world: ontology EWOnt. Some of the other (agent) ontologies will make use of EWOnt. Next, a language is used to represent facts concerning the state of the agent. The *agent input ontology* InOnt contains concepts for observation results and communication received. The following *input properties* are used for a given agent:

- a property expressing the observation result that some world statement holds; e.g., it rains	denoted by observation_result(p) where p denotes a state property of the external environment based on the ontology EWOnt
- a property expressing that agent C has communicated some world statement; e.g., agent C says to me that it rains	denoted by communicated_by(p, C) where p denotes a state property of the external environment based on the ontology EWOnt

Similarly, the *agent output ontology* OutOnt contains concepts to represent decisions to do actions within the external world, as well as concepts for outgoing communication and observations that the agent needs to obtain. The following *output properties* are used:

- a property expressing that the agent decides to perform action A; e.g., take an umbrella,	denoted by to_be_performed(A)
- a property expressing that the agent commu-nicates information to an agent C; e.g., I say to agent C that it rains	denoted by to_be_communicated_to(p, C) where p denotes a state property of the external environment based on the ontology EWOnt
- a property expressing that the agent decides to perform an observation to investigate the truth of a world state property; e.g., check whether it rains	denoted by by to_be_observed(p) where p denotes a state property of the external environment based on the ontology EWOnt

State properties, which model the interaction of the agent with its environment, are meta-properties: some of their arguments refer to state properties in an object-level language based on the ontology EWOnt. The *internal agent ontology* IntOnt is used for the internal (e.g., BDI) notions. The *agent interface ontology* is defined by InterfaceOnt = InOnt ∪ OutOnt; the *agent ontology* by AgOnt = InOnt ∪ IntOnt ∪ OutOnt, and the overall ontology by OvOnt = AgOnt ∪ EWOnt. The properties based on the overall state ontology are called *state properties*. All state properties based on a certain ontology Ont constitute the set SPROP(Ont).

2.2 Temporal and Spatial Language

Behaviour is described by changing states depending on time and on an agent's location. It is assumed that a state is characterised by the properties that hold in the state and those that do not hold.

Therefore, a *state* for ontology Ont is defined as an assignment of truth values to the set of atomic properties for Ont. The set of all possible states for ontology Ont is denoted by IS(Ont). We assume the time frame is the set of natural numbers or a finite initial segment of the natural numbers. An *overall trace* $\mathcal{M}$ over a time frame T is a sequence of states over the overall ontology OvOnt over time frame T. A *temporal domain description* $\mathcal{W}$ is a set of overall traces.

An *overall trace* $\mathcal{M}$ over a time frame **T** is a sequence of states $(M^t)_{t \in \mathbf{T}}$ in IS(OvOnt). Given an overall trace $\mathcal{M}$ the state of the input interface of agent A at time point t is denoted by state($\mathcal{M}$, t, input(A)). Analogously, state($\mathcal{M}$, t, output(A)) denotes the state of the output interface of the agent at time point t, and state($\mathcal{M}$, t, internal(A)) the internal state. We can also refer to the overall state of a system (agents and environment) at a certain moment; this is denoted by state($\mathcal{M}$, t).

States can be related to state properties via the satisfaction relation that expresses which properties hold in which state (comparable to the holds-relation in situation calculus); e.g., "at South of Amsterdam at 11 o'clock it rained". The *spatial state language* SSL is built on location state information such as "at South of Amsterdam it rains", using the usual logical connectives and quantification (for example, over locations and state properties). Quantification over these entities makes the language quite expressive.

state($\mathcal{M}$, t, input(A)) |= φ denotes that $\varphi \in$ SPROP(InOnt) is true in this state at time t, based on the strong Kleene semantics (e.g., [2]). The set S(Ont) is the set of all state statements that only make use of ontology Ont. We allow additional language elements as abbreviations of statements of the spatial language. Especially important are additional language elements, defining SSL, to express location information:

location_has_property(x, y, p)

denotes that location (x, y) has property p. A special case is the state property p given by present(A), expressing that agent A is present.

location_has_property(x, y, present(A)) expresses that agent A is present at location (x, y). Using this, for example,

state($\mathcal{M}$, t, input(A)) |=
observation_result(location_has_property(x, y, p))

denotes that at time t the agent A's input has the information that it observed that location (x, y) has property p.

A *past statement* for trace variable $\mathcal{M}$ and time variable t is a temporal statement $\psi(\mathcal{M}, t)$ such that each time variable different from t is restricted to the time interval before t. The set of past statements over ontology Ont w.r.t. $\mathcal{M}$ and t is PS(Ont, $\mathcal{M}$, t).

For past statements, for every time quantifier for a variable t' a restriction of the form $t' \leq t$, or $t' < t$ is required within the statement. Note that for any past statement $\psi(\mathcal{M}, t)$ it holds:

$$\forall \mathcal{M} \in \mathcal{W} \; \forall t \; \psi(\mathcal{M}_{[0, t]}, t) \iff \psi(\mathcal{M}, t).$$

To express that some state property has just become true, we use the qualifier *just*, denoted by $\oplus$. This is definable in other temporal terms: a state property has *just* become true at time t1 if and only if it is true at t1 and for some interval before t1 it was not true. Similarly it can be expressed that a state property just stopped to be true.

$\oplus$state($\mathcal{M}$, t1, *interface*) |= φ $\equiv$
    state($\mathcal{M}$, t1, *interface*) |= φ $\wedge$
    $\exists$t2<t1 $\forall$t [t2 $\leq$ t < t1 $\Rightarrow$
        state($\mathcal{M}$, t, *interface*) |$\neq$ φ]

$\oplus$state($\mathcal{M}$, t1, *interface*) |$\neq$ φ $\equiv$
    state($\mathcal{M}$, t1, *interface*) |$\neq$ φ $\wedge$
    $\exists$t2<t1 $\forall$t [t2 $\leq$ t < t1 $\Rightarrow$
        state($\mathcal{M}$, t, *interface*) |= φ

A *route* R is defined as a mapping from distances d (on the route) to locations (x, y), e.g., after 300 m on this route you are at location (E, 5) on the map. Note that a route is defined in a time-independent manner.

A route R is specified by the predicate
    at_ distance_at_location (R, d, x, y)
expressing that at route R after distance d you are at location (x, y).

A trace $\mathcal{M}$ of an agent walking in a city specifies an associated route R($\mathcal{M}$) in the following manner: at route after distance d you are at location (x, y) if and only if a time point t exists such that at t agent A has walked d from the start and is present at location (x, y). This abstracts from the specific trace the time information, keeping the spatial information.

Formally,

at_ distance_at_location (R($\mathcal{M}$), d, x, y) $\iff$

$\exists$t state($\mathcal{M}$, t, EW) |= distance_from_start(d) $\wedge$
    location_has_property(x, y, present(A))

Conversely, for a given route R the set of traces $\mathcal{M}$(R) can be defined as those traces that follow route R.

Formally,
    $\mathcal{M}$(R) = { $\mathcal{M}$ | R($\mathcal{M}$) = R }

3 External Representations of Beliefs, Desires, and Intentions

In this section, the assumed notions of belief, desire, and intention, and their interdependencies are discussed and formalised. Agents are considered to which external representations of intentional notions can be attributed. The interdepenedencies depicted in Fig. 2 will be interpreted as spatial interdependencies. Statements expressed in the spatial language defined above will be analysed on whether or not they are adequate candidates to express these interdependencies of intentional notions. In particular, conditions are given that formalise when a spatial statement represents a belief, desire or intention.

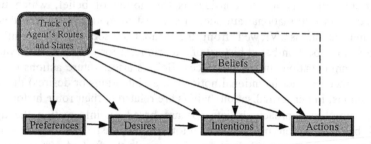

Fig. 1. Relationships between the BDI notions

A basic assumption made is that an agent's states functionally depend on the previous states and route(s) of the agent; i.e., two copies of the same agent build up exactly the same (internal) states if they have exactly the same inputs in the same time points and places. For a software agent, running on a deterministic machine, this Determinism Assumption can be considered a reasonable assumption. Differences between the behaviours of two copies of the same software agent will be created by their different histories, including having been at different locations. For most of the concepts defined below, this assumption is not strictly necessary, however, it is an assumption that strongly motivates the approach.

Comparing importance of temporal and spatial factors in determining behaviour we can say that depending on the context the importance can vary a lot. Consider example: there are two routes, one is related to temporal history of person A and the second one is related to the spatial history of the person B.

Person A (1981-1986 M.Sc. studies on Applied Mathematics; 1987-2000 – Ph.D. studies on Artificial Intelligence; 2001-2002 – Project Work on Ontology Engineering);

Person B (M.Sc. studies on Applied Mathematics in University of Jyvaskyla; Ph.D. studies on Artificial Intelligence in Massachusetts Technological Institute; Project Work on Ontology Engineering in Vrije Universiteit Amsterdam).

In this example the importance of spatial factor seem to be more powerful in the sense of providing more information about the person, which can be used for prediction of his future. Consider another example.

Person A (10:00 wants a cup of coffee; 15:00 wants to eat; 19:00 wants to watch TV News; 23:00 wants to sleep);
Person B (wants a cup of coffee in train "Jyvaskyla-Helsinki" near Pasila station; wants to eat in Helsinki University Conference Room; wants to watch TV News in the Irish Pub in Downtown Helsinki; wants to sleep in "Scandic" Hotel).

In this example we can see that temporal route is more predictive for the future behaviours because the person's desires in this case are more time - than spatially - related. In general, an integration of temporal (e.g., [9]) and spatial history routes would be the best background data for prediction of agent behaviour.

3.1   Beliefs

The first intentional notion to consider is the notion of belief, which usually is considered as an informational attitude, in contrast to motivational attitudes such as desires and intentions. Viewed from the spatial perspective an agent's beliefs originate from a location-based history of experiences; for example, observations and received communications in certain places. Beliefs affect future actions of the agent via their impact on other intentional notions (e.g., intentions or desires) that form the basis of actions. In our formalisation, beliefs are related to their route history.

In the simplest approach, beliefs (β) are based on information the agent has received by observation or communication in the past, and that has not been overridden by more recent information. This entails the first of our assumptions on beliefs: if the agent has received input in the past about a world fact, and no opposite input has been received since then, then the agent believes this world fact. The second assumption is the converse: for every belief on a world fact, there was a time at which the agent received input about this world fact (by sensing or communication), and no opposite input was received since then.

Before giving a temporal characterisation of the notion of belief an auxiliary definition is presented. The agent Ag gets information about a state property as *input* at time t if and only if it just received it at time t as an observation result or as information communicated by another agent B. This means that the agent has just received input that the state property is true at time point t.

Formally, let $p \in$ SPROP(Ont), then:

Input(p, t, $\mathcal{M}$, Ag) $\equiv$

$\oplus$state($\mathcal{M}$, t, input(Ag)) $\models$

observation_result(p)

$\vee \; \exists$ B $\in$ AGENT $\oplus$state($\mathcal{M}$, t, input(Ag)) $\models$

communicated_by(p, B)

Here AGENT is a sort for the agent names. For simplicity of notation, often the fourth argument Ag will be left out:

Input(p, t, $\mathcal{M}$)

Definition (Belief Statement)
The following characterisation of belief is based on the assumption that an agent believes a fact if and only if it received input about it in the past and the fact is not contradicted by later input of the opposite. Let $\alpha \in$ SPROP(Ont) be a state property

over Ont. The temporal statement $\beta(\mathcal{M}, t) \in$ TS is a *temporal belief statement* for state property α if and only if:

at each time point t and each trace $\mathcal{M}$ the statement $\beta(\mathcal{M}, t)$ is true if and only if at an earlier time point t1 the agent received input that α is true and after this time point did not receive input that α is false. Sometimes this belief statement is denoted by $\beta_\alpha(\mathcal{M}, t)$, to indicate it is a belief statement for α. In the specific case that $\beta(\mathcal{M}, t)$ is a temporal belief statement, and, in addition, $\beta(\mathcal{M}, t)$ is a temporal past statement (i.e., $\beta(\mathcal{M}, t) \in$ PS(InOnt, $\mathcal{M}$, t)), over ontology InOnt, then it is also called a *historical belief statement* for α.

Note that one particular historical belief statement for α is the temporal past statement Belief(α, t, $\mathcal{M}$) $\in$ PS(InOnt, $\mathcal{M}$, t) stating that 'at an earlier time point the agent received input that α is true and after this time point did not receive input that α is false'.

Formally, the temporal statement $\beta(\mathcal{M}, t1) \in$ TS is a *temporal belief statement* for α if and only if

$$\forall \mathcal{M} \in \mathcal{W} \; \forall t1 \; [\beta(\mathcal{M}, t1) \Leftrightarrow$$
$$\exists t0 \le t1 \; [\; \text{Input}(\alpha, t0, \mathcal{M}) \wedge$$
$$\forall t \in [t0, t1] \; \neg \; \text{Input}(\sim\alpha, t, \mathcal{M}) \;]\;]$$

Here for state property α, the *complementary property* $\sim \alpha$ is defined as
$$\sim \alpha = \alpha' \quad \text{if} \quad \alpha = \neg \alpha'$$
$$\sim \alpha = \neg \alpha \quad \text{otherwise}$$

The temporal past statement
$$\text{Belief}(\alpha, t, \mathcal{M}) \in \text{PS(InOnt, } \mathcal{M}, \text{ t)}$$
is formally defined by
$$\exists t0 \le t \; [\; \text{Input}(\alpha, t0, \mathcal{M}) \wedge$$
$$\forall t1 \in [t0, t] \; \neg \; \text{Input}(\sim\alpha, t1, \mathcal{M}) \;]$$

If required, these assumptions can also be replaced by less simple ones, possibly in a domain-dependent manner; for example, taking into account reliability of sensory processes in observation or reliability of other agents in communication.

3.2 Desires and Intentions

Also motivational attitudes can be viewed from a spatial perspective. Our assumptions on intentions are as follows. In the first place, under appropriate circumstances an intention leads to an action: an agent who intends to perform an action will execute the action in the nearest known location where an opportunity (α) occurs. Moreover, the second assumption is that when an action or communication (A) is performed (θ), the agent is assumed to have intended (γ) to do that.

Definition (Intention Statement)

An *action atom* $\theta(\mathcal{M}, t, Ag)$ is an atom stating that at time point t in trace $\mathcal{M}$ at the output of the agent Ag a specific generated action or communication can be found.

Let $\alpha \in$ SPROP(EWOnt) be an external state property and $\theta(\mathcal{M}, t, Ag)$ an action atom. The temporal statement $\gamma(\mathcal{M}, t) \in$

Formally, an *action atom* $\theta(\mathcal{M}, t, Ag)$ is an atom of the form
$$\text{state}(\mathcal{M}, t, \text{output}(Ag)) \models \psi$$

TS is called a *temporal intention statement* for action atom $\theta(\mathcal{M}, t, Ag)$ and *opportunity* α if and only if the following conditions are fulfilled:

with ψ an output atom: an atom of the form   to_be_performed(A),
         to_be_communicated_to(p, B),
or   to_be_observed(p).

Sufficiency condition for intention

If $\gamma(\mathcal{M}, t)$ holds for a given trace $\mathcal{M}$ and time point t1, and at some earlier time point the agent received input that α holds and since then the agent did not receive input that α does not hold, then there is a time point t2 later than t1 at which the action $\theta(\mathcal{M}, t2, Ag)$ occurs.

Formally, the *sufficiency condition for intention* is defined by:
$$\forall \mathcal{M} \in \mathcal{W} \; \forall t1 \; [\; \gamma(\mathcal{M}, t1) \; \wedge$$
$$\exists t0 \leq t1 \; [\; \text{Input}(\alpha, t0, \mathcal{M}) \; \wedge$$
$$\forall t \in [t0, t1] \; \neg \; \text{Input}(\sim\!\alpha, t, \mathcal{M})]$$
$$\Rightarrow \; \exists t2 \geq t1 \; \theta(\mathcal{M}, t2, Ag) \;]$$

Necessity condition for intention

If for a given trace $\mathcal{M}$ and time point t2 the action $\theta(\mathcal{M}, t, Ag)$ occurs, then $\gamma(\mathcal{M}, t1)$ holds at some earlier time point t1 and at a time point earlier than t1 the agent received input that α holds and since then until t1 the agent did not receive input that α does not hold.

Formally, the *necessity condition for intention* is defined by:
$$\forall \mathcal{M} \in \mathcal{W} \; \forall t2 \; [\; \theta(\mathcal{M}, t2, Ag) \; \Rightarrow$$
$$\exists t1 \leq t2 \; \gamma(\mathcal{M}, t1) \; \wedge$$
$$\exists t0 \leq t1 \; [\; \text{Input}(\alpha, t0, \mathcal{M}) \; \wedge$$
$$\forall t \in [t0, t1] \; \neg \; \text{Input}(\sim\!\alpha, t, \mathcal{M})]]$$

In the specific case that the past statement $\gamma_P(\mathcal{M}, t) \in PS(\text{InOnt}, \mathcal{M}, t)$ is a temporal intention statement for $\theta(\mathcal{M}, t, Ag)$ and opportunity α, it is also called a *historical intention statement* for action atom $\theta(\mathcal{M}, t, Ag)$ and opportunity α.

The above definition formalises the case that all actions are intended actions. However, it is not difficult to define weaker variants. For example, if also unintended actions are allowed, the second (necessity) condition can be left out. An agent can desire states of the world as well as actions to be performed. When the agent has a set of desires, it can choose to pursue some of them. A chosen desire for a state of the world can lead to an intention to do an action if, for example, expected effects of the action (partly) fulfil the desire. The first assumption on desires is that, given a desire (δ), for each relevant action there is an additional reason (ρ), so that if both the desire is present and the agent believes the additional reason, then the intention to perform the action will be generated. Having this additional reason prevents the agent from performing actions that do not make sense in the given situation; e.g., actions with contradicting effects. The second assumption formalised in the definition below is that every intention is based on a desire (δ), i.e., no intention occurs without desire. Based on these assumptions, desire statements are defined as follows:

Definition (Desire Statement)
Let an external state property $\rho \in \text{SPROP}(\text{EWOnt})$ and an intention statement $\gamma(\mathcal{M}, t)$ be given. The temporal statement $\delta(\mathcal{M}, t) \in TS$ is called a *temporal desire statement*

for intention $\gamma(\mathcal{M}, t)$ and *additional reason* ρ if and only if the following conditions are fulfilled:

Sufficiency condition for desire

If $\delta(\mathcal{M}, t1)$ holds for a given trace $\mathcal{M}$ and time point t1, and at some earlier time point the agent received input that ρ holds and since then the agent did not receive input that ρ does not hold, then there is a time point t2 later than t1 at which the intention $\gamma(\mathcal{M}, t2)$ occurs.

Formally, the *sufficiency condition for desire* is defined by:
$$\forall \mathcal{M} \in \mathcal{W} \; \forall t1 \; [\delta(\mathcal{M}, t1) \wedge$$
$$\exists t0 \leq t1 \; [\text{Input}(\rho, t0, \mathcal{M}) \wedge$$
$$\forall t \in [t0, t1] \; \neg \; \text{Input}(\sim\rho, t, \mathcal{M})]$$
$$\Rightarrow \exists t2 \geq t1 \; \gamma(\mathcal{M}, t2)]$$

Necessity condition for desire

If for a given trace $\mathcal{M}$ and time point t2 the intention $\gamma(\mathcal{M}, t2)$ occurs, then the desire $\delta(\mathcal{M}, t1)$ holds at some earlier time point t1 and at a time point earlier than t1 the agent received input that ρ holds and since then until t1 the agent did not receive input that ρ does not hold.

Formally, the *necessity condition for desire* is defined by:
$$\forall \mathcal{M} \in \mathcal{W} \; \forall t2 \; [\gamma(\mathcal{M}, t2) \Rightarrow$$
$$\exists t1 \leq t2 \; \delta(\mathcal{M}, t1) \wedge$$
$$\exists t0 \leq t1 \; [\; \text{Input}(\rho, t0, \mathcal{M}) \wedge$$
$$\forall t \in [t0, t1] \; \neg \; \text{Input}(\sim\rho, t, \mathcal{M})]\;]$$

If the past statement $\delta_P(\mathcal{M}, t) \in \text{PS}(\text{InOnt}, \mathcal{M}, t)$ is a temporal desire statement for intention $\gamma(\mathcal{M}, t)$ and additional reason ρ, it is called a *historical desire statement* for intention $\gamma(\mathcal{M}, t)$ and (additional) *reason* ρ.

As for intentions, weaker notions can be defined as well.

4 Tracking Spatial BDI Attributes in a Location Based System

In very general terms, the problem of predicting agent's states based on its spatial history can be described as follows (see Fig. 2). Given - set of routes M for the agent with observed agent state in different location points of each route; task – online prediction of agents next locations, BDI attributes and states for a new route.

In this chapter we are considering one case, where the necessary information about agent locations and states can be naturally tracked, observed or predicted. This case is a Mobile Location-Based Service (LBS), which is part of mobile commerce infrastructure.

In the general case, the location-based services can be defined as services utilizing the ability to dynamically determine and transmit the location of persons within a mobile network by the means of their terminals. From the mobile users' point of view, the LBSs are typically services accessed with or offered by her/his mobile terminal. Let us consider an example of LBSs: a visitor finding a suitable restaurant in a city being visited [14]. In this scenario you want to find a "near-by" restaurant where to eat. Using your mobile terminal you query for close moderately priced restaurants offering vegetable food. As a response, a map is presented on your

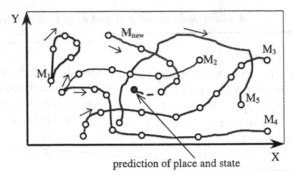

Fig. 2. Routes and states in agent's spatial history

terminal, displaying your current location and the locations of a few close restaurants offering vegetable food. By selecting a particular restaurant symbol on the map, you can get information about that restaurant, for example, the contact information and a lunch offer. After choosing one, you can ask for turn-by-turn navigation instructions to guide your way along the trip to the restaurant.

In mobile environment, a location service is one providing the location of the terminal for LBS. It computes the location estimate based on one or more positioning methods and delivers it to a service in a form of coordinates. Central component of the LBS itself is the content it provides, which can be divided into two categories: geographic data and location-based information [Virrantaus et al., 2001]. Geographic base data forms the data infrastructure of the services, consisting of the digital map data. Location based information is any value added information that can be joined to the base data, associated to a particular location. Geographic data is for example a street network and location-based information the information about restaurants.

4.1 Spatial BDI for Mobile Commerce Location-Based Application

Here we are finding an analogy of the previous considerations of agent's spatial behaviour with the behaviour of a LBS customer.

Agent – mobile customer.

Agent's location – can be tracked by positioning infrastructure.

Observable agents actions – e.g. clickstream (points of interest) on a map delivered to the mobile terminal, calls and downloads of information about points of interest, appropriate orders, reservations, payments, etc. - can be tracked by LBS.

Spatial BDI Axiom: "If a customer has absolutely same *beliefs* about content and quality of two different services, and such content and quality fits his recent *desires*, then this customer *intents* to select nearest one to get service from it".

Agent's Spatial Beliefs

Spatial Belief Axiom – customer believes QoS(q), i.e., that in the same location he can get likely the same quality of service q as he used to get in this location before (observation and communication results); formally:

$\forall \mathcal{M} \in \mathcal{W}$ $\forall t1$ [$\beta_{\text{location\_has\_property}(x, y, \text{QoS}(q))}(\mathcal{M}, t1) \Leftrightarrow$

$\exists t0 \leq t1$ [Input(location_has_property(x, y, QoS(q)), t0, $\mathcal{M}$) $\wedge$

$\forall t \in [t0, t1]$ $\neg$ Input(~location_has_property(x, y, QoS(q)), t, $\mathcal{M}$)]]

Tracking spatial beliefs – based on the Spatial Belief Axiom, the customer's beliefs can be tracked based on his current location coordinates by analyzing the history of his observations and actions (e.g., orders) in this or neighbour locations (see Fig. 3).

Fig. 3. Agent's spatial belief example

Agent's Spatial Desires

Spatial Desire Axiom – customer being in some location desires to get service q in some location x,y, i.e., he believes QoS(q), "turns his view" to location x,y and also believes that there is no such service q1 with better quality closer on his route to x,y; formally:

$\forall \mathcal{M} \in \mathcal{W}$ $\forall t, x, y, d, q$ { at_distance_at_location($\mathcal{R}(\mathcal{M}), d, x, y$) $\Rightarrow$

[$\delta_{\text{get\_service}(x, y, q)}(\mathcal{M}, t) \Leftrightarrow$

$\exists t0 \leq t$ $\forall t1 \in [t0, t]$ [($\beta_{\text{location\_has\_property}(x, y, \text{QoS}(q))}(\mathcal{M}, t1)$) $\wedge$

$\forall x1, y1, d1$ [(at_distance_at_location($\mathcal{R}(\mathcal{M}), d1, x1, y1$) $\wedge$ ($d > d1$)) $\Rightarrow$

$\neg \exists q1$ ($q1 < q$ $\wedge$ $\beta_{\text{location\_has\_property}(x1, y1, \text{QoS}(q1))}(\mathcal{M}, t1)$)] $\wedge$

$\exists t2 \in [t0, t]$ ($\theta_{\text{click\_location}(x, y)}(\mathcal{M}, t2)$)] }

where $\theta_{\text{click\_location}(x, y)}(\mathcal{M}, t2)$ denotes customers action «click to point x,y on his terminal screen», i.e. «turning view» to that point.

Tracking spatial desires – based on Spatial Desire Axiom, the customer's desires can be tracked based on types and coordinates of points of interest he clicks on the screen of mobile terminal (see Fig. 4).

Fig. 4. Agent's spatial desire example

Agent's Spatial Intentions

Spatial Intentions Axiom – customer intends to get some service at a certain location, i.e. he desires to get this service, and he either order/reserve this service online or moves towards this service location point.

$\forall \mathcal{M} \in \mathcal{W} \; \forall t, x, y, d, q \; \{ \text{at\_distance\_at\_location}(\mathcal{R}(\mathcal{M}), d, x, y) \Rightarrow$
$[\gamma_{\text{get\_service}(x, y, q)}(\mathcal{M}, t)] \Leftrightarrow$
$\exists t0 \leq t \; \forall t1 \in [t0, t] \; [(\delta_{\text{get\_service}(x, y, q)}(\mathcal{M}, t1)) \wedge \forall d1, d2 \; \text{at\_distance\_at\_location}(\mathcal{R}(\mathcal{M}),$
$d1, x, y) \wedge$
$[\forall t2 \in [t1, t] \; [\; (\text{at\_distance\_at\_location}(\mathcal{R}(\mathcal{M}), d2, x, y) \wedge (d1 > d2 > d))$
$\vee$
$\exists t3 \in [t1, t] \; (\theta_{\text{order\_service\_online}(q)}(\mathcal{M}, t3))]]] \}$

Tracking spatial intentions – based on Spatial Intentions Axiom, the customer's intentions can be tracked either based on the evidence of his ordering/reserving the desired service online or based on sequentially decreasing distance between customer location and desired service location (see Fig. 5).

Agent's Spatial Actions

Spatial Actions Axiom – a customer performs an action of getting some service, i.e. this service was intended, customer reaches the service location point and spends there at least minimal estimated time for this type of service or makes online electronic payment for this service.

$\forall \mathcal{M} \in \mathcal{W} \; \forall t, x, y, d, q \; \{ \text{at\_distance\_at\_location}(\mathcal{R}(\mathcal{M}), d, x, y) \Rightarrow$
$[\theta_{\text{get\_service}(x, y, q)}(\mathcal{M}, t)] \Leftrightarrow$
$\exists t0 \leq t \; \forall t1 \in [t0, t] \; [(\gamma_{\text{get\_service}(x, y, q)}(\mathcal{M}, t1)) \wedge \text{at\_distance\_at\_location}(\mathcal{R}(\mathcal{M}), d1, x,$
$y) \wedge$
$[\forall ti \in [t2, t3] \subset [t1, t] \; [\; (\text{at\_distance\_at\_location}(\mathcal{R}(\mathcal{M}), 0, x, y) \wedge (t3 - t2 >$
$\text{min\_time}(q))) \vee$
$\exists t3 \in [t1, t] \; (\theta_{\text{pay\_for\_service\_online}(q)}(\mathcal{M}, t3))]]] \}$

Fig. 5. Agent's spatial intentions examples

Tracking spatial actions – based on Spatial Actions Axiom, customer's actions can be tracked either based on the evidence of his electronic payment for the intended service online or based on a fact that customers coordinates are the same as intended service coordinates during minimal estimated time for this type of service (Fig. 6).

4.2 Mobile Commerce Location-Based Service Application

A Mobile Commerce (m-commerce) Location-Based Service Navigator (LBSN) helps its customers (mobile terminal users): (a) to navigate within unknown geographical locations, (b) to access information resources of real world services located in neighbourhood areas.

Fig. 6. Agent's spatial action example

The following transactions are typically expected from LBSN:

Changing Default Preferences (Input: built-in default preferences screen form, which consists of scale slices and types of services to be shown for each scale slice; Action: customer edits and saves form; Output: updated default customer preferences; Comment: for example at a Street Network scale slice customer wants to see museums, hotels and restaurants only, at a City Network scale slice he prefers to see only gasoline stations, at a Country Network scale he prefers to see only embassies).

Locating (Input: customer's request; Action: LBSN contacts positioning infrastructure, requests to locate customer, gets coordinates and delivers to customer; Output: customer's coordinates, four natural numbers (latitude, longitude, attitude, time point) according to agreed standard).

Showing Location (Input: customer's coordinates, scale of map visualizing; Action: LBSN selects appropriate geographical data, prepares it and delivers to customer's terminal; Output: screen with scaled map and pointed customer location on it; Comment: customer location supposes to be in the middle of screen, i.e. customer gets view of some scaled radius around his location).

Showing Services (Input: customer's coordinates, scale of map visualizing, preferences filter associated with scale; Action: LBSN selects appropriate geographical and service data, prepares it and delivers to customer's terminal; Output: screen with scaled map, pointed customer location on it and services, i.e. points of interest; Comment: all shown services are preliminary classified to types, displayed e.g. with different colours or different geometrical primitives for different type of service, and filtered against default user preferences).

Zooming (Input: screen with scaled map and pointed customer location on it, new scale of map visualizing; Output: screen with map updated according to a new scale and pointed customer location on it).

Intelligent Zooming (Input: screen with scaled map, pointed customer location and services on it, new scale of map visualizing, preferences filter associated with new scale; Output: screen with map and services updated according to a new scale and preference filter and pointed customer location on it; Comment: independently of selected scale LBSN is able to show in screen only limited number of points of interest, that is why the more big scale is used the more service points will be refused to be selected by preference filter).

Showing Point (Input: screen with scaled map, pointed customer location and services on it, customer's click to certain point of interest; Action: LBSN selects and downloads appropriate online data about requested service, prepares it and delivers to customer's terminal; Output: screen with online information about point of interest, e.g. recent offerings, prices, contact info, etc.).

Showing Route (Input: screen with scaled map, pointed customer location and services on it, customer's click to the point of interest on the map; Actions: LBSN discovers optimal routes from customer's location to selected point depending on map scale and available transport, prepares appropriate data and delivers it to customer's terminal; Output: screen with map with highlighted routes between the two points for all available transport facilities).

Call Point (Input: screen with online information about point of interest, customer's click to "call" button; Action: LBSN via mobile terminal dials telephone number of selected service; Output: Customer is connected to the point of interest.

Order Service (Input: screen with online information about point of interest, customer's click to "order" button; Action: LBSN via mobile terminal connects customer with appropriate service order web page of the selected service; Output: screen with online order form from the selected service web site).

4.3 Agent-Based Interpretation of the Location-Based Service Navigator

Location-Based Service Navigator (LBSN) for mobile customers is very similar to Autonomous Sensor Support for Agents (ASSA). Due to such autonomous sensor an agent is able to observe environment around his location, navigate within this environment, find, communicate with, get knowledge about, and services from other agents (services).

By keeping records of all transactions, ASSA is able to create really powerful collection of data about agents' behaviour. Appropriate data mining and knowledge discovery algorithms can be applied to discover useful patterns of each agent spatio-temporal behaviour and use these patterns for online prediction of agents' preferences, beliefs, desires, intentions and actions (see Fig. 2).

Now we can show what kind of information about agents ASSA can get from each transaction from the above-mentioned list of LBSN transactions:

1. *Changing Default Preferences* (ASSA gets explicitly agent's preferences, which can be treated as a set of possible agent's desires).
2. *Locating* (ASSA gets explicitly agent's location in different time points, i.e. can collect agent's routes within the environment and make grounded guesses based on this data about agent's spatial BDI).
3. *Showing Location* (ASSA gets explicitly the "picture of what the agent can see now", i.e. can discover some peace of the agent's knowledge).
4. *Showing Services* (ASSA gets explicitly data about "which services the agent can observe now", i.e. can discover some peace of the agent's knowledge).
5. *Zooming* (ASSA gets explicitly data about changing possible agents desires from one set of preferences to another one based on changes in scale. ASSA also gets new agent's view to the neighbouring environment).
6. *Intelligent Zooming* (ASSA gets explicitly data about changing possible agents desires from one set of preferences to another one based on changes in scale. ASSA also gets new agent's view to the services available in the neighbourhood).
7. *Showing Point* (ASSA gents explicitly focus of the agent's view, i.e. gets data about agent's desires, based on type of service the agent is observing now).
8. *Showing Route* (ASSA gets explicit information about agent's desire to move towards the selected point and to get appropriate service).
9. *Call Point* (ASSA gets explicit information about agent's intentions to get more information about appropriate service and agent's desire to get this service).
10. *Order Service* (ASSA gets explicit information about agent's intentions to get selected service).

5 Conclusions

The paper assumes that location of an agent effects on his beliefs desires and intentions and that the history of agent's mobility and observed states in different locations can be used to predict his future states if the location is being permanently observed. Formal spatial route language used in this paper is introduced. The assumptions made on the notions belief, desire and intention, and the way of their interactions are discussed and formalised: formal relationships between the intentional notions, and the spatial behaviour of an agent are defined. The case of using agent architecture for reasoning about the intentions of the customers of a mobile location-based service is also described.

The approach introduced here opens up a number of possibilities for further work. For example various electronic commerce applications are interested in personalizing their services to the customers by predicting and utilizing customer preferences. For location-aware applications the agent-based analogy of modelling customers' beliefs, desires and intention in tracked locations might be an important possibility. The model for beliefs, desires and intentions and their spatial dynamics can be made more complex if necessary. In particular, questions concerning revision and update of beliefs, desires and intentions can be addressed from the spatial perspective, for example in continuation of the exploratory investigations in modelling commitment strategies described in [3].

References

1. Berry, J.S., G. Belovsky, A. Joern, W.P. Kemp & J. Onsager, Object-Oriented Simulation Model of Rangeland Grasshopper Population Dynamics. In Proceedings of Fourth Annual Conference on AI, Simulation, and Planning in High Autonomy Systems, Tucson, AZ. September 20–22, 1993, pp. 102–108.
2. Blamey, S., Partial Logic. In: D. Gabbay and F. Guenthner (eds.), Handbook of Philosophical Logic, Vol. III, 1-70, Reidel, Dordrecht, 1986.
3. Brazier, F.M.T., Dunin-Keplicz, B.M., Treur, J., and Verbrugge, L.C., Modelling Internal Dynamic Behaviour of BDI agents. In: J.-J. Ch. Meyer and P.Y. Schobbes (eds.), Formal Models of Agents (Selected papers from final ModelAge Workshop). Lecture Notes in AI, vol. 1760, Springer Verlag, 1999, pp. 36–56.
4. Briggs, D., Westervelt, J., Levi, S., Harper, S., A Desert Tortoise Spatially Explicit Population Model. Third International Conference. Integrating GIS and Environmental Modeling. January 21–25, 1996. Santa Fe, NM.
5. Cohen, P.R. and Levesque, H.J., Intention is Choice with Commitment. Artificial Intelligence vol. 42 (1990), pp. 213–261.
6. Gimblett, H. R., R. M. Itami & D. Durnota. Some Practical Issues in Designing and Calibrating Artificial Human-Recreator Agents in GIS-based Simulated Worlds. Workshop on Comparing Reactive (ALife-ish) and Intentional Agents. Complexity International, vol. 3, 1996.
7. Green, D. G., Spatial Simulation of fire in Plant Communities. In Proceedings of National Symposium on Computer Modeling and Remote Sensing in Bushfire Prevention, 1987, pp. 36–41 (ed. P. Wise), National Mapping, Canberra.
8. Itami, R. M. & Gimblett, H. R., Intelligent recreation agents in a virtual GIS world. Complexity International, vol. 8, 2001.

9. Jonker, C.M., Treur, J., and Vries, W. de, Temporal Analysis of the Dynamics of Beliefs, Desires, and Intentions. Cognitive Science Quarterly, vol. 2, 2002, pp. 471–494.
10. Linder, B. van, Hoek, W. van der, Meyer, J.-J. Ch., How to motivate your agents: on making promises that you can keep. In: Wooldridge, M.J., Müller, J., Tambe, M. (eds.), Intell. Agents II. Proc. ATAL'95. LNAI, vol. 1037, Springer Verlag, 1996, pp. 17–32.
11. Rao, A.S. and Georgeff, M.P., Modelling Rational Agents within a BDI-Architecture. In: (J. Allen, R. Fikes and E. Sandewall, eds.), Proceedings of the Second International Conference on Principles of Knowledge Representation and Reasoning, (KR'91), Morgan Kaufmann, 1991, pp. 473–484.
12. Saarenmaa, H.; Perttunen, J.; Vakeva, J.; Nikula, A., Object-oriented modeling of the tasks and agent in integrated forest health management. *AI Applications in Natural Resource Management.* 8 (1), 1994, pp. 43–59.
13. Slothower, R. L.; Schwarz, P. A.; Johnson, K. M. , Some Guidelines for Implementing Spatially Explicit, Individual-Based Ecological Models within Location-Based Raster GIS. Third International Conference Integrating GIS and Environmental Modeling. January 21–25, 1996. Santa Fe, NM.
14. Virrantaus K., Veijalainen J., Markkula J., Katasonov A., Garmash A., Tirri H., Terziyan V., Developing GIS-Supported Location-Based Services, In: *Proceedings of WGIS 2001 - First International Workshop on Web Geographical Information Systems*, 3–6 December, 2001, Kyoto, Japan, pp. 423–432.

Meta-reasoning for Agents' Private Knowledge Detection

Jan Tožička[1], Jaroslav Bárta[2], and Michal Pěchouček[1]

[1] Gerstner Laboratory, Czech Technical University in Prague,
[2] Center of Applied Cybernetics, Czech Technical University in Prague,
Technicka 2, 166 27, Prague 6, Czech Republic
{tozicka, barta, pechouc}@labe.felk.cvut.cz

Abstract. Agent's meta-reasoning is a computational process that implements agent's capability to reason on a higher level about another agent or a community of agents. There is a potential for meta-reasoning in multi-agent systems. Meta-reasoning can be used for reconstructing agents' private knowledge, their mental states and for prediction of their future courses of action. Meta-agents should have the capability to reason about incomplete or imprecise information. Unlike the ordinary agents, the meta-agent may contemplate about the community of agents as a whole. This contribution presents application of the meta-reasoning process for the agent's private knowledge detection within the multi-agent system for planning of humanitarian relief operations.

1 Introduction

Multi-agent systems are collections of autonomous, heterogeneous agents with specialized functionalities. Distributed problem solving architectures provide important features, e.g. capability to find 'reasonably-good' solutions efficiently, robustness and a very high degree of fault-tolerance, reconfigurability capabilities, 'openness' of the community to integrate new agents or to replace the disappearing, etc.

We have demonstrated [1] that the concept of the multi-agent system is appropriate for planning humanitarian relief operations. The agents representing the humanitarian organizations control their actions with respect to their private restrictions. In this contribution, we focus on detection of these constrains by monitoring the community communication. We use a formal model of meta-agent presented in [2,3] for implementation of the meta-reasoning using different methods of artificial intelligence.

Section 1.1 introduces CPlanT – the target domain for meta-reasoning activities. In section 1.2, we define basic meta-reasoning terms. We describe used meta-reasoning architectures in section 2. In section 3, we describe the methods used in meta-reasoning implementation. In section 4, we summarize and briefly compare these methods.

M. Klusch et al. (Eds.): CIA 2003, LNAI 2782, pp. 316–323, 2003.

1.1   CPlanT Multi-agent System

Planning humanitarian relief operations [1] within a high number of hardly collaborating and vaguely linked non-governmental organizations is a challenging problem. Owing to the very special nature of this specific domain, where the agents may eventually agree to collaborate but are very often reluctant to share their knowledge and resources, we have combined classical negotiation mechanisms, teamwork theory [4] with the acquaintance models and social knowledge techniques[5].

Agents can create a *coalition*, a set of agents, which agreed to cooperate on a single, well-specified task.

We have defined agents' multi-level knowledge organization:

- **private knowledge** - accessible to no other agent,
- **semi-private knowledge** - accessible to other agents in a well-defined subset of the community and
- **public knowledge** - accessible to all agents in the community.

In the CPlanT system, every agent in the community decides in accordance to his private knowledge whether he will agree to participate in a coalition solving given task. The detection of this part of the agent's private information is the studied task of meta-reasoning. Its detection can help meta-agent to reduce necessary communication and to improve the quality of created coalitions. It is not necessary to find out the private knowledge in an exact form (e.g. as stored in the agent's memory), it is sufficient if we will be able to evaluate given task.

1.2   Shortly about Meta-Rrasoning and Meta-agents

We refer to **meta-reasoning** as an agent's capability to reason about the knowledge, mental states and reasoning processes of other members of the multi-agent community. We will refer to **object agents** which are subject of another agent's meta-reasoning process. Meta-reasoning can be carried out either by the object agent or by a specific agent, whose role is only to carry out the meta-reasoning related process. We will refer to **meta-agent** as to any agent with the meta-reasoning ability. Meta-reasoning is an important and inseparable part of reflective behavior of a multi-agent system [6]. A reflective system consists of object-level components and a reflective component.

According to the role/contribution of the object agents to the meta-reasoning process we distinguish between two different types of meta-reasoning. In **collaborative meta-reasoning**, the object agents are aware of being monitored, which is what they agree with and support. The purpose of collaborative meta-reasoning is very often an improvement of the object-agents' collective behavior. While in **non-collaborative meta-reasoning**, the object-agents do not want to be monitored and are not supporting the meta-reasoning process.

Meta-Agents. Many researchers have approached the problem of meta-agency from different points of view. Very often the agents, that reason or maintain knowledge about the community of object agents, are linked to the agents' interaction platform (e.g. *facilitators* [7]). However, meta-reasoning can be implemented also by loosely coupled agents such as *brokers* [8], *matchmakers* [9], or *mediators* [8]. If these agents are tightly connected to the implementation platform, they have been classified as *middle agents* [10].

Unlike the middle agents, the meta-agent is a loosely coupled agent that does not facilitate any functionality that is inevitable for operation of the object-agents. The meta-agent observes the behavior of the community and tries to draw some assumptions about the agents' behavior. This type of meta-agent can help other agents to make optimal decisions and therefore improve the performance of the multi-agent system as a whole. By introducing the concept of the meta-agent, one may get an overall view of the community's functionality.

2   Meta-agent Reasoning Architecture

The central point of the meta-agent's operation is an appropriate model of the community. This model has to be expressed in an appropriate language of adequate granularity. For any reasonable manipulation with the model we need to specify the relevant semantic properties of the object-level community it supposed to model. This is what we will refer to as the **background knowledge** – bk.

According to the model of social knowledge [5], the **agent's social neighborhood** $\mu(A)$ is a collection of agents that are subject of agent's A meta-reasoning processes. While $\mu^+(A)$ is a set of agents, which are monitored by the agent A, $\mu^-(A)$ is a set of all agents that monitor the agent A. Provided that A denotes any agent (including meta-agents), we can say that:

$$\forall A \in \mu^-(B) : B \in \mu^+(A). \tag{1}$$

Object-level community model. Let us define the model of the object-level community $\mathsf{model}(m)$ as a structure, that collects the facts that the meta-agent m knows about the group of agents $\theta \subseteq \mu^+(m)$. As we admit the meta-agent to be mistaken we do not require necessarily truthfulness of these facts, while we want the meta-agent to believe in their truthfulness: bel_m^θ.

Now, let us briefly mention how the model may be constructed and exploited. The meta-reasoning process in multi-agent system is built upon three mutually interconnected computational processes:

1. **monitoring** – process that makes sure that the meta-agent knows the most it can get from monitoring the community of object agents.
2. **reasoning** – this process manipulates the model of the community so that true facts (other than monitored) may be revealed.
3. **community revision** – a mechanism for influencing operation of the object agents' community.

In the following section, we will discuss the reasoning phase in more details. Description of the monitoring phase and the community revision phase can be found in [2].

2.1 Reasoning

The meta-reasoning agent's reasoning operation can be carried out in three different phases of the object agents' community life-cycle:

init-**time:** initialization time when the meta-agent starts to reason about the system before he receives any event from the community,

revision-**time:** the instance of the time when an event in the community happens and the community model is automatically revised or

inspection-**time:** when the user (or other agent possibly) queries the model in order to find out about truthfulness of the goal hypotheses.

Balancing the amount of computational processes in the *revision*-time and the *inspection*-time is really crucial. The proper design depends on the required meta-reasoning functionality. While for visualization and intrusion detection the most of computation is required in the *revision*-time, for explanation, simulation and prediction an important part of computational processes will be carried out in the *inspection*-time.

Community Model Revision. Let us introduce the **community model revision** operator - $\uplus$, that is expected to happen in the *revision*-time exclusively. The community model revision represents the change of the model $\mathsf{model}_t(m)$ in the time t with respect to the new formula event_t that describes an event in the community:

$$\mathsf{model}_{t+1}(m) = \mathsf{model}_t(m) \uplus \mathsf{event}_t \tag{2}$$

There are different types of events that initiate the community-model-revision process in the *revision*-time. We talk primarily about initiating a contract-net-protocol, offer for collaboration, accepting or rejection of the collaboration proposal, informing about actual resources, etc.

Community Model Inspection. During the *inspection*-time, the computational process of **community model inspection** provides the user (or any other agent) the reply for a queried question – about the truthfulness of the formula goal. We introduce an operator $\looparrowright$ for model inspection, which replies as follows:

$$\mathsf{model}(m) \looparrowright \mathsf{goal} = \begin{cases} yes & \text{if } \mathsf{model}(m) \text{ supports the truthfulness of } \mathsf{goal}, \\ no & \text{if } \mathsf{model}(m) \text{ supports the falseness of } \mathsf{goal}, \\ unsure & \text{otherwise.} \end{cases}$$

$$\tag{3}$$

If the goal formula contains variables, the reply can also contain their possible substitution.

3   Meta-reasoning Implementation

A meta-reasoning method consists of the structure model(m) describing community model, revision operator ⊎ and inspection operator ⤳. This abstract architecture has been used for agent's private knowledge detection in the CPlanT multi-agent system. We have implemented two meta-reasoning methods which represents two different possibilities of use of the theoretical background described above. First method uses explicit representation of true facts in the community and theorem proving algorithms as operators. The second one creates and manages hypothesis about every agent's decision rule, it uses machine learning algorithm to revise and inspect the model. Both methods uses the same monitoring and preprocessing to get events from the system.

3.1   Monitoring and Preprocessing

The meta-agent communicates with the object agents via TCP/IP connection by messages in ACL language in KIF format. The meta-agent subscribes the object agents for copies of their communication messages[1]. The meta-agent transforms results of the object agents' decision activity to the events, which are used by reasoning methods for further analysis.

Every agent shares with all other agents in his alliance his semi-private information - mainly for maintaining actual resources capacities. If an agent has not enough resources to satisfy task's demands, it is sure, that the agent will refuse the participation on this task. Because this rejection does not give us any information about agents private knowledge, so we can stop in dealing with this event - this functionality is added to the revision operator ⊎. On the other hand, during the model inspection (⤳ operator) we can directly reply, that the agent will refuse if we know, that he has not enough resources for a given task.

3.2   Theorem Proving and Automated Reasoning

We have experimented with the explicit representation of the true facts in the meta-reasoning model. We have defined the model of the object-level community as a set of true facts about the respective agents. We collect the facts that the meta-agent m knows about the agents θ into a belief-set bel_m^θ.

The model, managed by the meta-agent m, is then a set as follows:

$$\mathsf{model}(m) = \bigcup_{\theta \subseteq \mu^+(m)} \mathsf{bel}_m^\theta \tag{4}$$

It contains all beliefs about all subset of agents in the community. For the implementation of ⊎ and ⤳ operators, we have chosen a theorem proving method.

---

[1] We are talking about collaborative meta-reasoning.

Theorem Proving. Theorem proving and automated reasoning covers an important part of the traditional symbolic artificial intelligence, where the essence of building artificially intelligent systems is rooted in manipulation with the symbolic representation of the environment - the object level multi-agent system, in our case. The truthful facts about the object agents are represented by means of logical formulae and syntactical manipulation with these formulas is given by the rules of logical deduction.

Probably the most popular calculus used in the implementation of reasoning programs is based on the resolution principle [11]. All the logical formulas, that describe a model $\mathsf{model}_t(m)$, are supposed to be encoded as a conjunction of clauses, where each is a disjunction of literals – CNF (conjunctive normal form). By resolving clauses the inference machine tries to find a contradiction in the model with negation of the goal hypothesis. Had there been a contradiction found, the goal hypothesis is proved.

Community Model Revision. When designing the $\uplus$ operator, one needs to take into account the background knowledge – bk (mentioned in section 2). We may distinguish between two marginal effects of the meta-reasoning operation – $\uplus^{\max}$ and $\uplus^{\min}$ as follows (φ is a formula):

$$\mathsf{model}_t(m)\ \uplus^{\max}\ \mathsf{event}_t = \{\varphi : \mathsf{bk} \cup \mathsf{model}_t(m) \cup \{\mathsf{event}_t\} \vdash \varphi\} \qquad (5)$$

$$\mathsf{model}_t(m)\ \uplus^{\min}\ \mathsf{event}_t = \mathsf{model}_t(m) \cup \{\mathsf{event}_t\} \qquad (6)$$

The $\uplus^{\max}$ operator revises the model so that it contains all possible true facts that logically follow from the background knowledge – bk, actual model – $\mathsf{model}_t(m)$ in union with the new observation – event_t. The $\uplus^{\min}$ operator only appends the new formula to the model. In many cases, the $\uplus^{\max}$ operator is hard to achieve as the resulting model may be infinite - we introduce such a model as an abstract marginal concept. When designing the community-model-revision process, we seek such an operation $\uplus$ that

$$\mathsf{model}_t(m)\ \uplus^{\max}\ \mathsf{event}_t \supseteq \mathsf{model}_t(m)\ \uplus\ \mathsf{event}_t \supseteq \mathsf{model}_t(m)\ \uplus^{\min}\ \mathsf{event}_t. \qquad (7)$$

The closer our operation gets to $\uplus^{\min}$ the faster is the model revision process and more complex should be the computational process in the *inspection*-time. The closer we are to $\uplus^{\max}$ the easier should be the query process while the revision process is getting really complex. The concept of model revision is closely related to the concept of weak and strong update in the knowledge engineering area [12].

We have experimented with different model revision operators, all based on the suggested novel heuristic strategy – referring to as *minimization strategy*. This strategy generates a new clause only if the length of the new clause is smaller than one of its parents clauses (for experiments see [3]).

Community Model Inspection. The minimal version of the community model inspection process corresponds directly to *instantiation* of the goal formula within the model with no further reasoning:[2]

$$\text{model}(m) \looparrowright^{\min} \text{goal} = \begin{cases} yes & \text{if goal} \in \text{model}(m), \\ no & \text{if } \neg\text{goal} \in \text{model}(m), \\ unsure & \text{otherwise.} \end{cases} \tag{8}$$

In order to use the minimal version of the model inspection, we need to use the maximal (or close to maximal) model revision operator $\uplus^{\max}$.

If the reasoning triggered by the event has not produced the queried formula, the inspection process will be a more complex operation than simply parsing the existing model. The meta-agent is expected to employ reasoning in order to find out whether the requested goal formula logically follows from the model:

$$\text{model}(m) \looparrowright \text{goal} = \begin{cases} yes & \text{if model}(m) \vdash \text{goal}, \\ no & \text{if model}(m) \vdash \neg\text{goal}, \\ unsure & \text{otherwise.} \end{cases} \tag{9}$$

We have experimented with different theorem proving strategies for implementing the community model inspection operator.

3.3   Machine Learning Algorithm

Let us now talk about the reasoning about singleton object agent only. Watching object agent's reaction for a given tasks, we can learn how he is deciding. For this task it is possible to use a machine learning algorithm. Community model is then a structure used by the learning algorithm and model revision and inspection operators are represented by a learning and evaluation functions of chosen machine learning algorithm.

To allow the meta-agent using such a community model to reason about several agents, it is necessary to create this model for every object agent. But it can be very difficult (or even impossible) to implement more complicated interactions between several object agents. For our experiments, we have chosen version space algorithm [13] and inductive logic programming system. Both methods are able to learn and reply the query in a short time.

4   Conclusion and Comparison

We have presented two possible implementations the meta-reasoning process, i.e. representation of the community model and model revision and inspection operators. The first one is the resolution algorithm based on theorem proving paradigm. It tries to directly create a model containing formulas logical following

---

[2] The goal formula can contain free variables that get bound during the instantiation.

from the known facts. Second presented approach tries to learn how the object agent is deciding, it can be used with machine learning algorithms.

Next phases of our project will focus on abduction and multiple meta-agents cooperation. In [3], you can find methods and strategies comparison and some results of our experiments.

Acknowledgement. The project work has been co-funded by European Office for Aerospace Research and Development (EORD) Air Force Research Laboratory (AFRL) - contract number: FA8655-02-M-4056, Office of Naval Research (ONR) - award number: N00014-03-1-0292 and by the Grant No. LN00B096 of the Ministry of Education, Youth and Sports of the Czech Republic.

References

1. Pěchouček, M., Mařík, V., Bárta, J.: A knowledge-based approach to coalition formation. IEEE Intelligent Systems **17** (2002) 17–25
2. Pěchouček, M., Štěpánková, M., Mařík, O., Bárta, J.: Abstract architecture for meta-reasoning in multi-agent systems. In Mařík, Muller, P., ed.: Multi-Agent Systems and Applications III. Number 2691 in LNAI. Springer-Verlag, Heidelberg (2003)
3. Bárta, J., Tožička, J., Pěchouček, M., Štěpánková, O.: Meta-reasoning in CPlanT multi-agent system. Technical report, Technical Report of the Gerstner Laboratory ©, Czech Techical University in Prague (2003)
4. Tambe, M.: Towards flexible teamwork. Journal of Artificial Intelligence Research **7** (1997) 83–124
5. Mařík, V., Pěchouček, M., Štěpánková, O.: Social knowledge in multi-agent systems. In Luck, M., et al., eds.: Multi-Agent Systems and Applications. Number 2086 in LNAI. Springer-Verlag, Heidelberg (2001)
6. Pěchouček, M., Norrie, D.: Knowledge structures for reflective multi-agent systems: On reasoning about other agents. Research Report 538, Calgary: University of Calgary (2000)
7. McGuire, J., Kuokka, D., Weber, J., Tenebaum, J., Gruber, T., Olsen, G.: Shade: Technology for knowledge-based collaborative engineering. Concurrent Engineering: Research and Applications **1(3)** (1993)
8. Shen, W., Norrie, D., Barthes, J.: Multi-Agent Systems for Concurrent Intelligent Design and Manufacturing. Taylor and Francis, London (2001)
9. Decker, K., Sycara, K., Williamson, M.: Middle agents for internet. In: Proceedings of International Joint Conference on Artificial Intelligence 97, Japan (1997)
10. Sycara, K., Lu, J., Klusch, M., Widoff, S.: Dynamic service matchmaking among agents in open information environments. ACM SIGMOID Record 28 (1999) 211–246
11. Chang, C., Lee, C.R.: Symbolic Logic and Mechanical Theorem Proving. Academic Press New York and London (1973)
12. Pěchouček, M., Štěpánková, O., Mikšovský, P.: Maintenance of discovery knowledge. In Zitkow, R.J., ed.: Priciples of Data Mining and Knowledge Discovery. Springer-Verlag, Heidelberg (1999) 476–483
13. Mitchell, T.: Generalization as search. Artificial Intelligence (1982) 203–226

Formalizing Retrieval Goal Change by Prioritized Circumscription – Preliminary Report –

Ken Satoh

National Institute of Informatics
2-1-2 Hitotsubashi, Chiyoda-ku, Tokyo, 101-8430, Japan
ksatoh@nii.ac.jp

Abstract. We sometimes encounter a situation during a search over the Internet such that we change a retrieval goal. In this paper, we formalize this phenomena in terms of nonmonotonic reasoning (prioritized circumscription [McCarthy86]). The idea of formalization is as follows. We assume chain of causal rules to satisfy a purpose of the retrieval where bottom conditions are the context of retrieval results and/or retrieval goals such that executing some of the goals make a purpose of the retrieval purpose fulfilled. We also assume a prioritization over causal rules or success predictions of retrieval command which represents strength of satisfaction of rules. Then, given the current context of retrieval results obtained so far, we infer the most preferable retrieval command by prioritized circumscription. We believe that this formalization gives a theoretical basis of what is necessary in an intelligent user navigation tool.

1 Introduction

When we traverse over the Internet to search some information, we sometimes change an object which we are looking for, in other word, change a *retrieval goal* according to additional information obtained during search.

Consider the following motivating example of change of a retrieval goal[1].

- Prof. Tanaka would like to improve his English and he thinks that watching an English movie helps his purpose. So, he searches for a video recorder to watch a movie.
- He firstly searches a video recorder with a noise reduction facility to watch an English movie comfortably with the video recorder.
- During the search, he happens to know the existence of a video recorder with English closed caption facility and he changes a retrieval goal to try to find such video recorders with closed caption facility.

We would like to construct a system which supports this activity by invoking a retrieval goal change at an earlier stage of the activity since the new retrieval

---

[1] This example was given by Prof. Yuzuru Tanaka from Hokkaido University.

M. Klusch et al. (Eds.): CIA 2003, LNAI 2782, pp. 324–335, 2003.

goal is more effective according to the purpose. This means that the system predicts user's purpose for a retrieval activity and provides the most relevant retrieval command with the purpose. In order to make such a system, we need to model the phenomena of retrieval goal change in the first place. We believe that we could not get the overview of developing an intelligent advice system without such a modelling.

In this paper, we regard this kind of retrieval goal change as preference reasoning over rules with the assumption that we have the following rules and priority over the rules beforehand.

1. To improve English, watch an English movie.
2. To watch an English movie for English improvement, search a video recorder with a fine resolution or with a closed caption facility.
3. Search a video recorder with a fine resolution by default since we assume that the search for a video recorder with a closed caption facility will fail.
4. If we find a video recorder with a closed caption facility, we search other video recorders with a closed caption facility. This rule has a higher priority over the previous rule.
5. We search a video recorder either with a fine resolution or with a closed caption facility (not both simultaneously).

The first represents a causal rule for the ultimate purpose of the current information retrieval activity which is to improve English. This ultimate purpose is replaced by another sub-purpose which is to watch an English movie. There are two alternatives to watch an English movie; one is to find a video recorder with a fine resolution and the other is to find a video recorder with a closed caption facility. Although the video recorder with a closed caption facility is more preferable, we search a video recorder with a fine resolution firstly according to the third rule since we believe that finding a video recorder with a closed caption facility is very difficult. This means that the implausibility of a video recorder with a closed caption facility is stronger than the preference of the fourth rule.

In the current situation, we retrieve a video recorder with a fine resolution since it satisfies all the rules and preferences as follows. Firstly, we believe nonexistence of a video recorder with a closed caption facility. Then, the rule for finding a video recorder with a closed caption facility will not be used since the condition becomes false, although the rule itself is satisfied[2] Moreover, by searching a video recorder with a fine resolution, we can satisfy the rule concerning a search of a video recorder with a fine resolution. Therefore, all the preferred rules are satisfied and the most preferable retrieval goal is to search a video recorder with a fine resolution.

Suppose that, later after some retrieval activity, we happen to find a video recorder with a closed caption facility. Then, implausibility of existence of a video recorder with a closed caption facility is rebutted. Then, to satisfy the fourth rule, we need to make the retrieval of other video recorders with a closed caption facility. Since we consider a retrieval of one object at one time by the

---

[2] Note that the conditional sentence is logically true if the condition is false.

fifth rule, we also invalidate the third rule to retrieve a video recorder with a fine resolution.

This kind of inference cannot be formalized in a deductive way. Since the deduction is "monotonic", that is, once we get a inferred result, we can no longer retract the result in a deduction. Therefore, to understand the phenomena, we need other reasoning formalism. In this paper, we formalize this phenomena by prioritized circumscription [McCarthy86]. In prioritized circumscription, we can divide preference rules into hierarchy and this hierarchy gives a priority relation over rules. Therefore, we directly represent rules in the hierarchy in prioritized circumscription.

There are research of applying nonmonotonic reasoning to information retrieval and/or adaptive information filtering[Amati96,Brusa96,Hunter96, Bruza98,Lau99]. [Amati96,Brusa96,Bruza98,Lau99] formalize relevance (or in other words, aboutness) between terms by using preference reasoning. They regard information conveyed by information carrier as logical relation between the carrier and the information. Then, the system becomes nonmonotonic since information carriers of term t is not always information carriers of two terms t and s, that is, the system violates monotonicity. They formalize this phenomena in terms of preference relation over information carriers and relevant terms such that some carriers which are relevant with the term t becomes less preferable if we consider carriers having both t and s. Another work related with aboutness is [Hunter96] which formalizes the concept of aboutness by default logic. These research are regarded as a formalization to explain the behavior of the current system while we give a new formalization of user behavior.

The structure of this paper is as follows. Firstly, we give a formal definition of prioritized circumscription. Then, we show a formalization of goal change and give two examples; one is the above information retrieval example and the other is the goal change of the customer in the shop.

2   Prioritized Circumscription

We restrict our attention to propositional circumscription since we only consider the propositional case.

Let F and G be tuples of propositional formulas, $\langle F_1, F_2, ..., F_n \rangle$ and $\langle G_1, G_2, ..., G_n \rangle$. We define $F \leq G$ as $\bigwedge_{i=1}^{n} F_i \supset G_i$ where '$\supset$' is the material implication. We define $F < G$ as $F \leq G$ and $G \not\leq F$, and $F \equiv G$ as $F \leq G$ and $G \leq F$.

Let $A(P, Z)$ be a conjunction of formulas where P and Z are disjoint tuples of propositions used in A.

Circumscription of P for A with Z varied is defined as follows.

$$Circum(A; P; Z) = A(P, Z) \wedge \neg \exists p \exists z (A(p, z) \wedge p < P).$$

where p, z are tuple of propositional variables and $A(p, z)$ is obtained from $A(P, Z)$ by replacing each propositions by the corresponding variable. We call propositions in P *minimized propositions* and propositions in Z *varied propositions*.

For a model theory of circumscription, we define an order of interpretations to minimize P with Z varied is defined as follows. Let I be an interpretation and Φ be a tuple of propositional symbols. We define $I[\Phi]$ as $\{p \in \Phi | I \models p\}$ or, equivalently, $I \cap \Phi$.

Let I_1 and I_2 be interpretations.
$I_1 \leq^{P;Z} I_2$ if

1. $I_1[Q] = I_2[Q]$ where Q is a tuple of propositions neither in P nor in Z.
2. $I_1[P] \subseteq I_2[P]$.

Intuitively, the above order over models, $I_1 \leq^{P;Z} I_2$, means that I_1 falsifies more minimized propositions than I_2. We define $I_1 <^{P;Z} I_2$ as $I_1 \leq^{P;Z} I_2$ and $I_2 \nleq^{P;Z} I_1$.

A minimal model M of $A(P, Z)$ w.r.t. P with Z varied is defined as follows.

1. M is a model of $A(P, Z)$.
2. There is no model M' of $A(P, Z)$ such that $M' <^{P;Z} M$.

According to [Lifschitz85], I is a minimal model of $A(P, Z)$ w.r.t. P with Z varied if and only if I is a model of $Circum(A; P; Z)$.

We extend the above definition to prioritized circumscription as follows. We divide a set of propositions into n partitions and give an order over partitions. Suppose that this is $P_1 > P_2 > ... > P_n$. Intended meaning of this order is that we firstly minimize P_1, then P_2 .... ,then P_n. Let P and Q be a tuple of propositions which have orders $P_1 > P_2 > ... > P_n$ and $Q_1 > Q_2 > ... > Q_n$. We define $P \preceq^i Q$ as follows. If $i = 1$, $P \preceq^i Q$ is $P_1 \leq Q_1$ and if $i > 1$, $(\bigwedge_{j=1}^{i-1} P_j \equiv Q_j) \supset P_i \leq Q_i$. We define $P \preceq Q$ as $\bigwedge_{i=1}^{n} P \preceq^i Q$ and $P \prec Q$ as $P \preceq Q$ and $Q \npreceq P$.

Prioritized circumscription of $P_1 > P_2 > ... > P_n$ for A with Z varied is defined as follows.

$$Circum(A; P_1 > P_2 > ... > P_n; Z) = A(P, Z) \wedge \neg \exists p \exists z (A(p, z) \wedge p \prec P).$$

In a model theory of prioritized circumscription, we define an order over interpretations as follows.

Let I_1 and I_2 be interpretations and let $\mathcal{P}$ consist of disjoint sets $P_1, P_2, ..., P_n, Q, Z$.
$I_1 \preceq^{P_1 > P_2 > ... > P_n; Z} I_2$ if

1. $I_1[Q] = I_2[Q]$.
2. $I_1[P_1] \subseteq I_2[P_1]$.
3. For every i, if for every $1 \leq j \leq i - 1$, $I_1[P_j] = I_2[P_j]$, then $I_1[P_i] \subseteq I_2[P_i]$.

The above order means that I_1 falsifies more minimized propositions in the first place more than I_2, or if I_1 and I_2 falsifies the same minimized propositions in the first place, we consider the minimized propositions in the lower priority in the same way as the first place until some difference of minimization is found in I_1 and I_2.

We define $I_1 \prec^{P_1 > P_2 > ... > P_n; Z} I_2$ as $I_1 \preceq^{P_1 > P_2 > ... > P_n; Z} I_2$ and $I_2 \not\preceq^{P_1 > P_2 > ... > P_n; Z} I_1$.

A minimal model M of $A(P, Z)$ w.r.t. $P_1 > P_2 > ... > P_n$ with Z varied is defined as follows.

1. M is a model of $A(P, Z)$.
2. There is no model M' of $A(P, Z)$ such that $M' \prec^{P_1 > P_2 > ... > P_n; Z} M$.

According to [Lifschitz85], I is a minimal model of $A(P, Z)$ w.r.t. $P_1 > P_2 > ... > P_n$ with Z varied iff I is a model of $Circum(A; P_1 > P_2 > ... > P_n; Z)$.

3   Formalization

Now, we give a formal framework for a retrieval goal change. We divide propositions into four categories:

1. The first kind is called *purpose proposition* which expresses the ultimate purpose of the retrieval and a sub-purpose which leads to the ultimate purpose.
2. The second kind is called *context proposition* which expresses the current information context corresponding with the results obtained so far.
3. The third kind is called *retrieval proposition* which expresses retrieval command for the Internet or a database or even asked to other experts.
4. The fourth kind is called *abnormal proposition* which is used in the negated form in the conditional part of defeasible rules. If an abnormal proposition for a rule is true, then this expresses the abnormal situation for the rule and the rule becomes no longer applicable.

We allow the following rules expressing causal relation between purposes, contexts and retrieval commands:

1. $P_1 \wedge ... \wedge P_n \supset P$
   where each of $P_1, ..., P_n$ is either purpose proposition or retrieval proposition and P are purpose proposition. This means that P is decomposed into sub-purpose propositions or retrieval propositions.
2. $\neg Ab_\phi \wedge C_1 \wedge ... \wedge C_n \supset R$
   where Ab_ϕ is an abnormal proposition which is unique for this rule, and $C_1, ..., C_n$ are context propositions and R is a retrieval proposition. This means that if the context $C_1 \wedge ... \wedge C_n$ happens, we usually perform a retrieval corresponding with R.
3. $\neg Ab_\phi \wedge C_1 \wedge ... \wedge C_n \supset C$ or
   $\neg Ab_\phi \wedge C_1 \wedge ... \wedge C_n \supset \neg C$
   where Ab_ϕ is an abnormal proposition which is unique for this rule, and $C_1, , , C_n$ and C are context propositions. This means that if the context $C_1 \wedge ... \wedge C_n$ happens, some context information C usually becomes true (or false for the second rule).

We assume a preference over rules which is expressed by order of minimization of abnormal propositions. We also assume that only one retrieval command will be executed at one time.

Let $P_1, ..., P_n$ be the purpose propositions, and $R_1, ..., R_m$ be the retrieval propositions, and $C_1, ..., C_l$ be the context propositions, and $Ab_{11}, Ab_{12}, ..., Ab_{1k_1} ..., Ab_{hk_h}$ be the abnormal propositions and let the above conjunction of rules, together with the current context of retrieval results and the constraint that only one retrieval command will be executed at one time, be denoted as

$$A(Ab_{11}, Ab_{12}, ..., Ab_{1k_1} ..., Ab_{hk_h}, P_1, ..., P_n, R_1, ..., R_m, C_1, ...C_l).$$

Also let the priority over rules expressing by abnormal propositions be denoted as follows:

$$\langle Ab_{11}, Ab_{12}, ..., Ab_{1k_1} \rangle > \langle Ab_{21}, Ab_{22}, ..., Ab_{2k_2} \rangle > \langle Ab_{h1}, Ab_{h2}, ..., Ab_{hk_h} \rangle$$

Then, we compute models of the following circumscription:

$$Circum(A; \mathcal{A}_1 > \mathcal{A}_2 > ... > \mathcal{A}_h; Z)$$

where $\mathcal{A}_i$ denotes $\langle Ab_{i1}, Ab_{i2}, ..., Ab_{ik_i} \rangle$ and Z denotes $\langle P_1, ..., P_n, R_1, ..., R_m, C_1, ...C_l \rangle$. These models satisfy the preferable rules in the order specified by the prioritization of minimizing abnormal propositions as much as possible given the current context. Therefore, a retrieval proposition which is true in a model of the above circumscription becomes the most preferable retrieval command.

4 Examples

Now, we give a formalization of the video recorder example in the introduction using the above framework. We also show another example where introduction of a new rule and a priority are considered.

4.1 Video Recorder Example

We represent the rules of video recorder example in propositional logic as follows.

1. To improve English, watch an English movie:
   $W \supset I$
   where W means "watching an English movie" and I means "improving English".
2. To watch an English movie for English improvement, search a video recorder with a fine resolution:
   $F \supset W$
   where F means "searching a video recorder with a fine resolution".

3. To watch an English movie for English improvement, search a video recorder with a closed caption facility:

$C \supset W$

where C means "searching a video recorder with a closed caption facility".

4. Search a video recorder with a fine resolution by default. This rule is presented as:

$\neg Ab1 \supset F$

and we minimize $Ab1$ where $Ab1$ expresses an abnormal situation of this rule.

5. If we find a video recorder with a closed caption facility, we search other video recorders with a closed caption facility. This rule is presented as:

$\neg Ab2 \wedge E \supset C$

and we minimize $Ab2$ where E expresses an existence of a video recorder with a closed caption facility and $Ab2$ expresses an abnormal situation of this rule.

6. We assume that the search for a video recorder with a closed caption facility will fail. This rule is presented as:

$\neg Ab3 \supset \neg E$

and we minimize $Ab3$ where $Ab3$ expresses an abnormal situation of this rule.

7. We search a video recorder either with a fine resolution or with a closed caption facility (not both simultaneously):

$\neg(F \wedge C)$

Note that W and I are purpose propositions, and F and C are retrieval propositions and E is a context proposition. We also have the preference that $Ab3$ is firstly minimized and $Ab2$ is secondly minimized and $Ab1$ is thirdly minimized. This intuitively means that models which does not satisfy E (in other words, satisfies $\neg E$) are most preferable and if there is no such models, then models which satisfies $(E \supset C)$ are the secondly most preferable and if there is no such models, then models which satisfies F are the thirdly most preferable.

We denote the conjunction of the above rules as $A_1(Ab1, Ab2, Ab3, W, I, F, C, E)$ and compute the following prioritized circumscription:

$Circum(A_1; Ab3 > Ab2 > Ab1; W, I, F, C, E) =$
$\quad A_1(Ab1, Ab2, Ab3, W, I, F, C, E) \wedge$
$\quad \neg \exists ab3 \exists ab2 \exists ab1 \exists w \exists i \exists f \exists c \exists e($
$\qquad A_1(ab1, ab2, ab3, w, i, f, c, e) \wedge$
$\qquad (ab3 \supset Ab3) \wedge$
$\qquad ((ab3 \equiv Ab3) \supset (ab2 \supset Ab2)) \wedge$
$\qquad (((ab3 \equiv Ab3) \wedge (ab2 \equiv Ab2)) \supset (ab1 \supset Ab1)) \wedge$
$\qquad \neg((Ab3 \supset ab3) \wedge$
$\qquad\quad ((Ab3 \equiv ab3) \supset (Ab2 \supset ab2)) \wedge$
$\qquad\quad (((Ab3 \equiv ab3) \wedge (Ab2 \equiv ab2)) \supset (Ab1 \supset ab1))))$

where $ab1, ab2, ab3, w, i, f, c$ and e are propositional variables and $A_1(ab1, ab2, ab3, w, i, f, c, e)$ is obtained from $A_1(Ab1, Ab2, Ab3, W, I, F, C, E)$ by replacing each propositions by the corresponding variable.

We could delete all the existential quantifiers for propositional variables by the following translation[3]:

$$\exists x \phi(x) \Rightarrow \phi(\mathbf{T}) \vee \phi(\mathbf{F})$$

and compute the logical consequence of circumscription and then choose the consequence of retrieval command in a model which satisfies the retrieval purpose.

We intuitively explain how to compute the above circumscription. We firstly minimize $Ab3$ to obtain $\neg E$ Then, we secondly minimize $Ab2$ to obtain $E \supset C$. $E \supset C$ does not yield any result since $\neg E$ is true although $E \supset C$ itself is satisfied. Finally, we minimize $Ab3$ to obtain F. Therefore, the most preferable retrieval goal is to find a video recorder with a closed caption facility.

There is another way of computing minimal models based on the model-theory of circumscription. We firstly compute all the models of the axiom set and then, check each model whether there is no strictly preferable model than the model or not. For the video example, M_1 is strictly smaller than M_2 if one of the following conditions is satisfied:

- $M_1 \models \neg Ab3$ and $M_2 \models Ab3$.
- $((M_1 \models Ab3$ and $M_2 \models Ab3)$ or $(M_1 \models \neg Ab3$ and $M_2 \models \neg Ab3))$ and $M_1 \models \neg Ab2$ and $M_2 \models Ab2$.
- $((M_1 \models Ab3$ and $M_2 \models Ab3)$ or $(M_1 \models \neg Ab3$ and $M_2 \models \neg Ab3))$ and $((M_1 \models Ab2$ and $M_2 \models Ab2)$ or $(M_1 \models \neg Ab2$ and $M_2 \models \neg Ab2))$ and $M_1 \models \neg Ab1$ and $M_2 \models Ab1$.

There are 31 models satisfying $A_1(Ab1, Ab2, Ab3, W, I, F, C, E)$. Among them, a model[4]

$$\{\neg Ab1, \neg Ab2, \neg Ab3, W, I, F, \neg C, \neg E\}$$

is the unique minimal model since there is no other model which is strictly smaller than the model according to the order above.

Later, during the search, suppose that we happen to find a video recorder with a closed caption. Then, we add E to A_1. Let

$$A_2(Ab1, Ab2, Ab3, W, I, F, C, E) = A_1(Ab1, Ab2, Ab3, W, I, F, C, E) \wedge E$$

and compute the following prioritized circumscription:

$Circum(A_2; Ab3 > Ab2 > Ab1; W, I, F, C, E) =$
    $A_1(Ab1, Ab2, Ab3, W, I, F, C, E) \wedge E \wedge$
    $\neg \exists ab3 \exists ab2 \exists ab1 \exists w \exists i \exists f \exists c \exists e ($
        $A_1(ab1, ab2, ab3, w, i, f, c, e) \wedge e$
        $(ab3 \supset Ab3) \wedge$

---

[3] **T** represents "truth" and **F** represents "falsity".
[4] We denote a model as a set of literals which are true in the model.

$$((ab3 \equiv Ab3) \supset (ab2 \supset Ab2)) \wedge$$
$$(((ab3 \equiv Ab3) \wedge (ab2 \equiv Ab2)) \supset (ab1 \supset Ab1)) \wedge$$
$$\neg((Ab3 \supset ab3) \wedge$$
$$((Ab3 \equiv ab3) \supset (Ab2 \supset ab2)) \wedge$$
$$(((Ab3 \equiv ab3) \wedge (Ab2 \equiv ab2)) \supset (Ab1 \supset ab1))))$$

Then, we can no longer minimize $Ab3$ since E is true and therefore $Ab3$ becomes true. Minimizing $Ab2$ leads to derivation of the rule $E \supset C$ and therefore C becomes true. Then, since we can perform a retrieval only for one object, F becomes false and accordingly $Ab1$ becomes true by the rule $\neg Ab1 \supset F$. In this case, the most preferable retrieval goal is changed from F (to search a video recorder with a fine resolution) to C (to search a video recorder with closed caption facility).

Model-theoretically, there are 7 models for $A_1(Ab1, Ab2, Ab3, W, I, F, C, E) \wedge E$. Among them, a model

$$\{Ab1, \neg Ab2, Ab3, W, I, \neg F, C, E\}$$

is the unique minimal model. Note that there is a model

$$\{\neg Ab_1, Ab_2, Ab_3, W, I, F, \neg C, E\},$$

but this model is greater than the above model according to the order over models since minimizing $Ab2$ is more preferable to minimizing $Ab1$.

4.2   Salesclerk Example

This is not an example for information retrieval, but the real conversation happening in the store shown in [Shoji02]. We show this example in order to show not only generality of our analysis, but also possibility of giving new facility to the Internet shopping.

A Japanese female customer came to the store to buy a jacket, but the jacket under her consideration was short and then, the conversation happened as follows (the conversation is translated into English).

Customer: This (jacket) is a little short, isn't it?
Salesclerk: Such a design is popular this year. Almost every shop deals with short ones. Do you prefer longer one?
Customer: Too short to cover my waist...
Salesclerk: It depends on the balance with your skirt or pants. 'cause you're now wearing shorter tight skirt, you think that way, but if wearing a long skirt, you will feel better.

This conversation successfully led to the purchase of a jacket and Shoji et al. analyze this case as follows:

The customer's mental world was changed from one where the relevant attribute is length of jacket to another where different attribute called balance is relevant. Through the conversation, the capable salesclerk shown in the case could grasp the customer's wish that she make herself look as good-shaped as possible, and induce the appropriate goal (short but well-balanced jacket) in accordance with it.

This example is also a kind of retrieval goal change (from longer jacket to short jacket with well-balanced long skirt). If we assume the following causal rules, we can formalize this change as well.

1. A customer believes that normally the following holds:
   To have a good shape, find a long jacket.
2. A salesclerk have different rules to implement "good-shape" as follows:
   To have a good shape, find a short jacket and a well-balanced long skirt.

In this case, the causal rule is added and moreover the priority between rules dynamically; the second rule is more preferable to the first rule (because of the current boom). Note that the second rule is not in the customer's knowledge at the initial situation and only after the salesclerk's statement "It depends on the balance with your skirt or pants.", the customer came to know the rule and also higher priority of the new rule by the statement "Such a design is popular this year. Almost every shop deals with short ones."

We represent the rules of this example in propositional logic as follows.

1. To have a good shape, find a long jacket.
   $L \supset G$ where L means "finding a long jacket" G means "having a good shape.
2. Normally, we search a long jacket.
   $\neg Ab1 \supset L$ and we minimize $Ab1$ where $Ab1$ expresses an abnormal situation of this rule.

We denote the conjunction of the above rules as $A_3(Ab1; L, G)$ and compute the following circumscription:

$Circum(A_3; L, G) =$
   $A_3(Ab1, L, G) \wedge \neg \exists ab1 \exists l \exists g(A_3(ab1, l, g) \wedge (ab1 \supset Ab1) \wedge \neg(Ab1 \supset ab1))$

We minimize $Ab1$ and obtain L. Then G holds. Therefore, L (finding a longer jacket) is the most preferable retrieval command. Model-theoretically, there are 4 models for $A_3(Ab1, L, G)$. Among them, a model

$$\{\neg Ab1, L, G\}$$

is the unique minimal model.

Later, suppose that salesclerk says that the balanced combination of a short jacket and a long skirt also helps a good-shape. Then, we introduce the new rule according to the salesclerk.

3. To have a good shape, find a short jacket and well-balanced long skirt.
   $S \wedge W \supset G$
   where S means "finding a short jacket" and W means "finding a well-balanced long skirt".

4. Normally, we search a short skirt and well-balanced long skirt. $(\neg Ab2 \supset S) \wedge (\neg Ab2 \supset W)$ and we minimize $Ab2$ where $Ab2$ expresses an abnormal situation of this rule.
5. We search either a long jacket or a short jacket (not both simultaneously). $\neg(L \wedge S)$

We assume the preference of minimizing $Ab2$ over minimizing $Ab1$. We add the above rules to A_3. Let

$$A_4(Ab1, Ab2, L, G, S, W) =$$
$$A_3(Ab1, L, G) \wedge (S \wedge W \supset G) \wedge (\neg Ab2 \supset S) \wedge (\neg Ab2 \supset W) \wedge \neg(L \wedge S)$$

and compute the following prioritized circumscription:

$$Circum(A_4; Ab2 > Ab1; L, G, S, W) =$$
$$A_4(Ab1, Ab2, L, G, S, W) \wedge$$
$$\neg \exists ab2 \exists ab1 \exists l \exists g \exists s \exists w($$
$$A_4(ab1, ab2, l, g, s, w) \wedge$$
$$(ab2 \supset Ab2) \wedge ((ab2 \equiv Ab2) \supset (ab1 \supset Ab1)) \wedge$$
$$\neg((Ab2 \supset ab2) \wedge ((Ab2 \equiv ab2) \supset (Ab1 \supset ab1))))$$

Then, according to the minimization preference, $Ab2$ is minimized first. Then, $\neg Ab2$ becomes true and so are S and W. By $\neg(L \wedge S)$, L becomes false and $Ab1$ becomes true. Therefore the most preferable retrieval goals become S and W.

Model-theoretically, there are 12 models for $A_4(Ab1, Ab2, L, G, S, W)$. Among them, a model

$$\{Ab1, \neg Ab2, \neg L, G, S, W\}$$

is the unique minimal model. There are two models for $A_4(Ab1, Ab2, L, G, S, W)$ which falsify $Ab1$ and do not $Ab2$, but these models are not minimal models since minimizing $Ab2$ is more preferable to minimizimg $Ab1$.

5   Conclusion

This paper presents a formal analysis of retrieval goal change in information retrieval task. We demonstrated the appropriateness of the formalization using examples. We believe that this analysis will be a basis of intelligent agents which make more creative suggestion for information retrieval.

However, this is just the first step and there are a lot of things to be done:

- How to find a purpose?
- How to obtain causal rules?
- How to obtain preference over rules?
- How to change preferences if new information is obtained?

We would like to investigate the above concerns for an implementation of more helpful cooperative agent for information retrieval.

Acknowledgements This research is partly supported by the project "Intuitive Human Interface for Organizing and Accessing Intellectual Assets" which is the part of the Future Program of JSPS, "Kansei (Intuitive & Affective) Human Interface". I thank Yuzuru Tanaka from Hokkaido University for providing me an important motivating example for this research and Bob Kowalski from Imperial College for instructive comments on the research.

References

[Amati96] Amati, G., and Georgatos, K., Relevance as Deduction: A Logical View of Information Retrieval, *Proc. of the Second Workshop on Information Retrieval, Uncertainty and Logic (WIRUL'96)*, pp. 21–26 (1996).

[Brusa96] Bruza, P.D., and Huibers, T.W.C., A Study of Aboutness in Information Retrieval, *Artificial Intelligence Review*, Vol. 10, No. 5-6, pp. 381–407 (1996).

[Bruza98] Bruza, P.D., and van Linder, B., Preferential Models of Query by Navigation, F. Crestani, M. Lalmas, and C.J. van Rijsbergen (eds), *Information Retrieval: Uncertainty and Logics*, Kluwer Academic Publishers, pp. 73–96 (1998)

[Hunter96] Hunter, A., Intelligent Text Handling Using Default Logic, *Proc. of the Eighth IEEE International Conference on Tools with Artificial Intelligence (TAI'96)* pp. 34–40 (1996).

[Lau99] Lau, R., ter Hofstede, A.H.M., and Bruza, P.D., A Study of Belief Revision in the context of Adaptive Information Filtering, *Proc. of the 5th International Computer Science Conference ICSC'99 on Internet Applications*, LNCS 1749, pp. 1–10 (1999).

[Lifschitz85] Lifschitz, V., Computing Circumscription, *Proc. of IJCAI-85*, pp. 121–127 (1985).

[McCarthy86] McCarthy, J., "Application of Circumscription to Formalizing Common-sense Knowledge", Artificial Intelligence, Vol.28, pp. 89–116 (1986).

[Shoji02] Shoji, H., Mori, M., and Hori, K., "Concept Articulation as Chance Discovery by Shoppers", *Proc. of PRICAI Workshop on Chance Discovery*, pp. 103–114 (2002).

Organisational Change: Deliberation and Modification

Catholijn M. Jonker[1] , Martijn C. Schut[1], and Jan Treur[1,2]

[1]Vrije Universiteit Amsterdam, Department of Artificial Intelligence
De Boelelaan 1081a, NL-1081 HV Amsterdam, The Netherlands
{jonker, schut, treur}@cs.vu.nl
http://www.cs.vu.nl/~{jonker, schut, treur}
[2]Utrecht University, Department of Philosophy
Heidelberglaan 8, 3584 CS Utrecht

Abstract. For an information-agent-based system to support virtual (Internet-supported) organisations, changes in environmental conditions often demand changes in organisational behaviour, i.e., organisational changes. As organisational behaviour relates to organisational structure, rethinking the structure of an organisation as environmental conditions demand so, renders such an organisation imperatively flexible and adaptive. This paper presents a formal modelling approach for such organisational dynamics. The contributions of the reported research are (1) a formal model as a basis for simulation (2) formal specifications of dynamic properties of organisational behaviour at different aggregation levels, (3) logical interlevel relationships between these properties, (4) a prototype implementation, and (5) simulation and checking results.

1 Introduction

Within the field of Organisation Theory organisational structures regulating societal dynamics, and thus entailing organisational behaviour are studied; e.g., [6], [12], [14]. A particular area for which this field has become quite relevant is the area of virtual (Internet-supported) organisations. Supporting the design of virtual organisations based on information agents on the Internet asks for a dedicated organisation modelling approach. Within the area of Computational Organisation Theory and Artificial Intelligence, a number of organisation modelling approaches have been developed to simulate and analyse dynamics within organisations; e.g., [16], [13], [15], [3]. Some of these approaches explicitly focus on modelling organisational structure, abstracting from the detailed dynamics. Other approaches put less emphasis on organisational structure but focus on the dynamics in the sense of implementing and experimenting with simulation models. The Agent/Group/Role (AGR) approach as described in [3] is an example of an approach focussing on organisational structure, abstracting from the details of the dynamics. However, [4], [5] are some first steps to specify the organisational behaviour by adding specifications of dynamic properties to the organisational structure provided by AGR.

M. Klusch et al. (Eds.): CIA 2003, LNAI 2782, pp. 336–344, 2003.
© Springer-Verlag Berlin Heidelberg 2003

In [9] it is shown how the relation between an organisational structure and organisational behaviour can be founded formally. In [7] practical application of the connection between structure and behaviour is presented in the form of an approach that enables to derive organisation properties from role properties (and interaction properties), according to the organisational structure. However, in these papers it is not addressed how to model *organisational change*, i.e., an organisation that is changing its behaviour over time, a phenomenon that receives much attention in recent literature on Organisation Theory; e.g., [12], [13]. Organisational change is a process that allows an organisation to adapt its behaviour to changing environmental conditions. In virtual organisations such changes occur on a regular basis, and in fact may be part of the normal functioning of such an (evolving) organisation.

The initiative for changes of organisational structure usually lies within the organisation (in interaction with the environment). In organisations in human society, often the underlying decision process is embedded within the organisation in the form, e.g., of a director or management board supported by a strategic management department. In this sense, the process to obtain a changed organisation is itself part of the organised dynamics. This makes the organisational dynamics a reflective process.

To model the dynamics of this reflective process in order to support the evolution of virtual, information agent-based organisations is the challenge addressed in this paper. In Section 2 an overview of the modelling approach is presented, together with an example scenario. Section 3 provides more detail about the manner in which the strategic management for organisational change is modelled. Finally, Section 4 concludes, among others, by briefly discussing the prototype implementation and some simulation results.

2   Modelling Approach and Example Scenario

Processes of organisational change (in succession) realise an evolving organisation that is able to adapt to its (changing) environment; e.g., [12], [13]. From a strategic management perspective, this evolution is to be guided by deliberation. Based on such deliberation the organisational changes are initiated and accomplished. The deliberation may involve (the demands from) the environment, organisational goals, organisational structure, allocation of agents, and actions to achieve goals.

In the approach presented in this paper, to obtain a changed organisational structure is a means to achieve a goal. Such a goal concerns (dynamic) properties of the organisational behaviour. So, the deliberation starts by identifying the goals in terms of the required changes in organisational behaviour, given changed environmental conditions.

To model such a process, models are needed for deliberation and modification. Moreover, a number of explicit representations play a role: for organisational behaviour, organisational structure and relations between behaviour and structure. In the adopted modelling perspective two models play an important role. In the first place a goal-directed agent model is used to model the deliberative aspects of the organisational change, and in the second place a model for modification of the organisation structure and agent allocation. The deliberation model of the organisation-as-deliberative-agent is embedded within the organisation structure.

Representations of organisational behaviour play an important role both to describe existing (possibly undesired) behaviour as has been monitored, and to describe desired or required behaviour that can be taken as goal. A formalisation is needed of the dynamic properties that characterise organisational behaviour. To this end the formal specification language for dynamic properties of organisational behaviour as presented in [8] is adopted. An example of such a representation is:

> $\forall$ tid : TaskId, $\forall$ t1, tf : T
> $\forall$ C: CLIENT:client_service $\forall$ R: RECEPTIONIST: client_service
> [[t $\leq$ t1 $\leq$ t' & state(T , t1, output(C)) |= comm_from_to(requested(tid, tf), C, R) $\Rightarrow$
> $\exists$ t2 : T [t1 $\leq$ t2 $\leq$ t1 + d &
> [state(T , t2, input(C)) |= comm_from_to(rejected(tid), R, C) $\vee$
> state(T , t2, input(C)) |= comm_from_to(accepted(tid), R, C)]]]

This organisation behaviour property specifies that for trace T, at any point in time between t and t', if a client communicates a request to the receptionist, then within time duration d the receptionist will communicate either an acceptance or a rejection of the request to this client. Using the abstraction mechanism introduced in [10] such properties can be expressed in a conceptual high-level (but yet formal) language, without having to involve all (temporal) details. For example the property above can be represented in an abstract manner by

> has_maximal_request_response_time(T , t, t', d)

This abstraction mechanism allows the deliberation model to work with relatively simple expressions and relations between them.

To model the organisational aspects, the Agent-Group-Role (AGR) organisation modelling approach [3] was adopted. This approach abstracts from the behaviour of individual agents by considering organisational concepts as roles, groups and structures as first class citizens. As such, an agent is considered an active communicating entity which plays roles within groups. Groups are aggregated sets of agents and a role is an abstract representation of an agent function within a group. Organisational structure is considered at group and organisation level. On group level, a structure is an abstract description of a group, identifying all roles and interactions within the group. An organisational structure is a set of group structures together with intergroup interactions. The actual realisation of the organisation then constitutes the allocation of a set of agents to roles. The original aim of the AGR organisation modelling approach concentrates on organisation structure, while our concern is more with the actual dynamics. To incorporate the structure within the logical description of the internal dynamics of the organisation: firstly, for each element (e.g., group, role, interaction) in the organisational structure, a specific set of dynamic properties is introduced; secondly, relationships are identified between these sets, based on the structural relations between these elements; for further details on this formalisation, see [9].

The approach is illustrated by a toy example: a banking case study (see Figure 1). Clients put in requests, e.g., opening an account or withdrawing funds from an account, to the bank through a central call center. The call center forwards such a request to a bank in the region where the client resides. If a local bank then has fulfilled the request, the client is informed by the call center that the request is finished. Client requests come in via the Client Service group, from where they are forwarded to representatives of local banks. Client requests are allocated to local banks on the basis of the regions in which clients live. In local banks employees fulfill these requests. Interaction is bidirectional: requests go upstream from the clients to the employees and the different possible statuses of these requests (finished, accepted, rejected) go downstream.

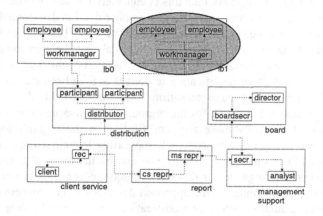

Fig. 1. Organisational AGR structure of the case study

Here, organisational change can be illustrated as follows. Assume that at some moment, the organisation has a single local bank called lb0 in region reg0, but dealing with client requests from reg0 and reg1. As the number of client requests increases over time, management may decide to open up another local bank, called lb1. After this reorganisation, lb0 deals with requests from region reg0 and lb1 deals with requests from region reg1. The Report group communicates statistics on the incoming requests, to the Management Support group. Based on this information within this group new organisational goals and actions are generated, upon which final decisions are made by the Director.

3   Strategic Management

Strategic management involves the deliberation process that takes into account (changed) environmental conditions, goals on the organisational behaviour, and organisational structure which is the vehicle to realise behavioural goals. In this section it is discussed how such a deliberation process takes place (Section 3.1) and how such a process is embedded within the organisational structure (Section 3.2).

3.1   Organisational Behaviour and Structure

The deliberation process is explained by means of an example scenario. Suppose in the period between t and t' a substantial increase in number of clients in a certain region occurs (for example due to an extension of a city). Based on monitor information this environmental change is detected. Moreover, as part of the analysis process it is found out that for the given organisation structure, the maximal response time has increased, i.e. the dynamic property has_maximal_request_response_time(T , t, t', d') holds, where d' is larger than before: d'>d. As part of the deliberation process on goals on the future organisational behaviour, this d' is considered much too high. Moreover, if an organisational change is performed, then this is considered as an opportunity to get the maximal response time even less than before: a number d"<d is determined such that a goal is that has_maximal_request_response_time(T , t', t", d") will hold. The new goal is this; without repeating this all the time, also the goal that the permanent costs per client are limited to some bound b will be imposed. As part of the deliberation process about organisational structure modification actions it is found out that this new combined goal will be achieved if the organisational structure is modified in the sense that a new location of the bank is set up for the region. As a consequence of this deliberation it is decided to actually make the modification to the organisation structure. Within the deliberation process as sketched, supporting techniques and tools can be used. First, within the monitor and analysis process, on the basis of a trace, dynamic properties of the current organisational behaviour and environment can be checked in a formal and automated manner by the approach described in [7]. Moreover, in deliberation about an organisation structure modification action it can be determined what the behavioural properties for a possible organisational structure are, also in a formal and automatically supported manner as in [7].

3.2   Embedding the Deliberation Model in the Organisation Model

The deliberation process consists of an analysis of the recent past (say of the last 3 months) of organisational behaviour, and a planning process to determine a goal and a modification action that will influence the organisation behaviour in the future. Both determination of a goal and determination of an action are performed by first generating one or more options and then select one (possibly with a slight change).

For the example organisation in the example domain the Management Support group is responsible for analysing the monitoring results, for suggesting goals for the future behaviour of the organisation, and for proposing modification actions to the organisation structure to satisfy certain goals. The Board is responsible for deciding on the goals and modification actions. Below, properties of groups will be indicated by GP and properties describing intergroup interaction by GI.

Proper transfer of information is important throughout the deliberation process and throughout the organisation. For all roles R1 and R2 that have to communicate with each other, a transfer property has been formulated:

TP(R1, R2, m) ≡ If R1 communicates m to R2 then R2 receives m.

If this holds for any m, this is denoted by TP(R1, R2), and two-way transfer by TTP(R1, R2). Witin each group, group properties can be related to transfer properties and role behaviour properties.

Monitoring

The monitoring requires that response time report is generated on a regular basis. The following properties show where in the organisation this is performed and how it can be specified that the monitoring results arrive timely at the appropriate places within the organisation.

Client Service Group

GP1 ≡ If in a certain week the Clients generate a number of requests, then the Receptionist will receive these requests in this week.

Client Service – Report Group Interaction

GI1 ≡ If in a certain week the Receptionist in the Client Service group receives a number of requests, then the Client Service representative in the Report group will communicate the weekly response time report to the Management Support group representative within the Report group.

Report Group Property

GP2 is the transfer property TP(CSrepr, MSrepr, weekreport)
Report - Management Support group interaction

GI2 ≡ If the Management Support representative in the Report group receives the weekly response time report, then the Secretary of the Management Support group communicates this report to the Analyst of the Management Support group.

Goal Determination

The goal determination process in our example is a joint responsibility of the Management Support group (generating options for goals) and the Board (selecting a goal). The following properties show a specification of the shared responsibilities, from receipt of monitoring information to formulation of new goals.

Management Support Group

GP3 ≡ If the Secretary within the Management Support group communicates a weekly response time report to the Analyst in which the maximal response time is unacceptable given the organisation's directions, and in the previous week report this was not the case, then the Secretary will receive one or more goal proposals from the Analyst.

Management Support – Board Group Interaction

GI3 ≡ If the Secretary of the Management Support group receives goal proposals from the Analyst, then the Secretary of the Board communicates these goal proposals to the Director.

Board Group

GP5 ≡ If the Secretary of the Board communicates goals proposed by the analyst to the Director, then the Secretary of the Board will receive a (possibly slightly altered) selected goal from the Director.

Board – Management Support Group Interaction

GI4 ≡ If the Secretary of the Board receives a goal from the Director, then the Secretary of the Management Support group communicates this goal to the Analyst.

Modification Action Determination

After a decision has been made as to what the goal for the organisational behaviour is, it is determined which modification action is used to satisfy that goal. In the example organisation that responsibility is shared by the Management Support group (generating options) and the Board (selecting an action).

Management Support Group

GP4 ≡ If the Secretary of the Management Support group communicates a director's goal to the Analyst, then the Secretary will receive from the Analyst one or more modification action proposals to satisfy this goal.

Management Support – Board Group Interaction

GI5 ≡ If the Secretary of the Management Support group receives a modification action proposal from the Analyst, then the Secretary of the Board communicates the proposal to the Director.

Board Group

GP6 ≡ If the Secretary of the Board communicates a modification action proposal (from the analyst), then the Director performs a (possibly slightly altered) modification action.

4 Discussion

The contribution of this paper is a rather complex model, designed as a specific type of composition of diverse ingredients. Due to this complexity, a rather simple (toy) example case study was used to illustrate the model. Moreover, given the model as a composition of various ingredients, one or more of the ingredients can be replaced by others without changing the overall model in an essential manner.

A prototype has been developed for validating the ideas introduced in this paper. This prototype involves temporal formalisation of the dynamics, part of which was described in Section 3, specified as an executable organisation model in 'leads to' format; cf. [11], and executed using the available software environment. The prototype includes some simplifications, without compromising the main ideas underlying the model presented in the paper. For example, the prototype does not include weekly response time reports. Instead, requests are communicated individually by the Receptionist to the Secretary of the Management Support group; subsequently, the Analyst accumulates the number of incoming requests and, if applicable, generates a corresponding goal proposal, e.g., to decrease the response time.

In [1] and [2] modification of a multi-agent system was addressed, both from the angle of simulation (the former paper) and analysis (the latter paper). Differences between these papers and the current paper are as follows. First of all, in these two papers no organisational structure is used within the multi-agent system, what is the focus of the current paper. As a consequence, what is modified in [1] and [2] is the multi-agent system, extending it by one new agent, not an organisational structure as in the current paper. Second, in these papers the deliberation about modification of the multi-agent system is performed within one of the agents, by a specific design agent including a task model for redesign, it is not distributed over the organisation and integrated within the organisation model. Furthermore, in [1] no explicit formalised representations and formal analysis of behaviour are used, and in [2] no simulation is performed. In the current paper, in the context of organisational structure both are addressed in an integrated manner.

Acknowledgements. Lourens van der Mey and Wouter Wijngaards have contributed to the development of the software environment.

References

1. Brazier, F.M.T., Jonker, C.M., Treur, J., and Wijngaards, N.J.E., Deliberative Evolution in Multi-Agent Systems. International Journal of Software Engineering and Knowledge Engineering, vol. 11, 2001, pp. 559–581.
2. Dastani, M., Jonker, C.M., and Treur, J., A Requirement Specification Language for Configuration Dynamics of Multi-Agent Systems. In: Wooldridge, M., Weiss, G., and Ciancarini, P. (eds.), Proc. of the 2nd International Workshop on Agent-Oriented Software Engineering, AOSE'01. Lecture Notes in Computer Science, vol. 2222. Springer Verlag, 2002, pp. 169–187.
3. Ferber, J. and Gutknecht, O. (1998). A meta-model for the analysis and design of organisations in multi-agent systems. In: Proceedings of the Third International Conference on Multi-Agent Systems (ICMAS'98), IEEE Computer Society Press, pp. 128–135.
4. Ferber, J., and Gutknecht, O. (1999). Operational Semantics of a role-based agent architecture. Proceedings of the 6th Int. Workshop on Agent Theories, Architectures and Languages (ATAL'1999). In: Jennings, N.R. & Lesperance, Y. (eds.) Intelligent Agents VI, Lecture Notes in AI, vol. 1757, Springer Verlag, 2000, pp. 205–217.
5. Ferber, J., Gutknecht, O., Jonker, C.M., Müller, J.P., and Treur, J., (2001). Organization Models and Behavioural Requirements Specification for Multi-Agent Systems. In: Y. Demazeau, F. Garijo (eds.), Multi-Agent System Organisations. Proceedings of MAAMAW'01, 2001.
6. Huczynski, A. and Buchanan, D. (1985). Organizational Behaviour, Prentice Hall
7. Jonker, C.M., Letia, I.A., and Treur, J., (2002). Diagnosis of the Dynamics within an Organisation by Trace Checking of Behavioural Requirements. In: Wooldridge, M., Weiss, G., and Ciancarini, P. (eds.), Agent-Oriented Software Engineering II, Proc. AOSE'01. Lecture Notes in Computer Science, vol. 2222. Springer Verlag, 2002, pp. 17–32.
8. Jonker, C.M., and Treur, J., Compositional Verification of Multi-Agent Systems: a Formal Analysis of Pro-activeness and Reactiveness. *International Journal of Cooperative Information Systems*, vol. 11, 2002, pp. 51–92.
9. Jonker, C.M., and Treur, J. (2002). Relating Structure and Dynamics in an Organisation Model. In: J.S. Sichman, F. Bousquet, and P. Davidson (eds.), Multi-Agent-Based Simulation II, Proc. of the Third International Workshop MABS'02. Lecture Notes in AI, vol. 2581, Springer Verlag, 2003, pp. 50–69.
10. Jonker, C.M., Treur, J., and Vries, W. de, Reuse and Abstraction in Verification: Agents Acting in a Dynamic Environment. In: P. Ciancarini, M.J. Wooldridge (eds.), Agent-Oriented Software Engineering, Proceedings of AOSE-2000. Lecture Notes in Computer Science, vol. 1957, Springer Verlag, 2001, pp. 253–268.

11. Jonker, C.M., Treur, J., and Wijngaards, W.C.A., (2001). Temporal Languages for Simulation and Analysis of the Dynamics Within an Organisation. In: B. Dunin-Keplicz and E. Nawarecki (eds.), From Theory to Practice in Multi-Agent Systems, Proceedings of the Second International Workshop of Central and Eastern Europe on Multi-Agent Systems, CEEMAS'01, 2001. Lecture Notes in AI, vol. 2296, Springer Verlag, 2002, pp. 151–160.
12. Kreitner, R., and Kunicki, A. (2001). Organisational Behavior, McGraw-Hill.
13. Lomi, A., and Larsen, E.R. (2001). Dynamics of Organizations: Computational Modeling and Organization Theories, AAAI Press, Menlo Park.
14. Mintzberg, H. (1979). The Structuring of Organisations, Prentice Hall, Englewood Cliffs, N.J.
15. Moss, S., Gaylard, H., Wallis, S., and Edmonds, B. (1998). SDML: A Multi-Agent Language for Organizational Modelling, Computational and Mathematical Organization Theory 4, (1), 43–70.
16. Prietula, M., Gasser, L., Carley, K. (1997). Simulating Organizations. MIT Press.

Author Index

Lecture Notes in Artificial Intelligence (LNAI)

Lecture Notes in Computer Science